Forms Interactivity for the World Wide Web

Forms

Creating HTML and PDF Form Documents

Interactivity for the World Wide Web

Malcolm Guthrie
Adobe Press, San Jose, California

This book consists of three sections. Each section is tailored to a different type of reader.

The first section of this book is comprised of Chapters One, Two, and Three. These chapters are presented as a discussion of the technical underpinnings of Web-based transactions. Although reading them is not required to benefit from sections two and three of the book, their content is a valuable resource in understanding why a form does or does not work. Even though the subject matter is technical, it is presented so that anyone can grasp the general principles.

The second section consists of Chapter Four. This section is a visual index of form examples. From these examples, specific form components are called out, pointing to their corresponding technical explanation in the book's third section. This section can be used to quickly identify a form you wish to implement, and can then be handed off to a technical person who can help implement the example.

The third section, and the bulk of the book, resides in Chapter Five. This chapter details the step-by-step process used to create each of the visual examples found in Chapter Four. Each example is treated as a stand-alone project. This makes it unnecessary to read another example to complete each project.

It is the goal of this book to cultivate many types of readers. Project managers or art directors might find a visual example and ask an IS manager to help them implement it. A programmer might have an idea and suggest it to management by showing them a visual example or a working sample on the companion Web site. Or the president of a company may see an example and follow the step-by-step instructions to create it on the company's Web site.

Whatever your technical level, this book is meant for you. Whether thumbing through the visual examples, following step-by-step instructions, or reading about the Web's technical foundation, read, discuss, enjoy.

For Catherine L. Norts

Acknowledgements

Behind every project of this size exists a team responsible for its completion. This book is no exception.

I am indebted to every member of our team for their assistance with this book.

For believing in me enough to sponsor the project, Patrick Ames.

For her tireless efforts without which many pieces of this book would never have become pages, Laura Swegles.

For his vigilant sentryship of the book's visual appeal and design, John Close.

For their playful goading and careful tutelage, Bill Hill and Terry Irwin.

And most importantly, for her support, encouragement and understanding throughout all phases of this project, Catherine L. Norts

November 1997
San Francisco, California
USA

Table of Contents

Cha

Getting Started–Setting up Shop

In this chapter we discuss how Web servers and client
browsers communicate. We explore several server software
options and examine structural issues concerning setup
of your site.

Overview

The purpose of this book is to help you add forms to your Web site. Before we get into the nuts and bolts of form and form-based application construction, it's necessary to briefly discuss how interaction on the Internet works. We won't go into a grueling technical discussion, but we will bring up several concepts important to understanding how people's browsers interact with your Web site.

If you're revamping an existing site or just setting up your own site, this chapter's information is intended to make your purchase, setup, and administration decisions a little easier.

Why are there HTML pages in my browser window?

Network computing, and the Internet, is based on a client/server model. The client/server concept isn't something new. In fact it's been around for quite a while and is very well understood. Your television operates under similar principles.

The concept is that a client makes requests from a server and the server replies to these requests. The client can be any simple, easy-to-use-and-administer device. The server handles the complicated and difficult-to-administer part of the transaction.

In the case of cable television, a signal is made available from a central dispatch station. This signal is viewable by any properly tuned-in television.

The dispatch station represents a server. This is where all the complicated equipment that transmits the signal lives. The upkeep of the dispatch station can be handled by trained professionals who spend forty hours a week concerned with these matters.

Your television is the client. You don't need to understand what happens at the dispatch station to access the signal it's sending. All that matters to you is that when you turn on your simple television and tune in the proper channel, you receive the program you desire.

The Internet is a bit different than television but it works on the same client/server principle. The Internet is a group of sophisticated machines that know how to look up and call one another. When I want to contact a specific machine, its number is looked up and my message is forwarded to it.

Currently there are millions of server machines connected to the Internet. These machines are connected by data communication lines and they do little more than listen for client requests. These client requests correspond to a user typing an address into a Web browser and hitting the enter key.

A typical request is where a client asks the server to locate a file and then return it. Another type of request is when a client asks the server to run a program and then return the results. This is how form processing is accomplished. Before we get too far ahead, let's identify how these clients and servers go about talking to each other.

How do clients and servers communicate?

http://www.w3.org/
hypertext/www/protocols/

They do it by having a few things in common. The first of these is the underlying structure of the way packets of information are transmitted between client and server. This transmission protocol is called TCP/IP (Transmission Control Protocol/Internet Protocol). How data is broken up into pieces that can be reassembled on another machine is the first element necessary for communication. The next is a common descriptive language of what we're sending. This is Hypertext Transmission Protocol (HTTP).

HTTP has been used by the World Wide Web since 1990. It is a lightweight, application-level protocol that defines how the WWW as a hypermedia information system communicates. HTTP operates in a very simple manner. A client initiates a request and the server returns a response. The client's request comes in the form of a Uniform Resource Identifier (URI). The full request form is outlined here:

Format of HTTP Request
URI
HTTP Version
MIME message
  request modifiers
  client information
  body content

The server responds to a request by returning information, as outlined here:

Format of HTTP Response
Status Line   HTTP 1.0 2000K
MIME Message
  server information
  entity meta information
  body content

In the real world of the Internet, communication usually isn't so simple. Commonly a gateway, proxy, or tunnel will receive and forward a client's request before it finds its destination. For our purposes we'll discuss a simple scenario where a client connects directly to the intended server and the server responds directly back to the client.

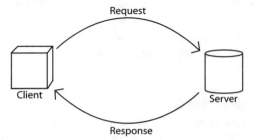

Figure 1.1: Client-Server Session

A simple client/server exchange

Let's look at a real world example of an HTTP exchange. An event initiates when a client sends an HTTP message to a server. This is equivalent to someone typing a text string into a browser and hitting the enter key. For instance, I might type http://forms.mix-media.com/ in my browser window and hit the enter key. What I've done is enter a text string requesting a resource located somewhere on the Internet. The text string is formatted so that I can remember what I'm requesting and the resource can be located by various computers on the network. This text string is a Uniform Resource Identifier (URI).

URIs and URLs

http://ds.internic.net/rfc/
rfc1630.txt

So what's the difference between all these acronyms? Actually it's very simple. They all belong in a single group called Uniform Resource Identifiers (URI). A Uniform Resource Locator (URL) is a type of URI. A URL gives specific instructions on what protocol to use to access the resource pointed at by any URI. For instance, a file named test.txt and a program named results.exe exist on an FTP server named ftp.mix-media.com. Both files reside in the /tests/iq directory. The URL for these files would be as follows:

ftp://ftp.mix-media.com/tests/iq/test.txt
ftp://ftp.mix-media.com/tests/iq/results.exe

Now let's say these files exist on an HTTP server named www.mix-media.com in the /tests/iq directory. The URL for these files would be as follows:

http://www.mix-media.com/tests/iq/test.txt
http://www.mix-media.com/tests/iq/results.exe

Each protocol operates on a specific port. Sometimes you'll see an HTTP address that looks like this:

http://www.mix-media.com:8080/index.html

The HTTP specification defines port number 80 as the default. If the HTTP server identifier doesn't indicate a specific port number it's assumed to be listening on the default port of 80. In the above example the number after the ":" is the port number this server is running on. It's possible there is another server running on the default port that when accessed would return a completely different file. For example, these two URLs would return two different files:

http://www.mix-media.com:8080/index.html
http://www.mix-media.com/index.html

It's possible to use partial path names once you're connected to a server. For instance, once connected to http://www.mix-media.com/, hypertext references to another file in the same directory are made by using only the file name. If another document existed named benefits.html, it could be referred to in the index.html file by its name alone. The same or current directory is automatically assumed. Documents in other directories can be referred to in the same way. For instance, an HTML document, http://www.mix-media.com/about/index.html, can be referred to by other hypertext documents on the same server as "/about/index.html". The path is assumed to be relative to the server root when it starts with a forward slash. If no slash is present, as in "about/ index.html", the about directory is assumed to exist in the current directory.

How does all of this relate to forms?
Well, the process involved with forms processing is the same. We'll always deal with what happens on the client and on the server.

The only difference from the client's perspective is that they're presented with a document that asks them to supply information. A form resource located on the Internet could be an HTML, PDF, or any document type available for viewing in a Web browser. On the front end of the process, once the desired information is entered, the client submits the data to the server.

Server processing of form submissions can take several paths. First, the server needs to have a mechanism for handling this submission of data. One mechanism is called the Common Gateway Interface (CGI). Using CGI, a server can launch a program and hand it the submission for processing. The CGI program executes and returns a response as text, HTML, FDF, etc., to the server. All this occurs on the server without user interaction.

From this simple request/response relationship, a complex array of possibilities has grown. Throughout the following chapters, we'll discuss creating forms and writing both scripts and programs to process client submissions. The rest of this chapter covers the physical elements needed to set up a server that will allow the publishing of documents and forms on the World Wide Web.

Choosing Your Server

Currently there are dozens of commercial and free Web servers for use and they're available on almost any computing platform. A few years ago, choosing a server could be hit or miss. Today, each server has been evaluated so thoroughly that any one's benefits and drawbacks could fill a volume itself. In this book we will discuss Netscape, Microsoft IIS, and Apache. Depending upon your host environment, any of these products provide all the functionality necessary to construct the forms-based examples in this book.

However, don't feel restricted by this list. If you do choose another server there are several issues to keep in mind. First of all, don't base your decision solely on cost. Apache, CERN, and NCSA servers are available on various UNIX platforms for free. Microsoft IIS server is available for Windows NT and Windows 95 for free. The price for these servers is attractive and they are all solid products. Just because they're free doesn't mean they're the best fit for your organization.

Although freeware applications offer cost advantages, they fall short in the area of support. When the unexpected occurs there is not a support line to call. For mission-critical applications it is advisable to choose a commercial server package with an established company and accessible technical support services. If you are a large company and you have the IS staff to maintain a freeware product, you have the added benefit of the complete source code at your disposal. Unfortunately, not everyone has the resources to dedicate several IS professionals to full-time Web server maintenance and development.

The final issue critical to selecting a server is security. US export regulations place strict controls on the export of encryption technology. Since most freeware providers do not restrict overseas downloading, they can not provide Secure Sockets Layer (SSL) support in their products. The commercial software vendors provide a US and foreign version of their products.

Any Web server can be configured to serve forms and process HTML, Adobe Forms Data (FDF) and other types of forms data. In the rest of this chapter we discuss several common Web servers.

Netscape

Netscape burst on the Internet scene with its Navigator browser. The company currently offers two Web servers, FastTrack and Enterprise. The FastTrack server is the low-cost server aimed at small to medium size organizations. The Enterprise server is Netscape's heavyweight Web server. It's the server Netscape runs its site with, and the server used to construct this book's Netscape examples.

Microsoft IIS

Microsoft's pursuit of server market share is spearheaded by its Internet Information Server. The server has rapidly developed as a viable server platform. It is tightly integrated with Microsoft's operating systems and mature software development tools. Implementing a site based with Internet Information Server is an attractive option if your organization is already well versed in Microsoft technology.

Apache

The Apache server is a freeware web server. It's currently maintained by a consortium of Internet enthusiasts dedicated to providing low-cost, sophisticated software for everybody. The Apache server comes as a set of source files you compile for your type of operating system. Compiled application files are available, but having the source code on hand for modification is a benefit unavailable with other products. This is the strength and weakness of a freeware product. When disaster strikes you must rely on yourself to fix it. There's no tech support line to call. If you have the know-how or the proper staff, maintaining a server from the source level can offer quite an advantage. If you don't have the luxury of a qualified staff, a commercial product may be a better choice.

Setting up Your Site's Structure

Two often overlooked but critical elements of your Web-based applications are the organization of your information and your underlying directory structure. If you are just constructing your site, a few hours of planning can save hundreds of hours of administration. If your site is already up and running it's never to late for a strategic reorganization. The hallmark of the Web is its complex organic nature. It's a seemingly endless connection of loosely related pieces of information. Managing a disorganized, ever-growing mass of electronic files can quickly become a nightmare.

Looking at your Data

More than likely the pool of information that is or will become your site is related in some way. A hierarchical approach to organization is by far the most common on the Web. It is human nature to look for similarities and hierarchies within groups of objects. By creating and maintaining understandable hierarchies, you can greatly enhance the usability of your site.

Simple hierarchy based on a home page

Most sites center around a home page that serves as a springboard to the rest of the site and related sites. Although there are dozens of other information architectures, variations of this simple tree make up the majority of Web sites today. It can't be overstated that the easier a user can understand and anticipate your site's structure, the more likely they are to enjoy and use it over and over again.

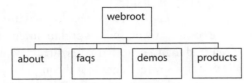

Figure 1.2: Sample Web site outline

Directory Structure

A simple hierarchy also serves as the best foundation for a site's directory structure. As a site grows, an ongoing effort to keep it simple will pay dividends to a site manager's mental health. A sample directory structure for the previous site map might look like the following illustration:

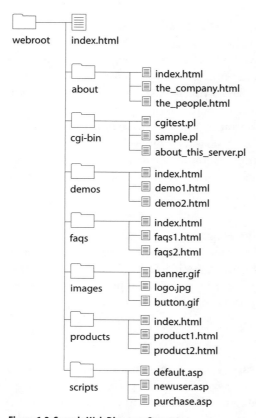

Figure 1.3: Sample Web Directory Structure

A bare minimum structure contains one directory that holds the entire site. This is the root directory. Inside this directory would be an images directory. By having one central directory for images, you avoid file duplication. Having multiple copies of an image located throughout your site compounds the complexity of updates and maintenance. By having one graphic file referred to in a central images directory, an update to this file automatically updates any reference to it throughout your site. Typically any directories that contain only HTML or PDF files do not require CGI programs to execute from their directory. Having a directory on your site that contains all files that require execution again simplifies administration. Instead of multiple directories requiring you to allow execution of files, you have one central repository of these special files.

Certainly another common solution is to have a separate directory for each type of script. Under this approach Perl scripts, C/C++ programs, Java applications, and Active Server Pages are stored in separate directories. As a site grows this approach may become necessary, but for most sites a single directory for CGIs should suffice.

In Figure 1.3, a sample directory structure is outlined. A good approach to site construction is to always simplify. Simplicity insures that as your site grows and as different people work on it, operations can be understood and problems can be addressed as they arise. A complex site soon becomes the responsibility of a handful of in-the-know people. This seems to be the goal of many IS departments or consultants, but as rapidly as Web services and needs change, I've found it wiser to have a simple strategy understood by as many employees as possible.

Permissions & Security

Without file permissions, any Internet prowler could scavenge your site, reading what they shouldn't, uploading whatever they want, and running any program they wish.

The three types of privileges you'll need to be familiar with are read, write, and execute. Most actions associated with Internet activities can be classified under those three categories. The first, read, is required to access any file. When a Web browser requests an HTML file, the server checks to see if the connected account has read access to the file. If it does, the file is returned by the server. A typical use requiring write permission is an FTP upload. A user desiring to upload a file to an FTP server must have write permission on the server for the directory where they want to place the file. The execute privilege determines if a connected user has the right to execute a script or program on the server machine. What rights or permissions a user has are stored on the host machine and are managed by authenticating a user when they connect.

You might not notice, but when your Web browser begins talking with a server, an authentication check occurs. If the file on the server resides in a directory that requires authentication, you're presented with a dialog that asks for a username and password. The process is similar for an FTP authentication sequence. There are several types of authentication available today. Basic authentication sends username and password as non-encrypted text across the network. This is a security hole for mission-critical information. Secure Sockets Layer (SSL) is the encrypted version of authentication. Username and password are encrypted before they are transmitted across the Internet. This is much better for locking out undesired users.

Microsoft servers offer an additional authentication scheme, the NT LAN Manager challenge/response (NTLM) security system. In this instance, username and password are encrypted using the NTLM method before they are sent to the receiving server. The NT Authentication scheme is tightly integrated into the operating system. This allows use of Windows user and group account information for authentication.

The most common access to your site is by the anonymous user. This visitor is classified as a guest usually with read-only privileges. It's also common for these non-authenticated users to access forms and submit data to a server. These forms often invoke scripts and programs that process a submission and return a reply. These scripts and programs must also have or reside in a directory that has execute permissions. A good strategy is to store all the scripts and programs in a single directory with execute privileges for web server users. This is an easier solution to maintain than individual privileges scattered on scripts throughout your site.

Again, a few hours of planning your security scheme will return your efforts many times over as your site begins to grow. A general rule to follow is to keep it simple by centralizing files with like privileges.

Cha

Chapter Two

Creating Form Applications and Documents

In this chapter we discuss the Common Gateway Interface
(CGI) and the most common languages and environ-
ments used to process submitted information. We'll discuss
each environment through a simple example and examine
several next-generation solutions.

Overview

The two most important parts of any form application are the document used to submit information and its corresponding script or program that processes the submitted information. This processing typically happens on the back or server end of the process. There are many architectures that allow a server to hand off a submission to a script or program. The original used on the Web is called the Common Gateway Interface (CGI). CGI is defined as the standard for interfacing external applications with your Web server. The specification is published and maintained by the National Center for Supercomputing Applications (NCSA).

http://hoohoo.ncsa.uiuc.edu/cgi/

http://www.w3.org/hypertext/www/CGI/

When a Web server is asked to return a plain HTML file, the file is located and returned. The data is read from disk and transmitted as it exists. A CGI program is capable of executing and then returning a response or an HTML page in real time. This allows pages to contain dynamic data rather than static information. A simple example of a CGI program is one that receives some data from a form and then emails the data to your Webmaster.

CGI is executable

By enabling CGI on your server you're enabling anyone that connects to your server to run an application on your system. This in itself raises several security concerns. This is why it's common practice to have a single directory where all of your CGI programs are stored. In this way your Webmaster can prohibit unauthorized people from adding to or changing your CGI programs.

How CGI works

CGI works within the boundaries of an HTTP session. Typically a client/browser will request a URL that points to a CGI on a server. The server receives the request and translates the URL into a path and file name. Next, the server recognizes the URL is actually a CGI program. The server has some additional responsibilities at this point. First it must prepare the environment variables it will pass to the CGI program. Then it must launch the CGI application and wait for its response. Once launched, the script takes over. A CGI program typically reads the environment variables passed to it, performs its intended function, returns its output, and terminates. Now the server notices the CGI program is finished. It returns the output to the client and then closes the connection. Finally the client receives the information and displays it for the user.

How to create CGI scripts and programs

Typically when we discuss CGI, we're talking about processing that happens on the server side of the transaction. Historically, all forms processing took place on the server. This was fine because most sites had only a couple of forms. As user interaction increased, server load did as well. The solution to the inevitable problem of overloading a server was to find a way to distribute part of the processing to the client machine making the request.

You can create a CGI application that executes on the server in any language you want. The two most common ways to create applications are to compile them into executable files, or to create them as scripts that can be executed by an interpreter. The only requirement for a CGI application is that the server has the ability to execute it.

Server Side Processing

CGIs that reside on the server can be broken up into two groups. First are the compiled CGI applications. These are created with a programming language such as C, C++, Visual Basic or even Fortran. They have the advantage of being speedy but they require more maintenance than a script. Each time you want to make a change you have to recompile before the CGI application will work.

On the other hand, scripting languages are sort of an intermediate step between programming languages and HTML. The main difference between scripting and programming languages is that scripting languages tend to be less intricate as far as syntax is concerned. Common CGI scripts are produced in Perl, C Shell, AppleScript, and Frontier. Perl is widely available on most platforms, C Shell is restricted to Unix, and AppleScript and Frontier are used solely on the Macintosh. JavaScript is also growing as a server-side scripting language. Microsoft has introduced VB Script as a scripting language for the millions of Visual Basic users.

Client Side

Realizing the untapped processing power of client machines, methods for client-side processing of form data have emerged. As Web sites grew, it became apparent that a large percentage of a server's CPU cycles was consumed validating data. Most of this processing could easily be performed by the client. Many web browsers began supporting script processing on the client side. JavaScript was the first and now VBScript and PerlScript have emerged. By adding a few simple script routines to HTML files, form validation and calculation can occur on the client side. This greatly reduces the amount of processing required on the server. This distribution of processing adds to the user experience by reducing undesired waiting time.

In the rest of this chapter we'll discuss popular programming and scripting languages used today. From this you'll create your site's CGI programs. You'll also be able to decide which part of your forms processing you'll elect to do on the server and which part you'll prefer to do on the client. Finally we'll discuss the different proposals and existing technologies that are promised by the next generation of CGI.

Choosing Your Scripting Language

Perl

http://www.perl.com/
http://www.perl.org/
http://www.perl.com/CPAN

To date, Perl is the most popular language used for writing CGI programs. It's a simple language for anyone with programming experience to learn and it offers excellent text processing capabilities. Perl is available for most platforms and can be downloaded free at http://www.perl.com/. There are innumerable sources of sample scripts posted on the Internet.

Perl is an interpreted language. This means Perl scripts aren't compiled on their host platform. This is a bonus in a rapidly changing environment like the World Wide Web. If each time a system variable changed it meant that all your Perl scripts needed to be recompiled, the luster of Perl would soon wear off.

A sample Perl script looks like this:

```
1.   #!/usr/local/bin/perl
2.
3.   print "Content-type: text/html", "\n\n";
4.
5.   print "<HTML>", "\n";
6.   print "<HEAD><TITLE>Perl Sample
     Script</TITLE></HEAD>", "\n";
7.   print "<BODY><H1>Perl Script Results!</H1><BR>",
     "\n";
8.   print "The server name is ", $ENV{'SERVER_NAME'},
     ".", "\n";
9.   print "</BODY>", "\n";
10.  print "</HTML>", "\n";
11.
12.  exit (0);
```

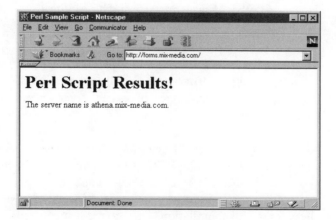

It looks simple, doesn't it? Let's walk through it a line at a time to see what happens.

The first line of the script instructs the server where the Perl interpreter is located. This is primarily for Unix systems. On Windows NT and Macintosh, the script is run according to its associated executable in the Windows NT registry, and its creator application on the Macintosh.

In the third line of our script we output data via the print function to standard output, STDOUT. The first thing we output is a valid HTTP header. At minimum the header must contain "Content-type:" followed by the MIME type of the remaining data. This script outputs HTML so the MIME type is "text/html". Two new lines characters follow the header.

Once we've output the header we can begin sending the body of our response. Lines five through seven of our script we print HTML to STDOUT. On line eight we output some text followed by the value returned by passing 'SERVER_NAME' to the $ENV{} function. Line nine is the final line of our HTML response. Line 12 instructs the Perl interpreter to exit with a return code of 0 (no error). From Perl we can access the environment variables through the $ENV associative array.

C/C++

There is certainly no shortage of programmers versed in C/C++. The languages have become the enterprise programmer's bread and butter. However, both languages are terse and have quite a learning curve for the uninitiated.

The languages offer flexibility and speed. A C/C++ program compiled for your server platform can be directly executed instead of interpreted. This requires fewer system resources and server performance is less impaired as usage scales.

The drawback to C/C++ development is that administration requirements increase. Individual C/C++ programs need to be recompiled any time a modification is necessary. When you're dealing with a half dozen executables, the maintenance increase is negligible. However, even at 50, the extra step of compilation begins to prove inconvenient.

A sample C program to generate an HTML page looks like this:

```
1.    #include <stdio.h>
2.    #include <stdlib.h>
3.    #include <string.h>
4.    void main (void)
5.    {
6.      char * the_server;
7.      the_server = getenv("SERVER_NAME");
8.      printf ("Content-type: text/html\n\n");
9.      printf ("<HTML><HEAD>\n");
10.     printf ("<TITLE>Sample C program.</TITLE>");
11.     printf ("<BODY><H1>C Program Results!</H1>\n");
12.     printf ("The server's name is ");
13.     printf ( (char*)the_server );
14.     printf (".\n");
15.     printf ("</BODY></HTML>\n");
16.   }
```

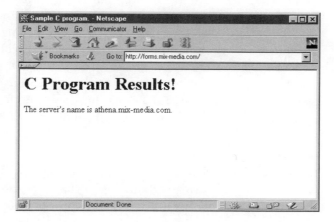

This looks similar to our Perl example, doesn't it? Let's walk through it to see what happens during program execution.

In this case the first three lines of our program are instructions directed at our C compiler. They indicate that the files stdio.h, stdlib.h, and string.h should be read and included when we compile the program into an executable. The stdio.h file defines routines we'll use to access standard input and output. The stdlib.h file defines routines in the standard library. The string.h file includes, as you may have suspected, routines used to manipulate strings. The fourth line of our program is different than anything in our Perl example. In every compiled C program there must be a main routine. It's the main routine that's called when the program is launched. Our main routine "void main (void)" defines our program as one that takes no input parameters "void" and returns no or "void" data. Line five of our program is an open parentheses. This tells our compiler that everything from this parentheses to the next matching close parentheses defines our main routine. Everything between these two is part of the main function. Our sixth and seventh lines define the variable the_server as a character pointer (don't worry about this right now), and then call the getenv() function. The getenv() is defined in our stdlib.h file. It takes a parameter, in this case "SERVER_NAME", and returns the matching value from our environment variables. What all this means is that the character pointer, the_server, is set to print to the SERVER_NAME as a string.

The eighth line is again where we print our response header to standard output. The response header is always followed by two new line characters. This is how your browser knows the header information has finished. Once the header is output we're free to start sending HTML. In the next three lines we're sending our document. On the twelfth line we begin printing the server's name to standard output. Next the printf function inserts "the_server" parameter as a string, then prints the remaining characters of the string to STDOUT. On line 15 we printf() the closing HTML tags to STDOUT, then we reach the end of our main routine.

JavaScript

You might wonder what the difference is between Java and JavaScript. Java is an object-oriented programming language. The language has strict syntax rules and an object framework consisting of predefined classes that allow inheritance. To create a Java application or applet you write and compile your program into a Java bytecode file. These bytecode executables can be referenced in an HTML file. When a browser that supports Java encounters an applet tag, it downloads and runs the compiled bytecode file.

JavaScript is an object-based scripting language with a set of built-in objects. These objects can be extended but they are not classes and they do not support inheritance. JavaScript commands get embedded in an

HTML file and are interpreted, not executed, by the client's browser. There is a mechanism to connect scripts to Java applets. The following lists compare JavaScript and Java.

JavaScript

Object-based. Code uses built-in, extensible objects, but no classes or inheritance.
Code integrated with, and embedded in, HTML.
Variable data types not declared (strong typing).
Dynamic binding. Object references checked at run-time.
Cannot automatically write to hard disk.

Java

Object-oriented. Applets consist of object classes with inheritance.
Applets distinct from HTML (accessed from HTML pages).
Variable data types must be declared (loose typing).
Static binding. Object references must exist at compile-time.
Cannot automatically write to hard disk.

From its beginnings, JavaScript was designed as an extension to HTML. JavaScript offers two main benefits. First it allows some processing to be shifted from the server to the client. The idea is that by reducing server load, waiting for server response can be diminished. Secondly, processing on the client side offers immediate user feedback. Users aren't asked to send data to the server and wait for a reply over and over again. JavaScript allows authors to embed scripts in HTML pages. When the pages are received by the client, the scripts are executed, allowing for run-time creation of HTML on the client. This is a great enhancement to the static world of plain HTML.

JavaScript can be used for arithmetic calculations, outputting strings, opening windows, and redirecting a browser to another URL. You might create a function that checks which browser the requesting client is using and directs the client to the page it can properly display. When the page loads, JavaScript can execute when certain events occur. For example, when a client clicks a submit button, a script can be triggered that checks the validity of an HTML form's submission fields.

Let's take a look at a simple HTML page that includes a JavaScript function generating an HTML page on the client.

```
1.    <HTML>
2.    <HEAD>
3.    <TITLE>Sample JavaScript program </TITLE>
4.    </HEAD>
5.    <BODY>
6.    <H1>JavaScript Results!</H1>
7.    <SCRIPT LANGUAGE = "JavaScript">
8.    <!--This hides the script from non-Script
      enabled browsers
9.      document.writeln("The server's name is " +
      location.hostname + ".");
10.   <!-- -->
11.   </SCRIPT>
12.   </BODY>
13.   </HTML>
```

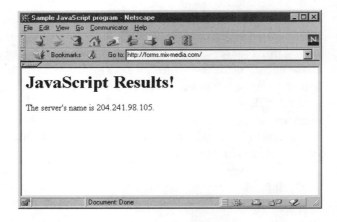

Now let's walk through the HTML page one line at a time.

Lines one through six are basic HTML tags to create our page, create its head and title, and to close the head section and begin the document's body. On line seven we see a <SCRIPT> tag that declares the language we're using as JavaScript. Line eight starts with an HTML comment marker. This is placed here so browsers that don't understand

JavaScript will ignore the following lines until it reaches the close comment tag (-->).

It's within the script tag where JavaScript takes over. This is a simple script where we only access two JavaScript objects, document and location. First we access the document.writeln member function to output some text. We pass the function the following parameter: "The server's name is" + location.hostname + "." The parameter we're using is broken into three parts separated by the "+" character. The "+" character concatenates strings. Before we actually write the line to our file, the browser interprets the parameter and notices it must assemble the string before it passes it to the document.writeln function. What happens next is that the first part of our string is copied and the second part is evaluated and concatenated to the end of the first part. Our second part is a reference to the JavaScript location object to return its hostname member. This is actually the name of the server we've retrieved the file from. This string is added to the end of the first part of our string and finally we add the remaining "." character. Now the string will look something like this, "The server's name is forms.mix-media.com." This is the string we pass to the document.writeln function. It writes the line to our browser's input stream and our script ends. We close the body section and file with the remaining two lines of HTML. If the client's browser doesn't support JavaScript, nothing is output. This is less than ideal and we should add a routine to check for JavaScript compatibility, but for this basic example we'll leave it how it is.

JavaScript is not only a client-side scripting language. JavaScript can be used in Microsoft's Active Server Pages and Netscape's LiveWire to execute on the server.

Java
When Java began being used on the Web, it was strictly a client-side service. Recently server-side Java APIs have begun showing up in Web servers. In this early stage of implementation, we suffer from having no standardized interface for constructing Java "servlets" for Web servers. Although JavaSoft is creating a "servlet" API, most developers have pledged compliance but plan to maintain their own API as well.

A sample server-side Java "servlet" looks like this:

```
1.   import java.io.*;
2.   import javax.servlet.*;
3.   import javax.servlet.http.*;
4.   class javatest extends HttpServlet {
5.     public void doGet (HttpServletRequest req,
     HttpServletResponse res)
6.     throws ServletException, IOException
7.     {
8.     ServletOutputStream out = res.getOutputStream();
9.       res.setContentType("text/html");
10.      out.println("<HTML><HEAD>");
11.      out.println("<TITLE>Sample Java
     Program</TITLE>");
12.      out.println("</HEAD><BODY>");
13.      out.println("<H1>Java Program Results</H1>");
14.      out.println("The server's name is " +
     req.getServerName() + ".");
15.      out.println("</BODY></HTML>");
16.      out.close();
17.    }
18.  }
```

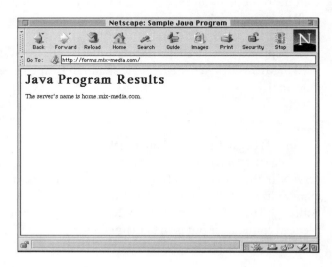

All of these examples are starting to look similar. Let's examine this "servlet" line by line.

The first three lines of this servlet import the Java classes we need to access standard input and output and the HTTP server utilities. The two javax classes were downloaded from Javasoft.

http://www.javasoft.com/

http://java.sun.com/

The fourth line declares our servlet's class name and which class it descends from. Our servlet's name is javatest and it descends from the HttpServlet class. What this means is that we'll have access to all the functions defined in the HttpServlet class. The sixth line of our program declares the doGet method. This is similar to our main routine in a C program. In servlets, the doGet method is called when the applet is launched. On line six we indicate that our applet will throw an exception if we encounter an error. If an exception occurs, error text is returned and information regarding the error is written to the server's error and access logs.

On line eight of our program, we retrieve the output stream for this servlet, and store a reference to it in the "out" variable. This is equivalent to standard output. Our next line accesses our servlet's response member and sets our response type to "text/html".

Now we're ready to print our HTML to the output stream. If you're not familiar with object-oriented programming, don't worry. We reference the println() member function of the out PrintStream. It's done by using out.println().

On line 14 we call the out.println() function, passing it the "the server name is" string. Then we use the "+" character to add the result of the next function to the end of the "The server's name" string. Here we access the request member's getServerName() member function. Again we concatenate the resulting string to the "The server's name is" string and out.println() it to the output stream. Finally we out.println() the closing HTML tags and the Java applet exits.

This is a server-side example, but don't forget that Java applets can also be used on the client side.

Visual Basic

Visual Basic has become the predominant platform used by Windows CGI developers. Visual Basic applications can access system variables and data stored in other programs. A major plus for Visual Basic is its robust development tools and scores of available controls. Not many other development platforms offer drag-and-drop application creation. Coupled with its ease of use, Visual Basic makes an attractive CGI development environment. The only drawback to Visual Basic is its lack of string processing functions.

Visual Basic supports DDE, ODBC, OLE, and Sockets, allowing communication with other applications and databases. Its support of ODBC allows communication with popular database applications.

Let's take a look at a simple CGI application that returns our sample page.

```
1.    Sub CGI_Main()
2.        Send ("HTTP/1.0 200")
3.        Send ("Content-type: text/html")
4.        Send ("")
5.        Send ("<HTML><HEAD>")
6.        Send ("<TITLE>Visual Basic Sample
          Program</TITLE>")
7.        Send ("</HEAD>")
8.        Send ("<BODY><H1>Visual Basic Program
          Results!</H1>")
9.        Send ("The server name is " + CGI_ServerName
          + ".")
10.       Send ("</BODY>")
11.       Send ("</HTML>")
12.   End Sub
```

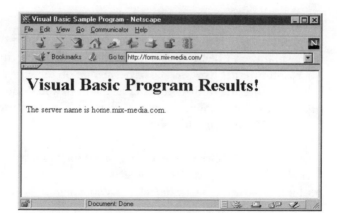

Our example here uses the CGI.BAS library with the Visual Basic environment. This library was developed by Bob Denny. The library contains a main function that stores our environment variables into variables prepended with CGI_. Then it calls our CGI_Main() sub routine. This is the first line of our example. In the following line, we output our header information, and each subsequent line outputs the HTML tags we need to generate our page in the client browser.

The ninth line of our example sends the string "The server name is" with the value of CGI_ServerName and "." concatenated to the string. An important point to remember is that Visual Basic and C/C++ are case sensitive languages. The environment variable 'SERVER_NAME' is referenced here as CGI_ServerName. If upper and lower case letters don't match exactly, the correct value won't be returned.

The final lines of our script output the tags we need to close the document's body section and then the document itself.

Once you're happy with your Visual Basic application, you compile it into an executable and it resides on your server as such. This, as in C/C++, adds an extra step in the CGI process. However, Visual Basic's rapid application development environment makes the process relatively painless.

Visual Basic Applications such as the example are server-side CGI programs. A derivative of this development platform is VBScript. VBScript can be executed using the Active Server Pages architecture on the server-side as well.

VBScript

http://www.microsoft.com/
vbscript/

http://www.vbscripts.com/

http://www.km-cd.com/scribe/

http://www.nac.net/~users/
mtadams/

VBScript is the newest member of the Visual Basic family of programming languages. VBScript is currently supported on the client side by Microsoft Internet Explorer 3.0 or newer and on the server side by Microsoft Internet Information Server 3.0 or newer. VBScript is a subset of the Visual Basic language. For this reason it's easy for anyone with Visual Basic experience to learn.

Like JavaScript, VBScript is an object-based scripting language with a predefined set of objects. These objects are not classes and do not support inheritance like a true object oriented language.

VBScript commands get embedded directly in an HTML file. These commands are interpreted by the browser. VBScript can connect to Java applets and ActiveX controls. VBScript, like JavaScript, does not support file input or file output or write access to the user's operating system.

VBScript shares the two benefits of client side processing that JavaScript enjoys. First VBScript shifts some processing from the server to the client. By reducing server load, frustrating waiting for the user can be diminished. Secondly, providing processing and validation on the client side allows immediate user feedback. This is much better than having a user post data to a server and then wait for a response.

VBScripts are transmitted to the client and interpreted upon arrival. This allows for runtime creation of HTML pages. VBScripts are enclosed by the HTML <SCRIPT> tags and are ignored by browsers that don't recognize the VBScript language. Currently Internet Explorer is the only browser supporting VBScript, but a plug-in for Netscape Navigator is available from NCompass Labs that lets Navigator users interpret VBScript and access ActiveX components.

http://www.ncompasslabs.
com/products.htm

VBScript can be used to perform calculations, output strings, open new windows, and redirect a browser to another URL. If your site focused on Internet Explorer users, you might create a script that checks for the browser type a requesting client is using, and returns a different page for those browsers that don't support VBScript.

VBScripts can execute when a page is loaded or when certain events occur. Events such as when a user clicks a button or URL, when the page is reloaded, or when a form is submitted are a few examples of when a script can be invoked. A common use is when a client clicks a button and a script is invoked that checks the validity of the forms fields. This processing is quickly done on the client, giving an immediate response either by submitting the form or reporting which field needs correction.

The following example is a simple HTML page that is meant to look similar to our JavaScript sample. On the client-side, it dynamically outputs the name of the server we contacted.

```
1.    <HTML>
2.    <HEAD>
3.    <TITLE>Sample VBScript Program</TITLE>
4.    </HEAD>
5.    <BODY>
6.    <H1>VBScript Results!</H1>
7.    <SCRIPT LANGUAGE="VBScript">
8.    <!-- This hides the script from non-script
      enabled browsers
9.    document.write "The server's name is " &
      Location.Hostname & "."
10.   <!-- End of comment line -->
11.   </SCRIPT>
12.   </BODY>
13.   </HTML>
```

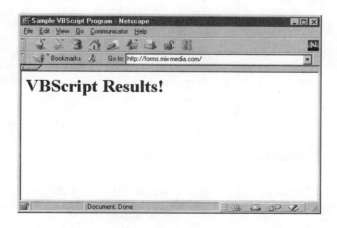

Let's look at this example in detail. In the first six lines of our HTML file, we have our basic tags declaring the file is HTML and the title in our header is "Sample VBScript Program". The sixth line is the first line in the body of our document. It's a level one header <H1> and the string is "VBScript Results!".

Lines seven through eleven are our script. On line seven we advise the browser that the script's language is VBScript. On line eight we begin with an HTML comment marker, making the following script invisible to browsers that don't support the <SCRIPT> tag. Line nine is where all of our work occurs. Here we access the write method of the browser's document object. The syntax we use is document.write. This is followed by the string we want to the browser window. This string is divided into three parts. "The server's name is" & Location.Hostname &".". In VBScript the "&" character is our concatenation operator. VBScript concatenates the string "." to the string returned when we evaluate the Location object's Hostname member. Next we concatenate our result to the "The server's name is" string. Now we're ready to write this out to our browser with the document.write method. That's all this VBScript does. Our next line closes the HTML comment. The last three lines of our file are the close tags for the script, the body of the file, and finally the HTML file itself.

This example just creates an HTML file that displays "VBScript Results!". if the client browser doesn't support VBScript. Ideally we should check for VB Script compatibility, and if the requesting browser doesn't support VBScript, we would return a static page informing the client that it can't view the output.

VBScript is not only a client-side scripting language. VBScript can be used on the server side through Microsoft's Active Server Pages technology.

Macintosh

The Macintosh is a unique computing platform in that it doesn't have a command line interface. This effects the mechanism of CGI. On the Macintosh, C/C++, Perl, AppleScript, and Frontier are the available solutions for creating CGI applications. C/C++ and Perl have been discussed.

AppleScript and Frontier are the two system-level scripting languages capable of creating CGI applications for use with Macintosh servers.

AppleScript

AppleScript is an object-oriented scripting language. It has the ability to communicate between and with programs and processes running on the Macintosh.

Its plain English syntax makes AppleScript easy to use. Its objects are based on familiar items such as words, sentences, shapes, and documents. AppleScript determines which objects and commands an application supports based on information contained in that application. There are many publicly available libraries that make CGI development a simple task.

Let's look at a simple CGI script in AppleScript that generates our familiar example.

```
1.   property lf : (ASCII character 10)
2.   property crlf : (ASCII character 13) & (ASCII
     character 10)
3.   property http_header : "HTTP/1.0 200 OK" & crlf
     & "Content-type: text/html" & crlf & crlf
4.   on <<event WWWΩsdoc>> path_args¬
5.     given <<class svpt>>:server_port
6.     set response_html_file to http_header & ¬
7.       "<HTML>" & lf & ¬
8.       "<HEAD>" & lf & ¬
9.       "<TITLE>Sample AppleScript Program</TITLE>"
10.      & lf & ¬
11.      "</HEAD>" & lf & ¬
12.      "<BODY>" & lf & ¬
13.      "<H1>AppleScript Results!</H1><BR>" & lf & ¬
14.      "The server port is " & server_port & "." &
         lf & ¬
15.      "</BODY>" & lf & ¬
16.      "</HTML>"
17.    return response_html_file
18.  end <<event WWWΩsdoc>>
```

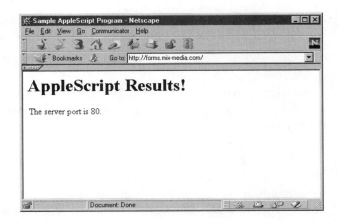

The first two lines of our script variables are created to hold certain values. The "crlf" variable stands for a carriage return and a line feed character. The second is our HTTP header. On the Macintosh we return a carriage return and line feed for cross platform compatibility. These variables are declared outside our event handler routine, making them a sort of global variable.

The sixth line of our script declares our event routine. The event our CGI script receives is of the WWWΩ's sdoc type. Several arguments are passed in here. Our example accepts the path_args and the server_name arguments. The following list shows the complete argument list available. If you don't accept any of these arguments it's okay. They are the only way to access the environment variables, so it is handy to have them around.

AppleScript Arguments

class kfor	http_search_args
class post	post_args
class meth	method
class addr	client_address
class user	username
class pass	password
class frmu	from_user
class svnm	server_name
class svpt	server_port
class scnm	script_name
class ctyp	content_type

Variables available for use:

http_search_args	stuff in the URL after a ?
post_args	stuff in the URL after a $
method	GET, POST, etc. Used to tell if post_args are valid
client_address	IP address or domain name of remote client's host
rom_user	e-mail address of remote user
username	authenticated user name
password	authenticated password
server_name	name or IP address of this server
server_port	TCP/IP port number being used by this server
script_name	URL name of this script
content_type	MIME content type of post_args

The eighth through fourteenth lines of our script create our response_html_file variable. This is really just one text string but our example breaks the script up into multiple lines by using the "¬" continued on the next line character. AppleScript uses the "&" as its concatenation operator so we output an HTML tag and append a return character to each line. We continue this process until the fifteenth line. On this line we concatenate the contents of the server_name argument to our "The server name is" string. Then we add the "." and a return character. In the final two lines we output the required closing HTML tags.

In the seventeenth line we instruct the routine to return the response_html_file variable to the calling application. Finally we reach the end of the handler and the script exits.

However simple AppleScript appears, its major drawback is a lack of string pattern matching operators. Scripting extensions are available to aid in CGI programming Open Scripting Architecture Extended (OSAX), but still they fall short of other languages, such as Perl.

Frontier

http://www.scripting.com/

Userland Software's Frontier is a development environment that contains a database scripting language, a debugger, and a text editor. Frontier is a popular CGI development environment on the Macintosh. To complement its Macintosh product, Userland has announced a Windows version of Frontier.

Frontier allows scripts to be constructed in AppleScript or in Frontier's own C-like language.

The following sample script is an example from the Frontier Web Scripting tutorial.

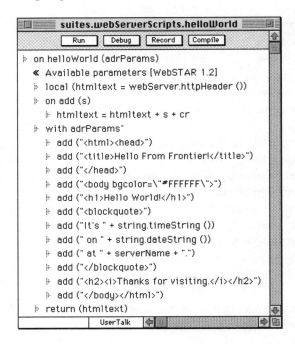

```
suites.webServerScripts.helloWorld
    Run    Debug    Record    Compile
on helloWorld (adrParams)
  « Available parameters [WebSTAR 1.2]
  local (htmltext = webServer.httpHeader ())
  on add (s)
    htmltext = htmltext + s + cr
  with adrParams^
    add ("<html><head>")
    add ("<title>Hello From Frontier!</title>")
    add ("</head>")
    add ("<body bgcolor=\"#FFFFFF\">")
    add ("<h1>Hello World!</h1>")
    add ("<blockquote>")
    add ("It's " + string.timeString ())
    add (" on " + string.dateString ())
    add (" at " + serverName + ".")
    add ("</blockquote>")
    add ("<h2><i>Thanks for visiting.</i></h2>")
    add ("</body></html>")
  return (htmltext)
                UserTalk
```

Configuring your server to run Frontier scripts is simple. The convention is that all Frontier scripts end in ".fcgi". By mapping the Frontier applica-tion to the fcgi file extension in your Web server, you can use the scripts you create to handle the CGI. This is conceptually how it's done but refer to your specific server's documentation for detailed setup instructions.

Creating new scripts is as simple as selecting New Script from the main menu. A dialog appears asking you to name the script and indicate what type of script it is. Indicate CGI script as the type and select the scripting language you want to use.

Clicking the okay button will open another window containing a stub you use to create your script.

Frontier's biggest drawback is that is platform specific. Although Frontier is limited to the Macintosh it still offers a robust environment for CGI and other forms of computer automation. With its string pattern matching and inter-application communication abilities, the Frontier environment is an outstanding alternative to AppleScript.

Active Server Pages

http://www.active-x.com/

http://webtoolz. webdeveloper.com/active.html

http://www.microsoft.com/iis/ LearnAboutIIS/ActiveServer/ default.asp

Active server pages are HTML pages with embedded scripting code. These embedded scripts are executed on the server. This offers the user a choice of scripting languages to execute, such as JavaScript, PerlScript, or VBScript. It doesn't matter what browser your user has because the scripts are evaluated on the server. VBScript is the default language for Active Server Page files. An interesting feature of Active Server Pages is that more than one scripting language can be used in a single file. To change scripting languages, all that is required is the alteration of a single tag. When an Active Server Page is encountered, it is read and any commands found are executed. An HTML page, text, or FDF data is returned to the client browser.

Active Server Pages (ASP) are files having the extension .asp. An ASP file is an ASCII text file that contains any text, HTML tags, and supported script commands.

An ASP is a series of commands. You can perform calculations, open windows, or redirect the server to another URL. Executing a script sends the series of commands to a scripting engine, which interprets and relays them to your computer. ASP Scripting provides scripting engines for the VBScript, JScript, and PerlScript scripting languages. VBScript is the default language for Active Server Pages.

Lets look at our simple example:

```
1.    <% Language=VBScript %>
2.    <% sname=Request.ServerVariables("SERVER_NAME")
      %>
3.    <% Response.ContentType="text/html" %>
4.    <HTML>
5.    <HEAD>
6.    <TITLE>Sample ASP Program</TITLE>
7.    </HEAD>
8.    <BODY>
9.    <H1>Active Server Page Results!</H1>
10.   The server name is <% =sname %>.
11.   </BODY>
12.   </HTML>
```

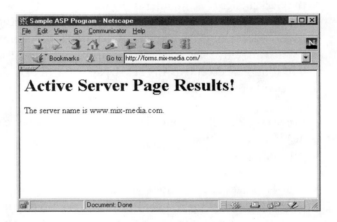

The third line of this ASP accesses the Content Type member function of the response object. It passes the function "text/html" as the response type. This constructs our HTTP header and prepares to send it to the browser. The next six lines output the text consisting of HTML tags opening the document, head, and title. The appropriate title is entered and the close head tag is output. We write the body and a level one header "Active Server Page Results!".

The eleventh line of the script is surrounded by "<%...%>". These are the ASP delimiters. This tells the ASP environment to process information contained within these tags. Line 11 references the document object's write member function. Here we take the string "The server name is" and concatenate the location object's ServerName member variable. Now we append the "." to the string and pass this new string to the document.write function. The string is written to the output stream and we continue processing the HTML file. The remaining two HTML close tags are added to the output stream and the resulting output is sent to the client.

The script is processed by the VBScript scripting language because it is the ASP default and we didn't indicate another language to use.

What Does the Future Hold?

When CGI was first proposed, it was a needed solution to interface with information gateways. Eventually, endless storehouses of information were accessible by Internet browsers. The development community rushed to create CGI access to database and other applications. It wasn't too long before some sites had hundreds or even thousands of CGI processes running at a time. Hardware requirements for servers increased and the drawbacks of CGI began to show. A search for alternatives to CGI began.

In direct response to this, it seems every server manufacturer created an API specific to their product. Despite proclaimed compatibility, these custom APIs were seldom usable with other products. Realizing the failure of CGI to meet the skyrocketing needs of today's dynamic Web sites, http://www.w3.org/ the World Wide Web Consortium is beginning to develop new standards that will address these issues. Although no standard has been approved, several have been proposed.

http://www.OpenMarket.com/ FastCGI is an open standard sponsored by OpenMarket. It is essentially an implementation of CGI with several extensions to improve performance. FastCGI is language independent, meaning many of the CGI applications that exist today can be easily ported to this environment. Unlike server-specific APIs, FastCGI spawns processes independent of the Web server. This adds extra safety in that an errant FastCGI script won't crash the server itself. Since FastCGI isn't tightly linked with any specific server software, it provides a consistent environment for Web application development.

FastCGI libraries are currently available for C/C++, Java, and Perl. FastCGI is a proposed open standard and these libraries are available free of charge.

http://www.digitalcreations.com/   Another possible solution is the ILU Requester proposed by Digital Creations. The ILU Requester is a model for extending Web servers through a standard, distributed object model. It creates an interface to a particular server's API. This object model is exposed through an infrastructure called API scripting.

API scripting services are accessed through objects receiving requests http://www.python.org/   from the ILU. Python is the current preferred scripting language. Support for maintained state, authorization and logging are incorporated. Performance is impressive compared to similar CGI applications. ILU Requester permits execution of a server process outside of its address space and even on another machine for flexible load balancing.

The ILU Requester is available for Netsite and Apache Servers. The Requesters are available on the Solaris, Digital Unix, Linux, AIX, and BSDI platforms. Support for Windows NT and OS/2 are also planned.

http://www.microsoft.com/IIS/   Microsoft ISAPI is an extension mechanism designed for Web server support/ISAPI/   manufacturers. Any server that supports ISAPI can load and run executable Dynamic Link Libraries (DLLs) in the HTTP server's address space. This architecture promises lower overhead because the process actually runs inside the server's memory space. On the other hand, CGI programs run as separate processes and communicate with the server across process boundaries.

Two types of DLLs are supported under ISAPI. The first are termed extensions. ISAPI server extensions are DLLs that are called by an HTTP server as the result of an HTTP request. A server extension might process form information, store it to a database, and return an HTML file to the client. The second type of DLLs are termed filters. ISAPI filters register with a server for notification of when certain types of events occur. When the requested event occurs, a server filter is called. It can then intercept and review or alter data being sent to the server or to the client. ISAPI filters can be used to implement a custom encryption or authentication method.

Microsoft and other third party developers provide tools for creating and debugging ISAPI DLLs. All ISAPI programs must be written in a language that can be compiled and is executable.

http://developer.netscape.com/

Netscape also has a server API, NSAPI. Netscape's API is designed for sites that experience significant CGI usage. Netscape NSAPI code libraries are compiled into DLLs on Windows NT and into shared objects on various Unix platforms. This multi-platform support is an advantage NSAPI enjoys.

NSAPI keeps a table of available functions a code library can access. These functions are described as steps of an HTTP request. Netscape identifies the six step categories available to the API:

Six Steps in NSAPI
1. Authorization translation
2. Name translation
3. Path checks
4. Object type
5. Respond to request
6. Log the transaction

The exposed functions help move data access away from the library, avoiding unnecessary parsing of cryptic data structures. Information is stored in a structure called a parameter block and retrieved by requesting name-value pairs stored in this block.

http://www.apache.org/api/

The Apache API is similar to NSAPI. It is designed to extend the Apache Server's capabilities. It categorizes request handling in a series of eight steps:

Eight Steps in Apache API
1. URI-Filename translation
2. Authorization ID checking
3. Authorization access checking
4. Access checking other than Authorization
5. Determining MIME type of the requested object
6. Fixups
7. Sending a response to the client
8. Logging the request

At each step or phase, the server looks through its list of registered Shared Objects to see if they have a handler for the step. If they have a Handle, Decline, or Signal handler, it is invoked. At this point a phase is terminated and the request-response process continues. Each step is handled by the first shared object registered for processing. Logging and Fixups phases continue through the list of shared objects, giving each an opportunity to do some processing.

The Apache API, like the Netscape API, runs shared objects inside the server's memory space.

http://developer.oracle.com/ wbsvr/wrb/

The final next generation API we'll discuss is Oracle's WRB. The Web Request Broker (WRB) is a higher application-level environment in contrast to the low-level ISAPI, Apache API, and NSAPI interfaces. The WRB refers to Web-based applications as cartridges. Each cartridge is run in its own memory space and can be started and stopped with no effect on the server itself or any other running cartridge. A cartridge is not dynamically linked into the HTTP server's memory space.

Central to the WRB architecture is the Web Request Broker Dispatcher. The dispatcher interacts with the server to locate the requested cartridge and forwards a request for execution to it. The Dispatcher manages multiple instances of a cartridge and balances load to enhance cartridge performance. The Dispatcher can also authenticate requests from broker database sessions.

WRB cartridges are developed as shared objects. These objects are registered with the WRB Application Engine. This engine can work with any WRB-enabled application.

The WRB allows construction of Web-based applications without requiring detailed knowledge of an HTTP transaction. Currently the Oracle Web Server product is the only one supporting the WRB architecture.

Many of these next generation alternatives are still developing. Before committing to one of these alternatives, check with its governing organization. Most API development is not for the timid. C programming experience is required. For this reason alone there is resistance to replacing CGI and its scripting-extensible environment, with something subtle, cryptic, and complex.

Creating HTML Forms

HTML forms can be created with any text editor or visual page creation application. In this section we'll discuss how HTML forms are created.

The front end of any form application is its user interface. HTML offers a complete set of Tags used in form construction. Radio buttons, check boxes, text areas, menus, and push buttons are all available items. All items in an HTML form are enclosed in the <FORM> tag.

```
<FORM> ACTION=? ENCTYPE=? METHOD=?
```

The form tag is a dynamic tag. All form elements that appear between it and its matching close tag </FORM> are included in that form. Multiple forms can be defined on one HTML page.

The HTML form tag defines three attributes. Action defines what the form should do when the form information is submitted. The action is typically an URL. The following URL directs form submission to a process.pl script.

```
<FORM ACTION='process.pl">
```

The ENCTYPE tag allows the form to specify in what format the form data is submitted. The most common ENCTYPE is text/HTML but application/vnd.fdf is another possibility. The final attribute of the form tag is METHOD. It defines the HTTP method used to pass data to the server. The two options for form submissions are GET and POST. For submissions of information larger than 1024 bytes, always use the POST method. A well-formed FORM tag would look like the following example:

```
<FORM ACTION="process.pl" ENCTYPE="text/html"
METHOD="POST">
...form fields go here...
</FORM>
```

There are eleven different types of form input fields. Nine of these fields are described as attributes of the <INPUT> tag.

Input field type	HTML
Checkbox	<INPUT TYPE="CHECKBOX">
File	<INPUT TYPE="FILE">
Hidden Text	<INPUT TYPE="HIDDEN">
Image	<INPUT TYPE="IMAGE">
Password Text	<INPUT TYPE="PASSWORD">
Radio Button	<INPUT TYPE="RADIO">
Rest	<INPUT TYPE="RESET">
Submit	<INPUT TYPE="SUBMIT">
Text Box	<INPUT TYPE="TEXT">
Menu	<SELECT><OPTION>Option 1</SELECT>
Multi-line Text	<TEXTAREA> </TEXTAREA>

To create a check box, a single line of HTML is required. Check boxes should be used to present a user with several choices. Check boxes choices aren't mutually exclusive. These choices can be selected or not without affecting the other options.

```
<INPUT TYPE="CHECKBOX" NAME="Checkbox1"
Value="email" CHECKED>
```

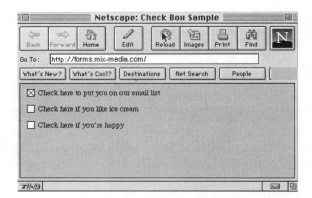

Check boxes differ from radio buttons in this way. A group of radio buttons ask a user to make a single selection from a group of choices. Once the user makes a selection, the other radio buttons in the group change to an unselected state. The choice of one radio button excludes others in the group.

The FILE tag is used to upload a file to the server. The FILE tag produces a text field and a button. When the button is clicked it activates a file browser window that asks a user to locate a file. Alternatively, the text field accepts the file name.

```
<INPUT TYPE="FILE" NAME=MY_FILE"
ACCEPT="image/+">
```

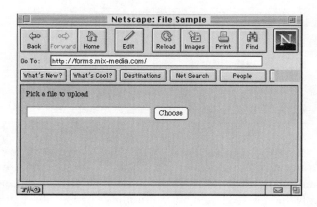

Hidden is an invisible field developed as a work-around for the stateless-ness of HTTP connections. This field type is passed back and forth between the client and the server and can be used to identify the client. Hidden fields aren't used for data input. Information from previous forms can be sent back to the client that include data from previous forms.

```
<INPUT TYPE="HIDDEN" NAME="user_id"
VALUE="0101-00-01">
```

The image input type is used to create graphic submit buttons. If you choose to use an IMAGE type as a submit button, form fields are sent to the server in name/value pairs, and the x and y coordinates of the mouse click are submitted as name/values of the IMAGE field's name appended with ".x" or ".y".

```
<INPUT TYPE="IMAGE" NAME="mouse_pt"
SRC="button.gif">
```

The Password type input field is a text field that substitutes "*" characters to hide the input from view. This maintains security from someone looking over your shoulder but not much more.

```
<INPUT TYPE="PASSWORD" NAME="Password">
```

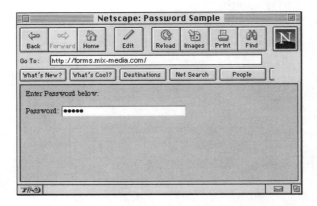

Radio buttons are designed to present a user with a set of alternatives from which a single choice is made. Radio buttons in a group all have the same name attribute but have a unique value attribute. Upon submission only the checked Radio button submits a name/value pair to the server.

```
<INPUT TYPE="RADIO" NAME="SELECTION" VALUE="1"
Checked>
<INPUT TYPE="RADIO" NAME="SELECTION" VALUE="2">
<INPUT TYPE="RADIO" NAME="SELECTION" VALUE="3" >
```

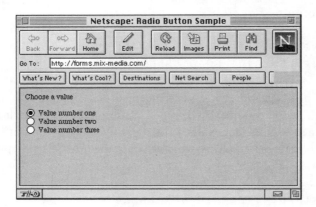

The TEXT input type allows the capture of keyboard input from the user. The field's size can be set to limit the viewable characters, and the maximum number of accepted characters can also be determined. By indicating an initial value, you can set the default text for the field.

```
<INPUT TYPE="TEXT" SIZE="50" NAME="USER"
VALUE="Enter your name here...">
```

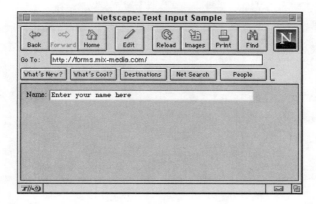

The RESET input type creates a button that resets the form's fields to its original default values. It's useful to include a reset button to allow users to start over in entering data.

```
<INPUT TYPE="RESET" VALUE="Reset this form">
```

The SUBMIT input type is used to create buttons that, when clicked, trigger the browser to submit the form information to the server.

```
<INPUT TYPE="SUBMIT" VALUE="Submit it...">
```

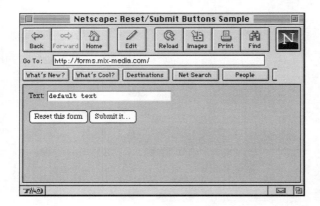

Another common interface element used in forms is menus. Menus are used to select one choice or multiple choices from a list. One-from-many menus are usually displayed as pop-up menus, and multiple choice menus are displayed as list boxes. Menus in HTML are created with the <SELECT> tag.

```
<SELECT NAME="PLANET">
<OPTION VALUE="1" Selected> Earth
<OPTION VALUE="2"> Mars
<OPTION VALUE="3"> Jupiter
<OPTION VALUE="4"> Uranus
<OPTION VALUE="5"> Pluto
</SELECT>
```

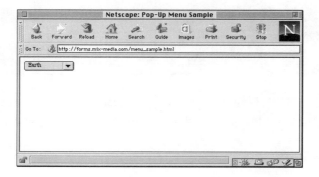

The final element type available in HTML is the multi-line text field. Multi-line text areas are created with the <TEXTAREA> tag. For anything more than one line of text this tag is required.

```
<TEXTAREA NAME="COMMENTS" ROW="3" COLUMNS="30">
This is the default text.
</TEXTAREA
```

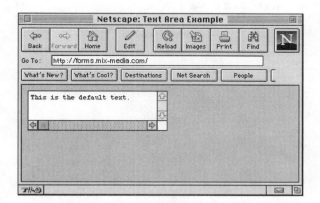

Attributes	Definition
NAME	Name used to identify the field when the form is submitted to the server
ROWS	Specifies the number of visible lines of text in the browser window.
COLS	Specifies the visible width of the window. The distance is figured in average character widths of the font the browser uses to display text.

Once you've created your forms, there are two ways you can submit the information to the server, GET and POST. The data is actually packaged up the same way. The difference is where the form data is stored when it's sent to the server.

Using the GET method, form fields are packaged up in key/value pairs and stored in the QUERY_STRING environment variable. This method places a 1-kilobyte limit on the amount of data that can be passed.

The POST method packages up the form fields in key/value pairs and sends the data to the server where it's stored in the standard input stream. The length of the data is stored in the CONTENT_LENGTH environment variable. This method is not restricted by the 1-kilobyte limit.

If a form is submitted to a server using GET, the field information is appended to the URL. It would look something like this:

```
http://home.mix-media.com/shell-cgi/form.pl?
name=Bill&age=40
```

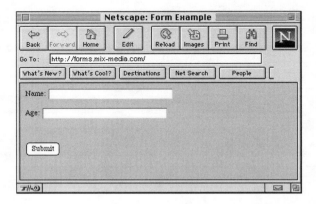

The string is further encoded if any field information contains spaces or any HTML control characters. If the user typed in Bill Clinton for a name, the URL would look like this:

```
http://home.mix-media.com/
shell-cgi/form.pl?name=Bill+Clinton&age=40
```

In the case of control characters, a "%" character is substituted followed by the ASCII value.

All this information is stored in the QUERY_STRING environment variable. The information appended to the URL after the "?" contains the key/value information. If the POST method is used, the same pre-packaging of information occurs. However, the place where data is stored differs.

Creating PDF Documents

A growing number of Internet sites are posting PDF documents as well as HTML pages. An interesting quality of PDF is that the design of printed pieces remains intact. As many people discovered, the rich visual language developed over hundreds of years of print use does not exist on the Internet in HTML. The inability to specify exact positions for placement of items in HTML has been found to be insufficient by graphic designers. Typographic excellence simply is unreachable with the tools available today for HTML page creation.

For these reasons, graphic documents such as annual reports, advertisements, and technical specifications, are most often posted as PDF documents. It is much easier to retain their original formatting using PDF.

Creating PDF documents is simple. If you have constructed the original document in any application that can print, you can convert the same document into PDF. Fonts and graphics can be embedded to insure the exact layout is recreated each time a user accesses the file no matter what computer platform they are using.

For simple documents, you choose the Acrobat PDF Writer as the printer you want to use and save the file to disk. If you have complex documents that contain EPS graphics, you are better off printing your file to disk as a postscript file and processing it with the Distiller application. I've found the Distiller produces smaller and cleaner PDF files and I use it exclusively for generation of PDF files.

With the release of Acrobat 3.0, Adobe has incorporated Forms technology similar to HTML forms. You can now set up and process your forms-based applications using PDF files to gather your information. The only difference with these PDF files is that an extra step is required to identify the form fields. This is done with the Forms tool inside the Acrobat Exchange environment.

Creating and formatting form fields

The forms tool is used to create fields that can be filled in by an Acrobat Exchange or Reader user. Form fields are created by defining the area of the field on the page and then naming it. After creating a field, use the form tool to format it, identify its type, define its appearance, and associate an action with it.

Adding form fields to a PDF document is simple

To create a form field, with the form tool selected, drag the cross-hair icon to make a box. When you release the mouse, a dialog appears asking you to give the field a name.

Available Field Types

As with HTML, there are a bevy of field types available in PDF. Buttons, checkboxes, menus, radio buttons, and text fields can additionally have their appearances, actions, and formats set.

Adding buttons

Buttons are the Internet's mechanism for invoking actions. PDF embraces and extends this methodology. In PDF, buttons are associated with actions or sequences of actions. These actions vary from opening a file, playing a sound, or submitting data to a CGI application for processing.

To add a button, create a form field and select Button from the Type menu in the Field Properties dialog box. Select the Button Options tab, and you are posed with attributes for the button.

The Highlight menu specifies the display of the button when the user clicks it. There are currently four options available for button highlighting:

Button Highlighting Options

Invert	inverts the colors in the button.
None	no change in the button appearance.
Outline	highlights the field border.
Push	creates a 3Dbutton using the text, the icon, or both entered in the pushed appearance.

The layout menu specifies the appearance of the button when it is at rest:

Resting Button Options

Text	displays the text entered in the Button Appearance section.
Icon	displays the icon chosen in the Button Appearance section.
Icon top, text bottom	displays the text and icon specified in the Button Appearance section in the relationship specified by the layout choice.

To choose an icon, click the Icon button beneath Button Appearance. Any page of a PDF file can be used as an Icon; however no other formats are currently supported.

Browse for a PDF file containing a page you want to use as an icon and Open it. Using the scrollbar, locate the page you wish to use and click the OK button. To make a button with another appearance when pushed, select an icon in the Pushed Appearance section. Locate the PDF file containing the page you wish to use. Again, use the scrollbar to navigate to the specific page and then click the OK button.

To complete the button's appearance, switch to the Appearance tab, and select border and text attributes for the button field.

Buttons do not require actions but most buttons make use of them. To specify an action for this button field, click the Actions tab and select the submit behavior from the When This Happens box on the tab. Then click Add, specify an action, and click Set Action.

You can select any combination of mouse behaviors for a field. You can also specify any combination of actions for mouse behavior. Adobe recommends these combinations be kept below ten for each individual field.

Click OK to close the Field Properties dialog box, and put into effect the appearance and actions we have established.

Adding check boxes

Check boxes are used to gather multiple choices presented to a user in a list. Radio buttons are used when a choice between two items must be made. To add a check box, with the form tool selected, create a form field and select Check Box from the Type menu in the Field Properties dialog box. Activate the Check Box Options tab and select a style for use when the check box is activated.

You should enter a value that will represent the item when it is sent to a CGI application. This is the same as the value key that is used in HTML.

If you want the check box to appear checked by default, choose Default.

Finally, activate the Appearance tab, and select border and text attributes for the check box.

To specify an action for this form field, first activate the Actions tab. Next, select the desired behavior from the When This Happens box on the tab and click the Add button. Finally, specify an action, and click the Set Action button.

To put your settings into effect, click OK to close the Field Properties dialog box and then test your checkbox.

Combo boxes/Pop-up menus

Combo boxes are used to provide the user with a list of items to choose from. To add a combo box, with the forms tool selected, create and name a form field. Choose Combo Box from the Type menu in the Field Properties dialog box.

Next, activate the Combo Box Options tab, and enter a value in the Item field. Click Add to commit your attributes for the Combo Box. Type in a value name that represents the Combo Box. It will be assigned the string value of the item chosen when the form is submitted to a CGI application. You can tell the Combo Box how you want the items it contains sorted.

If you want the items alphabetically ordered, select the Sort Items option. If you are happy with the way the items are ordered you can still move them around after they are entered by selecting the item and clicking the Up or Down button.

A type of Combo Box common on the Windows platform is one that allows the user to enter/edit text if they do not like the options given them. To enable editing of list items, select the Edit table option on the options tab.

Finally, activate the Appearance tab, and select the field's border and text attributes.

If you want to specify an action for the Combo Box, activate the Actions tab, choose the behavior you desire from the When This Happens box, and click Add. When this behavior occurs an action will be triggered.

Choose the action you want to invoke from the available list and click the Set Action button.

When you click OK and close the Field Properties dialog box, the selected attributes are applied to the Combo Box.

Radio buttons

Radio buttons are appropriate when you want a user to choose one item from a list of choices. If a user can select more than one item from your list, check boxes should be used. Related radio button field names must be the same, but for each button the values must be different.

Adding a radio button is simple. With the Forms tool selected, create and name a form field.

The Field Property dialog box will appear when you let up on the mouse button.

Select Radio Button from the Type menu to change the field to a radio button.

To customize the radio button, activate the Radio Buttons Options tab.

Select a style from the Style menu. The circle type is default but several options are available.

Enter a value that will be set if the radio button is chosen when the form is submitted to a CGI application.

You can indicate if the button is selected when the form is loaded by checking the default option. In this way you can set values that suggest what the user should choose.

To alter the radio button visual display, click the Appearance tab, and select the desired border and text attributes.

If you want to specify an action for this radio button, activate the Actions tab and select a behavior from the When This Happens box. Click the Add button and choose an available action. Click the Set Action button to add the action to the radio button.

To apply the selected attributes to the radio button, click OK to close the Field Properties dialog box.

Text fields

Text fields are used to gather textual information in single or multi-line formats. Text fields are most often used to gather information like a name, an address, or a phone number.

To add a text field, make sure the forms tool is selected in the Acrobat Exchange toolbar and create and name a form field.

Indicate the field will be a text field by selecting Text from the Type menu in the Field Properties dialog box.

To set the field's attributes, select the Text Options tab and choose from the options discussed below.

The default option specifies what text to display as the suggested default value for the field. By leaving this field blank, no default text is displayed. If you do not want the text to be editable, use the Appearance tab to make the field read-only.

Choosing an alignment sets the alignment of text inside the field. The Multi-line option allows your text box to have more than one line.

If you want to limit the number of characters in the text field, enter a number from 1 to 32,767. The default value is 32,767.

There are times when you want to conceal text entered into a field. The Password option allows for this. A field with the password attributes displays text as a series of asterisks to insure private entry of data.

Finally, activate the Appearance tab, and choose border and text attributes for the text field.

Occasionally you may want to specify an action to execute for this text field. To attach an action, activate the Actions tab and select a behavior from the When This Happens list. You specify an action by clicking on the Add button and choosing an action from the list. Once your desired action is highlighted, click the set action button to associate it with your text field.

To apply the attribute you have set, click OK to close the Field Properties dialog box.

Determining field appearances

Once a field is created, it is possible to alter the way your field appears from the Field Properties dialog box. You make choices based on the options available on the field's Appearance tab. With Acrobat 3.0 you can choose from the following options.

Set border color and background color by first clicking the Attributes checkbox. The color picker tile will activate, allowing you to choose a color based on the available system palette. Non-selection of a border or background color creates a transparent field. If you want the field to block out what it overlays, you must specify some background color. To choose a width for a border or a style, select from the pop-up menus listing the available options.

The attributes for text contained in the field are shown in the text sub-section of the field properties dialog box. Here you choose type size, color, and font. Currently Adobe's base 13 fonts are the only ones allowed for text fields. Any font can be used in a PDF document, but this base 13 restriction applies to text entered into form fields. The pop-up form field will only show the set of base 13 fonts you can choose from. The Auto size selection will fit entered type to the vertical size of your text field. In the case of multi-line fields, 12 point type is used by the Auto setting. There are four check boxes on the bottom of the Appearance tab.

Read Only
Hidden
Required
Don't Print

Selecting the read-only checkbox will deny the user data entry privileges. It is a read-only field. The hidden checkbox tells the PDF viewing application if it should show or hide the field. A neat feature of PDF is that fields can be viewed or shown at anytime. It is a great trick to hide several fields and make them visible after a certain action occurs. You can make it appear that a graphic has changed in this way.

The required attribute prompts the user to enter data if it has been omitted when a submission occurs. This is the same functionality found in a required field in HTML.

Lastly you can indicate if the contents of the field should be printed or not. Check the Don't Print box if you don't want information to print. It makes the entered text a sort of transparent ink.

Field Options

For each type of field, it is possible to set various option values. For instance, text fields accept a default value, and a type of alignment. A text field can be a single line or multi-line. Also, a limit can be placed on the number of characters the field accepts. The final option for a text field is to mark it as a password field. This substitutes asterisks for characters entered into the field.

Radio button and checkbox options include the style or shape of the radio button or checkbox, the value exported, and the button or checkbox's default state. Radio buttons and checkboxes can be set to show as selected or unselected.

List and combo box options include the values contained by the list box. Text entries can be added or subtracted from the list and export values can be set for each individual item. A default selection can be indicated and the list box can be set to sort the list entries alphabetically.

Button options indicate a highlighting method for a button in various states. The appearance of the button can be altered during a mouse up, mouse down, or a mouse rollover event. The layout of the button can be set to text, icon, or any combination of the two. Any PDF page can be selected as a button's appearance. The button icon can be resized to fit the button or scaled to show only a portion of the selected icon.

Field Actions

You can have a mouse event trigger any Acrobat action. By activating the Actions tab, you can select any action to execute when one of four mouse events occur. The four events in the When This Happens window are:

When This Happens Window Options

Mouse Up	when the mouse button is released
Mouse Down	when the mouse button is clicked
Mouse Enter	when the mouse moves over the field
Mouse Exit	when the mouse moves from inside to outside the field

Click one of the mouse event types and then click the Add button. The Actions dialog box appears, allowing you to set any action to execute from the pop-up list. Select an action, then click okay. Your choice will appear in the Do the Following window.

You can add as many actions as you want but no more than ten are recommended. Chosen actions appear in the Do the Following Things list box. The order actions are executed in the order they are displayed. Actions can be moved up or down by highlighting the action, then clicking the up or down arrow.

Once you have included an action, if you need to edit its properties, highlight it and then click the edit button. The Action dialog box appears, allowing you to make necessary changes to your action.

If you need to remove an action, highlight it in the list and click the delete button. This will remove the action from the Do The Following Things list box.

There are four actions that are specific to our purpose of creating forms:

Submit
Reset
Import Form Data
JavaScript

A typical form has several fields for data entry, a submit button and a reset button. To create the form, we create two button fields and assign the first one the submit action and the second the reset action. The button with the reset action, when invoked, will reset all the form fields to their default value. The button with the submit action, when invoked, will submit the data entered into the form fields to a URL. This URL is indicated when you set up the submit action. If you indicate a CGI application to process your form submission, the submit action packages up and sends the forms data to the selected CGI. You can send this information as HTML or FDF format. If you have an existing CGI application, PDF forms will function without modification as long as you send data in HTML format. Sending data as FDF allows for more options but requires a new version of your CGI to be constructed.

It is possible to import FDF data from an existing file. One reason to do this is it is easier for users to fill in repetitive information. For instance name, address, phone number, and email address can all be imported from a personal profile file located on the user's machine. This requires that fields in the personal profile match field names in the form that is importing the data. While importing from the file, data that matches field names is flowed into the matching fields and any other non-matching information is ignored. The most common way of implementing this lookup is to create a form that generates a personal profile for a user. Then each file that wants to use updating invokes an import action asking the user to locate a file to use to import the field information. By using a consistent field naming scheme, you can save your users time by not requiring repeated entry of matching data.

Additionally, list boxes can be set to execute a custom JavaScript when the list box selection changes.

Formatting Field Entries

Text fields can have a format. A format takes a user's input and when they select the next field on the form, the format take the entry and properly formats it.

There are built-in formats for numbers, percentages, dates and times. There are also several special formats for social security numbers and phone numbers.

If these built-in options aren't sufficient, custom JavaScript can be entered to perform the formatting.

Validating Field Entries

Number fields are capable of being validated. Input is gathered after a value is entered and run through a validation routine.

The built-in type of validation requires that a value must be between two values. If another type of validation is needed, it must be performed by a custom validation script. Custom scripts are written in JavaScript and can be entered in the Validate tab in the Field Properties dialog box.

Calculations From Field Entries

Field values can be the result of a calculation. From the Calculate tab in the Field Properties dialog box, basic calculations such as a sum, a product, an average, a minimum, or a maximum are indicated by selecting that type from a menu. The fields used in the calculation are chosen by clicking the pick button and selecting from a list. More complicated calculations are performed by entering a custom script. Again, all custom scripts are written in JavaScript.

Duplicating Fields

You can duplicate fields on the current page or across multiple pages. When you duplicate a form field, the fields can be set to have data duplicate into each instance of a duplicate field. The duplicate fields are allowed to have different appearances, but they must be named the same and they must have the same actions. Changing an action of a duplicate field will change the action for all fields with the same name.

To duplicate a field on the same page first, the form tool needs to be selected. The first way to duplicate a field is to press the Control key (Windows) or the Option key (Macintosh) while dragging the field to the new location. You can press the Shift key while dragging the field to constrain it horizontally or vertically. The second way is to select the field, choose Copy from the Edit menu, then Paste, and move the new field to its desired position. The third way to duplicate the field is, with the field selected, to choose Duplicate from the Edit menu in the Field sub-menu. A dialog appears asking you to enter the page number for the new field. Enter the current page number and click the OK button. To duplicate a field to a different page, choose select across all pages or type in a page range, and click the OK button.

Resizing Fields

Only the field selected is resized, even if other fields with the same name exist. Resizing fields is done graphically. To resize a field while the forms tool is selected, select a field and position the cursor over a corner anchor point. The cursor changes to a two-headed arrow. With the move button activated, drag the field's outline to resize it.

Note: Holding down the Shift key when re-sizing maintains the original properties of the field. Press Shift + Arrow Key to resize a field approximately 1/72 inch at a time.

Field Tab Order

The default tab order for form fields is the order in which the fields were created. It is possible to graphically change the order in which the user tabs through the fields. To change the current tab order of existing fields, select Set Tab Order from the fields sub-menu of the Edit menu. All fields display a number indicating the current tab order. To reorder the current tabbing order, click each field in the order that they should be encountered. To start renumbering at a field, press the Control key (Windows) or the Option key (Macintosh) and click the previous to the one you want to start with. Then continue clicking the remaining fields on your form.

Export Values

Each field can have a value that is exported during a submit action. The value is the actual information sent to a CGI application for processing. You need to define an export value field if the data will be collected or processed by a CGI application.

The default export value for a check box that has been selected is On. Both the Combo and List box's default value is the actual text of the item the user selects. Indicate an export value for combo or list boxes only if you want it to be different from the item selected in the list.

Radio buttons are special fields. Grouped radio buttons have the same field name but each button has a different export value. This ensures that the radio buttons display correctly in the browser.

Exporting and importing form data

Unlike HTML, you can export form data from a PDF form, creating a new file containing only the form field data. You can use this file as an archive, an electronic submission, or just to examine the values you are exporting. You can also import this data into PDF forms.

To export form data to a file, from the File menu choose the Form Data menu item from the Export sub-menu. You are presented with the save file dialog asking you to name the file you are saving. Enter a name for your data file and click the Save button.

You can import this file data to view or print by choosing the Form Data menu item from the Import menu item under the File menu. Note: if you import form data from a file, only the field values that match are updated. Any non-matching fields are ignored.

Chapt

Working with a Server–The Back End

In this chapter we discuss the mechanism used by HTTP servers to execute external scripts and programs. This is the same interface used to process form submissions and to return information to the client.

Overview

Web browsers and servers don't know much about the documents they handle. A browser requests a URL not knowing specifics about the document itself. The server isn't much smarter about the transaction. It locates the requested file and returns it to the browser. The server is courteous enough to include type information with the document it returns. This type information is called Multipurpose Internet Mail Extensions (MIME). The client browser uses this information to properly display the file that's returned. This is how static HTML pages are requested and returned.

On occasion, the URL requested is a script or program. In this instance the server recognizes the request is for a script or program and executes it. The standard interface for executing a program and returning its result to a browser is called the Common Gateway Interface (CGI).

Why would you need to run a program? CGI programs can read and write files and access databases or other programs. This allows the return of dynamic information to a client browser. The options seem almost limitless. In fact the only limiting factor is the stateless nature of HTTP connections. Each time a browser contacts a server, the server thinks it's the first time the two have ever spoken. This makes it difficult to store information between contacts. Several methods have been developed to maintain state with the server between HTTP requests.

The rest of this chapter concerns itself with what happens on the back end or server side of a request. We discuss how input is sent to the server and how output is returned to the client. We'll focus on the mechanics of CGI.

Common Gateway Interface

The Common Gateway Interface (CGI) is a publicly maintained specification from the National Center for Supercomputing Applications (NCSA). How the CGI process works is quite simple. The server recognizes that the requested URL is a script or program instead of a static file. Before the server launches the script, a number of environment variables are initialized. The variables are passed from server to script as parameters when the script is launched. The server may pass additional data to the script through the server's standard input STDIN stream. The CGI script reads these variables and if necessary the STDIN stream, and then processes information contained in them. When finished, it returns a result to the server through its standard output STDOUT stream.

http://hoohoo.ncsa.uiuc.edu/cgi/

For each instance of a script, the server passes it a set of environment variables. The server then waits for the script to finish. The script reads its environment variables and if necessary reads its STDIN stream. The script then returns its result through its STDOUT stream to the server. Finally, the server recognizes the script is finished and reads its result from the scripts STDOUT stream. This result is then returned to the requesting client's browser.

Getting Information
When a CGI program is invoked by the server, data is passed through the environment variables. The information is provided by one of two methods: GET or POST. The first task a CGI application performs is to determine in which way this data arrived. The CGI does this by accessing the REQUEST_METHOD environment variable.

In fact, the GET method is the same method a server uses to serve a static HTML document. The first of these two options is the GET method. GET appends data to the end of the URL. You've probably seen some really long URLs, such as:

```
http://forms.mix-media/welcome.pl?name=Name
```

The information following the '?' is what's received from a GET request and placed in the QUERY_STRING environment variable. For instance if the URL above is sent to a server for processing, the welcome.pl CGI is executed, GET is placed in the environment variable REQUEST_METHOD, and name=Name is placed in the QUERY_STRING environment variable.

The second way a CGI may receive information is through a POST. A POST invocation most often is received from a form document submitted by a browser. The REQUEST_METHOD for a POST is obviously POST. The difference with POST is that data is received through STDIN, your server's standard input stream. An interesting difference with receiving information via STDIN is that the data can be any length. The way to determine how much data you need to read from STDIN is to check another environment variable. CONTENT_LENGTH lets you know how much you need to read. An interesting note is that the QUERY_STRING in a POST method is not always empty. Depending on your server, information may be stored here that won't help accurate CGI processing. If CONTENT_TYPE is application/x-www-form-ulencoded, the STDIN stream must also be decoded.

What all this means is that each time a CGI program is called, it needs to do two things. First, determine which method invoked the CGI, and second, retrieve the data passed it. In addition, a POST must be checked to see if it is encoded, and if it is, it must be decoded.

CGI Environment Variables

http://hoohoo.ncsa.uiuc.edu/cgi/overview.html

http://www.w3.org/Protocols/

In order to pass data about the information request from the server to the script, the server uses command line arguments as well as environment variables. These environment variables are set when the server executes the gateway program. The following table lists the standard environment variables as defined by the NCSA specification.

Specification

The following environment variables are not request-specific and are set for all requests:

SERVER_SOFTWARE The name and version of the information server software answering the request (and running the gateway). Format: name/version

SERVER_NAME The server's hostname, DNS alias, or IP address as it would appear in self-referencing URLs.

GATEWAY_INTERFACE The revision of the CGI specification to which this server complies. Format: CGI/revision

The following environment variables are specific to the request being fulfilled by the gateway program:

SERVER_PROTOCOL The name and revision of the information protocol this request came in with. Format: protocol/revision

SERVER_PORT The port number to which the request was sent.

REQUEST_METHOD The method with which the request was made. For HTTP, this is "GET","HEAD","POST", etc.

PATH_INFO The extra path information, as given by the client. In other words, scripts can be accessed by their virtual pathname, followed by extra information at the end of this path. The extra information is sent as PATH_INFO. This information should be decoded by the server if it comes from an URL before it is passed to the CGI script.

PATH_TRANSLATED   The server provides a translated version of PATH_INFO, which takes the path and does any virtual-to-physical mapping to it.

SCRIPT_NAME   A virtual path to the script being executed, used for self-referencing URLs.

QUERY_STRING   The information which follows the "?" in the URL which referenced this script. This is the query information. It should not be decoded in any fashion. This variable should always be set when there is query information, regardless of command line decoding.

REMOTE_HOST   The hostname making the request. If the server does not have this information, it should set REMOTE_ADDR and leave this unset.

REMOTE_ADDR   The IP address of the remote host making the request.

AUTH_TYPE   If the server supports user authentication, and the script is protected, this is the protocol-specific authentication method used to validate the user.

REMOTE_USER   If the server supports user authentication, and the script is protected, this is the username the user is authenticated under.

REMOTE_IDENT   If the HTTP server supports RFC 931 identification, then this variable will be set to the remote user name retrieved from the server. Usage of this variable should be limited to logging only.

CONTENT_TYPE   For queries which have attached information, such as HTTP POST and PUT, this is the content type of the data.

CONTENT_LENGTH   The length of the said content as given by the client. In addition, the header lines received from the client, if any, are placed into the environment with the prefix HTTP_ followed by the header name. Any "-" characters in the header name are changed to "_" characters. The server may exclude any headers which it has already processed, such as Authorization, Content-type, and Content-length. If necessary, the server may choose to exclude any or all of these headers if including them would exceed any system environment limits.

An example of this is the HTTP_ACCEPT variable which was defined in CGI/1.0, or the header User-Agent.

HTTP_ACCEPT   The MIME types which the client will accept, as given by HTTP headers. Other protocols may need to get this information from elsewhere. Each item in this list should be separated by commas as per the HTTP spec. Format: type/subtype, type/subtype

HTTP_USER_AGENT   The browser the client is using to send the request. General format: software/version library/version.

Let's examine these variables through a simple example.

```
1.    #!/usr/local/bin/perl
2.    print "Content-type: text/html", "\n\n";
3.    print "<HTML>", "\n";
4.    print "<HEAD><TITLE>About this Server
      Environment</TITLE></HEAD>", "\n";
5.    print "<BODY><H1>About this Server</H1>", "\n";
6.    print "<HR>","\n","<PRE>";
7.    print "<br>", "Server Software:        ",
      $ENV{'SERVER_SOFTWARE'};
8.    print "<br>", "Server Name:            ",
      $ENV{'SERVER_NAME'};
9.    print "<br>", "Gateway Interface:      ",
      $ENV{'GATEWAY_INTERFACE'};
10.   print "<br>", "Server Protocol:        ",
      $ENV{'SERVER_PROTOCOL'};
```

```
11.    print "<br>", "Server Port:          ",
       $ENV{'SERVER_PORT'};
12.    print "<br>", "Request Method:       ",
       $ENV{'REQUEST_METHOD'};
13.    print "<br>", "Path Information:     ",
       $ENV{'PATH_INFO'};
14.    print "<br>", "Path Translated:      ",
       $ENV{'PATH_TRANSLATED'};
15.    print "<br>", "Script Name:          ",
       $ENV{'SCRIPT_NAME'};
16.    print "<br>", "Query String:         ",
       $ENV{'QUERY_STRING'};
17.    print "<br>", "Remote Host:          ",
       $ENV{'REMOTE_HOST'};
18.    print "<br>", "Remote Address:       ",
       $ENV{'REMOTE_ADDR'};
19.    print "<br>", "Authorization Type:   ",
       $ENV{'AUTH_TYPE'};
20.    print "<br>", "Remote User:          ",
       $ENV{'REMOTE_USER'};
21.    print "<br>", "Remote Identification: ",
       $ENV{'REMOTE_IDENT'};
22.    print "<br>", "Content Type:         ",
       $ENV{'CONTENT_TYPE'};
23.    print "<br>", "Content Length:       ",
       $ENV{'CONTENT_LENGTH'};
24.    print "<br>", "Mime Types Accepted:  ",
       $ENV{'HTTP_ACCEPT'};
25.    print "<br>", "User Agent:           ",
       $ENV{'HTTP_USER_AGENT'};
26.    print "<HR>","\n","</PRE>";
       print "</BODY></HTML>", "\n";
27.    exit (0);
```

Let's look at this Perl example a line at a time. The first line of this program instructs the server to use the Perl interpreter located with this
path. On Windows NT and Macintosh, this is ignored and the Perl interpreter associated with the file type is used.

The second line of this script outputs a bare minimum HTTP header. The header contains the MIME content_type of the response we generate. Here we are generating HTML so "text/html" is our content type. There are also two new line characters appended to the line. The first ends the "content-type: text/html" line, and the second creates a blank line indicating the end of our header.

Having printed our header to the standard output stream, we can access the environment variables through the %ENV associative array. After we print our HTML HEAD, TITLE, and BODY tags to standard output, we begin accessing the environment variables. We walk through each variable and output it to STDOUT.

Finally, we output our closing HTML tags and exit the Perl program with the "0" no error exit code.

Output from this program should look like this. However, your server environment variables might differ.

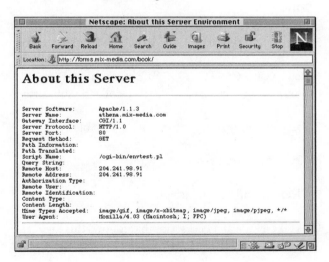

Accessing Input

A CGI script is evoked through one of four methods. POST and GET are the two concerned with passing form information. A script might receive a HEAD or PUT request but these are used infrequently by CGI.

The difference between GET and POST is slight. A GET request stores all information submitted by a client in the QUERY_STRING environment variable passed to the script. The POST method stores submitted information in the STDIN stream sent to the CGI script. A CGI script typically examines the REQUEST_METHOD environment variable.

No matter what language you use to construct your CGI scripts a similar process is followed. The following list describes the necessary steps to properly handle a CGI request.

1.Retrieve the script's environment variables.

2. Check the REQUEST_METHOD variable for the type of request.

3. If the request method is GET, retrieve the QUERY_STRING environment variable.

4. If the request method is POST, retrieve the CONTENT_LENGTH environment variable and read the content length number of bytes from STDIN.

5. If the request method is neither GET or POST, return an error.

6. Retrieve the CONTENT_TYPE environment variable and if it is application/x-www-form-urlencoded, decode the submitted information.

7. Parse the submission into separate variables.

8. Now do any processing you want.

9. Clean up and exit the script.

Let's take a look at a Perl script that follows this logic.

```
1.   #!/usr/local/bin/perl
2.   $request_method=$ENV {'REQUEST_METHOD'};
3.   $content_length=$ENV {'CONTENT_LENGTH'};
4.
5.   if ($request_method eq "GET")
6.   {
7.     $form_data=$ENV {'QUERY_STRING'};
```

```
8.      }
9.      elsif ($request_method eq "POST")
10.     {
11.       $form_data_length=$ENV{'CONTENT_LENGTH'};
12.       if ($form_data_length)
13.       {
14.         read(STDIN, $form_data, $form_data_length);
15.       }
16.     }
17.     else
18.     {
19.       ## send the user some error information
20.       exit (1);
21.     }
22.     if ($content_type eq "application/x-www-form-
        urlencoded")
23.     {
24.       $form_data=~ s/% ({\dA-Fa-f][\dA-Fa-f])
25.         /pack ("c", hex ($1))/eg;
26.     }
27.     @param_names=split (/&/, $form_data);
28.     for each $param_value (@param_names)
29.     {
30.       ($param, $value)=split (/=/, $param_value);
31.       $value=~ tr/+//;
32.       $value=~ s/%([\dA-Fa-f][\dA-Fa-f])/pack
33.         ('c", hex ($1))/eg;
34.     }
35.     ##
36.     ## Insert your processing statements here
37.     ##
38.
39.     print ("Content-type: text/html","\n\n");
40.     ##
41.     ##Send your output back to the server
42.     ##
43.     exit (0);
```

Output—Sending Information to a User
When a client requests an URL, it expects a valid HTTP response back

from the server. The fact that a server launches a CGI script and returns its output doesn't concern the client.

HTTP headers are used by your client browser to determine what type of information has returned and how to display it.

The structure of an HTTP header response block is loosely organized and very simple. First of all, the header information can be output in any order. The only real requirement is that the response header end with a blank line. The simplest response header is a one entry block describing the MIME content type of the file.

```
Content-type: text/html
```

This header describes the response file as a text/HTML MIME type. The following table is a listing of HTTP header types. A complete header includes HTTP protocol revision and server status, server name and version, and the MIME content type.

http://www.w3.org/

Header	Description
Content-length	Length in bytes. Most often found in a binary data response.
Content-type	MIME type of returned data
Expires	Expiration data and time of a document. Signals browser to reload after this date and time.
Location	Redirects response to another existing file. Send this header without other headers.
Pragma	Used to toggle document caching on and off.
Status	Status of request. Send this header alone.
Refresh	Specifies interval for client to reload document.
Set-Cookie	Client-stored data. Used to maintain state over multiple requests.

All our examples so far have shown simple examples of scripts returning HTML. CGI isn't limited here. In fact CGI scripts can return any type of document. Your CGI script might examine the HTTP_ACCEPT environment variable and return different documents, depending on what MIME types the requesting client browser supports. Each of the response headers is worth a brief discussion.

The Content-length header is used to inform the server of the size in bytes of the data sent. If you're sending image files or other binary data, Content-Length tells the server how much data to read even if there are end of file or end of line characters.

The Content-type header is used to identify the MIME type of the data that follows. This allows the requesting browser to identify and prepare for handling of the response. If the Content-type is text/plain or "text/html", the browser will display it in its window. If it's another type that is handled by a plug-in or helper application, the browser will forward the data appropriately.

The Expires header is a reference for browsers that cache files. The expired date is stored in the response header of a cache file. If the expired date hasn't passed, the URL will be loaded from its cached copy the next time it's requested. If your data is time sensitive, it's important to include an expiration date. A dynamically generated document will be reloaded from its static cached copy if the Expiry information is incorrectly recorded.

The Location header should not be included as part of a complete response header. This header is used to instruct the server to locate an existing document and return it. This is often used to return an error or a thank you document.

```
Location:/thank_you.html
```

This header instructs the server to look for a document named thank_you.html in the server's root directory. The path is not restricted to the machine the server runs on. Any URL can be the target of a Location response header.

The Pragma header is used to instruct the client how to handle caching the response document. The following example advises the client not to cache the document. This is directed at documents generated dynamically to avoid caching these documents displaying out of date information to a client.

```
Pragma: no-cache
```

The Status header is intended to give a bit more information on the request.

```
Status: One of the following status codes
```

The following table describes the available status codes.

Status Codes

http://www.ics.uci.edu/
pub/ietf/http/rfc1945.html
#Status-Codes

The data sections of messages Error, Forward and Redirection responses may be used to contain human-readable diagnostic information.

Success 2xx	These codes indicate success. The body section if present, is the object returned by the request. It is a MIME format object, and may only be in text/plain, text/html or one of the formats specified as acceptable in the request.
OK 200	The request was filled.
Created 201	Following a POST command, this indicates success, but the textual part of the response line indicates the URI by which the newly created document should be known.
Accepted 202	The request has been accepted for processing, but the processing has not been completed. The request may or may not eventually be acted upon, as it may be disallowed when processing actually takes place. There is no facility for status returns from synchronous operations such as this.
Partial Information 203	When received in response to a GET command, this indicates that the returned meta information is not a definitive set of the object from a server with a copy of the object, but is from a private overlaid Web. This may include annotation information about the object, for example.
No Response 204	Server has received the request but there is no information to send back, and the client should stay in the same document view. This is mainly to allow input for scripts without changing the document at the same time.

Error 4xx, 5xx	The 4xx codes are intended for cases in which the client seems to have erred, and the 5xx codes are for the cases in which the server is aware that it has erred. It is impossible to distinguish these cases in general, so the difference is only informational. The body section may contain a document describing the error in human readable form. The document is in MIME format, and may only be in text/plain, text/html or one of the formats specified as acceptable in the request.
Bad request 400	The request had bad syntax or was inherently impossible to satisfy.
Unauthorized 401	The parameter to this message gives a specification of authorization schemes which are acceptable. The client should retry the request with a suitable Authorization header.
Payment Required 402	The parameter to this message gives a specification of charging schemes acceptable. The client may retry the request with a suitable ChargeTo header.
Forbidden 403	The request is for something forbidden. Authorization will not help.
Not found 404	The server has not found anything matching the URI given.
Internal Error 500	The server encountered an unexpected condition which prevented it from fulfilling the request.
Not implemented 501	The server does not support the facility required.
Service temporarily overloaded 502	The server cannot process the request due to high load (whether HTTP servicing or other requests). The implication is that this is a temporary condition which may be alleviated at other times.
Gateway timeout 503	This is equivalent to Internal Error 500, but involves a server accessing some other service, and the response

from the other service did not return within a time acceptable to the gateway Since, from the point of view of the client and the HTTP transaction, the other service is hidden within the server, this may be treated identically to Internal error 500, but it has more diagnostic value.

Redirection 3xx	The codes in this section indicate action to be taken (normally automatically) by the client in order to fulfill the request.
Moved 301	The data requested has been assigned a new URI, and the change is permanent. (Note: this is an optimization, which must, pragmatically, be included in this definition. Browsers with link editing capability should automatically relink to the new reference, where possible.) The response contains one or more header lines of the form URI:<url> String CrLf which specify alternative addresses for the object in question. The String is an optional comment field. If the response is to indicate a set of variants which each correspond to the requested URI, then the multipart/alternative wrapping may be used to distinguish different sets.
Found 302	The data requested actually resides under a different URL; however, the redirection may be altered on occasion as for "Forward". (When making links to these kinds of documents, the browser should default to using the URI of the redirection document, but have the option of linking to the final document). The response format is the same as for Moved.
Method 303	Method: <method> <url> body section. Note: This status code is to be specified in more detail. For the moment it is for discussion only. Like the found response, this suggests that the client go try another network address. In this case, a different method may be used too, rather than GET. The body section contains the parameters to be used for the method. This allows the document to be a pointer to a complex query operation. The body may be preceded by the following additional fields as listed.

Not Modified 304	If the client has done a conditional GET and access is allowed, but the document has not been modified since the date and time specified in the If-Modified-Since field, the server responds with a 304 status code and does not send the document body to the client. Response headers are read as if the client had sent a HEAD request, but are limited to only those headers which are relevant to cache managers and which may have changed independently of the document's Last-Modified date. Examples include Date, Server, and Expires.
	The purpose of this feature is to allow efficient updates of local cache information (including relevant meta information) without requiring the overhead of multiple HTTP requests (e.g., a HEAD followed by a GET) and minimizing the transmittal of information already-known by the requesting client (usually a caching proxy).

The Refresh header is used to inform the client how often to reload the response document. Setting the Refresh header to 10 instructs the client to reload the response data every 10 seconds. It's useful in establishing a client pull. It's equivalent to having a user hit the reload button at a specified interval in their browser.

Finally, the Set-Cookie header instructs the client to store information on its own machine. This information can be requested later to identify a client. It's a process developed to work around the statelessness of HTTP communication. A server might store cookie information in a database and the next time an HTTP connection occurs, the supplied cookie is matched with information stored in the database and it's as if the client never broke its connection.

Security for CGI Applications—Secure Sockets Layer (SSL)

Information is sent whizzing around the Internet in packets. These packets bounce around before they reach their destination. The trouble with this is that anyone can put a program online that examines packets. If private information is transmitted in these packets, there's nothing to prevent it from being gathered by an unauthorized party. This security hole is the main reason that so much hesitation surrounds openly conducted business on the Internet.

As a possible solution SSL was developed by Netscape and RSA Data Security, Inc. SSL initiates a connection through a three phase procedure. First the client and server identities are verified. Certificates of authority are used. These digital signatures are issued by various companies whose job it is to verify identity and issue these IDs. Secondly, the client and server agree upon an encryption scheme they'll use to encrypt data before it's sent and decrypt it when it's received. This encryption is session specific. Lastly, as data is sent between the client and the server, SSL insures the integrity of the data itself. This prevents packet substitution by a malicious user or data loss due to transmission failure.

If security isn't a concern, SSL isn't necessary. If you plan to conduct transactions through your forms-based applications, SSL is certainly worth consideration as a secure method to augment CGI-based forms.

Server Side Includes

Another popular mechanism for dynamic generation of response data is Server Side Includes (SSI). Although SSI isn't considered part of CGI, it can be used to invoke a CGI script or include another file in the response data.

Server Side Includes are nothing more than bits of text embedded in HTML documents. SSI directories are embedded inside HTML comments. A typical SSI directive looks like the following:

```
<!--#echo var="SERVER_NAME"-->
```

Typically a Web server doesn't look at files it serves. It simply checks to see if the requesting user has the necessary security privileges to receive the file they desire, and if they do, the file is returned. However, there are situations when it is desirable for the server to read through a document before it is sent to a user. Depending on the file's content, the server could include differing information. This parsing of static HTML pages is what Server Side Includes is about.

A typical use for SSI is in a file that contains a company's copyright information. This information may need to be included on every page of your Web site. One solution is to type this information on every page. This isn't ideal for pieces of information that change very often. Wouldn't it be nice if you could store that bit of HTML that makes up the copyright information in one file and automatically have it included in each page? This is one thing SSI can accomplish.

A simple file that includes another file looks like the following:

```
1.   <HTML>
2.   <HEAD>
3.     <TITLE>A Typical Company Page</TITLE>
4.   </HEAD>
5.   <BODY>
6.   <H1>Welcome to Our Company Page</H1>
7.   Here is our company information.<BR>
8.   <BR>
9.   <HR>
10.  <!--#include file="footer.html"-->
11.  </BODY>
12.  </HTML>
```

The previous example includes a footer.html file at the bottom of the page. The information included in the footer.html can thereby be updated once and immediately is updated in any file that references it.

SSI isn't governed or maintained as a specification. This has led almost every server manufacturer to implement SSI in their own way.

To activate SSI, you should consult your particular server's documentation. For some servers you'll need to locate and modify various config files, while other servers just require you to click a checkbox to turn SSI on. Secondly, you'll need to add a MIME type of the SSI files. The NCSA server designates .SHTML as the file type that SSI processes and many others follow this lead. You can have your server process all HTML files by designating .HTML instead. You do this by adding text/x-server-parsed-html.html to the MIME type list. You'll also need to add a MIME type application/x-httpd-cgi.cgi if you want to enable the exe SSI command. The following example uses SSI to output the SSI Environment Variables.

Common SSI Commands

echo	<!-#echo var="SERVER_NAME"—>
include	<!—#include File="footer.html"—>virtual=
exec	<!—#exec cgi="/cgi-bin/counter.cgi"—>
	cmd="/bin/finger $
	REMOTE_USER@$REMOTE_HOST"
config	<!—#config errmsg="My message."—>
	<!—#config timefmt="%a%b%d%y"—>
	<!—#config sizefmt="bytes"—>
fsize	<!—#fsize file="/index.html"—>
flastmod	<!—#flastmod file="/index.html"—>
counter	<!—#counter type=" "—>

To configure your server to allow the above commands, you need to edit the configuration files. Specifically, the access.conf file needs to have options set for the directory you want processed. If you want the entire Web site processed, you'd set Options Includes ExecCGI on the server root directory. This enables SSI for the directory it's set on and all subdirectories.

Additional Variables in SSI

DOCUMENT_NAME	Name of the current file
DOCUMENT_URI	Path to the file
QUERY_STRING_ UNESCAPED	Undecoded query string
DATE_LOCAL	Date and Time in Local Time Zone
DATE_GMT	Date and Time in Greenwich Mean Time
LAST_MODIFIED	Last modification date and time of current file

The following example shows how to output CGI environment variables via SSI.

```
1.    <HTML>
2.    <HEAD>CGI Environment Variables - SSI
      </TITLE></HEAD>
3.    <TITLE>SSI Results!</TITLE>
4.    <BODY><H1>Here are the environment
      variables</H1><BR>
5.    Authentication type:     <!--#echo var="AUTHENTI-
      CATION_TYPE"--><BR>
6.    Document Name:     <!--#echo var="DOCUMENT_NAME"--
      ><BR>
7.    Document URI:     <!--#echo var="DOCUMENT_URI"--
      ><BR>
8.    Unescaped Query String:     <!--#echo
      var="QUERY_STRING_UNESCAPED"--><BR>
9.    Local Date:     <!--#echo var="DATE_LOCAL"--><BR>
      GMT Date:     <!--#echo var="DATE_GMT"--><BR>
10.   File Last Modified:     <!--#echo var="LAST_MODI-
      FIED"--><BR>
11.   <HR>
12.   </BODY>
13.   </HTML>
```

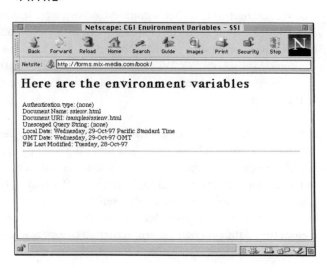

To use SSI, a server must be configured properly. It needs to know what file types to parse and which directives to allow. For proper configuration of SSI, refer to the documentation for your server.

Maintaining State with a Server

The stateless nature of HTTP makes it difficult to associate a series of connections into one visit. Forms-applications like a shopping cart or a multi-page survey need some way to track a client's previous actions.

Two main ways have developed to compensate for this inadequacy. The first method is to serve form-based applications through a CGI script. The second is by utilizing "cookies".

The first method involves sending information back and forth between client and server in hidden form fields. As a client fills out information in a succession of forms, all the previously gathered information is added to the next form in dynamically created hidden fields. This is the simplest method for carrying information between HTTP requests. A variation of this solution is to write the information to a temporary file and return only an identifier in a simple hidden field. This reduces the burden of transmitting large amounts of data between client and server.

http://developer.netscape.com
/cookies/

The second method is called a cookie. Cookies were invented by Netscape. A cookie is an HTTP header sent by a server to a client. A cookie-aware browser recognizes the Set-Cookie header and stores the cookie values on disk. When a browser next requests the URL, the client looks up the stored cookie value and returns it as a cookie header to the server.

A possible CGI solution might have a script check a requests header for a cookie. If it doesn't have a cookie, a new visit is set up and the Forms-based application begins. If a cookie is found, it's read and the visit is set to reflect information related to the cookie. After each action a client takes, the new cookie information is sent back and updated on the client. When a user decides to complete a transaction, the CGI reads all the transaction data, processes it, and returns a cookie reset for the next visit.

Cha

Visual Project index

This chapter presents a visual index of sample forms. It is intended to allow a reader to browse the samples to identify solutions similar to the reader's needs.

No amount of technical expertise is required to use this section. Callouts are provided to point the reader to following chapters that discuss the technical specifics of implementing the example.

Business Card Order

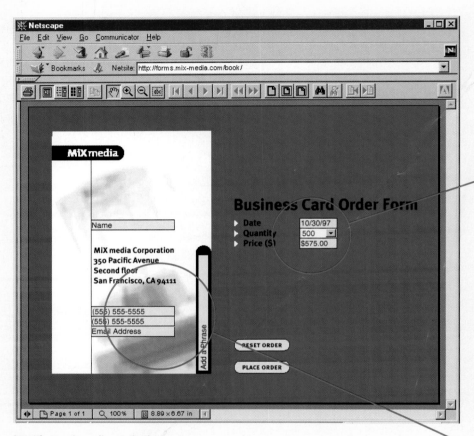

http//forms.mix-media.com/book/

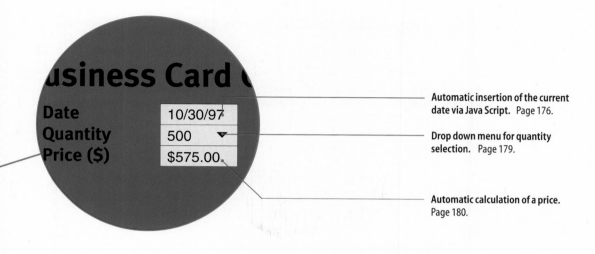

Business Card O

Date   10/30/97

Quantity   500 ▼

Price ($) $575.00

Automatic insertion of the current date via Java Script. Page 176.

Drop down menu for quantity selection. Page 179.

Automatic calculation of a price. Page 180.

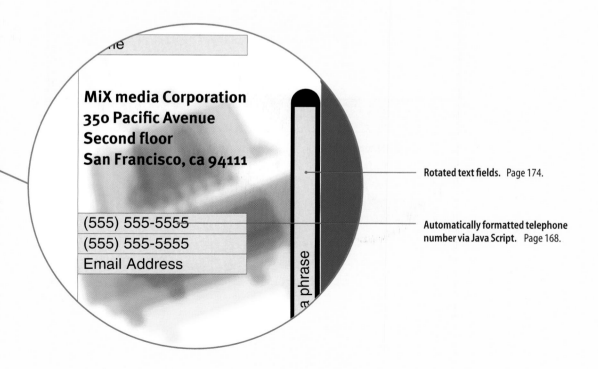

MiX media Corporation
350 Pacific Avenue
Second floor
San Francisco, ca 94111

(555) 555-5555
(555) 555-5555
Email Address

a phrase

Rotated text fields. Page 174.

Automatically formatted telephone number via Java Script. Page 168.

W4 Employer Form

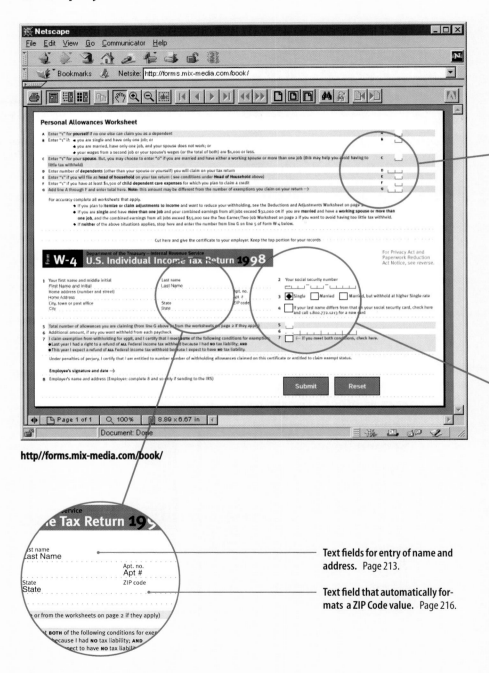

http//forms.mix-media.com/book/

Text fields for entry of name and address. Page 213.

Text field that automatically formats a ZIP Code value. Page 216.

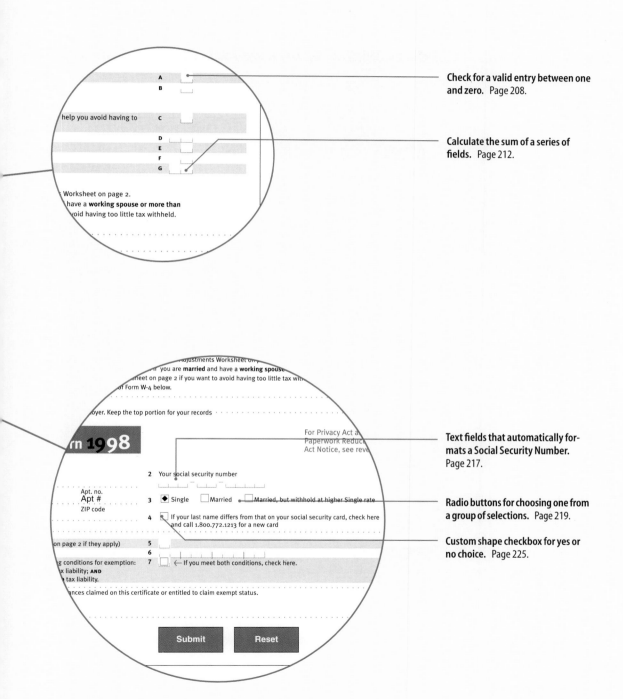

A
B

help you avoid having to C

D
E
F
G

Worksheet on page 2.
have a **working spouse or more than**
void having too little tax withheld.

Check for a valid entry between one and zero. Page 208.

Calculate the sum of a series of fields. Page 212.

...djustments Worksheet on
you are **married** and have a **working spouse**
...eet on page 2 if you want to avoid having too little tax wit...
...f Form W-4 below.

...oyer. Keep the top portion for your records

For Privacy Act a
Paperwork Reduc
Act Notice, see reve

rn 19 98

Apt. no.
Apt #
ZIP code

2   Your social security number

3   ◆ Single   ☐ Married   ☐ Married, but withhold at higher Single rate

4   ☐ If your last name differs from that on your social security card, check here
and call 1.800.772.1213 for a new card

on page 2 if they apply)   5
6

g conditions for exemption: 7   ☐ ← If you meet both conditions, check here.
x liability; **AND**
tax liability.

...nces claimed on this certificate or entitled to claim exempt status.

Submit   Reset

Text fields that automatically formats a Social Security Number. Page 217.

Radio buttons for choosing one from a group of selections. Page 219.

Custom shape checkbox for yes or no choice. Page 225.

1040 Tax Form

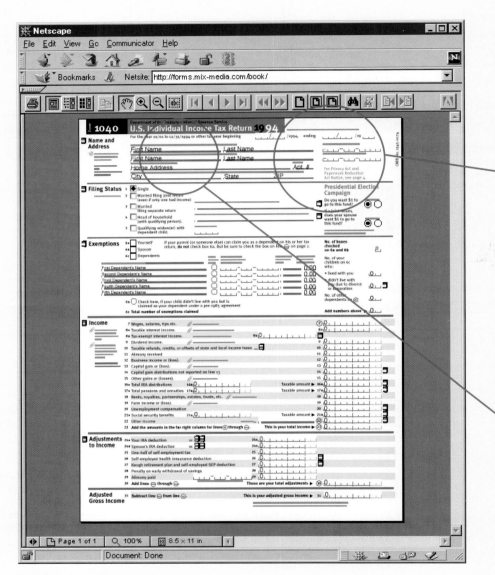

http//forms.mix-media.com/book/

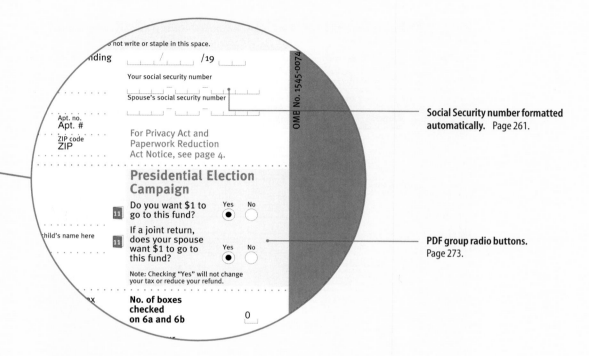

For Privacy Act and Paperwork Reduction Act Notice, see page 4.

Presidential Election Campaign

11 Do you want $1 to go to this fund?   Yes   No

11 If a joint return, does your spouse want $1 to go to this fund?   Yes   No

Note: Checking "Yes" will not change your tax or reduce your refund.

No. of boxes checked on 6a and 6b   0

Social Security number formatted automatically.   Page 261.

PDF group radio buttons. Page 273.

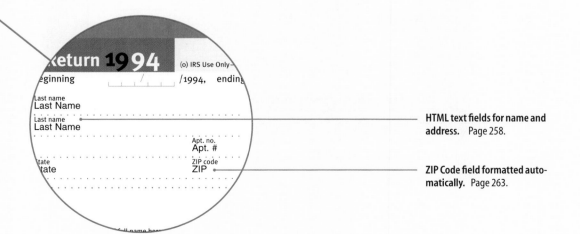

HTML text fields for name and address.   Page 258.

ZIP Code field formatted automatically.   Page 263.

1040 Tax Form, cont.

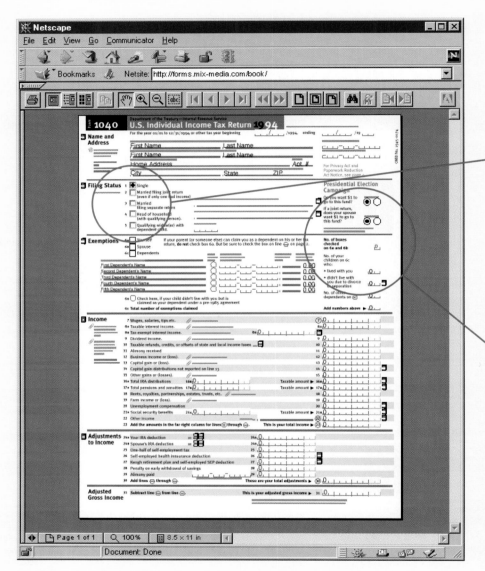

http//forms.mix-media.com/book/

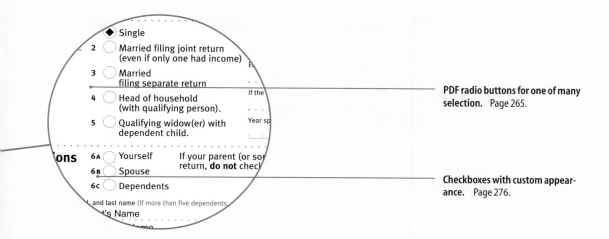

PDF radio buttons for one of many selection. Page 265.

Checkboxes with custom appearance. Page 276.

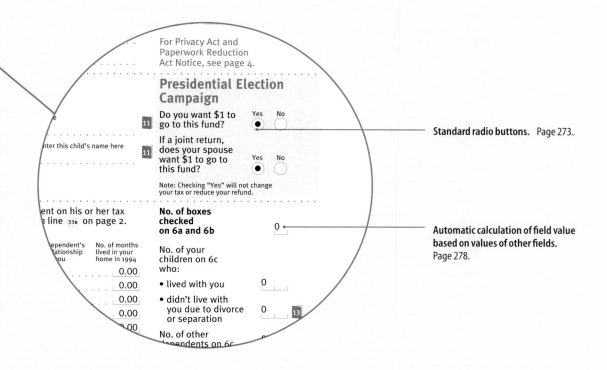

Standard radio buttons. Page 273.

Automatic calculation of field value based on values of other fields. Page 278.

1040 Tax Form, cont.

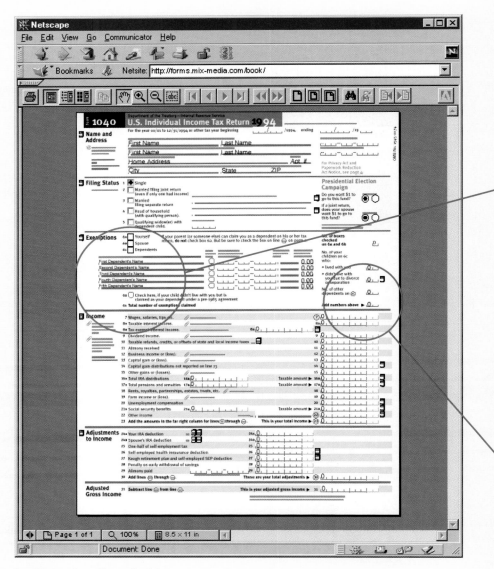

http//forms.mix-media.com/book/

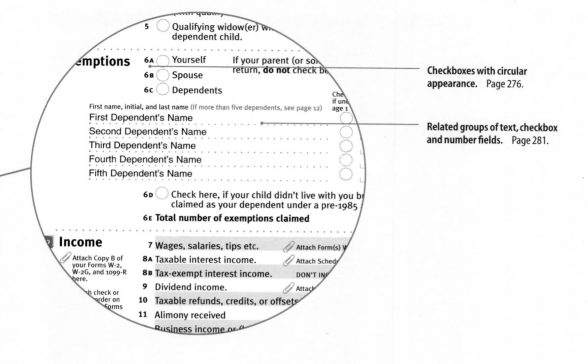

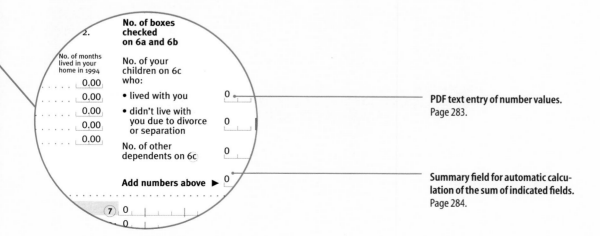

Checkboxes with circular appearance.   Page 276.

Related groups of text, checkbox and number fields.   Page 281.

PDF text entry of number values. Page 283.

Summary field for automatic calculation of the sum of indicated fields. Page 284.

1040 Tax Form, cont.

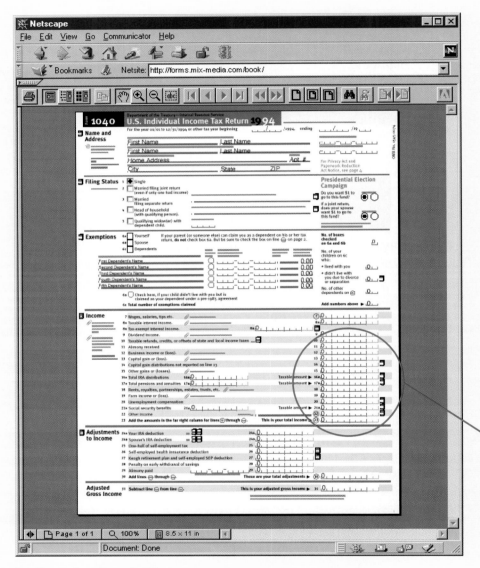

http//forms.mix-media.com/book/

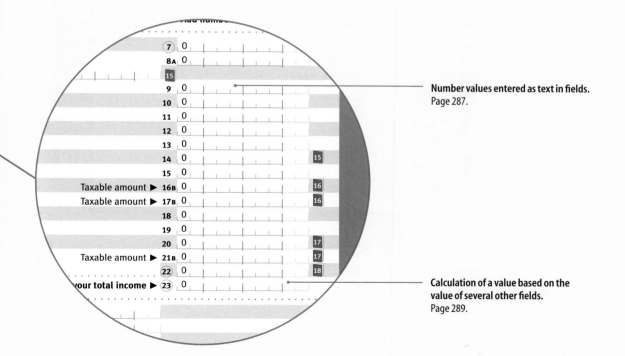

Number values entered as text in fields.
Page 287.

Calculation of a value based on the value of several other fields.
Page 289.

1040 Tax Form, cont.

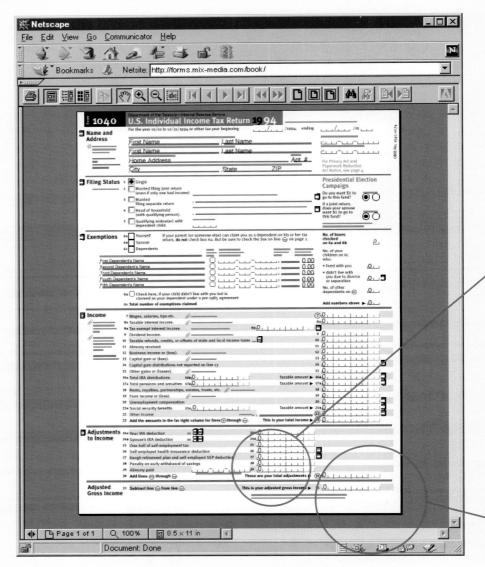

http//forms.mix-media.com/book/

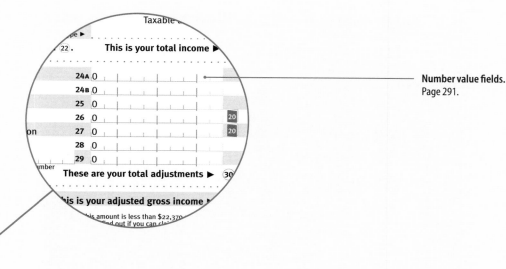

Taxable

pe ▶

22 .   **This is your total income ▶**

24A 0

24B 0

25 0

26 0   20

on   **27** 0   20

28 0

29 0

mber   **These are your total adjustments ▶** 30

his is your adjusted gross income ▶

his amount is less than $22,370
d out if you can clai

Number value fields.
Page 291.

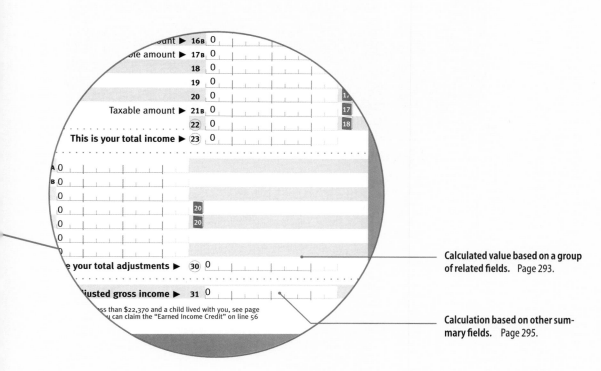

unt ▶ **16B** 0

le amount ▶ **17B** 0

18 0

19 0

20 0   1,

Taxable amount ▶ **21B** 0   17

22 0   18

This is your total income ▶ 23 0

A 0

B 0

0

0   20

0   20

0

0

e your total adjustments ▶ 30 0

justed gross income ▶ 31 0

ss than $22,370 and a child lived with you, see page
u can claim the "Earned Income Credit" on line 56

**Calculated value based on a group
of related fields.** Page 293.

**Calculation based on other sum-
mary fields.** Page 295.

Driver License Order

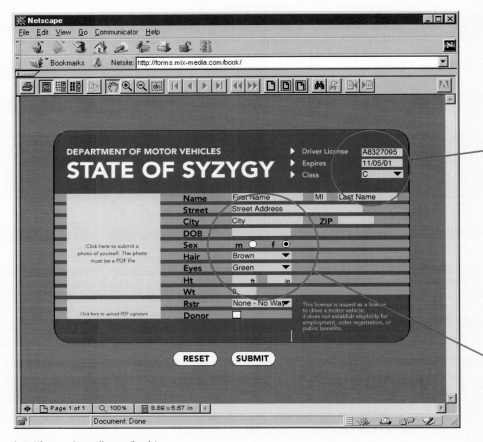

http//forms.mix-media.com/book/

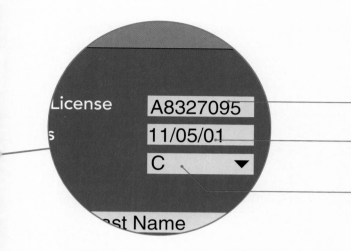

Automatic generation of a license number. Page 327.

Automatic calculation of an expiration date. Page 330.

PDF drop down menu for selecting a type of license. Page 332.

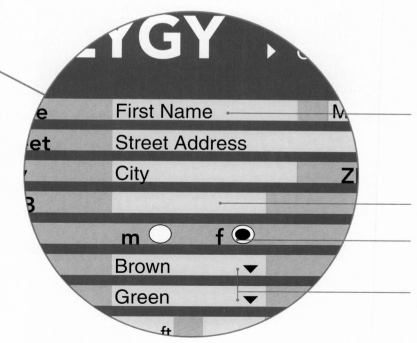

PDF text field for first name entry. Page 302.

PDF text field that automatically formats a date value. Page 316.

Radio buttons used for an either or selection. Page 307.

Drop down menus for selection from a list. Page 310.

Driver License Order Form, cont.

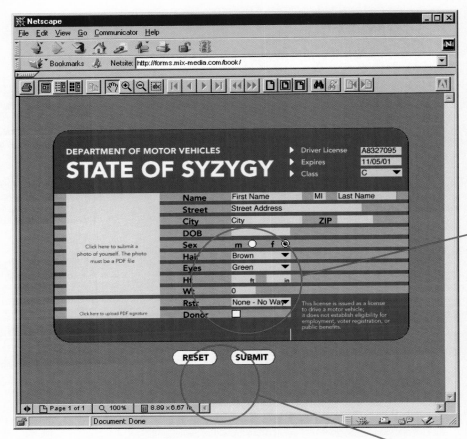

http//forms.mix-media.com/book/

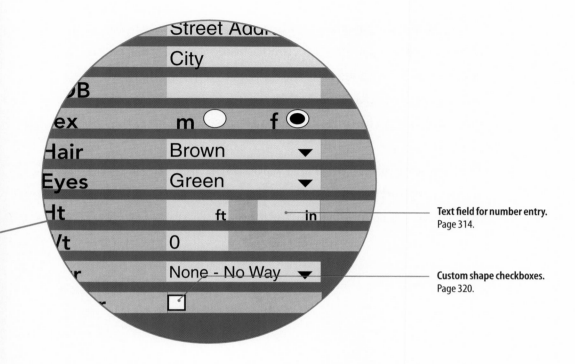

Text field for number entry.
Page 314.

Custom shape checkboxes.
Page 320.

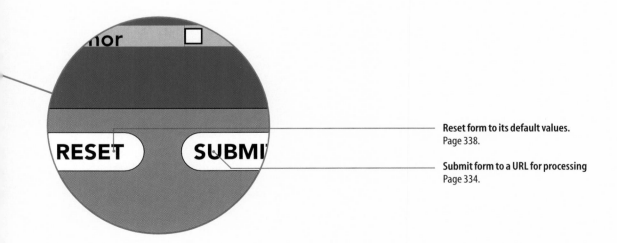

Reset form to its default values.
Page 338.

Submit form to a URL for processing
Page 334.

Employee Benefits

This example constructs a multi-page form application to track employee benefits information. Medical, Dental, Vision and general Employee Information are available. The methods used to construct the employee information form and the Medical Plan information path are discussed here.

The two additional dental and vision paths are available for viewing and downloading on the companion Web site, http://forms.mix-media.com/book/

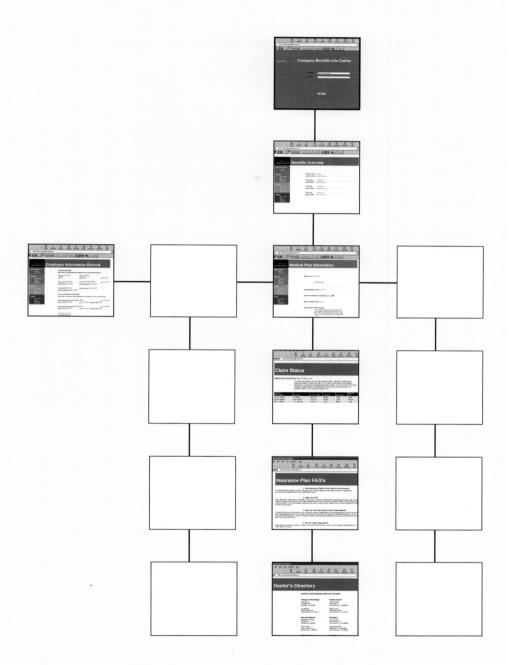

Employee Benefits

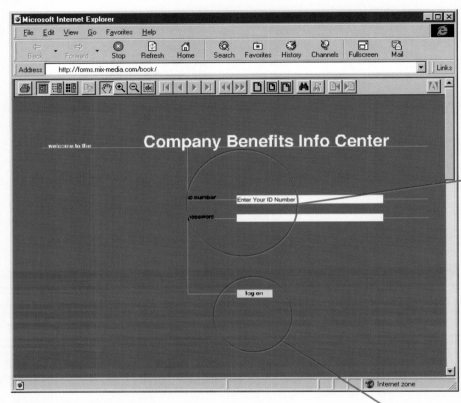

http//forms.mix-media.com/book/

id number

Enter Your ID Number

PDF text field.
Page 363.

password

Password field for hidden text.
Page 365.

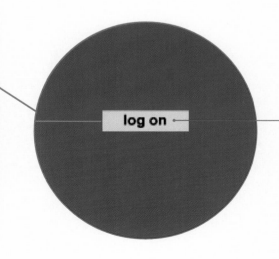

log on

Custom submit button queries database of authorized users.
Page 367.

Employee Benefits, cont.

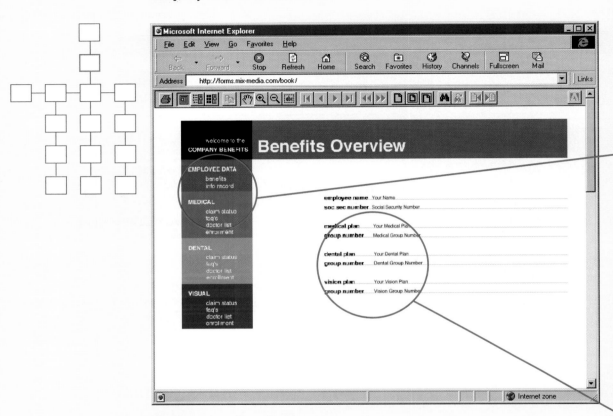

http//forms.mix-media.com/book/

welcome to the
COMPANY BENEFITS

EMPLOYEE DATA
benefits
info record

**PDF links to other documents in this
application.** Page 372.

employee name	Your Name
soc. sec. number	Social Security Nu
medical plan	Your Medical Plan
group number	Medical Group Num
dental plan	Your Dental Plan
group number	Dental Group Nu
vision plan	Your Visio
number	Vi

**Text information flowed into PDF
file following successful logon.**
Page 394.

**Returned data from database query
flowed into the PDF file.**
Page 394.

Employee Benefits, cont.

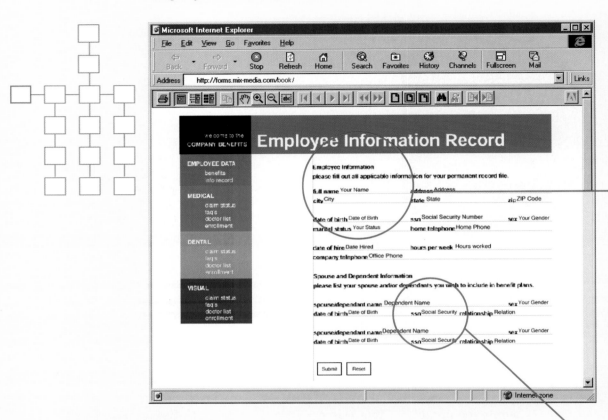

http//forms.mix-media.com/book/

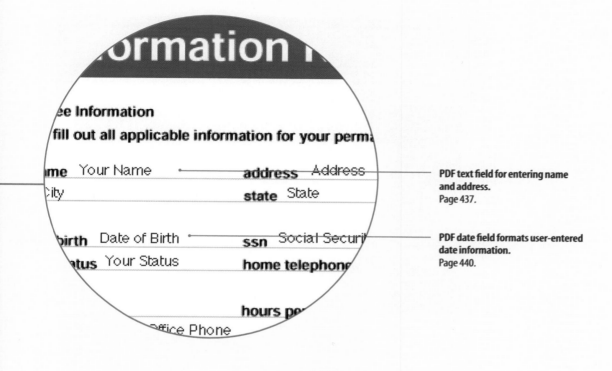

ormation

ee Information

fill out all applicable information for your perma

me Your Name   **address** Address

City   **state** State

birth Date of Birth   **ssn** Social Securi

tus Your Status   **home telephone**

hours pe

ffice Phone

PDF text field for entering name and address.
Page 437.

PDF date field formats user-entered date information.
Page 440.

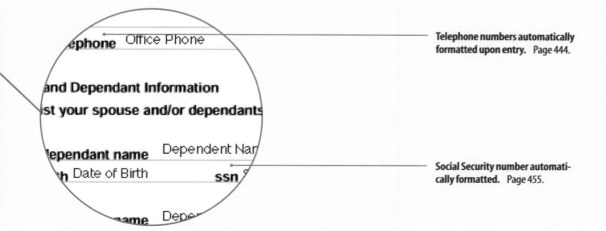

phone Office Phone

and Dependant Information

st your spouse and/or dependants

ependant name Dependent Nar

h Date of Birth   **ssn**

ame Depe

Telephone numbers automatically formatted upon entry. Page 444.

Social Security number automatically formatted. Page 455.

Employee Benefits, cont.

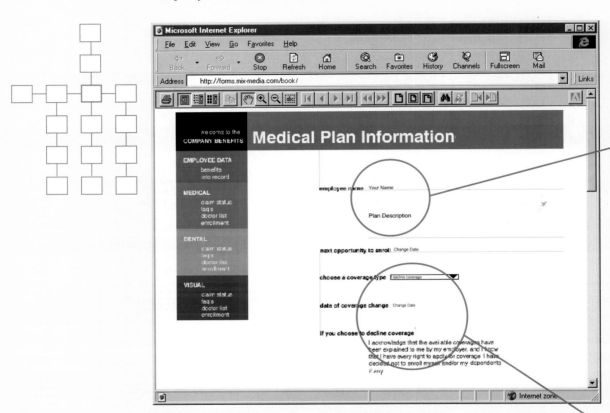

http//forms.mix-media.com/book/

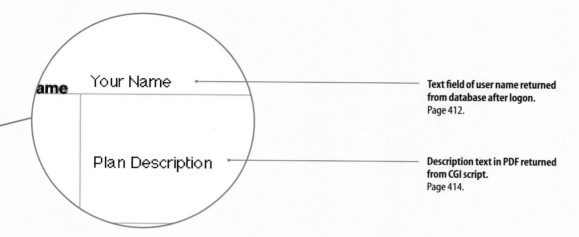

ame

Your Name

Plan Description

Text field of user name returned from database after logon.
Page 412.

Description text in PDF returned from CGI script.
Page 414.

type

I decline coverage

age change   Change Date

Date calculated from a Perl script and flowed into the PDF file.
Page 415.

to decline coverage

I acknowledge that the available coverag
been explained to me by my employer,
at I have every right to apply for co
ided not to enroll myself and/o

Employee Benefits, cont.

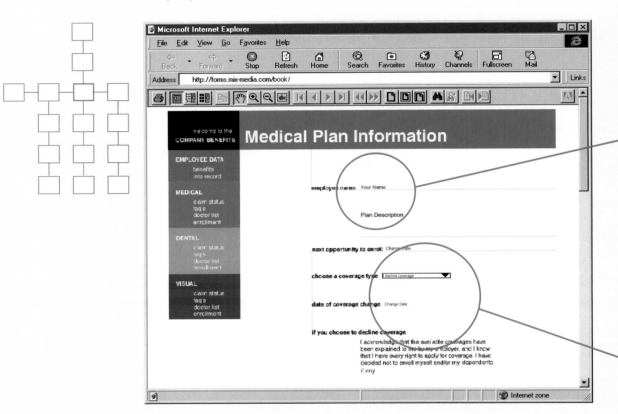

http//forms.mix-media.com/book/

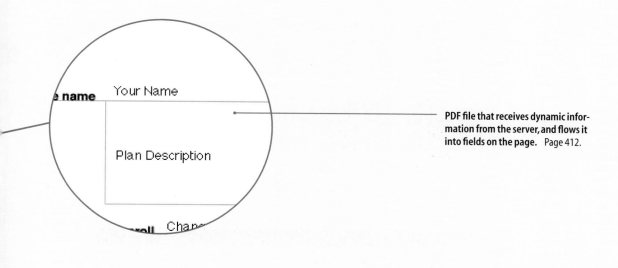

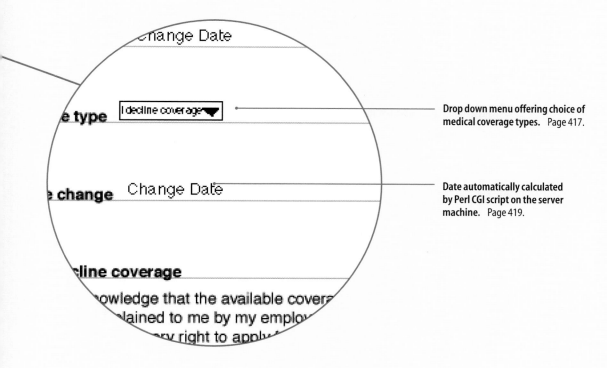

e name

Your Name

Plan Description

PDF file that receives dynamic information from the server, and flows it into fields on the page.   Page 412.

e type

Change Date

I decline coverage

Drop down menu offering choice of medical coverage types.   Page 417.

e change

Change Date

Date automatically calculated by Perl CGI script on the server machine.   Page 419.

cline coverage

owledge that the available covera
lained to me by my employ
ry right to appl

Employee Benefits, cont.

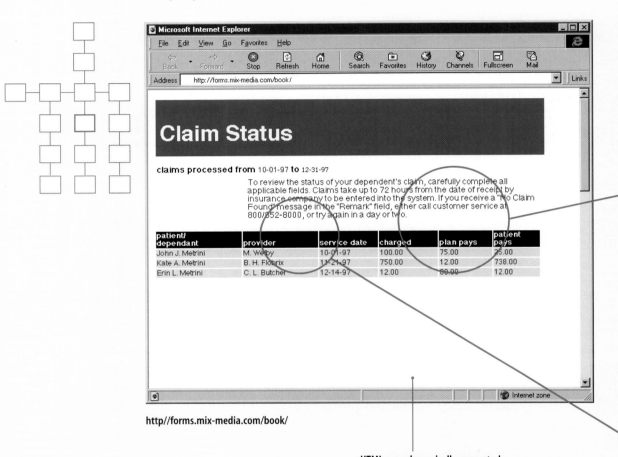

http//forms.mix-media.com/book/

HTML page dynamically generated
from information in an Oracle
database.

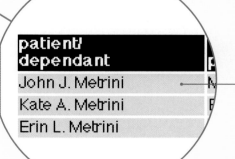

ur dependent's claim, care
s take up to 72 hours from the d
be entered into the system. If you
he "Remark" field, either call custome
y again in a day or two.

service date	charged	plan pay
10-01-97	100.00	75.00
1-21-97	750.00	12.00
8-14-97	12.00	00.00

HTML table dynamically generated
by a Perl script that queries an
Oracle database.
Page 424.

patient/ dependant	
John J. Metrini	N
Kate A. Metrini	E
Erin L. Metrini	

Claim records returned from
database query.   Page 424.

Employee Benefits, cont.

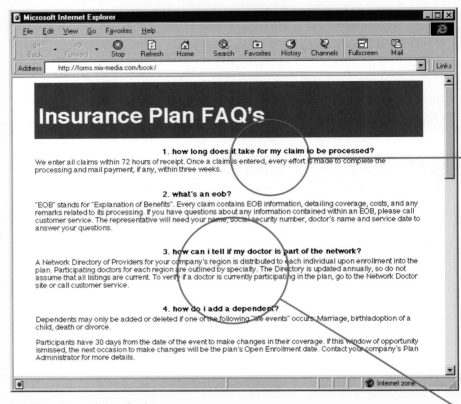

Insurance Plan FAQ's

1. how long does it take for my claim to be processed?
We enter all claims within 72 hours of receipt. Once a claim is entered, every effort is made to complete the processing and mail payment, if any, within three weeks.

2. what's an eob?
"EOB" stands for "Explanation of Benefits". Every claim contains EOB information, detailing coverage, costs, and any remarks related to its processing. If you have questions about any information contained within an EOB, please call customer service. The representative will need your name, social security number, doctor's name and service date to answer your questions.

3. how can i tell if my doctor is part of the network?
A Network Directory of Providers for your company's region is distributed to each individual upon enrollment into the plan. Participating doctors for each region are outlined by specialty. The Directory is updated annually, so do not assume that all listings are current. To verify if a doctor is currently participating in the plan, go to the Network Doctor site or call customer service.

4. how do i add a dependent?
Dependents may only be added or deleted if one of the following "life events" occurs: Marriage, birth/adoption of a child, death or divorce.

Participants have 30 days from the date of the event to make changes in their coverage. If this window of opportunity is missed, the next occasion to make changes will be the plan's Open Enrollment date. Contact your company's Plan Administrator for more details.

http//forms.mix-media.com/book/

1. how long doe

hours of receipt. Once a claim
t, if any, within three weeks.

2. what's an eob

of Benefits". Every claim co
If you have questions
e will need your

Static HTML page for frequently
asked questions.   Page 425.

ation of Benefits". Ever
processing. If you have ques
he representative will need your
stions.

3. how can i tell

rectory of Providers for your company's region
ating doctors for each region are outlined by s
all listings are current. To verify if a doctor is cu
stomer service.

HTML table simulating indented
first line of text.
Page 428.

4. how do i ad

nly be added or deleted if one of t

the date

Employee Benefits, cont.

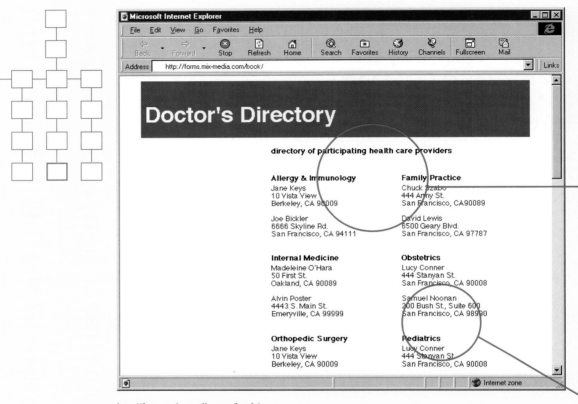

http//forms.mix-media.com/book/

of participating health care pro

y & Immunology

Keys
ta View
ey, CA 90009

kler
yline Rd.
cisco, CA 94111

ine

Family Pra

Chuck Szabc
444 Army St.
San Francisc

David Lewis
6500 Gear
San Fran

C

Three column HTML table simulating multi-column text.   Page 434.

Lucy Conner
444 Stanyan St.
San Francisco, CA

Samuel Noonan
200 Bush St., Suite 60
San Francisco, CA 989

Pediatrics

Lucy Conner
444 Stanyan S

Third column in an HTML table.
Page 435.

Stock Photo Library

http//forms.mix-media.com/book/

PDF document in frame for visual representation of printed document. Page 520.

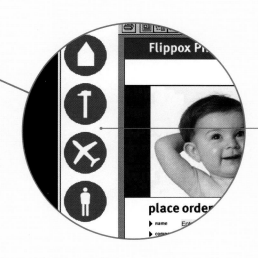

HTML frame used for navigation between section documents.
Page 518.

Stock Photo Library, cont.

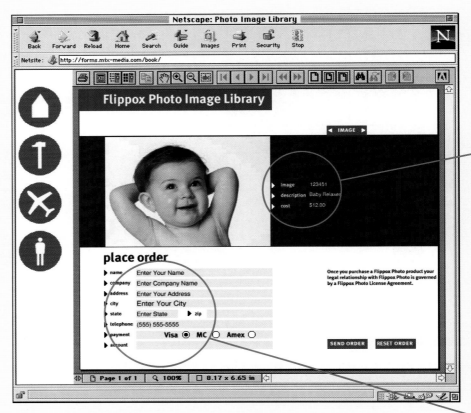

http//forms.mix-media.com/book/

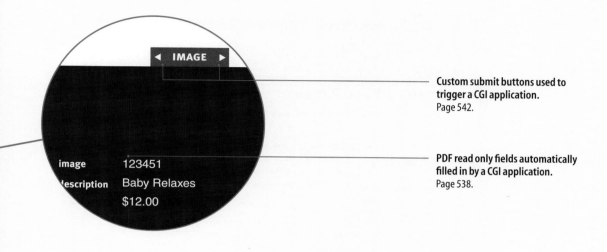

Custom submit buttons used to
trigger a CGI application.
Page 542.

PDF read only fields automatically
filled in by a CGI application.
Page 538.

image   123451
description   Baby Relaxes
    $12.00

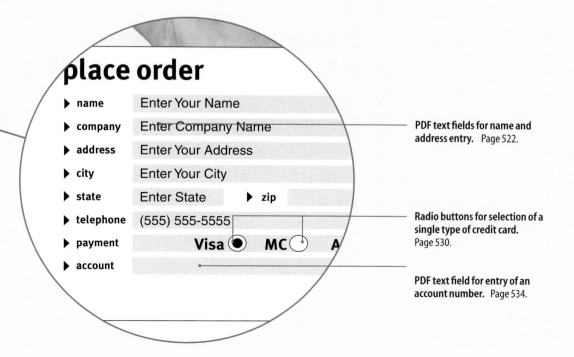

place order

▶ **name**   Enter Your Name
▶ **company**   Enter Company Name
▶ **address**   Enter Your Address
▶ **city**   Enter Your City
▶ **state**   Enter State   ▶ **zip**
▶ **telephone**   (555) 555-5555
▶ **payment**   Visa ● MC ○   A
▶ **account**

PDF text fields for name and
address entry.   Page 522.

Radio buttons for selection of a
single type of credit card.
Page 530.

PDF text field for entry of an
account number.   Page 534.

Résumé Submission

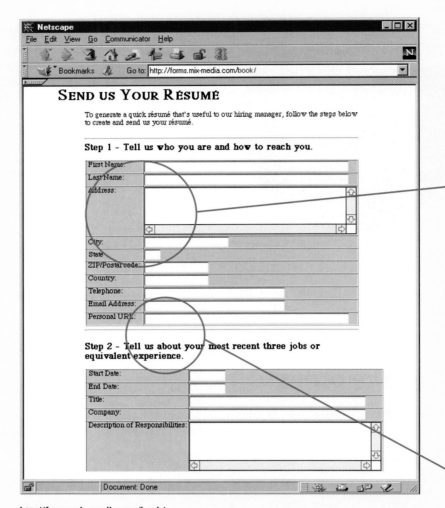

http//forms.mix-media.com/book/

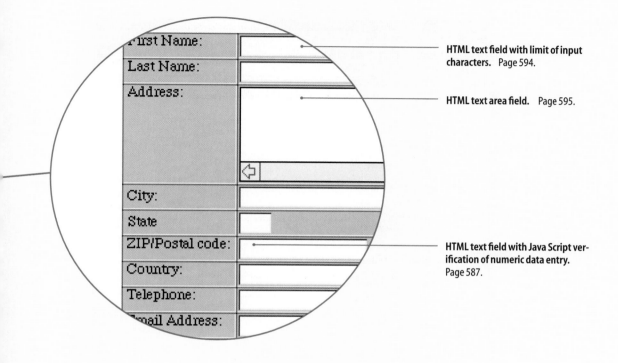

First Name:

HTML text field with limit of input characters. Page 594.

Last Name:

Address:

HTML text area field. Page 595.

City:

State

ZIP/Postal code:

HTML text field with Java Script verification of numeric data entry. Page 587.

Country:

Telephone:

Email Address:

ll us about
nt experience.

Date:

HTML text as a date field. Page 596.

Date:

any:

tion of Responsibilities:

Verification of text length by JavaScript. Page 587.

Résumé Submission, cont.

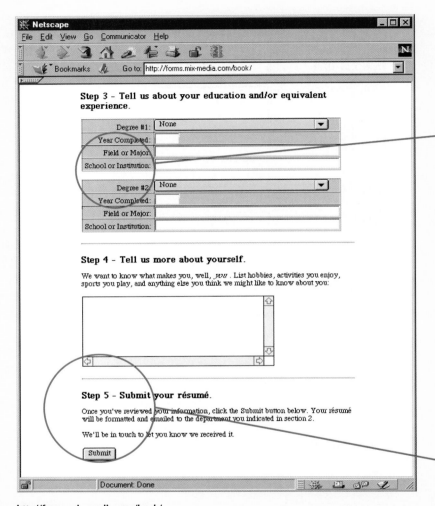

http//forms.mix-media.com/book/

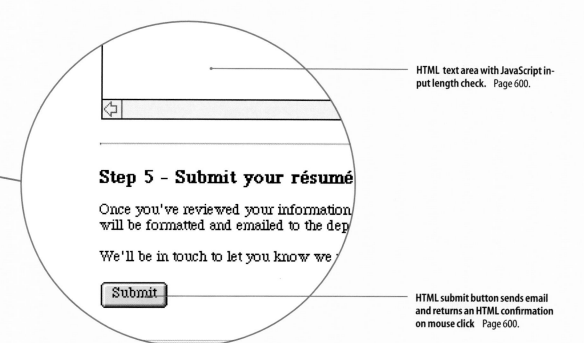

Tell us about ...
...rience.

Degree #1:	None
Year Completed:	
Field or Major:	
...ol or Institution:	
...gree #2:	Non...

HTML drop down menu, offering the user choices from a list. Page 598.

HTML text area with JavaScript input length check. Page 600.

Step 5 – Submit your résumé

Once you've reviewed your information will be formatted and emailed to the dep...

We'll be in touch to let you know we ...

Submit

HTML submit button sends email and returns an HTML confirmation on mouse click Page 600.

University Course Enrollment

This example demonstrates how a fictional university might construct a course registration forms application. The example allows a student to view available courses, register for a course, view a list of students that are enrolled in a course, and view courses in which they're enrolled.

The complete sample Web site can be viewed and downloaded on the companion Web site to this book, http://forms.mix-media.com/book/.

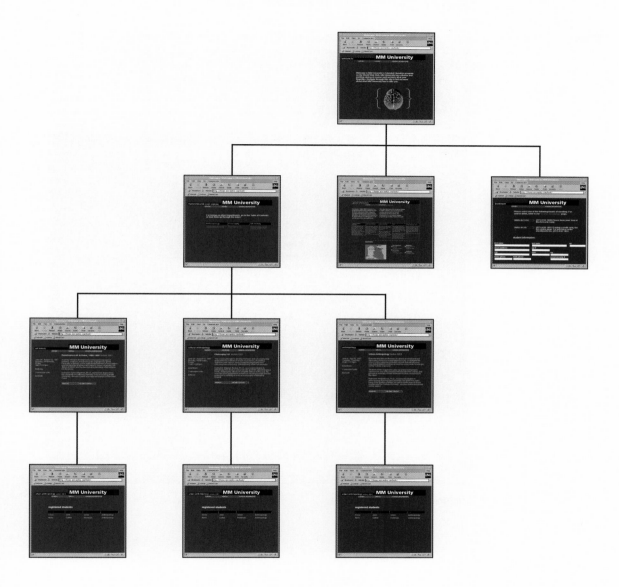

University Course Enrollment, cont.

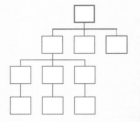

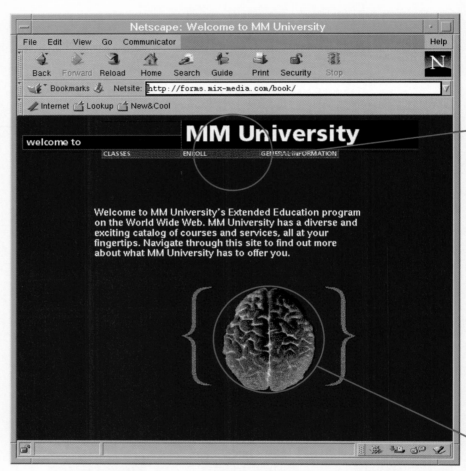

http//forms.mix-media.com/book/

HTML image map contains multiple
links. Page 622.

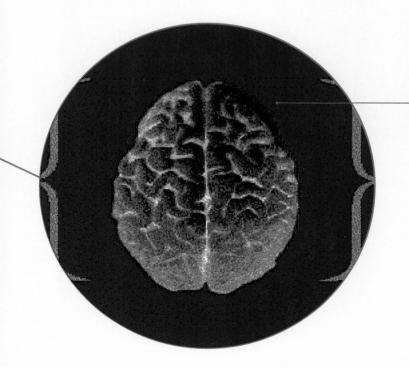

HTML table containing text and
images. Page 624.

University Course Enrollment, cont.

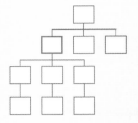

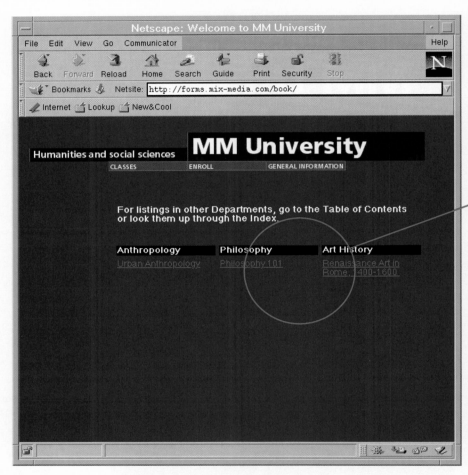

http//forms.mix-media.com/book/

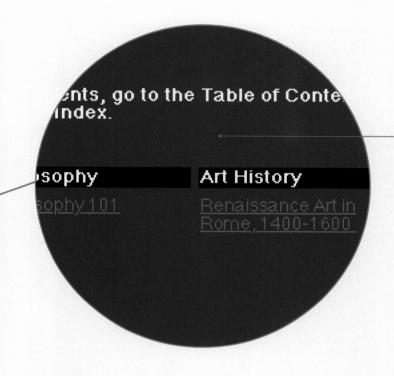

ents, go to the Table of Conte
Index.

sophy   Art History

sophy 101   Renaissance Art in
                         Rome, 1400-1600

HTML table containing text and
hypertext links.   Page 629.

University Course Enrollment, cont.

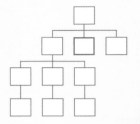

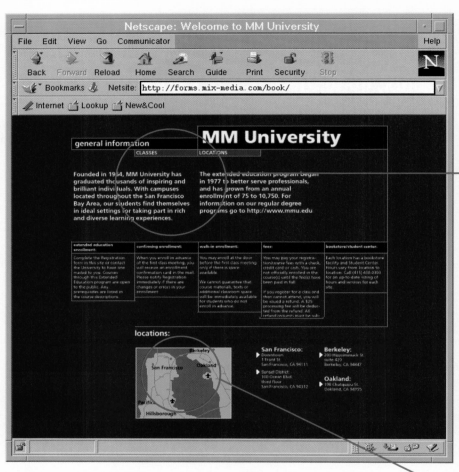

http//forms.mix-media.com/book/

nformation

CLASSES · LOCA

ed in 1964, MM University has
ated thousands of inspiring and
nt individuals. With campuses
d throughout the San Francisco
ea, our students find themselves
settings for taking part in rich
rse learning experiences.

The ex
in 1977
and has
enrollm
inform
progr

confirming enrollmen

Hypertext links simulating an
image map in a PDF file .   Page 637.

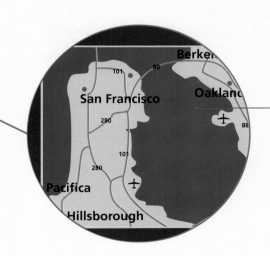

Berke

San Francisco

Oakland

Pacifica

Hillsborough

Scalable illustration in PDF file for
high-resolution printing.   Page 637.

University Course Enrollment, cont.

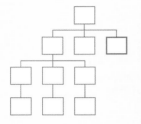

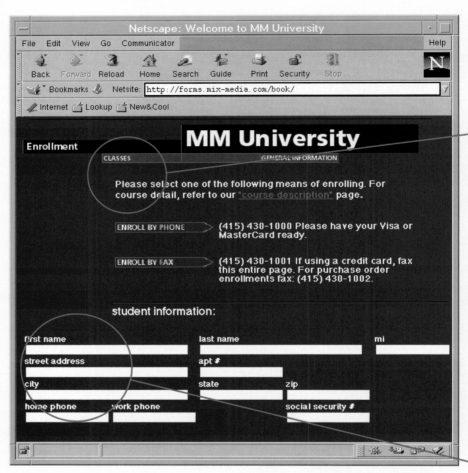

http//forms.mix-media.com/book/

HTML table containing multi-column text and graphics.
Page 639.

HTML text form fields for entering a user's name and address.
Page 651.

University Course Enrollment, cont.

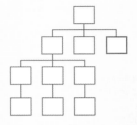

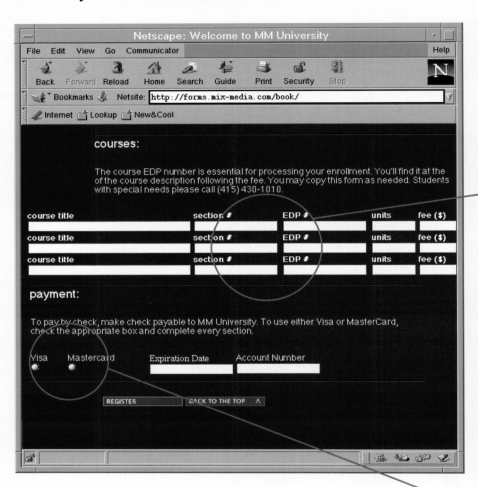

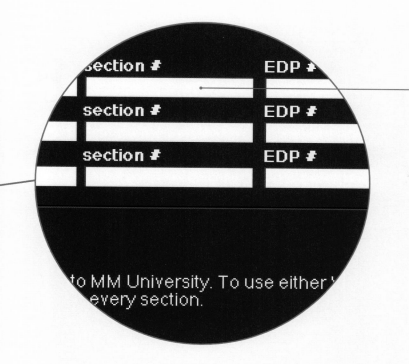

section ⌗   EDP ⌗

section ⌗   EDP ⌗

section ⌗   EDP ⌗

to MM University. To use either
every section.

HTML text form fields used to insert data into an Access database. Page 653.

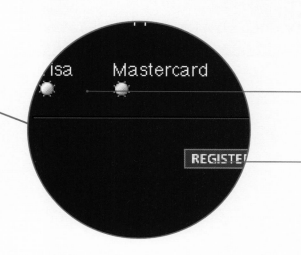

isa   Mastercard

REGISTER

HTML custom radio button group. Page 647.

HTML submit button linking to an Active Server Page that registers a student by inserting their information in an ODBC database and then returning an HTML page listing all courses in which the student is registered. Page 654.

University Course Enrollment, cont.

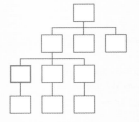

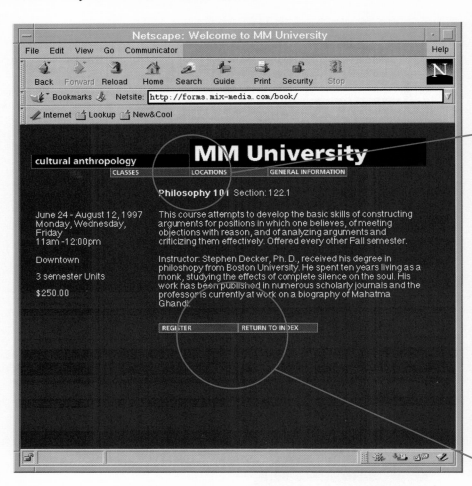

LOCATIONS

Philosophy 101 Se

This course attem
arguments for n

HTML table containing multi-
column text and graphics.
Page 634.

with reason,
zing them effectively.

nstructor: Stephen Decker, Ph. L
philoshopy from Boston University
monk, studying the effects of comp
work has been published in numero
professor is currently at work on a bi
Ghandi.

REGISTER   RETURN TO INDEX

HTML image map linked to an
Active Server Page that queries a
database and displays the list of
students enrolled in this course.
Page 637.

University Course Enrollment, cont.

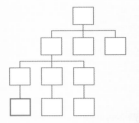

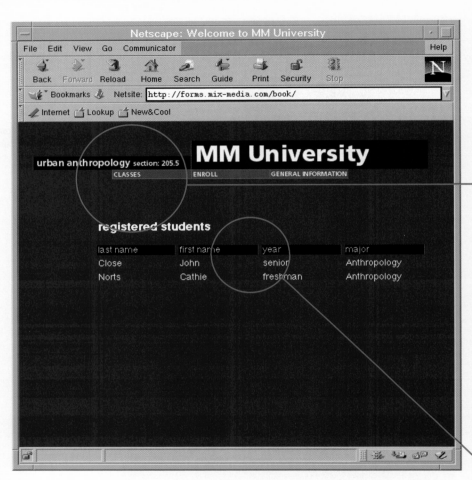

Netscape: Welcome to MM University

File   Edit   View   Go   Communicator   Help

Back   Forward   Reload   Home   Search   Guide   Print   Security   Stop

Bookmarks   Netsite: http://forms.mix-media.com/book/

Internet   Lookup   New&Cool

urban anthropology section: 205.5

MM University

CLASSES   ENROLL   GENERAL INFORMATION

registered students

last name	first name	year	major
Close	John	senior	Anthropology
Norts	Cathie	freshman	Anthropology

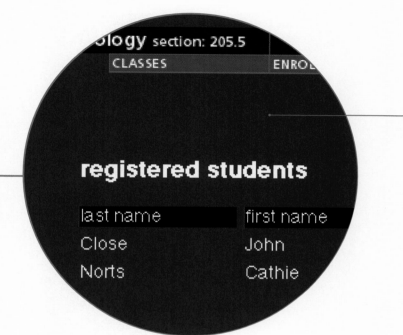

HTML page generated by Active Server Page. Page 659.

HTML table generated and formatted by a database query from an Active Server Page. Page 659.

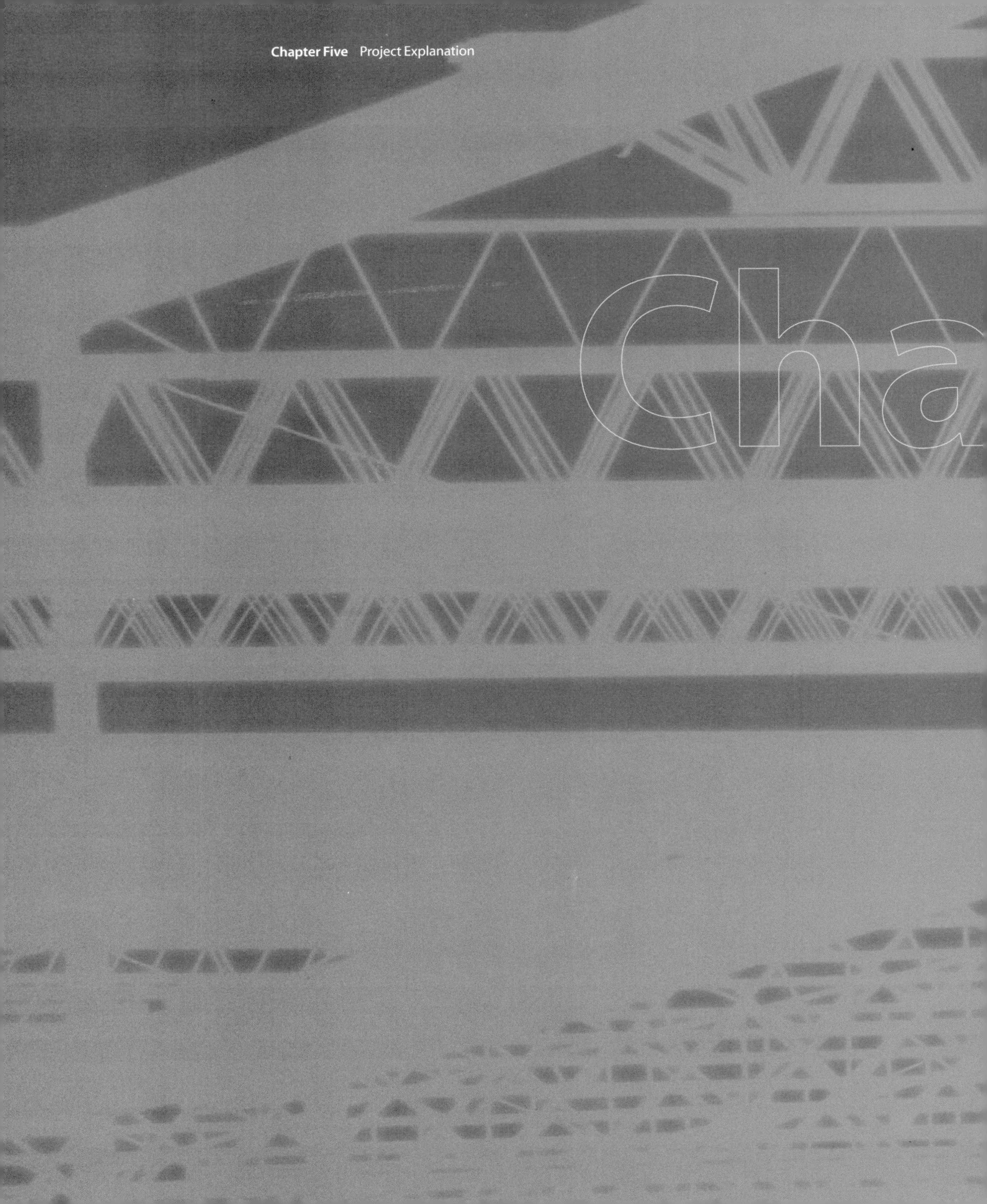
Cha

Project Explanation

This chapter discusses in detail the nuts and bolts of creating
the visual examples from the previous chapter.

Platform specifics and software requirements are defined
for each project. It is possible to recreate the examples
on a different platform by comparing the setup of another
project.

A complete working model of each project is posted on the
book's companion Web site. The companion Web site can be
viewed at: http://forms.mix-media.com/

Business Card Order

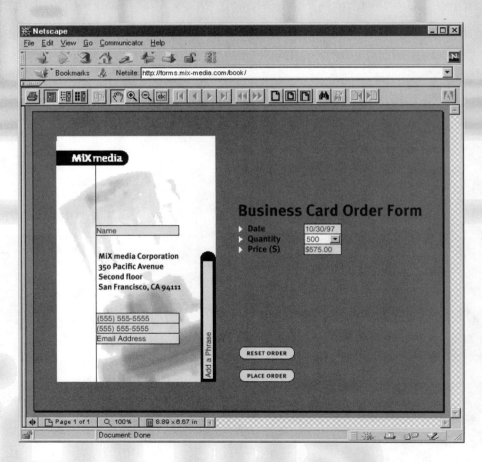

Overview

This example demonstrates how to construct an order form that sends an email upon submission. The example allows the user to enter information into a PDF document that resembles what the actual business card will look like. This way a user can get a preview before committing to an order.

Physical Requirements

The following list is a description of the setup used to create this example. The actual components are:

Windows NT Server version 4.0 for the Intel platform
Netscape Enterprise Server 3.0
Perl 5.0 for Win32
Netscape Navigator 3.x or Netscape Communicator 4.04 or newer with Acrobat Plug-in or Microsoft Internet Explorer 4.0 or newer with Acrobat Plug-in
Adobe Acrobat Reader or Exchange 3.1 or newer with Adobe Forms Plug-in 3.5

Physical Setup the Example Uses

The example is served on a Netscape Enterprise server running on Windows NT 4.0 Server. Perl 5.0 is installed on the Windows NT machine. During the installation, the ".pl" file extension type was selected to be associated with Perl script files.

The Netscape server is set to use the operating system file extensions associations to recognize the program with which to run the CGI script. This requires that the "b_card.pl" script we use to process the form's submission reside in the "shell-cgi" directory in the root folder for our Web server.

Netscape Communicator 4.04 and Acrobat Reader 3.01 are installed on our client machine. Additionally, Netscape Communicator has the Acrobat plug-in in Communicator's plug-in directory. This allows PDF files to be viewed directly in the Communicator window.

Creating the Necessary Files

To get this example to work we need to put two files on the server. The first is a PDF file that is the form the client interacts with, and the second is the Perl script we'll use to process the form submission.

Creating the PDF File

This example uses a PDF file as its form interface to the user. This form allows users to enter information relevant to placing a business card order. The form takes a name, phone number, fax number, e-mail address, phrase, date, and quantity, and e-mails the data to a predetermined recipient. For this example we had a graphic designer create the example file. The designer constructed the file in Adobe Illustrator and then distilled it into PDF format. The next ten steps discuss creating the form for interaction on the client side of this transaction.

Step 1

The Form Field Names

Once we have the final PDF document, we need to add the following form fields using Acrobat Exchange's form creation tool:

name
phone
fax
email
phrase
date
quantity
price
reset
submit

Step 2

Name Field

The first field we'll create is the name field. To create the field choose the forms tool button on the Acrobat Exchange toolbar. The cursor changes to a crosshair. Click the mouse button and drag out a rectangle defining the area where you want the user to enter name text. The Field Properties dialog box appears asking for specifics about the text field we're creating.

Step 2: Field Properties Dialog - Appearance Tab

Enter "name" as the field name and select Text as the field type. We left the User Name field blank. It's used if we want to have a different field name exported with this field's value when the form is submitted.

Activate the Appearance tab. Here we're presented with options that affect the field's appearance. Our designer decided to create the fields as a graphic so we don't have a Border or Background Color selected. If we want to create a field that hasn't been drawn in our document, Acrobat forms provides several options to create a field with an outline or a background. Select a color the text will display by clicking the Text Color chip. Select Helvetica as the Font and Auto as the Size. Finally check the Required checkbox. The user will be warned if they don't fill out this field before submitting the form to the server.

Click the OK button. The dialog closes, adding the field to the document.

Step 3

Phone Field
Next we'll create the phone field. To create the field, choose the forms tool button on the Acrobat Exchange toolbar. The cursor changes to a

crosshair. Click the mouse button and drag out a rectangle defining the area where you want the user to enter a phone number. The Field Properties dialog box appears asking for specifics about the text field we're creating.

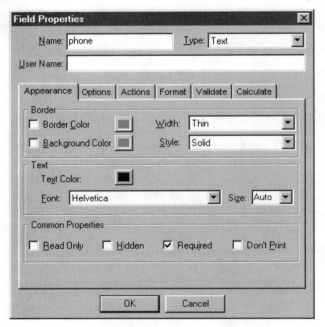

Step 3: Field Properties Dialog-Appearance Tab

Enter "phone" as the field name and select Text as the field type. We left the User Name field blank. It's used if we want to have a different field name exported with this field's value when the form is submitted.

Activate the Appearance tab. The field exists as a graphic so we don't select a Border or Background Color. Select a color the text will display by clicking the Text Color chip. Select Helvetica as the Font and Auto as the Size. Finally check the Required checkbox. The user will be warned if they don't fill out this field before submitting the form to the server.

Now activate the Format tab. The Format tab allows us to regulate the format of information entered into the field. Choose Special from the Category list and Phone Number from the Special Options list. Phone format is a pre-defined field type that insures the user only enters numbers and dash characters. If they try to enter anything else, the system beeps to alert them that the entry wasn't accepted.

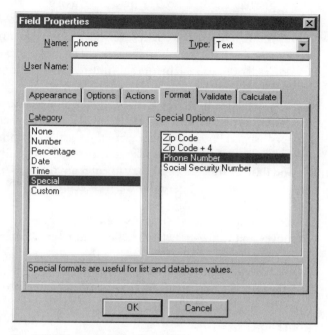

Step 3: Field Properties Dialog-Format Tab

After the user enters their phone information and moves on to another field, the phone number is formatted in the following form: (555) 555-5555

Click the OK button. The dialog closes, adding the field to the document.

Step 4

Fax Field

Next create the fax field by repeating the process we used to create the phone field but name the field "fax". Create the field by choosing the forms tool button on the Acrobat Exchange toolbar. Click the mouse button and drag out a rectangle defining the area where you want the user to enter a fax number. The Field Properties dialog box appears, asking for specifics about the text field we're creating.

Enter "fax" as the field name and select Text as the field type. We left the User Name field blank. It's used if we want to have a different field name exported with this field's value when the form is submitted.

Activate the Appearance tab. The field exists as a graphic so we don't se-lect a Border or Background Color. Select a color the text will display by clicking the Text Color chip. Select Helvetica as the Font and Auto as the Size. Finally check the Required checkbox. The user will be warned if they don't fill out this field before submitting the form to the server.

Now activate the Format tab. The Format tab allows us to regulate the format of information entered into the field. Choose Special from the Category list and Phone Number from the Special Options List. Phone format is a pre-defined field type that insures the user only enters num-bers and dash characters. If they try to enter anything else, the system beeps to alert them that the entry wasn't accepted.

As with the phone field, after the user enters their phone information and moves on to another field, the phone number is formatted in the fol-lowing form: (555) 555-5555

Click the OK button. The dialog closes, adding the field to the document.

Step 5

Email Field
To create the email field, choose the forms tool button on the Acrobat Exchange toolbar. Click the mouse button and drag out a rectangle defining the area where you want the user to enter an email address. The Field Properties dialog box appears, asking for specifics about the text field we're creating.

Step 5: Field Properties Dialog-Appearance Tab

Enter "email" as the field name and select Text as the field type. We left
the User Name field blank. It's used if we want to have a different field
name exported with this field's value when the form is submitted.
Activate the Appearance tab. These options affect the field's appearance.
Again we don't have a Border or Background Color selected. Select a
color the text will display by clicking the Text Color chip. Select Helvetica
as the Font and Auto as the Size. Finally check the Required checkbox.
The user will be warned if they don't fill out the email field before submitting the form to the server.

For this field, let's set a limit to how many characters a user can enter.
Activate the Options tab in the dialog. Here you can enter default text
that the field will show before a user enters any information. You can also
choose an alignment for text in the field. Choose Left for this example.
Next check the Limit checkbox and enter 64 for the number of characters
we'll allow. Leave the Password checkbox unchecked, otherwise text entered will be shown as asterisks.

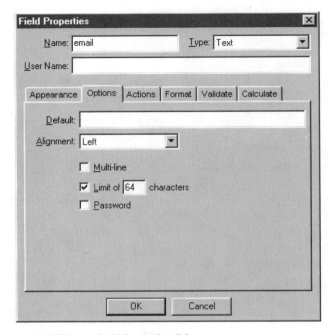

Step 5: Field Properties Dialog-Options Tab

Click the OK button. The dialog closes, adding the field to the document.

Step 6

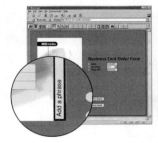

Phrase Field—Rotated Text

The next text field we'll add is a little more complex. It demonstrates how to add a rotated text field to a document. The first task is to rotate the entire page. This is a little awkward but not difficult. From the Acrobat Menu Bar choose the Document menu. Choose Rotate Pages from the Document Menu. The Rotate Pages Dialog appears.

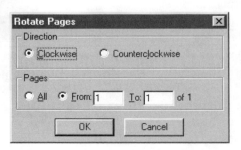

Step 6: Rotate Pages Dialog

Rotate the page Clockwise. Our goal is to orient the page so we can add a text field for the business card phrase. Currently all fields must be added in a left to right data entry orientation.

Now we'll add the phrase text field. To create the field, choose the forms tool button on the Acrobat Exchange toolbar. Click the mouse button and drag out a rectangle defining the area where you want the user to enter the phrase. The Field Properties dialog box appears asking for specifics about the text field we're creating.

Step 6: Field Properties Dialog-Appearance Tab

Enter "phrase" as the field name and select Text as the field type. Leave the User Name field blank. We don't want to have a different field name exported with this field's value when the form is submitted.

Activate the Appearance tab. Here we're presented with options that affect the field's appearance. Our designer decided to create the fields as a graphic so we don't have a Border or Background Color selected. Click the color chip next to the Text Color setting and select white. Select Helvetica as the Font and Auto as the Size. Finally, check the Required checkbox. The user will be warned if they don't fill out this field before submitting the form to the server.

Click the OK button. The dialog closes, adding the field to the document.

Now we need to return the page to its original orientation. From the Acrobat Menu Bar choose the Document menu. Choose Rotate Pages from the Document Menu. The Rotate Pages Dialog appears.

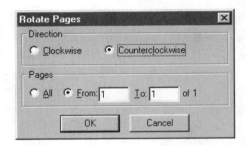

Step 6: Rotate Pages Dialog

Rotate the page Counterclockwise, returning it to its original position.

Step 7

Date Field—Read Only

Now we'll add a date field. This is a read-only field that inserts the date the order is constructed. With Acrobat Exchange's forms tool button selected, drag out a rectangle defining the area where you want to display the date. The Field Properties dialog box appears asking for specifics about the field we're creating.

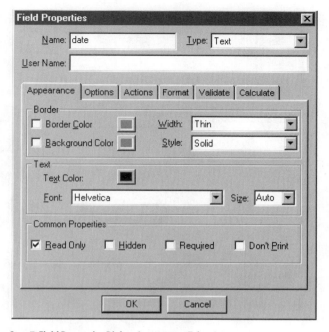

Step 7: Field Properties Dialog-Appearance Tab

Enter "date" as the field name and select Text as the field type. We left the User Name field blank. It's used only if we want to have a different field name exported with this field's value when the form is submitted.

Activate the Appearance tab. Here we're presented with options that affect the field's appearance. Our designer decided to create the fields as a graphic so we don't have a Border or Background Color selected. Select a color the text will display by clicking the Text Color chip. Select Helvetica as the Font and Auto as the Size. Finally check the Read Only checkbox. This text box will hold and display text but it won't allow a user to enter any information.

Now activate the Format tab. The Format tab allows us to regulate the formatting of information entered into the field. Choose Date from the category list and pick a date format from the Date Options List.

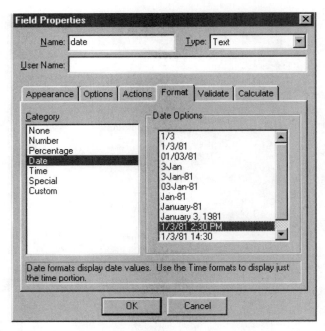

Step 7: Field Properties Dialog-Format Tab

Right now we have a date field, but to make it useful we'll need to attach a bit of JavaScript. To do this, while still in the Format tab, select the Custom Category and click the Edit button. The Acrobat JavaScript editing window appears. Type in the following code:

```
1.    var d = new Date();
2.    d.setDate(d.getDate());
3.    event.value = util.printd("mm/dd/yy", d);
```

This script gets today's date and set the current field's value to the date. The first line of this script creates a new date value. A reference to this date is stored in the variable "d". The second line of this script uses two member functions of the date object. The second line calls the setDate() member function to actually set the numeric value of the date. The parameter passed into the function is the result of the getDate() member function. In short, we're setting the date to the value returned by getDate(). This value is today's date. The third line of this script formats and prints the value in our "d" variable. We've formatted it as "mm/dd/yy", two digits for month, two digits for day, and two digits for year. This formatted string is stored in the event.value field of the current event. In this case, the script is called whenever the field is asked to format its contents.

Click the OK button. The dialog closes, adding the field to the document.

Step 8

Quantity Field—Combo Box

Now we'll add a combo box to allow the user to select a quantity of cards to order. With the Acrobat Exchange forms tool selected, drag out a rectangle defining the area where you want the quantity combo box to appear. The Field Properties dialog box appears asking for specifics about the field we're creating.

Step 8: Field Properties Dialog-Appearance Tab

Enter "quantity" as the field name and select Combo Box as the field type. Again leave the User Name field blank. We want this fields name to be exported as "quantity" when the form is submitted.

Activate the Appearance tab. We don't have a Border but select Background Color and choose white as its color. Select black as the text color by clicking the Text Color chip if it isn't already black. Select Helvetica as the Font and 12 as the Size. Finally check the Required checkbox.

Now activate the Options tab. Here we'll enter the items to display in our combo box. We want the drop down list to contain four items. Enter each item and its corresponding export value that the form will send to the server and click the Add button. If you enter the items out of order, you can move them around in the list by selecting an item and clicking the up or down button. If you need to change an item or its value, select the item in the list and its associated value and item appearance in the entry fields above it. When the four values are entered, select 500 as the default and click the OK button to save the field to the document.

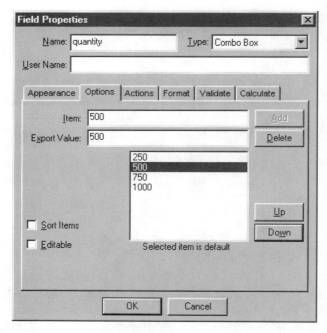

Step 8: Field Properties Dialog-Options Tab

Step 9

Price Field—Read Only

Now we'll add a price field. This is a read-only field where we calculate the price based on the quantity of cards ordered. With the Acrobat Exchange forms tool selected, drag out a rectangle defining the area where you want to display the price. The Field Properties dialog box appears asking for specifics about the field we're creating.

Step 9: Field Properties Dialog-Appearance Tab

Enter "price" as the field name and select Text as the field type. Again we leave the User Name field blank. It's only used if we want to have a different field name exported with this field's value when the form is submitted.

Activate the Appearance tab. We don't need to select a Border or Background Color due to our form's design. Make sure the text color is black. If it isn't, change it to black by clicking the Text Color chip. Select Helvetica as the Font and 12 as the Size. Finally check the Read Only checkbox. This text box will hold and display text but it won't allow a user to enter any information.

Now activate the Format tab. The Format tab allows us to regulate the formatting of information entered into the field. Choose Number from the category list. Set the number of decimal places we'll display to two. Choose Dollar as the currency symbol we want to use. Pick a separator style and choose how negative numbers are to be displayed.

Step 9: Field Properties Dialog-Format Tab

Finally, activate the Calculate tab. The Calculate tab lets us set up a field to calculate the value of this field. There are several simple calculation options available, including calculating the sum of several fields, calculating the product of fields, and even averaging field values.

Our calculation is a little more complex. We need to add a custom calculation. To do this, click the Custom calculation script radio button and then click the Edit button. The Acrobat Javascript editing window appears. Type in the following code.

```
1.    var f = this.getField("quantity");
2.    event.value = f.value * 1.15;
```

This simple script calculates the value of our price field based on the value of the quantity combo box. The first line of this script gets a reference to the quantity field and stores it in the variable "f". The second line accesses the "value" member of "f" and multiplies it by 1.15. The result is stored in the event.value field of the event that is happening. This event is the price field being asked to calculate its value. All fields on a page receive a request to calculate their value when any field on the same page commits to a new value.

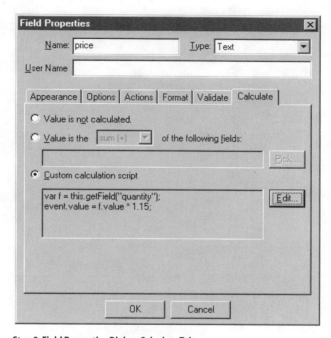

Step 9: Field Properties Dialog-Calculate Tab

Once the script is entered, close the Javascript window by clicking the OK button. You will be able to see the script in the Calculate tab. If you can't see the script, go back and enter the script again.

Now click the Field Properties dialog's OK button. The dialog closes, adding the field to the document.

Step 10

Submit Button
Our two remaining fields correspond to the submit and reset buttons. First we'll create the submit button. With the Acrobat Exchange forms tool selected, drag out a rectangle defining the area where the submit button is located. The Field Properties dialog box appears asking for specifics about the field we're creating.

Step 10: Field Properties Dialog-Appearance Tab

Activate the Appearance tab. Again we don't need to select a Border or Background Color due to our form's design. The button's text color isn't important because we aren't displaying the buttons' title.

Step 10: Field Properties Dialog-Options Tab

The Options tab is where you select any special appearance options for the button. In this instance, we set the Highlight option to Invert. The Layout option is set to Text only. Because we don't want any text to show over our buttons, the Text entry for the Button Face Attributes is left blank. The Button Face When option determines when the appearance we set up is invoked. Here we want it to Invert on a mouse up event.

Step 10: Field Properties Dialog-Actions Tab

The Actions tab is where you select any action this field will invoke. Here we choose the Mouse Up event. Click the Add button and choose Submit Form from the list of available action types.

Step 10: Edit an Action Dialog

Now we need to identify the URL that will process the form submission. Click the Select URL button and enter the URL you will use to process this form.

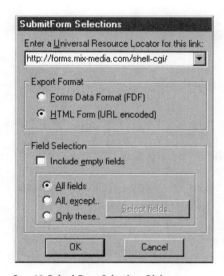

Step 10: SubmitForm Selections Dialog

Here we also choose to submit the data to the server in HTML format. We could submit in the FDF format but the Perl script we'll use to process the submission is set up to receive the data in HTML format. We also want to send all fields, even though we have the option to just send a subset of the fields from the form. Once the proper selections are made, click the OK buttons in the SubmitForm Selections, Edit an Action, and Field Properties dialogs.

Step 11

Reset Button

Our final field is the reset button. With the Acrobat Exchange forms tool selected, drag out a rectangle defining the area where the reset button is located. The Field Properties dialog box appears asking for specifics about the field we're creating.

Step 11: Field Properties Dialog-Appearance Tab

Activate the Appearance tab. Again, we don't need to select a Border or Background Color due to our form's design. The button's text color isn't important because we aren't displaying the button's title.

Step 11: Field Properties Dialog-Options Tab

The Options tab is where you select any special appearance options for the button. In this instance we set the Highlight option to Invert. The Layout option is set to Text only. Because we don't want any text to show over our buttons, the Text entry for the Button Face Attributes is left blank. The Button Face When option determines when the appearance we set up is invoked. Here we want it to Invert on a mouse up event.

Step 11: Field Properties Dialog-Actions Tab

The Actions tab is where you select any action this field will invoke. Here we choose the Mouse Up event. Click the Add button and choose Reset Form from the list of available action types.

Step 11: Edit an Action Dialog

Here we can choose the fields we want to reset. All Fields is the default. Once the proper selections are made, click the OK buttons in the Edit an Action and Field Properties dialogs.

Now we're ready to discuss setting up the back end of the process to receive information from this form.

Creating the Perl Script

This example uses a PDF file as its interface to the user. The form gathers a name, phone number, fax number, email address, phrase, date, and quantity, and sends it to the server for processing by a CGI script. This example uses a Perl script to process the submitted information. The Perl script decodes the submission, prepares the information, and then emails the data to a predetermined recipient.

The following pages discuss creating the Perl script used for processing the form's submission on the server side of this transaction. The complete script is shown below. For this example to work, the script must exist as a file named "b_card.pl". This file is placed in the "shell-cgi" directory in the Netscape Enterprise Server's root directory. Of course the Netscape Server's root directory and shell-cgi directory were created automatically when we installed the Web server on our Windows NT machine.

Code Example: b_card.pl

```
1.   #!/usr/local/bin/perl
2.
3.   $sendto   = "info\@mix-media.com";
4.   $sentfrom = "admin\@mix-media";
5.   $mailpath = "Blat.exe ";
6.
7.   &parse_form_data(*FORM_DATA);
8.   &send_mail();
9.   &send_thank_you();
10.  exit(0);
11.
12.  sub parse_form_data
13.  {
```

```
14.        local (*FORM_DATA) = @_;
15.
16.        local ( $request_method, $query_string,
           @key_value_pairs, $key_value, $key,
           $value);
17.
18.        $request_method = $ENV{'REQUEST_METHOD'};
19.
20.        if($request_method eq "GET")
21.        {
22.            $query_string = $ENV{'QUERY_STRING'};
23.        }
24.        elsif($request_method eq "POST")
25.        {
26.            read(STDIN, $query_string,
               $ENV{'CONTENT_LENGTH'});
27.        }
28.        else
29.        {
30.            &return_error (500, "Server Error",
               "Server uses unsupported method");
31.        }
32.
33.        @key_value_pairs = split(/&/,
           $query_string);
34.
35.        foreach $key_value (@key_value_pairs)
36.        {
37.            ($key, $value) = split (/=/,
             $key_value);
38.            $value =~ tr/+/ /;
39.            $value =~ s/%([\dA-Fa-f][\dA-Fa-f])/pack
               ("C", hex ($1))/eg;
40.
41.            if (defined($FORM_DATA{$key}))
42.        {
43.                $FORM_DATA{$key} = join ("\0",
                   $FORM_DATA{$key}, $value);
44.            }
45.        else
```

```
46.        {
47.                $FORM_DATA{$key} = $value;
48.            }
49.          }
50.      }
51.
52.    sub send_mail
53.    {
54.      local (*FORM_DATA) = @_;
55.
56.      $commandLine = $mailpath;
57.      $filepath = "C:\\temp\\";
58.      $filepath .= int(rand 100000000) + 1;
59.      $filepath .= ".tmp";
60.
61.      open(TMPFILE, ">" . $filepath) or die
         "Couldn't create file: $!";
62.      print TMPFILE "\n\nThe following business
         card order was placed\.", "\n";
63.      print TMPFILE "Date submitted:
         ",$FORM_DATA{'date'}, "\n";
64.      print TMPFILE "Full Name:  ",
         $FORM_DATA{'name'}, "\n";
65.      print TMPFILE "Phone:      ",
         $FORM_DATA{'phone'}, "\n";
66.      print TMPFILE "Fax:        ",
         $FORM_DATA{'fax'}, "\n";
67.      print TMPFILE "E-mail:     ",
         $FORM_DATA{'email'}, "\n";
68.      print TMPFILE "Phrase:     ",
         $FORM_DATA{'phrase'}, "\n";
69.      print TMPFILE "Quantity:   ",
         $FORM_DATA{'quantity'}, "\n";
70.      print TMPFILE "\r\n\r\n";
71.      close(TMPFILE);
72.
73.      $commandLine = $mailpath;
74.      $commandLine .= $filepath . " ";
75.      $commandLine .= "-s \"Resume Submission\" ";
76.      $commandLine .= "-i \"admin\@mix-media.com\" ";
```

```
77.      $commandLine .= "-t \"info\@mix-media.com\" ";
78.
79.      system($commandLine);
80.      unlink($filepath);
81.  }
82.  sub send_thank_you
83.  {
84.      local (*FORM_DATA) = @_;
85.
86.      print "Content-type: text/html\n\n";
87.
88.      print "<HTML>\n";
89.      print "<HEAD>\n";
90.      print "<TITLE>CGI Business Card
         Order</TITLE>\n";
91.      print "</HEAD>\n";
92.      print "<BODY><BR>\n";
93.      print "<H1>Thanks for Your Business Card
         Order</H1>\n";
94.      print "<PRE>\n";
95.      print "Your information was submitted,
         ",$FORM_DATA{'date'}, ".<BR>\n";
96.      print "Your information we received
         was:<BR>\n";
97.      print "Full Name:  ", $FORM_DATA{'name'},
         "<BR>\n";
98.      print "Phone:      ", $FORM_DATA{'phone'},
         "<BR>\n";
99.      print "Fax:        ", $FORM_DATA{'fax'},
         "<BR>\n";
100.     print "E-mail:     ", $FORM_DATA{'email'},
         "<BR>\n";
101.     print "Phrase:     ", $FORM_DATA{'phrase'},
         "<BR>\n";
102.     print "Quantity:   ", $FORM_DATA{'quantity'},
         "<BR>\n";
103.     print "</PRE>\n";
104.     print "<HR>\n";
105.     print "<BR>\n";
106.     print "</BODY></HTML>\n";
```

```
107.  }
108.  sub return_error
109.  {
110.     local ($status, $errtype, $message) = @_;
111.
112.     print "Content-type: text/html\n";
113.     print "Status: ", $status, " ", $errtype,
         "\n\n";
114.     print "<HTML>\n";
115.     print "<HEAD>\n";
116.     print "<TITLE>CGI Program Error</TITLE>\n";
117.     print "</HEAD>\n";
118.     print "<BODY><BR>\n";
119.     print "<H1>This CGI program encountered a ",
         $errtype, "</H1>\n";
120.     print $message;
121.     print "<HR>\n";
122.     print "<BR>\n";
123.     print "</BODY></HTML>\n";
124.     exit(1);
125.  }
```

The Example Script

Let's take a detailed look at our example script. Line one of our script is used to declare the location of the Perl interpreter to use when running this script. In a UNIX environment, this line would look something like this: #!/usr/local/bin/perl. Windows NT keeps track of which programs run which type of files, so we don't need to point out the path of the Perl interpreter to use.

Line three sets the variable we'll use to direct our email. Here we'll send it to "info@mix-media.com". Notice the "@" has a "\" before it. This character actually has meaning to a computer. Characters like this can cause programs to execute certain functions. To prevent this from happening we put a "\" character in front of them announcing the next character is in fact a character and not a command we want executed. This is called escaping characters in a string.

```
1.    #!/usr/local/bin/perl
2.
```

```
3.      $sendto   = "info\@mix-media.com";
4.      $sentfrom = "admin\@mix-media";
5.      $mailpath = "Blat.exe ";
6.
7.      &parse_form_data(*FORM_DATA);
8.      &send_mail();
9.      &send_thank_you();
10.     exit(0);
```

Lines seven to ten are the core of our script. They are three sub routines we use to do some work for us. The first, parse_form_data(), gathers and decodes the information sent to us by the client. Next, the send_mail() routine packages the decoded data and sends it via email to "info@mix-media.com". When this is completed, the sub routine send_thank_you() returns an HTML thank you page to the client that submitted the information. Finally, the Perl script exits, returning a result code of zero. This signals that everything has been executed without a problem.

The parse_form_data() Sub Routine

Now let's take a detailed look at our parse_form_data() sub routine. Line 12 of our script is used to declare the instructions following it are part of our parse_form_data() sub routine. Every instruction between the open curly bracket on line 13 and the close curly bracket on line 50 is included in this routine. On line 14 we call the Perl local routine to create a reference to the argument passed to the routine. Perl passes arguments to its routines through the @_ associative array. If this is unfamiliar to you, we've simply created a reference to the submitted form data that this sub routine and the main routine can share. On line 16 we create some more local space to store information we'll copy out of the submission.

```
12.     sub parse_form_data
13.     {
14.         local (*FORM_DATA) = @_;
15.
16.         local ( $request_method, $query_string,
            @key_value_pairs, $key_value, $key,
            $value);
```

The two most popular methods for submitting information to an HTTP server are POST and GET. Information sent to a server via the GET method is stored in the QUERY_STRING environment variable. If it's sent via a POST to the server, the data is placed in the STDIN buffer and its length is placed in the CONTENT_LENGTH environment variable. This architecture requires that we check for the method of submission in order to locate the form data. On line 18 we determine just how the information was sent to this script by calling the $ENV{} function and passing "REQUEST_METHOD" as the parameter. This returns the submission method and stores it in the $request_method local variable. On line 20 we compare what's stored in $request_method with the string "GET". If they're equal, we again call $ENV{} but this time with "QUERY_STRING" as the parameter. This stores the submission information in the local variable $query_string.

```
18.      $request_method = $ENV{'REQUEST_METHOD'};
19.
20.      if($request_method eq "GET")
21.      {
22.          $query_string = $ENV{'QUERY_STRING'};
23.      }
```

If what's stored in $request_method isn't equal to "GET", on line 24 we check to see if it's equal to "POST". If it is, we need to read the form data from the standard input buffer. This is done by calling the read() command. However, the read command requires three parameters. First, it needs to know from where it is to read the information. Second, it must know where to put the information it reads, and third, it needs to know how much information it's supposed to read.

Invoking the read() command and passing it STDIN (the standard input buffer) provides the instruction as to where to read from, and $query_string as where to store the information that is read, while calling $ENV{'CONTENT_LENGTH'} retrieves the length of the data that should be read.

```
24.      elsif($request_method eq "POST")
25.      {
26.          read(STDIN, $query_string,
             $ENV{'CONTENT_LENGTH'});
27.      }
```

In case the $request_method isn't either GET or POST we provide a catch-all that calls our return_error() sub routine. This returns an HTML page informing the user we didn't know what to do with their request. It then exits the script without processing the submission.

```
28.     else
29.     {
30.         &return_error (500, "Server Error",
            "Server uses unsupported method");
31.     }
```

After we receive the information and properly store it in the $query_string local variable, our next task is to format and decode it. We know the HTTP protocol requires the client to separate each key/value pair with the ampersand character. Using this information, we can use the Perl split() command to store each key/value pair in an array. Line 26 accomplishes this by splitting the query string at each ampersand and storing it in the key_value_pairs array.

```
33.     @key_value_pairs = split(/&/,
        $query_string);
```

Once we have the key/value information in an array, we need to break it into its key and value components. The HTTP protocol requires each key or field and its value to be separated by the equals character. As we loop through each entry, line 37 splits the field name and its value and stores the two in the $key and $value local variables. Line 38 uses the Perl translate command to replace any "+" characters with a space. This is necessary because the client has done the reverse and replaced any space with "+" characters before transmitting the data to the server. Line 39 is another type of translation. Here we use the substitute command to revert all characters that have been converted to their hexadecimal equivalent back to their original ASCII values. The substitute command contains a regular expression that looks for a "%" followed by two characters. These two characters are stored in a variable $1. The expression then is evaluated by the "e" option, converting the value stored in $1 into its ASCII equivalent. Finally, the "g" option searches the initial string and replaces all occurrences on the hexadecimal value with its ASCII equivalent. As you can see, a lot happens in this little line.

We finally have our data in a state that we're ready to store. Line 41 checks for an existing entry for this key. If there is already an entry, we call the join command to append this value to the existing values in our array on line 43. If the key doesn't yet exist, we add it and its value to the $FORM_DATA associative array on line 47.

```
35.     foreach $key_value (@key_value_pairs)
36.     {
37.         ($key, $value) = split (/=/,
            $key_value);
38.         $value =~ tr/+/ /;
39.         $value =~ s/%([\dA-Fa-f][\dA-Fa-f])/pack
            ("C", hex ($1))/eg;
40.
41.         if (defined($FORM_DATA{$key}))
42.     {
43.             $FORM_DATA{$key} = join ("\0",
                $FORM_DATA{$key}, $value);
44.         }
45.     else
46.     {
47.             $FORM_DATA{$key} = $value;
48.         }
49.     }
50. }
```

The entire purpose of the parse_form_data() sub routine is to format and decode the form submission data. At this point that task is accomplished. Now let's examine our send_mail() subroutine.

The send_mail() Sub Routine

This sub routine's purpose is to package the decoded information and email it to a pre-determined email address. The routine begins by creating a reference to the associative array passed to the script's main routine.

http://gepasi.dbs.aber.ac.uk/ softw/blat.html

On line 56 we begin assembling the arguments necessary to send the email. In the Windows operating system we'll use a free program called Blat. Blat is a Standard Mail Transfer Protocol program that can email a file to a list of recipients.

```
56.     $commandLine = $mailpath;
57.     $filepath = "C:\\temp\\";
58.     $filepath .= int(rand 100000000) + 1;
59.     $filepath .= ".tmp";
```

On line 57 we add the path to our temp directory to the path we'll use to create a temp file to hold our email. On line 58 we generate a random number to use as a file name, and concatenate it to our temp path. Finally, we place a suffix on the path on line 59. To effectively handle the creation of thousand of files, we'd need to check if the random file name we generated already exists. If so, we'd loop, trying file names until we generate one that's available. This doesn't happen in our script because we don't expect thousands of submissions, but you might.

```
61.     open(TMPFILE, ">" . $filepath) or die
        "Couldn't create file: $!";
62.     print TMPFILE "\n\nThe following business
        card order was placed\.", "\n";
63.     print TMPFILE "Date submitted:
        ",$FORM_DATA{'date'}, "\n";
64.     print TMPFILE "Full Name:  ",
        $FORM_DATA{'name'}, "\n";
65.     print TMPFILE "Phone:       ",
        $FORM_DATA{'phone'}, "\n";
66.     print TMPFILE "Fax:         ",
        $FORM_DATA{'fax'}, "\n";
67.     print TMPFILE "E-mail:      ",
        $FORM_DATA{'email'}, "\n";
68.     print TMPFILE "Phrase:      ",
        $FORM_DATA{'phrase'}, "\n";
69.     print TMPFILE "Quantity:    ",
        $FORM_DATA{'quantity'}, "\n";
70.     print TMPFILE "\r\n\r\n";
71.      close(TMPFILE);
```

Line 61 opens the file we use to store the email information. If the file open fails, the script places a message in the server's error log and exits. If the file is successfully opened, we print the submission information to the temp file. Each field is printed to the file and then the temporary file is closed.

```
73.    $commandLine = $mailpath;
74.    $commandLine .= $filepath . " ";
75.    $commandLine .= "-s \"Resume Submission\" ";
76.    $commandLine .= "-i \"admin\@mix-media.com\" ";
77.    $commandLine .= "-t \"info\@mix-media.com\" ";
```

On line 73 we begin constructing the command line we'll use to invoke our email program. Lines 73 to 77 add the Blat.exe path, the path to the file we placed our information in, the subject of the email, the address the email is from, and the address where the email is sent.

On line 79 we use the Perl system call and pass the command line we created. The routing executes the Blat program, sending the email.

```
79.    system($commandLine);
80.    unlink($filepath);
```

On line 80 we use the unlink routine to delete the temporary file, in effect cleaning up after ourselves. At this point, the routine exits, having completed its task.

The send_thank_you() Sub Routine

Line 82 of our script is used to declare the following instructions are part of our send_thank_you() sub routine. On line 84 we call the Perl local command to create a reference to the associative array passed to this script's main routine. Again we create a reference to the submitted form data that this sub routine and the main routine can share. By the time we call this routine, we've formatted and decoded the information in the parse_form_data() routine.

On line 86 we use the print command to output a minimum HTTP response header. The line informs the client the file they're about to receive is of the "text/html" MIME type. The print command sends data to the standard output buffer (STDOUT). This is where the server looks for a response to send back to the client.

```
82.    sub send_thank_you
83.    {
84.      local (*FORM_DATA) = @_;
85.
```

```
86.      print "Content-type: text/html\n\n";
87.
88.      print "<HTML>\n";
89.      print "<HEAD>\n";
90.      print "<TITLE>CGI Business Card
         Order</TITLE>\n";
91.      print "</HEAD>\n";
92.      print "<BODY><BR>\n";
93.      print "<H1>Thanks for Your Business Card
         Order</H1>\n";
```

On lines 88-94 we begin printing HTML to STDOUT as our reply. On line 95 we include information from the array we prepared in the parse_form_data() sub routine. We start with some text and concatenate the value store in $FORM_DATA{'date'}. To this we concatenate the closing period for the sentence, and an HTML line break followed by a new line character. All this is then printed to STDOUT as part of our reply.

```
95.      print "Your information was submitted,
         ",$FORM_DATA{'date'}, ".<BR>\n";
```

On lines 96-107 we continue printing HTML combined with our $FORM_DATA to STDOUT as our reply. On lines 106 we print the required closing HTML, and on line 107 the routine ends. Pretty simple!

```
96.      print "Your information we received
         was:<BR>\n";
97.      print "Full Name:  ", $FORM_DATA{'name'},
         "<BR>\n";
98.      print "Phone:      ", $FORM_DATA{'phone'},
         "<BR>\n";
99.      print "Fax:        ", $FORM_DATA{'fax'},
         "<BR>\n";
100.     print "E-mail:     ", $FORM_DATA{'email'},
         "<BR>\n";
101.     print "Phrase:     ", $FORM_DATA{'phrase'},
         "<BR>\n";
102.     print "Quantity:   ", $FORM_DATA{'quantity'},
         "<BR>\n";
103.     print "</PRE>\n";
```

```
104.    print "<HR>\n";
105.    print "<BR>\n";
106.    print "</BODY></HTML>\n";
107. }
```

The return_error() Sub Routine

Our return_error() sub routine is a very simple solution that sends an HTML response to the client advising them that an error occurred. Line 108 of our script is used to declare the instructions that follow are part of our send_thank_you() sub routine. On line 110 we call the Perl local command to create local references to the three parameters passed to this routine.

On line 112 we use the print command to output the content-type member of the HTTP response header. On line 113 we add the status to the header and append two new line characters signifying the response header's end. Lines 114-117 output the opening HTML needed to construct the reply. On lines 119 and 120, we combine the $errtype and $message into our response and then print the HTML required to complete the response file. In conclusion we call the Perl exit() command, passing it "1" so the script will exit knowing an error has been encountered.

```
108. sub return_error
109. {
110.    local ($status, $errtype, $message) = @_;
111.
112.    print "Content-type: text/html\n";
113.    print "Status: ", $status, " ", $errtype,
        "\n\n";
114.    print "<HTML>\n";
115.    print "<HEAD>\n";
116.    print "<TITLE>CGI Program Error</TITLE>\n";
117.    print "</HEAD>\n";
118.    print "<BODY><BR>\n";
119.    print "<H1>This CGI program encountered a ",
        $errtype, "</H1>\n";
120.    print $message;
121.    print "<HR>\n";
122.    print "<BR>\n";
```

```
123.    print "</BODY></HTML>\n";
124.    exit(1);
125. }
```

Run the Example

To run the example, place the "b_card.pl" Perl script in your Netscape Server's "shell-cgi" directory. Place the "business_card.pdf" on your server in a directory that you can access through your browser.

Now enter the form's URL in your browser window. Enter some information into the form fields and click the submit button.

W4 Employer Form

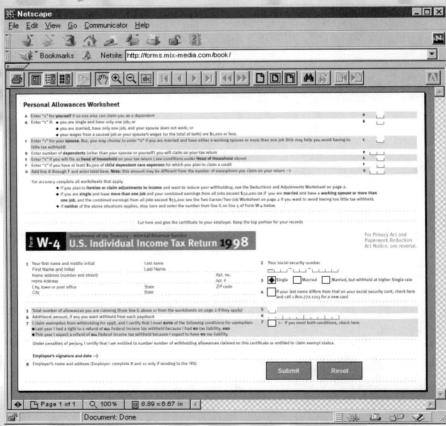

Overview

This example demonstrates how to construct a form that gathers tax filing information and stores the information in a database upon submission. The example allows the user to enter information into a PDF document that resembles an actual US Treasury W4 form. The user can submit their information and a graphic representation of their signature.

Physical Requirements

The following list is a description of the setup used to create this example. The actual components are:

Windows NT Server version 4.0
Perl 5.0 for Win32
Netscape Enterprise Server 3.01/JavaScript Application
Microsoft Access ODBC Driver
Netscape Navigator 3.x or Netscape Communicator 4.04 or newer with Acrobat Plug-in or Microsoft Internet Explorer 4.0 or newer with Acrobat Plug-in
Adobe Acrobat Exchange or Reader 3.0 or newer, with Adobe Forms Plug-in 3.5

Physical Setup the Example Uses

The example runs on Netscape Enterprise Server 3.01 running on a Windows NT 4.0 server. A server-side JavaScript application is used to access a Microsoft Access database. The Netscape Enterprise Server's JavaScript Application Manager is used to install the application.

We've created a Microsoft Access database and added one table titled "taxinfo". We'll use this table to store employee submissions. The database is configured to accept connections from user, "adobe" with a password "book". The table has twenty-one fields that correspond to the fields of our submission form. They are: "A", "B", "C", "D", "E", "F", "AF", "fname", "lname", "address", "apt", "city", "state", "ZIP", "ssnumber", "status", "diffname", "additional", "exempt", "signature", and "date". For security reasons, the "taxinfo" table is the only one this user and password can access.

For this example we're using a JavaScript application to manage the connection to the database. The application is compiled into a file of platform-independent bytecodes, which generate HTML. A JavaScript Web application uses JavaScript on the server side to issue SQL commands to a database. These commands are communicated through a database's native driver or through ODBC.

We have installed Netscape Communicator 4.04 and Acrobat Exchange on our client machine. Additionally, Netscape Navigator has the Acrobat plug-in located in its plug_in directory. This allows PDF files to be viewed directly in the Navigator window.

Creating the Necessary Files

To get this example to work we need to place several files on the server. The first is a PDF file that is the form the client interacts with. The second is the w4_result.html file we'll use to process the form submission. The third file is the compiled bytecode file. To create this file, it's handy to also create a "build.bat" file. Instead of typing the command line to compile the ".web" file, the process can be automated via a batch file. In addition, we need to create the Access database and set up a connection through an ODBC driver.

Creating the PDF File

This example uses a PDF file as its client-side form interface. This form allows users to enter information relevant to submitting their W4 employment information. The form collects the results from the personal allowances worksheet, a first name, last name, street address, city, state, ZIP code, social security number, marital status, name difference, additional deduction amount, exempt status, date, and signature. This information is then submitted to a server and stored in a database. The form file was constructed in Adobe Illustrator and then distilled into PDF format. The next steps discuss creating the client side form of this transaction.

Step 1

The Form Field Names

Once we have the final PDF document created by our designer we need to add the following form fields using Acrobat Exchange's form creation tool.

A
B
C
D
E
F
AF
fname
lname
address
apt
city
state
zip
ssnumber
status
diffname
additional
exempt
signature
date
submit

Step 2

"A" Field

First we'll create the "A" field. The "A" field will hold the value that corresponds to line A of the Personal allowances worksheet portion of the form. To create the field, choose the forms tool button on the Acrobat Exchange toolbar. The cursor changes to a crosshair. Click the mouse button and drag out a rectangle defining the area where you want the user to enter their first name. The Field Properties dialog box appears asking for specifics about the text field we're creating.

Step 2: Field Properties Dialog-Appearance Tab

Enter "A" as the field name and select Text as the field type. Leave the User Name field blank. It's only used to export a different field name with this field's value when the form is submitted.

Activate the Appearance tab. Here we're presented with options that affect the field's appearance. The design of our form draws the field as a graphic so we don't need to have a Border or Background Color. Select a color the text will display by clicking the Text Color chip. Select Helvetica as the Font and 12 as the Size. Finally check the Required checkbox. The user will be warned if they don't fill out this field before submitting the form to the server.

Now activate the Format tab. The Format tab allows us to regulate the formatting of information entered into the field. Choose Number from the Category list and select "None" from the Currency Symbol list.

Field Properties

Name: A Type: Text

User Name

Appearance | Options | Actions | Format | Validate | Calculate

○ Value is not validated.

● Value must be greater than or equal to [0]

and less than or equal to [1]

○ Custom validate script:

[Edit...]

[OK] [Cancel]

Step 2: Field Properties Dialog-Validate Tab

Now activate the Validate tab. Here we'll enter the value range the field accepts. Click the second radio button and enter zero and one as the limits. We want the user to enter either of these numbers.

Once you're happy with your choices, click the OK button. The dialog closes adding the field to the document.

Step 3

"B", "C", "D", "E", and "F" Fields

Now we'll create the "B", "C", "D", "E", and "F" fields. To create these fields we'll repeat step two for each field. The Field Properties dialog box appears each time we create a field, asking for specifics about the text field we're creating.

As you create each field, activate the Appearance tab, enter the field name and be sure to select Text as the field type. Select Helvetica as the Font and 12 as the Size.

For each field we add, activate the Validate tab. Enter the value range the field accepts. Click the second radio button and enter zero and one as the limits for each field except field "D". Field "D" needs to be a little more flexible. We'll set the limit between 0 and 100. I suppose someone might have 100 dependents.

For each field, click the OK button, closing the dialog and adding the field to the document.

Step 4

"AF" field

Now we'll create the "AF" field. The "AF" field will hold the value that corresponds to the sum of lines A through F of the Personal allowances worksheet portion of the form. To create the field, choose the forms tool button on the Acrobat Exchange toolbar. The cursor changes to a crosshair. Click the mouse button and drag out a rectangle defining the area where you want the user to enter their first name. The Field Properties dialog box appears asking for specifics about the text field we're creating.

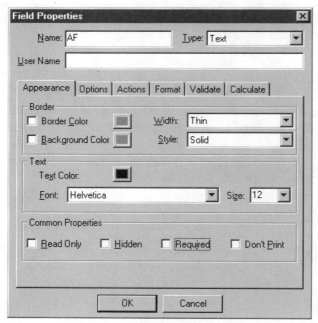

Step 4: Field Properties Dialog-Appearance Tab

Enter "AF" as the field name and select Text as the field type. Leave the User Name field blank. It's only used to export a different field name with this field's value when the form is submitted.

Activate the Appearance tab. Here we're presented with options that affect the field's appearance. The design of our form draws the field as a graphic so we don't need to have a Border or Background Color. Select a color the text will display by clicking the Text Color chip. Select Helvetica as the Font and 12 as the Size. Finally check the Read Only checkbox.

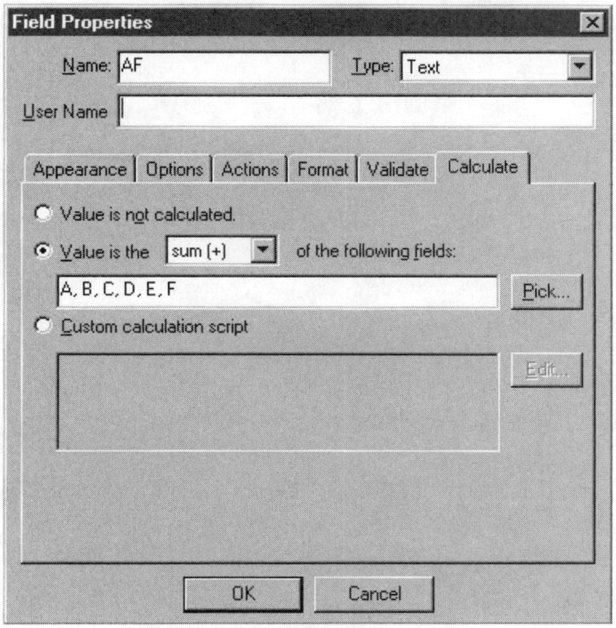

Step 4: Field Properties Dialog-Calculate Tab

Now activate the Calculate tab. Here we'll enter the value definition for the field. The "AF" field is the sum of fields "A" through "F", so click the second radio button and select sum from the list of predefined calculations. On the line below enter all the fields we want included in this summary calculation.

Once you're happy with your choices, click the OK button. The dialog closes, adding the field to the document.

Step 5

"fname" Field

Next we'll create the "fname" field. To create the field, choose the forms tool button on the Acrobat Exchange toolbar. The cursor changes to a crosshair. Click the mouse button and drag out a rectangle defining the

area where you want the user to enter their first name. The Field Properties dialog box appears asking for specifics about the text field we're creating.

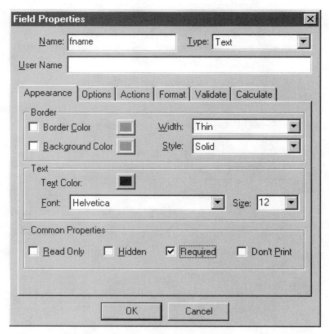

Step 5: Field Properties Dialog-Appearance Tab

Enter "fname" as the field name and select Text as the field type. Leave the User Name field blank. It's only used to export a different field name with this field's value when the form is submitted.

Activate the Appearance tab. Here we're presented with options that affect the field's appearance. Our designer decided to create the fields as a graphic so we don't have a Border or Background Color selected. If the designer didn't add a field graphic, Acrobat forms provides options to create a field with an outline or a background color. Select a color the text will display by clicking the Text Color chip. Select Helvetica as the Font and 12 as the Size. Finally check the Required checkbox. The user will be warned if they don't fill out this field before submitting the form to the server.

Field Properties   ×

Name: fname   Type: Text ▼

User Name: |

| Appearance | Options | Actions | Format | Validate | Calculate |

Default: First Name

Alignment: Left ▼

☐ Multi-line

☐ Limit of [   ] characters

☐ Password

[OK]   [Cancel]

Step 5: Field Properties Dialog-Options Tab

Now activate the Options tab, where we'll enter the default text displayed in the field. Here we've entered "First Name". This gives the user a little hint to guide them in their entry. We could also limit the number of characters or change this to a password field if we desired. Let's leave them blank for now.

Once you're happy with your choices, click the OK button. The dialog closes, adding the field to the document.

Step 6

"lname", Address, Apt, City, and State Fields

Now we'll create the "lname", address, apt, city, and state fields. To create these fields we'll repeat step two for each field. The Field Properties dialog box appears each time we create a field, asking for specifics about the text field we're creating.

As you create each field, activate the Appearance tab, enter its name, and be sure to select Text as the field type. Select Helvetica as the Font and 12 as the Size. Finally check the Required checkbox. The user will be warned if they don't fill out this field before submitting the form to the server.

For each field we add, activate the Options tab. Here we'll enter the default text displayed in the field. Enter some unique identifier, giving the user a hint about what to enter. Leave the limit on the number of characters and the password field unchecked for now.

For each field, click the OK button, closing the dialog and adding the field to the document.

Step 7

ZIP Code Field

Now we'll add a ZIP code field. With Acrobat Exchange's forms tool selected, drag out a rectangle defining the area where you want to display the ZIP code. The Field Properties dialog box appears asking for specifics about the field we're creating.

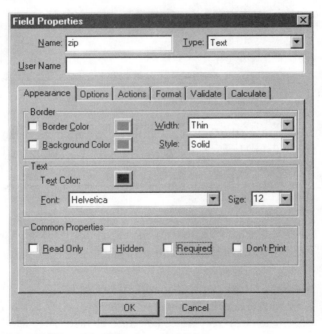

Step 7: Field Properties Dialog-Appearance Tab

Enter "zip" as the field name and select Text as the field type. We left the User Name field blank because we want the field name to be "zip" when the form is submitted.

Activate the Appearance tab. Make sure the Border or Background

Colors aren't selected. Select a color the text will display by clicking the Text Color chip. Select Helvetica as the Font and 12 as the Size.

Next activate the Options tab. Enter the default text to display in the field. Leave the limit on the number of characters and the password field unchecked for now.

Now activate the Format tab. The Format tab allows us to regulate the formatting of information entered into the field. Choose Special from the Category list and pick a ZIP code from the Special Options list. This insures users only enter five digits. If they try to enter letters, the system beeps and doesn't enter the character in the field.

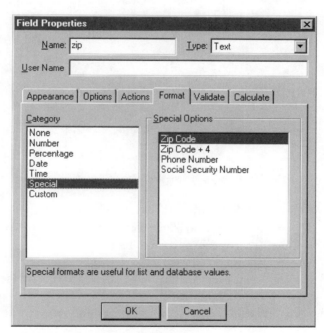

Step 7: Field Properties Dialog-Format Tab

Click the OK button. The dialog closes, adding the field to the document.

Step 8

"ssnumber" Field

Now we'll add a "ssnumber" field. With Acrobat Exchange's forms tool selected, drag out a rectangle defining the area where you want to display

the social security number. The Field Properties dialog box appears asking for specifics about the field we're creating.

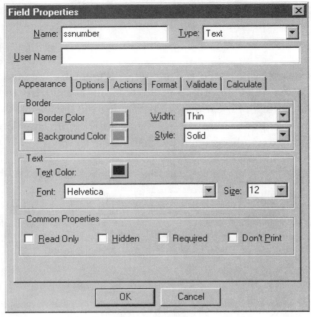

Step 8: Field Properties Dialog-Appearance Tab

Enter "ssnumber" as the field name and select Text as the field type. We left the User Name field blank because we want the field name to be "ssnumber" when the form is submitted.

Activate the Appearance tab. Make sure the Border or Background Colors aren't selected. Select a color the text will display by clicking the Text Color chip. Select Helvetica as the Font and 12 as the Size.

Next activate the Options tab. Enter the default text to display in the field. Leave the limit on the number of characters and the password field unchecked for now.

Now Activate the Format tab. The Format tab allows us to regulate the formatting of information entered into the field. Choose Special from the Category list and pick Social Security Number from the Special Options list. This insures users only enter nine digits. If they try to enter letters, the system beeps and doesn't enter the character in the field. It also formats the entry, inserting hyphens after the first three digits and the first five digits.

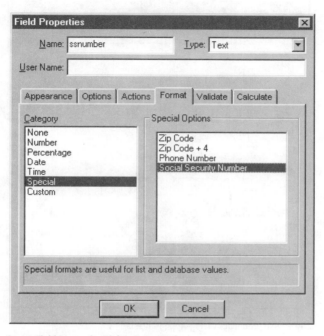

Step 8: Field Properties Dialog-Format Tab

Click the OK button. The dialog closes, adding the field to the document.

Step 9

"Single","Married" and "Married But Withhold A Higher Rate" Radio Buttons

In this step we'll add "Single" and "Married" and "Married But Withhold A Higher Rate" radio buttons to our document. These radio buttons are in a group, meaning only one of them can be selected at a time. This is accomplished in HTML by naming the buttons the same but having the value they export when selected differ. The same is true for PDF radio buttons. In this step we'll add one of three radio buttons that allow the user to indicate their marital status.

With the Acrobat Exchange forms tool selected, drag out a rectangle defining the area where you want the "Single" radio button to appear. The

Field Properties dialog box appears asking for specifics about the field we're creating.

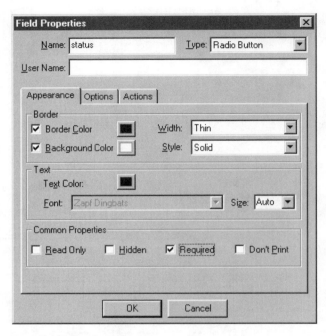

Step 9: Field Properties Dialog-Appearance Tab

Enter "status" as the field name and select Radio Button as the field type. Again leave the User Name field blank. We want this field's name to be exported as "status" when the form is submitted.

Activate the Appearance tab. Make sure to select the Border Color check-box. In addition, choose a color for the outline of the radio button by clicking the color chip next to the Border Color checkbox. Select black or any dark color so we'll be able to see it. Now select the background checkbox and choose a background color for the radio button by clicking the color chip next to it. Select white or any light color so we'll be able to see when the radio button is chosen. You can play with combinations of the Width and Style options to produce radio buttons with different looks. Our example uses the Thin Width and Solid Style options. Font selection is disabled for radio buttons but you might see Zapf Dingbats as the disabled selection. Finally check the Required checkbox.

Now activate the Options tab. Here we choose the look of the radio button we'll create, identify the value to export if this radio button is selected, and indicate if this button is selected as the default. Choose the list's default value by selecting it.

The Radio Style option presents us with half a dozen options for radio button styles. Let's be a little fancy and select "Diamond". Enter "single" as the Export Value and select the Default is Checked checkbox. When the form is initially opened, the "Single" radio button will now be selected.

Step 9: Field Properties Dialog-Options Tab

We've finished the first of three Radio buttons, so click the OK button closing the dialog and adding our work to the document.

Now we need to add the second status radio button to our document. With the Acrobat Exchange forms tool selected, drag out a rectangle defining the area where you want the "Married" radio button to appear. The Field Properties dialog box appears.

```
┌─────────────────────────────────────────────────────────┐
│ Field Properties                                      [X] │
│                                                           │
│        Name: │status          │    Type: │Radio Button ▼│ │
│                                                           │
│  User Name: │                                           │ │
│                                                           │
│  ┌─Appearance─┐ Options │ Actions │                       │
│  │ ┌─Border────────────────────────────────────────────┐ │
│  │ │ ☑ Border Color      ■      Width: │Thin         ▼│ │ │
│  │ │ ☑ Background Color  □      Style: │Solid        ▼│ │ │
│  │ └────────────────────────────────────────────────────┘ │
│  │ ┌─Text──────────────────────────────────────────────┐ │
│  │ │   Text Color:      ■                              │ │
│  │ │      Font: │Zapf Dingbats       ▼│ Size: │Auto ▼│ │ │
│  │ └────────────────────────────────────────────────────┘ │
│  │ ┌─Common Properties─────────────────────────────────┐ │
│  │ │ ☐ Read Only   ☐ Hidden   ☑ Required   ☐ Don't Print│ │
│  │ └────────────────────────────────────────────────────┘ │
│                                                           │
│              │   OK   │      │ Cancel │                   │
└─────────────────────────────────────────────────────────┘
```

Step 9: Field Properties Dialog-Appearance Tab

Enter "status" as the field name and select Radio Button as the field type. Again leave the User Name field blank. We want this field's name to be exported as "status" when the form is submitted.

Activate the Appearance tab. Make sure to select the Border Color checkbox. In addition, choose a color for the outline of the radio button by clicking the color chip next to the Border Color checkbox. Select black or any dark color so we'll be able to see it. Now select the Background Color checkbox and choose a background color for the radio button by clicking the color chip next to it. Select white or any light color so we'll be able to see when the radio button is chosen.

Up to this point, does everything look the same? If it doesn't, go back and walk through the steps for the radio buttons again.

Activate the Options tab and select "Diamond" as the Radio Style. Enter "married" as the Export Value. Be sure the Default is Checked checkbox is not selected. If this radio button is selected when the form is submitted the status field will contain the value "married".

Now we need to add the third status radio button to our document. With the Acrobat Exchange forms tool selected drag out a rectangle defining the area where you want the "Married But Withhold At Higher Rate" radio button to appear. The Field Properties dialog box appears.

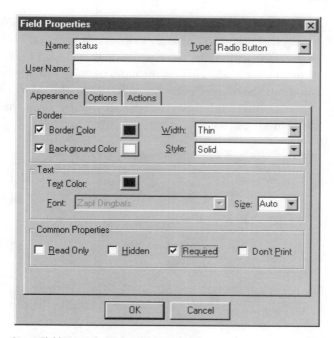

Step 9: Field Properties Dialog-Appearance Tab

Enter "status" as the field name and select Radio Button as the field type. Again leave the User Name field blank. We want this fields name to be exported as "status" when the form is submitted.

Activate the Appearance tab. Make sure to select the Border Color checkbox. In addition, choose a color for the outline of the radio button by clicking the color chip next to the Border Color checkbox. Select black or any dark color so we'll be able to see it. Now select the Background Color checkbox and choose a background color for the radio button by clicking the color chip next to it. Select white or any light color so we'll be able to see when the radio button is chosen.

Again, up to this point does everything look the same? If it doesn't, go back and walk through the steps for the radio buttons again.

Activate the Options tab and select "Diamond" as the Radio Style. Enter "higher" as the Export Value. Be sure the Default is Checked checkbox is not selected. If this radio button is selected when the form is submitted, the status field will have the value, "married but withhold at higher rate".

We've finished this group of Radio buttons, so click the OK button, closing the dialog and adding our work to the document. This is a good time to test if the buttons are working. To do this, choose the Hand tool on the Acrobat toolbar and click on the radio buttons. Initially the "Single" button should be selected and when you click on the "Married" or the "Married But Withhold At Higher Rate" radio button, the "Single" button should deselect.

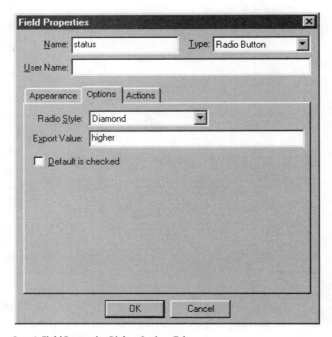

Step 9: Field Properties Dialog-Options Tab

Step 10

"diffname" Field—Check Box

Let's create a check box to track if the user's last name differs from the one on their social security card. To create the field, use the form tool to draw a rectangle defining the area where the check box is located. The Field Properties dialog box appears.

Step 10: Field Properties Dialog-Appearance Tab

Enter "diffname" as the field name and select Check Box as the field type.

Activate the Appearance tab. Make sure to select the Border Color checkbox. In addition choose a color for the outline of the Check Box by clicking the color chip next to the Border Color Check Box. Select black or any dark color so we'll be able to see it. Now select the Background Color checkbox and choose a background color for the Check Box by clicking the color chip next to it. Select white or any light color so we'll be able to see when the Check Box is chosen. You can play with combinations of the Width and Style options to produce checkboxes with different looks. Our example uses the Thin Width and Solid Style options. Font selection is also disabled for Check Boxes but you might see Zapf Dingbats as the disabled selection. Finally check the Required check box.

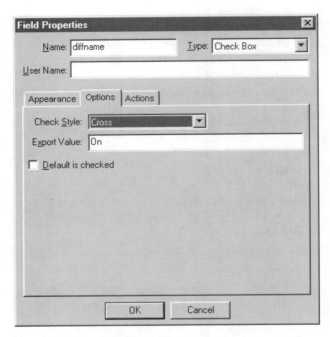

Step 10: Field Properties Dialog-Options Tab

Now activate the Options tab. Make sure to indicate this button is not selected as the default.

The Check Box option presents us with half a dozen different options for Check Box styles. Let's make this Check Box look like a Radio Button so select "Cross". Enter "On" as the export value.

When the proper settings are in place, click the OK button. The dialog closes, adding the field to the document.

Step 11

Duplicate the Summary Field

Now let's duplicate the summary field ("AF" field) from the worksheet and place it next to item five on the bottom of the form. With Acrobat Exchange's forms tool selected, click and select the summary field we created in step four. When the field is selected, click on it and continue to hold the mouse button down. Next, press the control key on Windows and UNIX or the option key on Macintosh and move your mouse to a new location on the page. When you reach the proper location, release the mouse button and a duplicate field appears. This field has the same name and properties as the one we created earlier. It will also contain the same value as our step four summary field when the form is being filled out.

Step 12

Additional Dollar Amount Field

Now we'll add an additional field. This field is used to enter an additional dollar amount the user might want withheld from their paycheck. With Acrobat Exchange's forms tool selected, drag out a rectangle defining the area where you want to display the dollar amount. The Field Properties dialog box appears asking for specifics about the field we're creating.

Step 12: Field Properties Dialog-Appearance Tab

Enter "additional" as the field name and select Text as the field type. Again we leave the User Name field blank. It's only used if we want to have a different field name exported with this field's value when the form is submitted.

Activate the Appearance tab. We don't need to select a Border or Background Color due to our form's design. Make sure the text color is black. If it isn't, change it to black by clicking the Text Color chip. Select Helvetica as the Font and Auto as the Size. Finally check the Read Only checkbox. This text box will hold and display text but it won't allow a user to enter any information.

Now Activate the Format tab. The Format tab allows us to regulate the formatting of information entered into the field. Choose Number from the Category list. Set the number of Decimal Places we'll display to two. Choose Dollar as the Currency Symbol we want to use. Pick a Separator Style and choose how Negative Numbers are to be displayed.

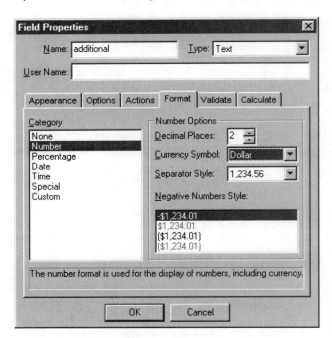

Step 12: Field Properties Dialog-Format Tab

Now click the Field Properties dialog's OK button. The dialog closes, adding the field to the document.

Step 13

Exempt Status Field—Check Box

Now we'll create a Check Box to track the exempt status. To create the field, use the form tool to draw a rectangle defining the area where the check box is located. The Field Properties dialog box appears.

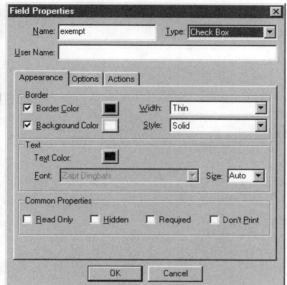

Step 13: Field Properties Dialog-Appearance Tab

Enter "exempt" as the field name and select Check Box as the field type.

Activate the Appearance tab. Make sure to select the Border Color check-box. In addition choose a color for the outline of the Check Box by click-ing the color chip next to the Border Color checkbox. Select black or any dark color so we'll be able to see it. Now select the Background Color Check Box and choose a background color for the Check Box by clicking the color chip next to it. Select white or any light color so we'll be able to see when the Check Box is chosen. You can play with combinations of the Width and Style options to produce Check Boxes with different looks. Our example uses the Thin Width and Solid Style options. Font selection is also disabled for Check Boxes but you might see Zapf Dingbats as the disabled selection. Finally, check the Required checkbox.

Step 13: Field Properties Dialog-Options Tab

Now activate the Options tab. Make sure to indicate this button is not selected as the default.

The Check Box option presents us with half a dozen different options for Check Box styles. Let's make this Check Box look like a Radio Button so select "Cross". Enter "On" as the export value.

When the proper settings are in place, click the OK button. The dialog closes, adding the field to the document.

Step 14

Signature Field—Button

The next field is a button. The button allows a user to click the signature field and insert a PDF file containing the user's signature.

To start, select the Acrobat Exchange forms and define a rectangle where the signature button is located. The Field Properties dialog box appears asking for specifics about the field.

Step 14: Field Properties Dialog-Appearance Tab

Activate the Appearance tab. Again we don't need to select a Border or Background Color due to our form's design. The button's text color isn't important because we aren't displaying the button's title. We aren't going to require the signature for a submission, so make sure Required isn't checked.

Step 14: Field Properties Dialog-Options Tab

The Options tab allows you to select how the button appears when it's clicked and the general layout of the button. In this instance we set the Highlight option to Invert. Here we want the button to Invert when the user clicks the photo and then lets the mouse button up. The Layout option is set to Icon only. When Icon only is chosen, the Advanced Layout button activates.

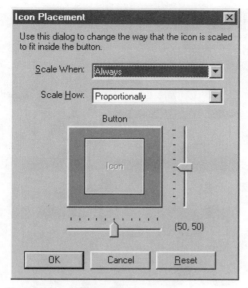

Step 14: Advanced Layout Dialog

The Advanced Layout dialog lets us scale an image we'll import into this button. Scaling can be done if the image is larger or smaller than the button's size. Scaling can also be set to be proportional or it can vary horizontally and vertically. Here we choose to Always scale an image to fit the button and to scale it Proportionally. Click OK to return to the Field Properties dialog box.

We won't set an initial icon for the button because we'll add a JavaScript that asks the user to select a button appearance.

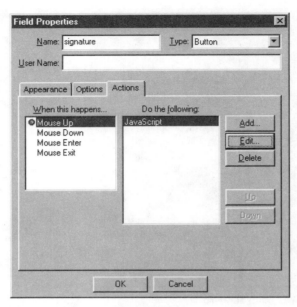

Step 14: Field Properties Dialog-Actions Tab

Since our buttons load another PDF image and this isn't normal button behavior, we need to add a JavaScript action to accomplish this. From the Field Properties Dialog Actions Tab, we add the action Mouse Up from the When this happens list.

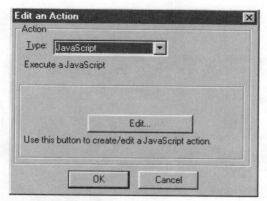

Step 14: Edit an Action Dialog

In the Edit an Action dialog choose the JavaScript Action Type and click the Edit button. Enter the following lines of JavaScript code and close the window.

```
1.   var f = this.getField("photo");
2.   f.bgColor = color.white;
3.   f.buttonImportIcon();
```

This simple script instructs Acrobat to reset the value of the button's icon. The first line of this script gets a reference to the photo field and stores it in the variable "f". The second line sets the background color of the field to white. The third line calls the field's buttonImportIcon() routine, which asks the user to locate a single page of a PDF file to insert as the field's appearance.

Once the script is entered, close the JavaScript window by clicking the OK button. Now click the Set Action button in the Add an Action dialog. If you're pleased with your selections, click the Field Properties dialog's OK button. The dialog closes, adding the field to the document. Don't forget to repeat the process for the signature field.

Step 15

Date Field

Now we'll add a date field. This field allows a user to enter a date and formats it in the way we specify. Error checking is performed and the user is warned if they try to enter information that can't be converted into a date. With Acrobat Exchange's forms tool, define the area where the user

will enter the date. The Field Properties dialog box appears asking for specifics about the field we're creating.

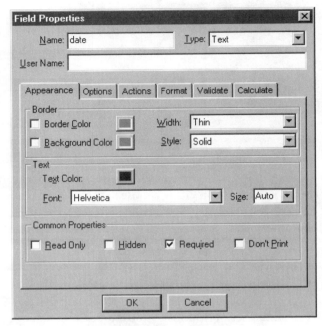

Step 15: Field Properties Dialog-Appearance Tab

Enter "date" as the field name and select Text as the field type. Leave the User Name field blank.

Activate the Appearance tab. We don't need a Border or Background Color. Select a color the text will display by clicking the Text Color chip. Select Helvetica as the Font and Auto as the Size. Be sure to check the Required checkbox.

Now Activate the Format tab. The Format tab allows us to regulate the formatting of information entered into the field. Choose Date from the Category list and pick a date format from the Date Options list.

Field Properties ☒

_N_ame: date   _T_ype: Text ▼

_U_ser Name:

| Appearance | Options | Actions | Format | Validate | Calculate |

_C_ategory

None
Number
Percentage
Date
Time
Special
Custom

Date Options

1/3
1/3/81
01/03/81
3-Jan
3-Jan-81
03-Jan-81
Jan-81
January-81
January 3, 1981
1/3/81 2:30 PM
1/3/81 14:30

Date formats display date values. Use the Time formats to display just the time portion.

OK   Cancel

Step 15: Field Properties Dialog-Format Tab

Click the OK button. The dialog closes, adding the field to the document.

Step 16

Submit Button

Our remaining field corresponds to the submit button. With Acrobat Exchange's forms tool selected, drag out a rectangle defining the area where the submit button is located. The Field Properties dialog box appears asking for specifics about the field we're creating.

Step 16: Field Properties Dialog-Appearance Tab

Activate the Appearance tab. Again we don't need to select a Border or Background Color due to our form's design. The button's text color isn't important because we aren't displaying the button's title.

Step 16: Field Properties Dialog-Options Tab

The Options tab is where you select any special appearance options for the button. In this instance we set the Highlight option to Invert. The Layout option is set to Text only. Because we don't want any text to show over our buttons, the Text entry for the Button Face Attributes is left blank. The Button Face When option determines when the appearance we set up is invoked. Here we want it to Invert on a mouse up event.

Step 16: Field Properties Dialog-Actions Tab

The actions tab is where you select any action this field will invoke. Here we choose the Mouse Up event. Click the Add button and choose Submit Form from the list of available action types.

Step 16: Edit an Action Dialog

Now we need to identify the URL that will process the form submission.

Click the Select URL button and enter the URL we'll use to process this form.

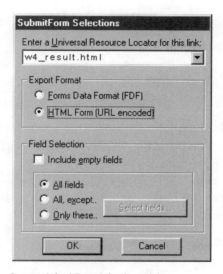

Step 16: SubmitForm Selections Dialog

Here we also choose to submit the data to the server in HTML format. We could submit in the FDF format but the Perl script we'll use to process the submission is set up to receive the data in HTML format. We also want to send all fields even though we have the option to just send a subset of the fields from the form. Once the proper selections are made, click the OK buttons in the SubmitForm Selections, Edit an Action, and Field Properties dialogs.

We're now ready to discuss setting up the back end of the process to receive information from this form.

Creating the Access Database

This example uses a Microsoft Access database to store information submitted by a client. Although Access is a popular database, it isn't recommended as an industrial-strength Web database. If your site demands thousands of transactions per day, another database designed to handle higher levels of transactions is a better choice. However, for our simple employee tax information example, Access's architecture is more than sufficient.

In this example we'll create a database using the Microsoft Access application and add a table named "taxinfo" to it. This database will exist on our server and we'll connect to it using ODBC drivers.

Step 1

Create the Database

Our first step is to create the database. Open Microsoft Access and choose new from the file menu. Create a blank database. Name it "w_four.mdb" and save it on the Web server machine.

Step 2

Add the "taxinfo" Table

Now we need to add the "taxinfo" table where we'll store the employee information that is submitted via our form. To do this we choose Table from the Insert menu. I like to add tables using the design view option but use whatever method you're most familiar with. Add the following fields to the table we just created.

Field Name	Data Type	Description
A	Text	Personal deduction
B	Text	One job
C	Text	Spouse
D	Text	Number of dependents
E	Text	Head of household
F	Text	Child dependent care expenses
AF	Text	Summary of Fields A-F
fname	Text	First Name
lname	Text	Last Name
address	Text	Address
apt	Text	Apartment Number
city	Text	City
state	Text	State
zip	Text	ZIP Code
ssnumber	Text	Social Security Number
status	Text	Status
diffname	Text	Different Last Name
additional	Text	Additional Deduction
exempt	Text	Exempt Status
signature	Text	Signature file path
date	Text	Submission date

Step 3

Create the ODBC Data Source

Once the database is created, we must create the ODBC data source. The first step is to verify that the Microsoft Access ODBC driver is installed on the Windows NT server. To check for this, open the ODBC Administrator in the server's control panel. The list of available drivers is displayed on the ODBC drivers tab of the dialog. If you don't see Microsoft Access Driver (*.mdb) in the list, install it from the Microsoft Access setup program. When you run the setup program, choose the custom setup option and install the Data Access Object. This will install the Access ODBC drivers. After you've performed this installation, check back in the ODBC Administrator control panel to verify the installation was a success.

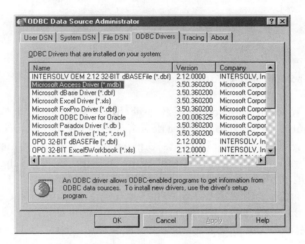

Step 3: ODBC DataSource Administrator Set up

Step 4

Open the ODBC Administrator

Once you've verified the correct drivers are installed, open the ODBC Administrator again. It lists all registered user data sources. User data sources are set up for individual users that log onto the system. This isn't what we want. We need a data source that's available to processes running on the server. These type of data sources are called system data sources. To create a new system data source, click the "System DSN" tab. The System Data Sources dialog tab lists available system data sources.

Now click the "Add..." button. The Create a New Data Source dialog appears and asks you to select an ODBC driver. Select the Microsoft Access Driver and click the OK or Finish button.

Step 5

Configure the Data Source

Now we should be presented with the ODBC Microsoft Access Setup dialog.

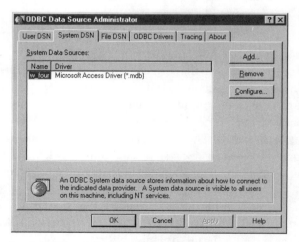

Step 5: ODBC Microsoft Assess 97 Set up

Here we need to accomplish three things. We need to name the data source, we need to supply a description of the data source, and we need to select the file for this data source. Enter "w_four" as the name and "Employee W4 Information" as the description. Then click the Select button and locate the database file we created in step 2. To enact the settings, click the OK button. The "w_four" data source should be viewable in the System Data Sources Dialog. When the w_four data source is visible, close the dialog. It's now available through ODBC connectivity.

Step 5: ODBC DataSource Administrator Set up

Creating the JavaScript Web Application

This example uses a PDF file as its interface to the user. The form gathers A, B, C, D, E, F, AF, fname, lname, address, apt, city, state, zip, ssnumber, status, diffname, additional, exempt, signature, and date and sends it to the server for processing by a compiled JavaScript application.

Creating a JavaScript application on a Netscape Enterprise 3.0 or newer server is a three-step process. The first step is to create the source files. These files can either be HTML with embedded JavaScript or files of pure JavaScript. The second step is to compile the application's source files into a platform-independent bytecode file. This is stored on the server as a ".web" file. The third step is to install the JavaScript application using the JavaScript Application Manager module of the Web Server.

The following pages discuss creating the files needed to run the application. The JavaScript application consists of a single file, w4_result.html. This file contains the HTML and JavaScript that queries the Access database and returns the resulting HTML page.

The complete page is shown below. For this example to work, the script must be compiled using the jsac.exe application. The resulting w_four.web file is what the server uses when the URL is accessed.

Code Example: w4_form.html

```
1.    <HTML>
2.    <HEAD>
3.    <TITLE>W4 SQL Query Result </TITLE>
4.    </HEAD>
5.    <BODY BGCOLOR=white>
6.    <SERVER>
7.    project.lock()
8.    project.name="w_four"
9.    project.desc="Database connection sample
      application."
10.   project.unlock()
11.
12.   // Construct the values needed for our connection
13.   client.type    = "ODBC";
```

```
14.    client.server   = "w_four";
15.    client.id       = "adobe";
16.    client.password = "book";
17.    client.database = "";
18.
19.    client.sql = "INSERT INTO taxinfo VALUES("
20.    + "\'" + request.A
21.    + "\', \'" + request.B
22.    + "\', \'" + request.C
23.    + "\', \'" + request.D
24.    + "\', \'" + request.E
25.    + "\', \'" + request.F
26.    + "\', \'" + request.AF
27.    + "\', \'" + request.fname
28.    + "\', \'" + request.lname
29.    + "\', \'" + request.address
30.    + "\', \'" + request.apt
31.    + "\', \'" + request.city
32.    + "\', \'" + request.state
33.    + "\', \'" + request.zip
34.    + "\', \'" + request.ssnumber
35.    + "\', \'" + request.status
36.    + "\', \'" + request.diffname
37.    + "\', \'" + request.additional
38.    + "\', \'" + request.exempt
39.    + "\', \'" + request.signature
40.    + "\', \'" + request.date + "\');";
41.
42.    project.lock();
43.    database.connect(client.type,
44.                     client.server,
45.                     client.id,
46.                     client.password,
47.                     client.database);
48.
49.    if(!database.connected())
50.    {
51.      project.unlock();
52.    write("<H1>Error</H1><BR>;
53.    write("There was an error connecting!");
```

```
54.     }
55.     else
56.     {
57.       client.status = database.execute(client.sql);
58.       project.unlock();
59.       client.majorNumber = database.majorErrorCode();
60.       client.majorText   =
          database.majorErrorMessage();
61.       client.minorNumber = database.minorErrorCode();
62.       client.minorText   =
          database.minorErrorMessage();
63.
64.       write("<H1>Server-side JavaScript
          Results</H1><BR>");
65.       if(client.status != 0)
66.       {
67.         write("<BR>An error was
            encountered.<BR>\r\n");
68.         write("<BR>Client Status: <B>" + client.status
            + "</B><BR>\r\n");
69.
70.         write("<BR>Major error number for this query:
            <B>" + client.majorNumber + "</B><BR>\n");
71.         write("<BR>Major error message for this query:
            <B>" + client.majorText  + "</B><BR>\n");
72.         write("<BR>Minor error number for this query:
            <B>" + client.minorNumber + "</B><BR>\n");
73.         write("<BR>Minor error message for this query:
            <B>" + client.minorText   + "</B><BR><BR>\n");
74.       }
75.       else
76.       {
77.         client.sql = "SELECT * FROM taxinfo";
78.
79.         project.lock();
80.         database.SQLTable(client.sql);
81.         database.disconnect();
82.         project.unlock();
83.       }
84.     }
```

```
85.   </SERVER>
86.   </BODY>
87.   </HTML>
```

The Example Script

Let's take a detailed look at our example script. Lines one through five are standard HTML. On line six of the file we encounter a new tag. The <SERVER> tag is used to inform the jsac.exe compiler that the following information is embedded JavaScript. When the compiler processes the file, any JavaScript statements within the <SERVER></SERVER> tags are evaluated and compile with the rest of the file. The only way to output HTML to the file from inside these tags is to call the write() function.

```
6.    <SERVER>
7.    project.lock()
8.    project.name="w_four"
9.    project.desc="Database connection sample
      application."
10.   project.unlock()
11.
```

Line seven locks the project object of this JavaScript application. This insures no other users access the object while we're using it. Lines eight and nine assign values to the name and desc members of the property object. On line ten we unlock the object since we're done setting its values.

```
12.   // Construct the values needed for our connection
13.   client.type     = "ODBC";
14.   client.server   = "w_four";
15.   client.id       = "adobe";
16.   client.password = "book";
17.   client.database = "";
18.
```

Line 12 is a comment. Any information found after a pair of forward slashes "//" is not used. This contains all information from the slashes to the end of that line.

In lines 13 through 17 we set members of the client object to values we'll use to connect to our database. Here we're using ODBC to connect to our w_four database. We'll connect as the "adobe" user with a password "book". The database member of the client object is set to the null string. Its value is used with some databases, but not for Microsoft Access.

The client object is a global object that is automatically created for each project. There is also a request object that contains any information submitted to the application by a form.

```
19.   client.sql = "INSERT INTO taxinfo VALUES("
20.   + "\'" + request.A
21.   + "\', \'" + request.B
22.   + "\', \'" + request.C
23.   + "\', \'" + request.D
24.   + "\', \'" + request.E
25.   + "\', \'" + request.F
26.   + "\', \'" + request.AF
27.   + "\', \'" + request.fname
28.   + "\', \'" + request.lname
29.   + "\', \'" + request.address
30.   + "\', \'" + request.apt
31.   + "\', \'" + request.city
32.   + "\', \'" + request.state
33.   + "\', \'" + request.zip
34.   + "\', \'" + request.ssnumber
35.   + "\', \'" + request.status
36.   + "\', \'" + request.diffname
37.   + "\', \'" + request.additional
38.   + "\', \'" + request.exempt
39.   + "\', \'" + request.signature
40.   + "\', \'" + request.date + "\');";
41.
```

On lines 19 through 40 we construct the SQL statement we'll use to insert the form's submission in the database. Each field of the request is accessed and concatenated to the string we store in the SQL member of the client object. Once assembled, the SQL statement will look something like this:

```
INSERT INFO taxinfo VALUES ('1', '1', '1', '1', '1', '1', '6'
                            'first name',
                            'last name',
                            'address',
                            'apt',
                            'city',
                            'state',
                            'zip',
                            'ssnumber',
                            'status',
                            'diffname',
                            'additional',
                            'exempt',
                            'signature',
                            'date');
```

This statement instructs the database to insert the enclosed values in a new row. Notice the single quotes that surround each value. They are preceded by a "\" character. This informs the compiler the following character is in fact a single quote and not a character that has any special meaning to the compiler.

```
42.   project.lock();
43.   database.connect(client.type,
44.              client.server,
45.              client.id,
46.              client.password,
47.              client.database);
```

On line 42 we again lock the project. We're ready to connect to the database and we want exclusive access while we read and write to it. On line 43 we connect to the database using the values we stored in our client object at the beginning of the file.

```
49.   if(!database.connected())
50.   {
51.     project.unlock();
52.     write("<H1>Error</H1><BR>;
53.     write("There was an error connecting!;
54.   }
```

Line 49 checks to see if we're connected. If we aren't, we unlock the project and write an error message as our response. If the connection is successfully established, we travel down the else branch that starts on line 55.

```
55.   else
56.   {
57.     client.status = database.execute(client.sql);
58.     project.unlock();
59.     client.majorNumber = database.majorErrorCode();
60.     client.majorText   =
        database.majorErrorMessage();
61.     client.minorNumber = database.minorErrorCode();
62.     client.minorText   =
        database.minorErrorMessage();
63.
64.     write("<H1>Server-side JavaScript
        Results</H1><BR>");
```

If line 57 is reached, we have a successful connection, so we call the database.execute() function, passing it the SQL string we stored in our client object. Any status code is stored in our client object in the status member. At this point we can unlock the project object for others to use. Next, we retrieve any error codes resulting from the last database function. Again, we store these in the client object. Now we're ready to start returning a response. On line 64 we write a level one head and then we prepare to write our full response.

```
65.     if(client.status != 0)
66.     {
67.       write("<BR>An error was
          encountered.<BR>\r\n");
68.       write("<BR>Client Status: <B>" + client.status
          + "</B><BR>\r\n");
69.
70.       write("<BR>Major error number for this query:
          <B>" + client.majorNumber + "</B><BR>\n");
71.       write("<BR>Major error message for this query:
          <B>" + client.majorText  + "</B><BR>\n");
72.       write("<BR>Minor error number for this query:
          <B>" + client.minorNumber + "</B><BR>\n");
```

```
73.      write("<BR>Minor error message for this query:
         <B>" + client.minorText  + "</B><BR><BR>\n");
74.    }
75.    else
76.    {
77.      client.sql = "SELECT * FROM taxinfo";
78.
79.      project.lock();
80.      database.SQLTable(client.sql);
81.      database.disconnect();
82.      project.unlock();
83.    }
84.  }
85.  </SERVER>
86.  </BODY>
87.  </HTML>
```

On line 65 the status code returned is checked and if it isn't zero, we write the error information as our response. Line 67 outputs a text message and then on line 68 we write a piece of HTML. This HTML is concatenated with the value stored in the client.status member and then another string of HTML is concatenated to the entire string. To concatenate strings in JavaScript we use the "+" character. It's just like adding two strings together. This process is repeated on lines 70 to 73 to output the error codes and messages we stored from our last database function call.

If the client.status is zero, no error occurred and we travel through the else block that starts on line 75. If we enter this block we've inserted a new row in our database. On line 77 we construct a new SQL statement that selects all information from the taxinfo table. Again, we store it in the SQL member of our client object.

On line 79 we again lock the project and on line 80 we call the built-in database.SQLTable() function. Passing this function select statement outputs an HTML table based on the database information returned. You can construct your own methods to do this, but the built-in method is a quick and dirty way to output a table.

On line 81 we disconnect from the database and then we once again unlock the project.

Line 85 contains our closing server tag and the following two lines close the body of the document and finally, the document itself.

This is the entire JavaScript application. Our next step is to generate the w_four.web file. This is done by selecting your project's directory as the current directory and calling the jsac.exe from the command line:

```
jsac -v -o w_four.web w4_result.html
```

Entered on a command line, the above example calls the JavaScript Application Compiler, telling it to output verbose "-v" comments to the object file "-o" named w_four.web. The remaining parameters are the file names to include in the application. On the Windows platform it's helpful to construct this as a batch file. During development, recompilation is frequent and a batch file saves a lot of typing.

Now that we have a w_four.web file, we need to install it in the server. To add the application, we need to access the administration pages of the Netscape Server. To do this, enter the following URL, substituting your server's name and domain.

```
http://server.domain/appmgr/
```

This will present you with your server's authentication dialog screen. You need to enter a user name and password to administer the server. Next, you'll click the Add Application button.

Enter the application's name, w_four. The path to the w_four.web file we created will be something like this:

```
C:\Netscape\Suitespot\js\w_four\w_four.web
```

It will be the path to wherever you choose to store items on your machine. Enter the default page to return to whenever the path to the application is accessed. Enter w4_form.pdf. We'll leave our initial page blank, the maximum database connections set to one, and external libraries blank. Finally, leave the Client Object Maintenance at its default. The JavaScript Application Manager can set cookies for connected clients, but we don't make use of this in our example. When all is set, click the OK button to install the application.

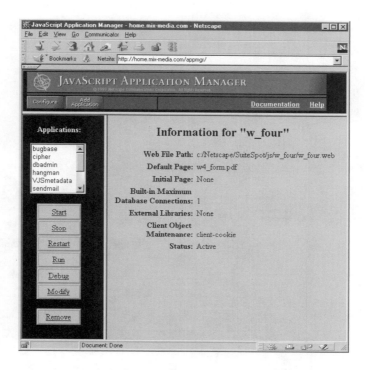

When you install the application for the first time, the entire server must be restarted for the application to become accessible.

At this point restart your server from your administration server in the Windows NT services Control Panel, or by restarting your machine.

Run the Example

Once the server has restarted, type in the URL;

```
http://server.domain/w_four/
```

to access the JavaScript application. If something goes wrong, you can return to the application manager page to stop, start, run, and debug your application.

1040 Tax Form

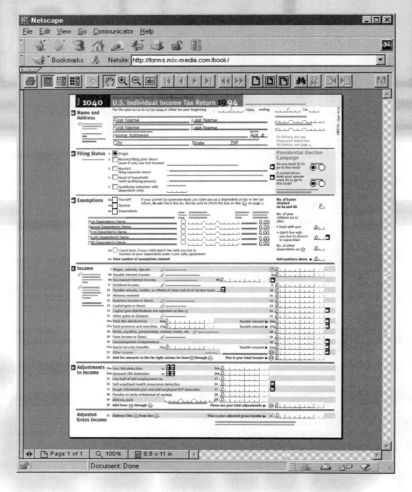

Overview

This example demonstrates how to construct a form that gathers individual tax filing information and stores the information in a file on the user's machine. This file can then be used to import the stored information into the form at a later time. The example allows the user to enter information into a PDF form that resembles what their actual US Treasury 1040 form will look like.

Physical Requirements

The following list is a description of the setup used to create this example. The actual components are:

Windows NT Server version 4.0
Netscape Enterprise Server 3.01
Netscape Navigator 3.x or Netscape Communicator 4.04 or newer with Acrobat Plug-in or Microsoft Internet Explorer 4.0 or newer with Acrobat Plug-in
Adobe Acrobat Exchange 3.1 or newer with Adobe Forms Plug-in 3.5

Physical Setup the Example Uses

The example runs on a Netscape Enterprise Server 3.01 running on Windows NT 4.0 Server

We have installed Netscape Communicator 4.04 and Acrobat Reader 3.1 on our client machine. Additionally, Netscape Communicator has the Acrobat plug-in located in its plug_in directory. This allows PDF files to be viewed directly in the Navigator window.

Creating the Necessary Files

To get this example to work we need to put one file on the server. The form is a PDF file designed to print out or to save field data to a user's hard drive.

Creating the PDF File

This example uses a PDF file as its client side form interface. This form allows users to enter information relevant to submitting their individual tax information.

The form mimics the current US Treasury 1040 tax form. It is used for collection of personal tax information for an individual. There are 53 fields on our simulation of the form. The next 15 steps group the fields into common field types. We'll walk through the creation of one field for each group, then ask you to repeat the process for each remaining field in the group. Otherwise the step by step instruction required to construct this form would require more pages than we've been allotted and that you would want to read.

This information can be printed and saved to disk. If the form information is saved to disk, it can be reloaded into the form at a later time. This form doesn't have any back end process, so no action is taken by the server except that the form is sent to the client when it is requested.

The form file was constructed in Adobe Illustrator and then distilled into PDF format. The next steps discuss creating the client side form of this transaction.

Step 1

The Form Field Names
Once we have the final PDF document designed and created we need to add the following form fields using Acrobat Exchange's form creation tool.

fname1	status
lname1	fund1
fname2	fund2
lname2	6A
address	6B
apt	6C
city	exempt
state	livewith
zip	liveaway
ssnumber1	other
ssnumber2	6D

6E	19
7	20
8A	21A
8B	21B
9	22
10	23
11	24A
12	24B
13	25
14	26
15	27
16A	28
16B	29
17A	30
17B	31
18	

Step 2

"fname1","lname1","fname2","lname2","Address","Apt","City", and "State" Fields

First we'll create the "fname1", "lname1", "fname2", "lname2", "address", "apt", "city", and "state" fields. We'll walk through creating the "fname1" text field. It will hold the user's first name. The process we define should be repeated for the other seven fields. The "fname1" field will hold the value that corresponds to the "Your first name" field of the Name and Address section of the form.

```
┌─────────────────────────────────────────────────────────┐
│ ■ Field Properties                                    ×  │
├─────────────────────────────────────────────────────────┤
│                                                           │
│        Name: [fname1         ]      Type: [Text      ▼]   │
│                                                           │
│   User Name [                                         ]   │
│                                                           │
│   ┌─────────┬────────┬────────┬────────┬────────┬────────┐│
│   │Appearance│ Options│ Actions│ Format │Validate│Calculate││
│   │─────────────────────────────────────────────────────┐│
│   │ ┌ Border ──────────────────────────────────────────┐││
│   │ │ □ Border Color     ■      Width: [Thin      ▼]   │││
│   │ │ □ Background Color ■      Style: [Solid      ▼]   │││
│   │ └───────────────────────────────────────────────────┘││
│   │ ┌ Text ────────────────────────────────────────────┐││
│   │ │    Text Color:    ■                               │││
│   │ │    Font: [Helvetica          ▼]  Size: [12   ▼]  │││
│   │ └───────────────────────────────────────────────────┘││
│   │ ┌ Common Properties ───────────────────────────────┐││
│   │ │ □ Read Only   □ Hidden   ☑ Required  □ Don't Print│││
│   │ └───────────────────────────────────────────────────┘││
│   └───────────────────────────────────────────────────────┘│
│                                                           │
│            [    OK    ]      [   Cancel   ]               │
│                                                           │
└─────────────────────────────────────────────────────────┘
```

Step 2: Field Properties Dialog-Appearance Tab

Enter "fname1" as the field name and select Text as the field type. As you create the other fields, be sure to enter their names instead of "fname1". Leave the User Name field blank. It's only used to export a different field name with this field's value when the form is submitted.

Activate the Appearance tab. Here we're presented with options that affect the field's appearance. Our designer decided to create the fields as a graphic so we don't have a Border or Background Color selected. If the designer didn't add a field graphic, Acrobat forms provides options to create a field with an outline or a background color. Select a color the text will display by clicking the Text Color chip. Select Helvetica as the Font and 12 as the Size. Finally check the Required checkbox. The user will be warned if they don't fill out this field before submitting the form to the server.

Field Properties ⊠

Name: [fname1]   Type: [Text ▾]

User Name [   ]

| Appearance | **Options** | Actions | Format | Validate | Calculate |

Default: [First Name   ]

Alignment: [Left   ▾]

☐ Multi-line
☐ Limit of [   ] characters
☐ Password

[OK]   [Cancel]

Step 2: Field Properties Dialog-Options Tab

Now activate the Options tab, where we'll enter the default text displayed in the field. Here we've entered "First Name". This gives the user a little hint to guide them in their entry. We could also limit the number of characters or change this to a password field if we desired. Let's leave them blank for now.

Once you're happy with your choices, click the OK button. The dialog closes, adding the field to the document.

Step 3

"ssnumber1" and "ssnumber2" Fields

Now we'll add the "ssnumber1" and "ssnumber2" fields. We'll create the "ssnumber1" field that corresponds to the social security number field in the form's Name and Address section. You'll need to repeat the steps to create the "ssnumber2" field that holds a spouse's social security number. With Acrobat Exchange's forms tool selected, drag out a rectangle defining the area where you want to display the Social Security Number. The Field Properties dialog box appears asking for specifics about the field we're creating.

Step 3: Field Properties Dialog-Appearance Tab

Enter "ssnumber1" as the field name and select Text as the field type. We left the User Name field blank because we want the field name to be "ssnumber1" when the form is submitted. Don't forget to use "ssnumber2" as the field's name when you repeat these steps.

Activate the Appearance tab. Make sure the Border or Background Colors aren't selected. Select a color the text will display by clicking the Text Color chip. Select Helvetica as the Font and 12 as the Size.

Next activate the Options tab. Enter the default text to display in the field. Leave the limit on the number of characters and the password field unchecked for now.

Now activate the Format tab. The format tab allows us to regulate the formatting of information entered into the field. Choose Special from the category list and pick Social Security Number from the Special Options List. This insures users only enter digits. If they try to enter letters, the system beeps and doesn't enter the character in the field. It also formats the entry inserting hyphens after the first three digits and the first five digits.

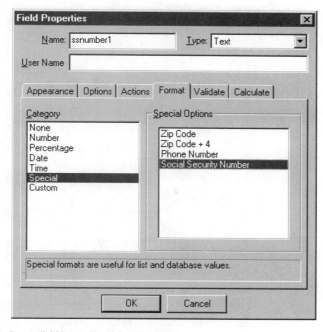

Step 3: Field Properties Dialog-Format Tab

Click the OK button. The dialog closes adding the field to the document. Now repeat the process for the "ssnumber2" field.

Step 4

ZIP Code Field

Now we'll add a ZIP code field. With Acrobat Exchange's forms tool selected, drag out a rectangle defining the area where you want to display the ZIP code. The Field Properties dialog box appears asking for specifics about the field we're creating.

Step 4: Field Properties Dialog-Appearance Tab

Enter "zip" as the field name and select Text as the field type. We left the User Name field blank because we want the field name to be "zip" when the form is submitted.

Activate the Appearance tab. Make sure the Border or Background Colors aren't selected. Select a color the text will display by clicking the Text Color chip. Select Helvetica as the Font and 12 as the Size.

Next activate the Options tab. Enter the default text to display in the field. Leave the limit on the number of characters and the password field unchecked for now.

Now activate the Format tab. The format tab allows us to regulate the formatting of information entered into the field. Choose Special from the Category list and pick a ZIP code from the Special Options list. This insures users only enter five digits. If they try to enter letters, the system beeps and doesn't enter the character in the field.

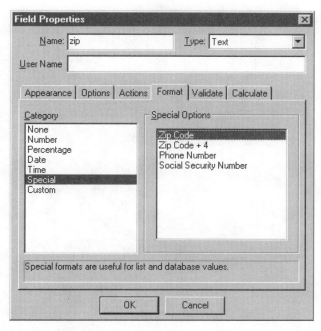

Step 4: Field Properties Dialog-Format Tab

Click the OK button. The dialog closes, adding the field to the document.

Step 5

"Single", "Married", "Married Filing Joint Return", "Head of Household", and "Qualifying Widow(er)" Radio Buttons

In this step we'll add "Single", "Married", "Married Filing Joint Return", "Head of Household" and "Qualifying widow(er)" radio buttons to our document. These radio buttons are in a group, meaning only one of them can be selected at a time. This is accomplished in HTML by naming the buttons the same but having the value they export when selected differ. The same is true for PDF radio buttons. In this step we'll add one of five radio buttons that allow the user to indicate their filing status.

With the Acrobat Exchange forms tool selected, drag out a rectangle defining the area where you want the radio button to appear. The Field Properties dialog box appears asking for specifics about the field we're creating.

Step 5: Field Properties Dialog-Appearance Tab

Enter "status" as the field name and select Radio Button as the field type. Again leave the User Name field blank. We want this field's name to be exported as "status" when the form is submitted.

Activate the Appearance tab. Make sure to select the Border Color checkbox. In addition, choose a color for the outline of the radio button by clicking the color chip next to the Border Color checkbox. Select black or any dark color so we'll be able to see it. Now select the Background Color checkbox and choose a background color for the radio button by clicking the color chip next to it. Select white or any light color so we'll be able to see when the radio button is chosen. You can play with combinations of the Width and Style options to produce radio buttons with different looks. Our example uses the Thin Width and Solid Style options. Font selection is disabled for radio buttons but you might see Zapf Dingbats as the disabled selection. Finally check the Required checkbox.

Now activate the Options tab. Here we choose the look of the radio button we'll create, identify the value to export if this radio button is selected, and indicate if this button is selected as the default. Choose the list's default value by selecting it.

The Radio Style option presents us with half a dozen options for radio button styles. Let's be a little fancy and select "Diamond". Enter "single" as the Export Value and select the Default is Checked checkbox. When the form is initially opened, the "Single" radio button will now be selected.

Step 5: Field Properties Dialog-Options Tab

We've finished the first of five radio buttons, so click the OK button, closing the dialog and adding our work to the document.

Now we need to add the second status radio button to our document. With the Acrobat Exchange forms tool selected, drag out a rectangle defining the area where you want the Married filing joint return radio button to appear. The Field Properties dialog box appears.

Enter "status" as the field name and select Radio Button as the field type. Again leave the User Name field blank. We want this field's name to be exported as "status" when the form is submitted.

Activate the Appearance tab. Make sure to select the Border Color check-box and choose a color for the outline of the radio button by clicking the color chip next to the checkbox. Select black or any dark color so we'll be able to see it. Now select the Background Color checkbox and choose a background color for the radio button by clicking the color chip next to it. Select white or any light color so we'll be able to see when the radio button is chosen.

Up to this point does everything look the same? If it doesn't, go back and walk through the steps for the radio buttons again.

Activate the Options tab and select "Diamond" as the Radio Style. Enter "joint" as the export value. Be sure the Default is Checked checkbox is not selected. If this radio button is selected when the form is submitted the status field will contain the value, "joint".

Step 5: Field Properties Dialog-Options Tab

Now we need to add the third status radio button to our document. With the Acrobat Exchange forms tool selected drag out a rectangle defining the area where you want the "Married filing separate return" radio button to appear. The Field Properties dialog box appears.

Enter "status" as the field name and select Radio Button as the field type. Again leave the User Name field blank. We want this field's name to be exported as "status", not another, when the form is submitted.

Activate the Appearance tab. Make sure to select the Border Color checkbox and choose a color for the outline of the radio button by clicking the color chip next to the checkbox. Select black or any dark color so we'll be able to see it. Now select the background checkbox and choose a background color for the radio button by clicking the color chip next to it. Select white or any light color so we'll be able to see when the radio button is chosen.

Up to this point if everything doesn't look the same, go back and walk through the steps for the radio buttons again.

Activate the Options tab and select "Diamond" as the Radio Style. Enter "separate" as the export value. Be sure the Default is Checked checkbox is not selected. If this radio button is selected when the form is submitted the status field will contain the value, "separate".

Step 5: Field Properties Dialog-Options Tab

Now we need to add the fourth status radio button to our document. With the Acrobat Exchange forms tool selected, drag out a rectangle defining the area where you want the "Head of household" radio button to appear. The Field Properties dialog box appears.

Enter "status" as the field name and select Radio Button as the field type. Again leave the User Name field blank. We want this fields name to be exported as "status", not another, when the form is submitted.

Activate the Appearance tab. Make sure to select the Border Color checkbox. In addition, choose a color for the outline of the radio button by clicking the color chip next to the checkbox. Select black or any dark color so we'll be able to see it. Now select the Background Color checkbox and choose a background color for the radio button by clicking the color chip next to it. Select white or any light color so we'll be able to see when the radio button is chosen.

Again, up to this point, does everything look the same? If it doesn't, go back and walk through the steps for the radio buttons again.

Activate the Options tab and select "Diamond" as the Radio Style. Enter "head" as the Export Value. Be sure the Default is checked checkbox is not selected. If this radio button is selected when the form is submitted, the status field will contain the value, "head".

Step 5: Field Properties Dialog-Options Tab

Now we need to add the fifth and last status radio button to our document. With the Acrobat Exchange forms tool selected, drag out a rectangle defining the area where you want the "Qualifying widow(er) with dependent child" radio button to appear. The Field Properties dialog box appears.

Enter "status" as the field name and select Radio Button as the field type. Again leave the User Name field blank. We want this field's name to be exported as "status" when the form is submitted.

Activate the Appearance tab. Make sure to select the Border Color checkbox. In addition choose a color for the outline of the radio button by clicking the color chip next to the Border Color checkbox. Select black or any dark color so we'll be able to see it. Now select the Background Color checkbox and choose a background color for the radio button by clicking the color chip next to it. Select white or any light color so we'll be able to see when the radio button is chosen.

Again, up to this point, does everything look the same? If it doesn't, go back and walk through the steps for the radio buttons again.

Activate the Options tab and select "Diamond" as the Radio Style. Enter "widow" as the Export Value. Be sure the Default is checked checkbox is not selected. If this radio button is selected when the form is submitted, the status field will have the value, "widow".

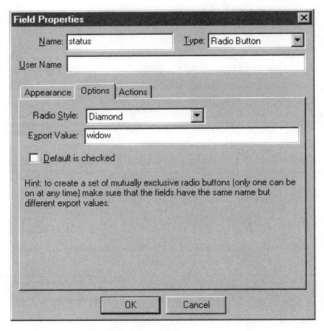

Step 5: Field Properties Dialog-Options Tab

We've finished this group of Radio buttons, so click the OK button, closing the dialog and adding our work to the document. This is a good time to test if the buttons are working. To do this, choose the Hand tool on the Acrobat toolbar and click on the radio buttons. Initially the "Single" button should be selected, and when you click on the "Married Filing Separate Return" or the "Head of Household" radio button, the "Single" button should deselect.

Step 6

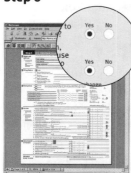

Yes and No Radio Buttons

In this step we'll add Yes and No radio buttons to our document, allowing the user to choose whether they want to contribute one dollar to the presidential election campaign fund. These radio buttons are in a group meaning only one of them can be selected at a time. This is accomplished in HTML by naming the buttons the same, but the value they export when selected is different. The same is true for PDF radio buttons.

With the Acrobat Exchange forms tool selected, drag out a rectangle defining the area where you want the radio button to appear. The Field Properties dialog box appears asking for specifics about the field we're creating.

Step 6: Field Properties Dialog-Appearance Tab

Enter "fund1" as the field name and select Radio Button as the field type. Again leave the User Name field blank. We want this field's name to be exported as "fund1" when the form is submitted.

Activate the Appearance tab. Make sure to select the Border Color checkbox. In addition, choose a color for the outline of the radio button by clicking the color chip next to the Border Color checkbox. Select black or any dark color so we'll be able to see it. Now select the Background Color checkbox and choose a background color for the radio button by clicking the color chip next to it. Select white or any light color so we'll be able to see when the radio button is chosen. You can play with combinations of the Width and Style options to produce radio buttons with different looks. Our example uses the Thin Width and Solid Style options. Font selection is disabled for radio buttons but you might see Zapf Dingbats as the disabled selection. Finally check the Required checkbox.

Now activate the Options tab. Here we choose the look of the radio button we'll create, identify the value to export if this radio button is selected, and indicate if this button is selected as the default. Choose the list's default value by selecting it.

The Radio Style option presents us with half a dozen different options for radio button styles. Let's stick to the basics for now and select "Circle". Enter "yes" as the export value and select the Default is checked checkbox. When the form is initially opened, the "Yes" radio button will now be selected.

Step 6: Field Properties Dialog-Options Tab

We've finished the first of two radio buttons, so click the OK button, closing the dialog and adding our work to the document.

Now we need to add another radio button to our document. This button will allow the user to choose not to contribute to the presidential election fund. With the Acrobat Exchange forms tool selected, drag out a rectangle defining the area where you want the "No" radio button to appear. The Field Properties dialog box appears.

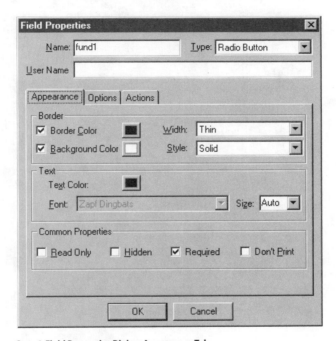

Step 6: Field Properties Dialog-Appearance Tab

Enter "fund1" as the field name and select Radio Button as the field type. Again leave the User Name field blank. We want this field's name to be exported as "fund1" when the form is submitted.

Activate the Appearance tab. Make sure to select the Border Color checkbox. In addition choose a color for the outline of the radio button by clicking the color chip next to the Border Color checkbox. Select black or any dark color so we'll be able to see it. Now select the Background Color checkbox and choose a background color for the radio button by clicking the color chip next to it. Select white or any light color so we'll be able to see when the radio button is chosen.

Activate the Options tab and select "Circle" as the Radio Style. Enter "no" as the Export Value. Be sure the Default is checked checkbox is not selected. If this radio button is selected when the form is submitted, the "fund1" field will contain the value, "no".

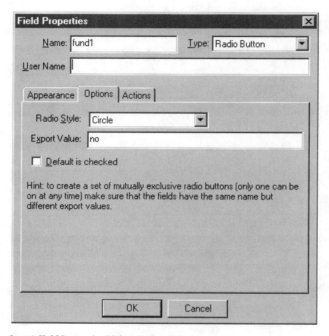

Step 6: Field Properties Dialog-Options Tab

We've finished the group of Radio buttons we'll use to indicate if the user wants to donate one dollar to the presidential election fund.Click the OK button, closing the dialog and adding our work to the document. Once this is done, we'll need to repeat the steps for the "fund2" field.

This is a good time to test if the buttons are working. To do this choose the Hand tool on the Acrobat toolbar and click on the radio buttons. Initially the "Yes" button should be selected and when you click on the "No" radio the "Yes" button should deselect.

Step 7

Three Exemption Check Boxes
Let's create three check boxes to begin tracking how many exemptions a

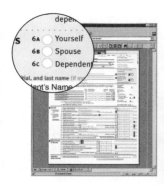

user can claim. To create the first of three fields, use the form tool to draw a rectangle defining the area where the check box is located. The Field Properties dialog box appears.

Field Properties

Name: self   Type: Check Box

User Name

Appearance | Options | Actions

Border
☑ Border Color   ■   Width: Thin
☑ Background Color □   Style: Solid

Text
Text Color: ■
Font: Zapf Dingbats   Size: Auto

Common Properties
☐ Read Only   ☐ Hidden   ☑ Required   ☐ Don't Print

OK   Cancel

Step 7: Field Properties Dialog-Appearance Tab

Enter "self" as the field name and select Check Box as the field type.

Activate the Appearance tab. Make sure to select the Border Color checkbox. In addition, choose a color for the outline of the Check Box by clicking the color chip next to the Border Color checkbox. Select black or any dark color so we'll be able to see it. Now select the Background Color checkbox and choose a background color for the Check Box by clicking the color chip next to it. Select white or any light color so we'll be able to see when the Check Box is chosen. You can play with combinations of the Width and Style options to produce Check Boxes with different looks. Our example uses the Thin Width and Solid Style options. Font selection is also disabled for Check Boxes but you might see Zapf Dingbats as the disabled selection. Finally check the Required checkbox.

Step 7: Field Properties Dialog-Options Tab

Now activate the Options tab. Here choose the look of the Check Box. Identify the value to export by entering it into the proper text field. Make sure to indicate this button is not selected as the default.

The Check Box option presents us with half a dozen different options for Check Box styles. Let's make this Check Box look like a Radio Button, so select Cross. Enter "on" as the export value.

When the proper settings are in place, click the OK button. The dialog closes, adding the field to the document.

If the field appears properly, repeat the above steps in creating checkboxes for the "Spouse" and "Dependents" fields.

Step 8

Sub-total of Exemptions Field—Read only
Now we'll add a field to track the sub-total of exemptions selected by the user. This is a read-only field. The field value is calculated based on how many checkboxes the user clicked in the exemptions group.

With Acrobat Exchange's forms tool selected, drag out a rectangle defining the area where you want to display the number. The Field Properties dialog box appears asking for specifics about the field we're creating.

Step 8: Field Properties Dialog-Appearance Tab

Enter "exempt" as the field name and select Text as the field type. Again we leave the User Name field blank. It's only used if we want to have a different field name exported with this field's value when the form is submitted.

Activate the Appearance tab. We don't need to select a Border or Background Color due to our form's design. Make sure the text color is black. If it isn't, change it to black by clicking the Text Color chip. Select Helvetica as the Font and Auto as the Size. Finally check the Read Only checkbox. This text box will hold and display text but it won't allow a user to enter any information.

Activate the Format tab. Choose Number from the category list. Set the number of decimal places we'll display to two. Choose Dollar as the currency symbol we want to use. Pick a separator style and choose how negative numbers are to be displayed.

Activate the Calculate tab. The calculate tab lets us set up a field to calculate the value of this field. There are several simple calculation options available, including calculating the sum of several fields, calculating the product of fields, and even averaging field values.

Our calculation is a little more complex. We need to add a custom calculation. To do this, click the Custom calculation script radio button and then click the Edit button. The Acrobat JavaScript editing window appears. Type in the following code:

```
1.    var count = 0;
2.    var f = this.getField("self");
3.    count += f.value;
4.    var g = this.getField("spouse");
5.    count += g.value;
6.    event.value += count;
```

This simple script calculates the sub-total of our exemptions based on the values of the self and spouse checkboxes. The first line of this script declares a variable and initializes it to zero. The second line gets a reference to the "self" field and stores it in the variable "f". The third line adds the value of the "f" field to the count variable. The fourth line gets a reference to the "spouse" field and stores it in the variable "g". The fifth line adds the value of the "g" field to the count variable. The sixth stores the "count" in the "event.value" field of the current event. The current event is the "exempt" field being asked to calculate its value. All fields on a page receive a request to calculate their value when any field on the same page commits to a new value.

Field Properties

Name: exempt   Type: Text

User Name:

Appearance | Options | Actions | Format | Validate | **Calculate**

○ Value is not calculated.

○ Value is the [sum (+) ▼] of the following fields:

[   ] [Pick...]

● Custom calculation script

```
var count = 0;
var f = this.getField("self");
count += f.value;
var g = this.getField("spouse");
```
[Edit...]

[OK]   [Cancel]

Step 8: Field Properties Dialog-Calculate Tab

Once the script is entered, close the JavaScript window by clicking the OK button. You will be able to see the script in the Calculate tab. If you can't see the script, go back and enter the script again.

Now click the Field Properties dialog's OK button. The dialog closes, adding the field to the document.

Step 9

"Dependent1","Months1","Dependent2","Months2","Dependent3", "Months3","Dependent4","Months4","Dependent5",and "Months5" Fields

In this step we'll create the "dependent1", "months1", "dependent2", "months2", "dependent3", "months3", "dependent4", "months4", "dependent5" and "months5" fields. We'll walk through creating the "dependent1" text field. It will hold the first dependent's name. The remaining nine fields should be created by repeating this procedure. The "dependent1" field will hold the value that corresponds to the "First dependent's name" field of the Exemptions section of the form.

Step 9: Field Properties Dialog-Appearance Tab

Enter "dependent1" as the field name and select Text as the field type. As you create the other fields, be sure to enter their names instead of "dependent1". Leave the User Name field blank. It's only used to export a different field name with this field's value when the form is submitted.

Activate the Appearance tab. Here we're presented with options that affect the field's appearance. Our designer decided to create the fields as a graphic so we don't have a Border or Background Color selected. If the designer didn't add a field graphic, Acrobat forms provides options to create a field with an outline or a background color. Select a color the text will display by clicking the Text Color chip. Select Helvetica as the Font and 12 as the Size.

Field Properties ☒

Name: dependent1   Type: Text ▾

User Name |

| Appearance | Options | Actions | Format | Validate | Calculate |

Default: First Dependent's Name

Alignment: Left ▾

☐ Multi-line
☐ Limit of [   ] characters
☐ Password

[OK]   [Cancel]

Step 9: Field Properties Dialog-Options Tab

Now activate the Options tab, where we'll enter the default text displayed in the field. Here we've entered "First Dependent's Name". This gives the user a little hint to guide them in their entry. We could also limit the number of characters or change this to a password field if we desired. Leave them blank for now.

Once you're happy with your choices, click the OK button. The dialog closes, adding the field to the document.

Before you go on, repeat these steps for the other nine fields.

Step 10

Number of Dependents Fields

Now we'll add three number fields. They allow entry of how many dependents live with you, how many didn't live with you because of divorce or separation, and the number of other dependents. The three fields are located on the far right of the Exemptions section of the 1040 form. Once again we'll walk through the creation of the "livewith" field, which will guide you in repeating the process for the "liveaway" and the "other dependents" fields.

With Acrobat Exchange's form tool selected, drag out a rectangle defining the area where you want to display the "livewith" field information. The Field Properties dialog box appears asking for specifics about the field we're creating.

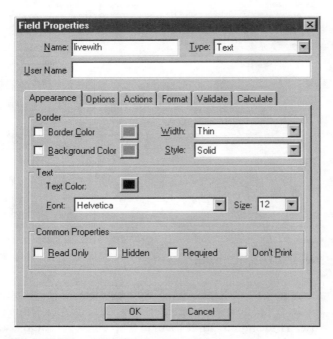

Step 10: Field Properties Dialog-Appearance Tab

Enter "livewith" as the field name and select Text as the field type. We left the User Name field blank because we want the field name to be "livewith" when the form is submitted.

Activate the Appearance tab. Make sure the Border or Background Colors aren't selected. Select a color the text will display by clicking the Text Color chip. Select Helvetica as the Font and 12 as the Size.

Next activate the Options tab. Enter the default text to display in the field. Leave the limit on the number of characters and the password field unchecked for now.

Now activate the Format tab. The format tab allows us to regulate the formatting of information entered into the field. Choose Number from the Category list and Pick "0" for the number of decimal places and choose None for the Currency Symbol. This is a basic method of authentication that insures users only enter digits. We'll do a more detailed check on the server side of the transaction.

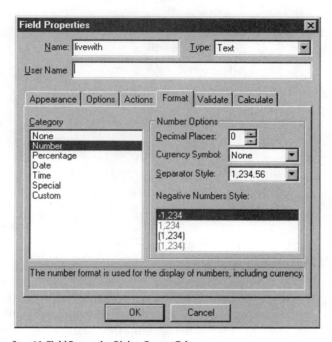

Step 10: Field Properties Dialog-Format Tab

Click the OK button. The dialog closes, adding the field to the document. Repeat this for the "liveaway" and the "other dependents" fields, each time closing the dialogs and saving the fields to the document.

Step 11

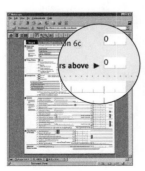

"6E" Field

Next we'll create the "6E" field. The "6E" field will hold the the sum of the "livewith", "liveaway", and the "other dependents" fields of the form. To create the field, choose the forms tool button on the Acrobat Exchange toolbar. The cursor changes to a crosshair. Click the mouse button and drag out a rectangle defining the field location. The Field Properties dialog box appears asking for specifics about the text field we're creating.

Step 11: Field Properties Dialog-Appearance Tab

Enter "6E" as the field name and select Text as the field type. Leave the User Name field blank. It's only used to export a different field name with this field's value when the form is submitted.

Activate the Appearance tab. Here we're presented with options that affect the field's appearance. The design of our form draws the field as a graphic so we don't need to have a Border or Background Color. Select a color the text will display by clicking the Text Color chip. Select Helvetica as the Font and 12 as the Size.

Field Properties   [X]

Name: [6E]   Type: [Text   ▼]

User Name [|]

| Appearance | Options | Actions | Format | Validate | **Calculate** |

○ Value is n**o**t calculated.

● **V**alue is the [sum (+) ▼] of the following **f**ields:

[livewith, liveaway, otherdependents   ]   [Pick...]

○ **C**ustom calculation script

[   ]   [Edit...]

[OK   ]   [Cancel]

Step 11: Field Properties Dialog-Calculate Tab

Now activate the Calculate tab. Here we'll enter the value definition for the field. The "6E" field is the sum of the "livewith", "liveaway", and the "other dependents" fields, so click the second radio button and select sum from the list of predefined calculations. On the line below, enter all the fields we want included in this summary calculation, separated by commas.

Once you're happy with your choices click the OK button. The dialog closes, adding the field to the document.

Step 12

Add Eighteen Number Fields

Now we'll add eighteen number fields. The fields allow entry of different types of income needed to calculate a person's total income. The eighteen fields are located on the far right side of the Income section of the 1040 form. Once again we'll walk through the creation of the "7" field, which will guide you in repeating the process for fields "8A" through "22".

With Acrobat Exchange's form tool selected, drag out a rectangle defining the area where you want to display the "7" field information. The

Field Properties dialog box appears asking for specifics about the field we're creating.

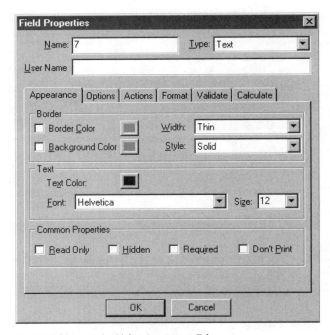

Step 12: Field Properties Dialog-Appearance Tab

The fields in this step are named for the corresponding line number located on the form. Enter "7" as the field name and select Text as the field type. We left the User Name field blank because we want the field name to be "7" when the form is submitted.

Activate the Appearance tab. Make sure the Border or Background Colors aren't selected. Select a color the text will display by clicking the Text Color chip. Select Helvetica as the Font and 12 as the Size.

Next activate the Options tab. Enter the default text to display in the field. Leave the limit on the number of characters and the password field unchecked for now.

Now activate the Format tab. The Format tab allows us to regulate the formatting of information entered into the field. Choose Number from the Category list and pick "0" for the number of decimal places and choose None for the Currency Symbol. This is a basic method of authentication that insures users only enter digits. We'll do a more detailed check on the server side of the transaction.

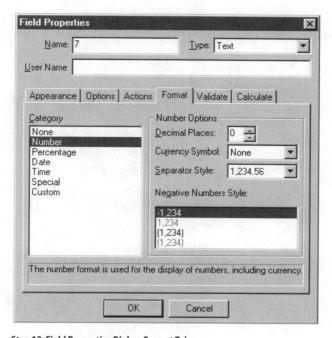

Step 12: Field Properties Dialog-Format Tab

Click the OK button. The dialog closes, adding the field to the document. You can stop here but to exactly duplicate the example, repeat this for "8A" through "22".

Step 13

"23" Field

Next we'll create the "23" field. The "23" field will hold the sum of fields "7", "8A", "9", "10", "11", "12", "13", "14", "15", "16B", "17B", "18", "19", "20", "21", and "22" fields of the form. To create the field, choose the forms tool button on the Acrobat Exchange toolbar. The cursor changes to a crosshair. Click the mouse button and drag out a rectangle defining where you want to display the field information. The Field Properties dialog box appears asking for specifics about the text field we're creating.

Step 13: Field Properties Dialog-Appearance Tab

Enter "23" as the field name and select Text as the field type. Leave the User Name field blank. It's only used to export a different field name with this field's value when the form is submitted.

Activate the Appearance tab. Here we're presented with options that affect the field's appearance. The design of our form draws the field as a graphic so we don't need to have a Border or Background Color. Select a color the text will display by clicking the Text Color chip. Select Helvetica as the Font and 12 as the Size.

Step 13: Field Properties Dialog-Calculate Tab

Now activate the Calculate tab. Here we'll enter the value definition for the field. The "23" field is the sum of the "7", "8A", "9", "10", "11", "12", "13", "14", "15", "16B", "17B", "18", "19", "20", "21", and "22" fields, so click the second radio button and select sum from the list of predefined calculations. On the line below, enter all the fields we want included in this summary calculation, separated by commas.

Once you're happy with your choices, click the OK button. The dialog closes, adding the field to the document.

Step 14

Income Adjustment Fields

Now we'll add seven more number fields. They allow entry of different types of income adjustments necessary to calculate a person's gross income. The seven fields are located on the middle of the Adjustments to Income section of the 1040 form. Once again we'll walk through the creation of one, the "24A" field, which will guide you in repeating the process for fields "24B" through "29".

With Acrobat Exchange's form tool selected, drag out a rectangle defining the area where you want to display the field information. The Field Properties dialog box appears, asking for specifics about the field we're creating.

Step 14: Field Properties Dialog-Appearance Tab

The fields in this step are named for the corresponding line number on the form. Enter "24A" as the field name and select Text as the field type. We left the User Name field blank because we want the field name to be "24A" when the form is submitted.

Activate the Appearance tab. Make sure the Border or Background Colors aren't selected. Select a color the text will display by clicking the Text Color chip. Select Helvetica as the Font and 12 as the Size.

Next activate the Options tab. Enter the default text to display in the field. Leave the limit on the number of characters and the password field unchecked for now.

Now activate the Format tab. The Format tab allows us to regulate the formatting of information entered into the field. Choose Number from the Category list and pick "0" for the number of decimal places and choose None for the Currency Symbol. This is a basic method of authentication that insures users only enter digits. We'll do a more detailed check on the server side of the transaction.

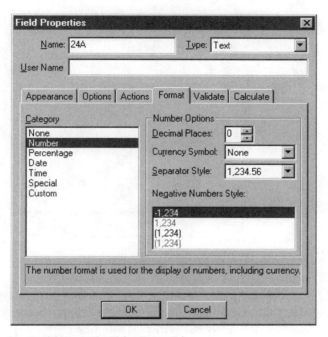

Step 14: Field Properties Dialog-Format Tab

Click the OK button. The dialog closes, adding the field to the document. You can stop here, but to exactly duplicate the example, repeat this for "24B" through "29".

Step 15

"30" field

Next we'll create the "30" field. The "30" field will hold the sum of fields "24A", "24B", "25", "26", "27", "28", and "29" of the form. To create the field, choose the forms tool button on the Acrobat Exchange toolbar. The cursor changes to a crosshair. Click the mouse button and drag out a rectangle defining the area where you want to display the field information. The Field Properties dialog box appears asking for specifics about the text field we're creating.

Step 15: Field Properties Dialog-Appearance Tab

Enter "30" as the field name and select Text as the field type. Leave the User Name field blank. It's only used to export a different field name with this field's value when the form is submitted.

Activate the Appearance tab. Here we're presented with options that affect the field's appearance. Since the field is drawn as a graphic, we don't need to have a Border or Background Color. Select a color the text will display by clicking the Text Color chip. Select Helvetica as the Font and 12 as the Size.

Field Properties   ☒

Name: [30]   Type: [Text   ▼]

User Name [   ]

Appearance | Options | Actions | Format | Validate | Calculate |

○ Value is not calculated.

◉ Value is the [sum (+) ▼] of the following fields:

[24A, 24B, 25, 26, 27, 28, 29   ]   [Pick...]

○ Custom calculation script

[   ]   [Edit...]

[OK   ]   [Cancel   ]

Step 15: Field Properties Dialog-Calculate Tab

Now activate the Calculate tab. Here we'll enter the value definition for the field. The "30" field is the sum of the "24A", "24B", "25", "26", "27", "28", and "29" fields, so click the second radio button and select sum from the list of predefined calculations. On the line below, enter all the fields we want included in this summary calculation.

Once you're happy with your choices, click the OK button. The dialog closes, adding the field to the document.

Step 16

"31" field

Next we'll create the "31" field. The "31" field will calculate the value of field "23" less the value of field "30". To create the field, choose the forms tool button on the Acrobat Exchange toolbar. The cursor changes to a crosshair. Click the mouse button and drag out a rectangle defining the area where you want to display the field information. The Field Properties dialog box appears asking for specifics about the text field we're creating.

Step 16: Field Properties Dialog-Appearance Tab

Enter "31" as the field name and select Text as the field type. Leave the User Name field blank. It's only used to export a different field name with this field's value when the form is submitted.

Activate the Appearance tab. Here we're presented with options that affect the field's appearance. Since the field is drawn as a graphic, we don't need to have a Border or Background Color. Select a color the text will display by clicking the Text Color chip. Select Helvetica as the Font and 12 as the Size.

Step 16: Field Properties Dialog-Calculate Tab

Next activate the Calculate tab. The Calculate tab lets us set up a field to calculate the value of this field. Choose the Custom calculation script radio button and then click the Edit button. The Acrobat JavaScript editing window appears. Type in the following code:

```
1.   var f = this.getField("23");
2.   var g = this.getField("30");
3.   var income = f.value;
4.   var adjust = g.value;
5.   event.value = income - adjust;
```

This simple script calculates the user's total gross income. This value is calculated by subtracting the value of the total adjustment field from the value of the total income field. The first line gets a reference to the "23" field and stores it in the variable "f". The second line gets a reference to the "30" field and stores it in the variable "g". The third line stores the value of the "f" field to the income variable. The fourth line stores the value of the "g" field to the adjust variable. The fifth line subtracts the value of the adjust from income variable, and stores the result in the "event.value" field of the current event. The current event is the "31" field being asked to calculate its value. All fields on a page receive a request to calculate their value when any field on the same page commits to a new value.

Once the script is entered, close the JavaScript window by clicking the OK button. You will be able to see the script in the Calculate tab. If you can't see the script, go back and enter the script again.

Now click the Field Properties dialog's OK button. The dialog closes, adding the field to the document.

Run the Example

To run the example, place the "1040_form.pdf" on your server in a directory that you can access through your browser. Enter the URL to access the PDF form. When the document appears in your browser window, enter your information to insure your form is functioning properly.

Take the time to print the form, verifying the information prints as you've entered it. A feature of PDF is that from the file menu, you can export the form information, or the form and the information. If you save just the form data, a file is placed at the location you indicate that contains only your entered data. The file also contains a reference to where the original form is located. When you open the form data file, Acrobat attempts to locate the form and fill in the field information.

Another option is to save the entire form to disk with your information intact, providing later reference to forms you've already filled out.

Saving only the field information in FDF format is a compact solution, but be careful to guarantee access to the original form. The FDF field data is of little use without it.

Driver License Order

Overview

This example demonstrates how to construct a form that writes information to a file on the server machine upon submission. The example allows the user to enter their information into a PDF document that resembles their actual driver license. The user can submit a custom photo of themselves and a graphic representation of their signature.

Physical Requirements

The following list is a description of the setup used to create this example. The actual components are:

Sun Solaris Server
Netscape Enterprise Server 3.0
Perl 5.0 for Unix
Adobe Acrobat Reader or Exchange 3.1 or newer
Netscape Navigator 3.x or Netscape Communicator 4.04 or newer with Acrobat
Plug-in or Microsoft Internet Explorer 4.0 or newer with Acrobat Plug-in 3.5
Adobe Acrobat Reader or Exchange 3.1 or newer
Adobe Acrobat Exchange 3.1 or newer with Adobe Forms Plug-in 3.5

Physical set-up the example uses

The example is served on a Netscape Enterprise Server 3.0 running on a Sun Solaris server. Perl 5.0 is installed on the server.

The Netscape server is set to execute CGI scripts from the cgi-bin directory. This requires that the "d_license.pl" script we use to process the form's submission reside in the "cgi-bin" directory in the root folder for our Web server.

Netscape Communicator 4.04 and Acrobat Reader 3.01 are installed on our client machine. Additionally, Netscape Communicator has the Acrobat plug-in located in its plug_in directory. This allows PDF files to be viewed directly in the Navigator window.

Creating the Necessary Files
To get this example to work, we need to put two files on the server. The first is a PDF file that is the form the client interacts with, and the second is the Perl script we'll use to process the form submission.

Creating the PDF File

This example uses a PDF file as its client side form interface. This form allows users to enter information relevant to submitting their driver license information. The form takes a first name, last name, middle initial, street address, city, state, ZIP code, sex, hair color, eye color, height in feet and inches, weight, date of birth, restriction, donor status, photograph and signature, and writes the information to a file on the server. The designer constructed the form file in Adobe Illustrator and then distilled it into PDF format. The next steps discuss creating the client-side form of this transaction.

Step 1

The Form Field Names
On the final PDF document created by our designer, we need to add the following form fields using Acrobat Exchange's form creation tool:

fname	weight
lname	dob
mname	restriction
address	donor
city	photograph
state	signature
zip	number
sex	class
hair	expiration
eye	reset
hfeet	submit
hinches	

Step 2

"fname" Field

First we'll create the "fname"field. To create the field, choose the forms tool button on the Acrobat Exchange toolbar. The cursor changes to a crosshair. Click the mouse button and drag out a rectangle defining the area where you want the user to enter their first name. The Field Properties dialog box appears asking for specifics about the text field we're creating.

Step 2: Field Properties Dialog-Appearance Tab

Enter "fname" as the field name and select Text as the field type. Leave the User Name field blank. It's only used to export a different field name with this field's value when the form is submitted.

Activate the Appearance tab. Here we're presented with options that affect the field's appearance. Our designer decided to create the fields as a graphic so we don't have a Border or Background Color selected. If the designer didn't add a field graphic, Acrobat forms provides options to create a field with an outline or a background color. Select a color the text will display by clicking the Text Color chip. Select Helvetica as the Font and 12 as the Size. Finally check the Required checkbox. The user will be warned if they don't fill out this field before submitting the form to the server.

Step 2: Field Properties Dialog-Options Tab

Now activate the Options tab, where we'll enter the default text displayed in the field. Here we've entered "First Name". This gives the user a little hint to guide them in their entry. We could also limit the number of characters or change this to a password field if we desired. Let's leave them blank for now.

Once you're happy with your choices click the OK button. The dialog closes, adding the field to the document.

Step 3

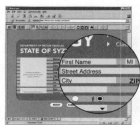

"lname," "mname," Address, and City Fields

Now we'll create the "lname", "mname", address, and city fields. To create these fields, we'll repeat step two for each field. The Field Properties dialog box appears each time we create a field asking for specifics about the text field we're creating.

As you create each field, activate the Appearance tab, enter the field's name, and be sure to select Text as the field type. Select Helvetica as the Font and 12 as the Size. Finally check the Required checkbox. The user will be warned if they don't fill out this field before submitting the form to the server.

For each field we add, activate the Options tab. Here we'll enter the default text displayed in the field. Enter some unique identifier, giving the user a hint about what to enter. Leave the limit on the number of characters and the password field unchecked for now.

For each field, click the OK button, closing the dialog and adding the field to the document.

Step 4

ZIP Code Field

Now we'll add a ZIP code field. With Acrobat Exchange's forms tool selected, drag out a rectangle defining the area where you want to display the ZIP code. The Field Properties dialog box appears asking for specifics about the field we're creating.

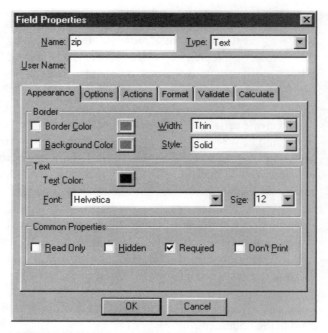

Step 4: Field Properties Dialog-Appearance Tab

Enter "zip" as the field name and select Text as the field type. We left the User Name field blank because we want the field name to be "zip" when the form is submitted.

Activate the Appearance tab. Make sure the Border or Background Colors aren't selected. Select a color the text will display by clicking the Text Color chip. Select Helvetica as the Font and 12 as the Size.

Next activate the Options tab. Enter the default text to display in the field. Leave the limit on the number of characters and the password field unchecked for now.

Now activate the Format tab. The Format tab allows us to regulate the formatting of information entered into the field. Choose Special from the Category list and pick ZIP Code from the Special Options list. This insures users only enter five digits. If they try to enter letters, the system beeps and doesn't enter the character in the field.

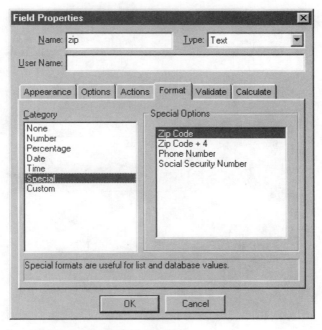

Step 4: Field Properties Dialog-Format Tab

Click the OK button. The dialog closes, adding the field to the document.

Step 5

Gender Radio Buttons

In this step we'll add Male and Female radio buttons to our document. These radio buttons are in a group, meaning only one of them can be selected at a time. This is accomplished in HTML by naming the buttons the same. But the value they export when selected is different. The same is true for PDF radio buttons. In this step we'll add one of two radio buttons that allow the user to indicate their gender.

With the Acrobat Exchange forms tool selected, drag out a rectangle defining the area where you want the radio button to appear. The Field Properties dialog box appears asking for specifics about the field we're creating.

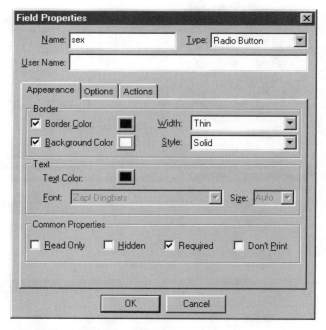

Step 5: Field Properties Dialog-Appearance Tab

Enter "sex" as the field name and select Radio Button as the field type.
Again leave the User Name field blank. We want this field's name to be
exported as "sex" when the form is submitted.

Activate the Appearance tab. Make sure to select the Border checkbox. In
addition, choose a color for the outline of the radio button by clicking
the color chip next to the Border Color checkbox. Select black or any
dark color so we'll be able to see it. Now select the background checkbox
and choose a background color for the radio button by clicking the color
chip next to it. Select white or any light color so we'll be able to see when
the radio button is chosen. You can play with combinations of the Width
and Style options to produce radio buttons with different looks. Our example uses the Thin Width and Solid Style options. Font selection is disabled for radio buttons but you might see Zapf Dingbats as the disabled
selection. Finally check the Required checkbox.

Now activate the Options tab. Here we choose the look of the radio button we'll create, identify the value to export if this radio button is selected,
and indicate if this button is selected as the default.

The Radio Style option presents us with half a dozen different options for radio button styles. Let's stick to the basics for now and select "Circle". Enter "male" as the Export Value and select the Default is Checked checkbox. When the form is initially opened, the "male" radio button will now be selected.

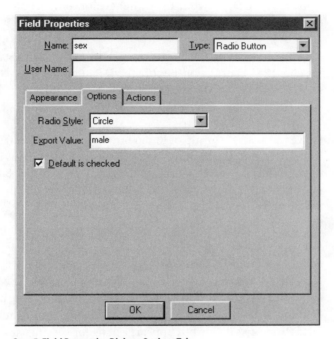

Step 5: Field Properties Dialog–Options Tab

We've finished the first of our two radio buttons, so click the OK button, closing the dialog and adding our work to the document.

Now we need to add another gender radio button to our document. With the Acrobat Exchange forms tool selected, drag out a rectangle defining the area where you want the female radio button to appear. The Field Properties dialog box appears.

Enter "sex" as the field name and select Radio Button as the field type. Again leave the User Name field blank. We want this field's name to be exported as "sex" when the form is submitted.

Activate the Appearance tab. Make sure to select the Border checkbox. In addition, choose a color for the outline of the radio button by clicking the color chip next to the Border Color checkbox. Select black or any dark color so we'll be able to see it. Now select the background checkbox and choose a background color for the radio button by clicking the color chip next to it. Select white or any light color so we'll be able to see when the radio button is chosen.

Activate the Options tab and select "Circle" as the Radio Style. Enter "female" as the Export Value. Be sure the Default is Checked checkbox is not selected. If this radio button is selected when the form is submitted, the "sex" field will contain the value "female".

We've finished this group of Radio buttons, so click the OK button, closing the dialog and adding our work to the document. This is a good time to test if the buttons are working. To do this, choose the Hand tool on the Acrobat toolbar and click on the radio buttons. Initially the "male" button should be selected and when you click on the "female" radio button, the "male" button should deselect.

Step 6

Hair Color Field—Combo Box

Now we'll add a combo box to allow the user to select the color of their hair. With the Acrobat Exchange forms tool selected, drag out a rectangle defining the area where you want the hair combo box to appear. The Field Properties dialog box appears asking for specifics about the field we're creating.

Step 6: Field Properties Dialog-Appearance Tab

Enter "hair" as the field name and select Combo Box as the field type.
Leave the User Name field blank. We want this field's name to be exported as "hair" when the form is submitted.

Activate the Appearance tab. We don't have a Border but select
Background Color and choose white as its color. Select black as the text
color by clicking the Text Color chip if it isn't already black. Select
Helvetica as the Font and 12 as the Size. Finally check the Required
checkbox.

Now activate the Options tab. Here we'll enter the items to display in our
combo box. We want the drop down list to contain five items. Enter each
item and its corresponding export value that the form will send to the
server, and click the Add button. If you enter the items out of order, you
can move them around in the list by selecting them and clicking the up
or down button. If you need to change an item or its value, select it in the
list. Its associated value and item appear in the entry fields above it.
Choose the "hair" combo box default value by selecting it and closing the

dialog. When the five values are entered, select Brown as the default we want and click the OK button to save the field to the document.

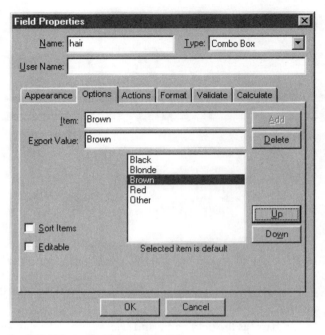

Step 6: Field Properties Dialog-Options Tab

Step 7

Eye Color Field—Combo Box

Now we'll add a combo box to allow the user to select the color of their eyes. The process is the same as the combo we created for hair choice. With the Acrobat Exchange forms tool selected, drag out a rectangle defining the area where you want the hair combo box to appear. The Field Properties dialog box appears asking for specifics about the field we're creating.

Step 7: Field Properties Dialog-Appearance Tab

Enter "eyes" as the field name and select Combo Box as the field type. Again leave the User Name field blank. We want this field's name to be exported as "eyes" when the form is submitted.

Activate the Appearance tab. We don't have a Border but select Background Color and choose white as its color. Select black as the text color by clicking the Text Color chip if it isn't already black. Select Helvetica as the Font and 12 as the Size. Finally check the Required checkbox.

Now activate the Options tab. Here we'll enter the items to display in our combo box. We want the drop-down list to contain four items. Enter each item and its corresponding export value that the form will send to the server, and click the Add button. If you enter the items out of order, you can move them around in the list by selecting them and clicking the up or down button. Choose the combo box's default value by selecting it and closing the dialog. When the four values are entered, select Green as the default, and click the OK button to save the field to the document.

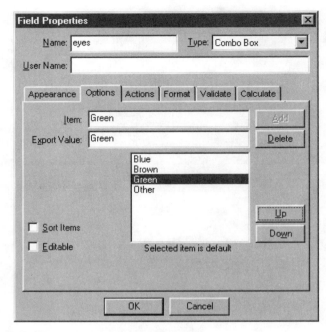

Step 7: Field Properties Dialog-Options Tab

Step 8

"hfeet", "hinches" and Weight Fields

Now we'll create the "hfeet", "hinches" and weight fields. To create these three fields, we'll repeat the following procedure for each field. With the Acrobat Exchange Forms tool, define a rectangle where you want the field to appear. The Field Properties dialog box appears each time we create a field, asking for specifics about the field we're creating.

Step 8: Field Properties Dialog-Appearance Tab

As you create each field, activate the Appearance tab. Enter its name and be sure to select Text as the field type. Select Helvetica as the Font and 12 as the Size. Finally check the Required checkbox. The user will be warned if they don't fill out this field before submitting the form to the server.

Now Activate the Format tab. The Format tab allows us to regulate the formatting of information entered into the field. Choose Number from the Category list and set Decimal places to "0" from the Number Options list.

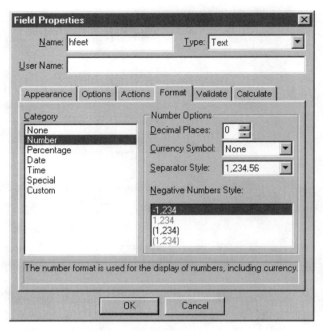

Step 8: Field Properties Dialog-Format Tab

For each field, click the OK button, closing the dialog and adding the field to the document.

Step 9

Date of Birth Field

Now we'll add a date of birth field. This field allows a user to enter their date of birth, and then formats it. Error checking is performed and the user is warned if they try to enter information that can't be converted into a date. With Acrobat Exchange's forms tool, define the area where the user will enter their birthdate. The Field Properties dialog box appears asking for specifics about the field we're creating.

Field Properties   ☒

Name: dob   Type: Text   ▼

User Name:

| Appearance | Options | Actions | Format | Validate | Calculate |

Border
☐ Border Color ▨   Width: Thin   ▼
☐ Background Color ▨   Style: Solid   ▼

Text
Text Color: ■
Font: Helvetica   ▼   Size: Auto ▼

Common Properties
☐ Read Only   ☐ Hidden   ☑ Required   ☐ Don't Print

OK   Cancel

Step 9: Field Properties Dialog-Appearance Tab

Enter "dob" as the field name and select Text as the field type. Leave the User Name field blank.

Activate the Appearance tab. We don't need a Border or Background Color. Select a color the text will display by clicking the Text Color chip. Select Helvetica as the Font and Auto as the Size. Be sure to check the Required checkbox.

Now activate the Format tab. The Format tab allows us to regulate the formatting of information entered into the field. Choose Date from the Category list and pick a date format from the Date Options list.

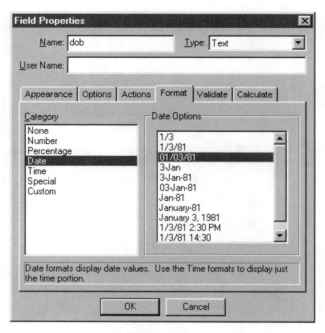

Step 9: Field Properties Dialog-Format Tab

Click the OK button. The dialog closes, adding the field to the document.

Step 10

Restriction Field—Combo Box

Next we'll add a combo box to allow the user to select a restriction placed on their driving. With the Acrobat Exchange forms tool, create a rectangle where you want the restriction combo box to appear. The Field Properties dialog box appears asking for specifics about the field we're creating.

Step 10: Field Properties Dialog-Appearance Tab

Enter "restriction" as the field name and select Combo Box as the field type. Again leave the User Name field blank. We want this field's name to be exported as "restriction" and not anything else when the form is submitted.

Activate the Appearance tab. We don't have a Border but select Background Color and choose white as its color. Select black as the text color by clicking the Text Color chip if it isn't already black. Select Helvetica as the Font and 12 as the Size. Finally check the Required checkbox.

Now activate the Options tab. Here we'll enter the items to display in our combo box. We want the drop-down list to contain four items. Enter each item and its corresponding export value that the form will send to the server and click the Add button. If you enter the items out of order, you can move them around in the list by selecting them and clicking the up or down button. Choose the combo box's default value by selecting it. When the four values are entered, select "None-No Way" as the default we want and click the OK button to save the field to the document.

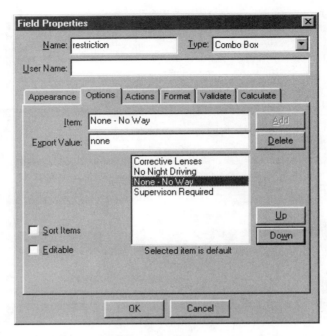

Step 10: Field Properties Dialog-Options Tab

Step 11

Donor Field—Checkbox

Let's create a checkbox to track the user's donor status. To create the field, use the form tool to draw a rectangle defining the area where the check box is located. The Field Properties dialog box appears.

Field Properties   ⊠

Name: donor   Type: Check Box   ▼

User Name:

| Appearance | Options | Actions |

Border
☑ Border Color   ■   Width: Thin   ▼
☑ Background Color ☐   Style: Solid   ▼

Text
Text Color: ■
Font: Zapf Dingbats   ▼   Size: Auto ▼

Common Properties
☐ Read Only   ☐ Hidden   ☑ Required   ☐ Don't Print

OK   Cancel

Step 11: Field Properties Dialog-Appearance Tab

Enter "donor" as the field name and select Check Box as the field type.

Activate the Appearance tab. Make sure to select the Border checkbox. In addition, choose a color for the outline of the Check Box by clicking the color chip next to the Border Color checkbox. Select black or any dark color so we'll be able to see it. Now select the Background color checkbox and choose a background color by clicking the color chip next to it. Select white or any light color so we'll be able to see when the Check Box is chosen. You can play with combinations of the Width and Style options to produce Check Boxes with different looks. Our example uses the Thin Width and Solid Style options. Font selection is also disabled for Check Boxes but you might see Zapf Dingbats as the disabled selection. Finally check the Required checkbox.

Step 11: Field Properties Dialog-Options Tab

Now activate the Options tab. Here choose the look of the Check Box. Identify the value to export by entering it into the proper text field. Make sure to indicate this button is not selected as the default

The Check Box option presents us with half a dozen different options for Check Box styles. Let's make this Check Box look like a radio button. Select "Circle" and enter "On" as the export value.

When the proper settings are in place, click the OK button. The dialog closes, adding the field to the document.

Step 12

Button Fields—Images

The next two fields are both buttons. The first button allows a user to click it and select a PDF file to insert in the photo field. The second allows a user to click the signature field and insert a PDF file containing the user's signature. We'll walk through the process with the photo field, which will guide you in repeating the process for the signature field.

To start, select the Acrobat Exchange forms tool and define a rectangle where the photo button is located. The Field Properties dialog box appears asking for specifics about the field.

Step 12: Field Properties Dialog-Appearance Tab

Activate the Appearance tab. We don't need to select a Border or Background Color due to our form's design. The button's text color isn't important because we aren't displaying the button's title. We aren't going to require the photo for a submission, so make sure Required isn't checked.

Step 12: Field Properties Dialog-Options Tab

The Options tab allows you to select how the button appears when it's clicked and the general layout of the button. Is this instance we set the Highlight option to Invert. Here we want the button to Invert when the user clicks the photo and then lets the mouse button up. The Layout option is set to Icon only. When Icon Only is chosen, the Advanced Layout button activates.

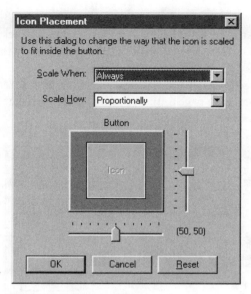

Step 12: Advanced Layout Dialog

The Advanced Layout dialog lets us scale an image we'll import into this button. Scaling can be done if the image is larger or smaller than the button's size. Scaling can also be set to be proportional or it can vary horizontally and vertically. Here we choose to Always scale an image to fit the button, and to scale it Proportionally.

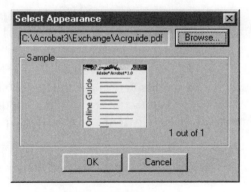

Step 12: Select Appearance Dialog

After determining the scaling options, we need to select the button's icon. We do this back in the Field Properties dialog. Click the Select Icon button and you're asked to choose a PDF file to browse through. Here we've selected the Acrguide.pdf file that ships with Acrobat. If the selected PDF contains multiple pages, a scroll bar appears, allowing you to scroll through each page until you find the one you want. Click the OK button to confirm the selection.

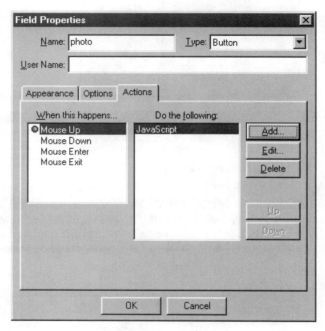

Step 12: Field Properties Dialog-Actions Tab

Since our buttons load another PDF image and this isn't normal button behavior, we need to add a JavaScript action to prevent this. From the Actions Tab we select Mouse Up from the When this happens list.

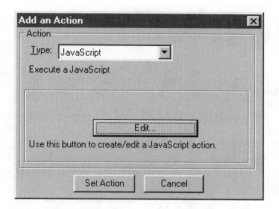

Step 12: Add an Action Dialog

In the Add an Action dialog, choose the JavaScript action type and click the Edit button. Enter the following lines of JavaScript code and close the window.

```
1.   var f = this.getField("photo");
2.   f.bgColor = color.white;
3.   f.buttonImportIcon();
```

This simple script instructs Acrobat to reset the value of the button's icon. The first line of this script gets a reference to the photo field and stores it in the variable "f". The second line sets the background color of the field to white. The third line calls the field's buttonImportIcon() routine, which asks the user to locate a single page of a PDF file to insert as the field's appearance.

Once the script is entered, close the JavaScript window by clicking the OK button. Now click the Set Action button in the Add an Action dialog. If you are pleased with your selections, click the Field Properties dialog's OK button. The dialog closes, adding the field to the document. Don't forget to repeat the process for the signature field.

Step 13

Driver License Number Field—Read Only

Now we'll add a driver license number field. This is a read-only field where we calculate a driver license number. For this example we a create pseudo random number. With the Acrobat Exchange forms tool, create

the field where the License Number will be placed. The Field Properties dialog box appears asking for specifics about the new Driver License number field.

Step 13: Field Properties Dialog-Appearance Tab

Enter "number" as the field name and select Text as the field type. We leave the User Name field blank.

Activate the Appearance tab. We don't need to select a Border or Background Color due to our form's design. Make sure the text color is black. If it isn't, change it to black by clicking the Text Color chip. Select Courier Bold as the Font and 12 as the Size. Finally select the Read Only checkbox. This text box will hold and display text, but it won't allow a user to enter any information.

Next activate the Calculate tab. The Calculate tab lets us set up a field to calculate the value of this field. Choose the custom calculation script radio button and then click the Edit button. The Acrobat JavaScript editing window appears. Type in the following code.

```
1.    var f = this.getField("number");
2.    f.value = "A" + Math.round(Math.random() *
              10000000);
3.    event.value = f.value;
```

This simple script calculates the driver license number based on a random number. The first line of this script gets a reference to the number field and stores it in the variable "f". The second line calculates a random number. The global JavaScript Math object has several methods we use to calculate this number. Inside our parentheses we first call the Math.random() method to return a random number between zero and one. We then multiply this value by 10,000,000 to produce a seven digit whole number. Next, we round our number, eliminating its fractional part. This numeric value is then added to the string "A" to produce our license number. This string value is placed in the field's value member. The result is stored in the "event.value" field of the occurring event. The current event is the number field being asked to calculate its value. All fields on a page receive a request to calculate their value when any field on the same page commits to a new value.

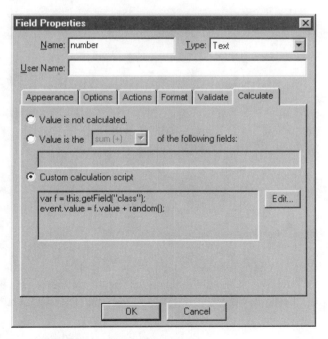

Step 13: Field Properties Dialog-Calculate Tab

Once the script is entered, close the JavaScript window by clicking the OK button. You will be able to see the script in the Calculate tab. If you can't see the script, go back and enter the script again.

Now click the Field Properties dialog's OK button. The dialog closes, adding the field to the document.

Step 14

Expiration Date Field—Read Only

Now we'll add an expiration date field. This is a read-only field where we insert the expiration of the license. With Acrobat Exchange's Forms tool, create a rectangle defining the area where you want to display the date. The Field Properties dialog box appears.

Step 14: Field Properties Dialog-Appearance Tab

Enter "expiration" as the field name and select Text as the field type. We left the User Name field blank. It's used if we want to have a different field name exported with this field's value when the form is submitted.

Activate the Appearance tab. We don't want a Border or Background Color so make sure they're not selected. Select a color the text will display by clicking the Text Color chip. Select Courier Bold as the Font and 12 as the Size. Finally select the Read Only checkbox. This text box will hold and display text but it won't allow a user to enter any information.

Now activate the Format tab. The Format tab allows us to regulate the formatting of information entered into the field. Choose Date from the Category list and pick a date format from the Date Options list.

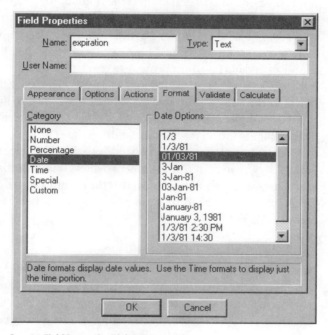

Step 14: Field Properties Dialog-Format Tab

Click the OK button. The dialog closes, adding the field to the document.

Right now we have a date field, but to make it useful we'll need to attach a bit of JavaScript. To do this, select the custom category and click the Edit button. The Acrobat JavaScript editing window appears. Type in the following code.

```
1.   var d = new Date();
2.   d.setDate(d.getDate());
3.   var yr = d.getYear() + 4;
4.   if(yr >= 100) yr = yr - 100;
```

```
5.   d.setYear(yr);
6.   event.value = util.printd("mm/dd/yy", d);
```

The first line of this script creates a new date value. A reference to this date is stored in the variable "d". The second line of this script uses two member functions of the date object. The second line calls the setDate() member function to actually set the numeric value of the date. The parameter passed into the function is the result of the getDate() member function. In short, we're setting the date to the value returned by getDate(). This value is today's date. Line three of the script gets the year from our date and adds four. Our new license will expire four years from the renewal date. Line four provides a check to see if the year has gone over 100. We're only interested in the last two digits, so if the "yr" variable is greater than 100 we subtract 100 to reduce our year to an acceptable number of digits. Finally, on line five, the new year value is placed in our date by calling the setYear() member function. The last line of this script formats and prints the value in our "d" variable. We've formatted it as "mm/dd/yy", two digits for month, two digits for day, and two digits for year. This formatted string is stored in the event.value field of the current event. In this case, the script is called whenever the field is asked to format its contents.

Step 15

License Class Field—Combo Box
Next we'll add another combo box to allow the user to select the class of license. Select the Acrobat Exchange forms tool, and create a rectangle where you want the class combo box to appear. The Field Properties dialog box appears asking for specifics about the field we're creating.

Field Properties   [×]

Name: class   Type: Combo Box ▼

User Name:

Appearance | Options | Actions | Format | Validate | Calculate |

Border
☑ Border Color   [■]   Width: Thin ▼
☑ Background Color [ ]   Style: Solid ▼

Text
Text Color: [■]
Font: Helvetica ▼   Size: 12 ▼

Common Properties
☐ Read Only   ☐ Hidden   ☑ Required   ☐ Don't Print

OK   Cancel

Step 15: Field Properties Dialog-Appearance Tab

Enter "class" as the field name and select Combo Box as the field type. Leave the User Name field blank. We want this field's name to be exported as "class" and not anything else when the form is submitted.

Activate the Appearance tab. Select a Border and a Background Color. Try black as the border and white as the background color. Select black as the text color by clicking the Text Color chip. Select Helvetica as the Font and 12 as the Size. Finally check the Required checkbox.

Now activate the Options tab. Here we'll enter the items to display in our combo box. We want the drop-down list to contain four items. Enter each item and the corresponding export value that the form will send to the server, and click the Add button. If you enter the items out of order, you can move them around in the list by selecting them and clicking the up or down button. Choose the combo box's default value by selecting it. When the four values are entered, select "C" as the default and click the OK button to save the field to the document.

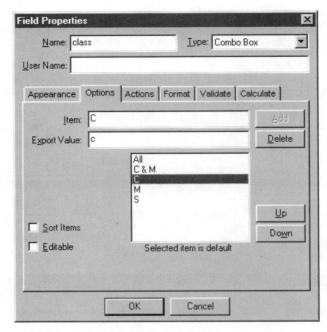

Step 15: Field Properties Dialog-Options Tab

Step 16

Submit Button

Our two remaining fields correspond to the Submit and Reset buttons. First we'll create the Submit button. With Acrobat Exchange's forms tool selected, drag out a rectangle defining the area where the Submit button is located. The Field Properties dialog box appears asking for specifics about the field we're creating.

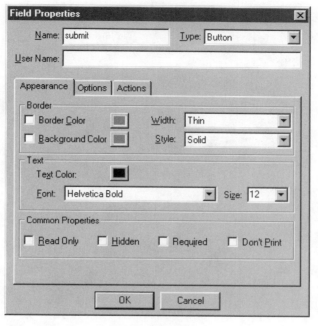

Step 16: Field Properties Dialog-Appearance Tab

Activate the Appearance tab. We don't need to select a Border or Background Color due to our form's design. The button's text color isn't important because we aren't displaying the button's title.

Step 16: Field Properties Dialog-Options Tab

The Options tab is where you select any special appearance options for the button. Is this instance we set the Highlight option to Invert. The Layout option is set to Text only. Because we don't want any text to show over our buttons, the Text entry for the Button Face Attributes is left blank. The Button Face When option determines when the appearance we set up is invoked. Here we want it to Invert on a mouse up event.

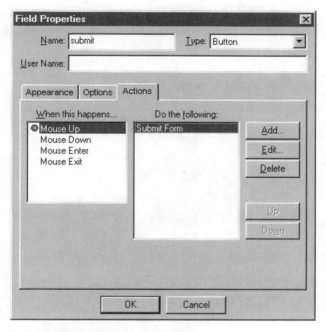

Step 16: Field Properties Dialog-Actions Tab

The Actions tab is where you select any action this field will invoke. Here we choose the Mouse up event. Click the Add button and choose Submit Form from the list of available action types.

Step 16: Edit an Action Dialog

Now we need to identify the URL that will process the form submission. Click the Select URL button and enter the URL we'll use to process this form.

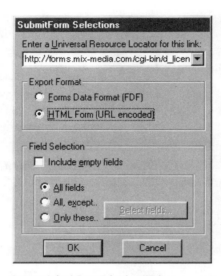

Step 16: SubmitForm Selections Dialog

Here we also choose to submit the data to the server in HTML format. We could submit in the FDF format, but the Perl script we'll use to process the submission is set up to receive the data in HTML format. We also want to send all fields even though we have the option to just send a subset of the fields from the form. Once the proper selections are made, click the OK buttons in the SubmitForm Selections, Edit an Action, and Field Properties dialogs.

Step 17

Reset Button

Our final field is the reset button. With Acrobat Exchange's form tool selected, drag out a rectangle defining the area where the reset button is located. The Field Properties dialog box appears asking for specifics about the field we're creating.

Step 17: Field Properties Dialog-Appearance Tab

Activate the Appearance tab. We don't need to select a Border or Background Color due to our form's design. The button's text color isn't important because we aren't displaying the button's title.

Step 17: Field Properties Dialog-Options Tab

The Options tab is where you select any special appearance options for the button. In this instance we set the Highlight option to Invert. The Layout option is set to Text only. Because we don't want any text to show over our buttons, the Text entry for the Button Face Attributes is left blank. The Button Face When option determines when the appearance we set up is invoked. Here we want it to Invert on a Mouse Up event.

Step 17: Field Properties Dialog-Actions Tab

The Actions tab is where you select any action this field will invoke. Here we choose the Mouse up event. Click the Add button and choose Reset Form from the list of available action types.

Step 17: Edit an Action Dialog

Here we can choose the fields we want to reset. All fields is the default. Once the proper selections are made, click the OK buttons in the Edit an Action and Field Properties dialogs.

We're ready to discuss setting up the back end of the process to receive information from this form.

Creating the Perl Script

This example uses a PDF file as its interface to the user. The form gathers fname, lname, mname, address, city, zip, sex, hair, eye, hfeet, hinches, weight, dob, restriction, donor, photograph, signature, number, class, and expiration and sends it to the server for processing by a CGI script. This example uses a Perl script to process the submitted information. The Perl script decodes the submission, formats the information, and writes it to a file on the server.

The following pages discuss creating the Perl script used for processing the form's submission on the server side of this transaction. The complete script is shown below. For this example to work, the script must exist as a file named "d_license.pl". This file is placed in the "cgi-bin" directory in the Netscape Enterprise Server's root directory. Of course the Netscape Server's root directory and cgi-bin directory were created automatically when we installed the Web server on our server machine.

Code Example: d_license.pl

```
1.    #!/usr/local/bin/perl
2.
3.    &parse_form_data(*FORM_DATA);
4.    &write_file();
5.    &send_thank_you();
6.    exit(0);
7.
8.    sub parse_form_data
9.    {
10.       local (*FORM_DATA) = @_;
11.
```

```
12.        local ( $request_method, $query_string,
           @key_value_pairs, $key_value, $key, $value);
13.
14.        $request_method = $ENV{'REQUEST_METHOD'};
15.
16.        if($request_method eq "GET")
17.        {
18.            $query_string = $ENV{'QUERY_STRING'};
19.        }
20.        elsif($request_method eq "POST")
21.        {
22.            read(STDIN, $query_string,
                 $ENV{'CONTENT_LENGTH'});
23.        }
24.        else
25.        {
26.            &return_error (500, "Server Error",
                 "Server uses unsupported method");
27.        }
28.
29.        @key_value_pairs = split(/&/,
           $query_string);
30.
31.        foreach $key_value (@key_value_pairs)
32.        {
33.            ($key, $value) = split (/=/,
                $key_value);
34.            $value =~ tr/+/ /;
35.            $value =~ s/%([\dA-Fa-f][\dA-Fa-f])/pack
                ("C", hex ($1))/eg;
36.
37.            if (defined($FORM_DATA{$key}))
38.        {
39.                $FORM_DATA{$key} = join ("\0",
                   $FORM_DATA{$key}, $value);
40.            }
41.        else
42.        {
43.                $FORM_DATA{$key} = $value;
44.            }
```

```
45.        }
46.    }
47.
48.    sub write_file
49.    {
50.      local (*FORM_DATA) = a_;
51.
52.      $filepath = "C:\\license\\";
53.      $filepath .= $FORM_DATA{'number'};
54.      $filepath .= ".lic";
55.
56.      open(TMPFILE, ">" . $filepath) or die
             "Couldn't create file: $!";
57.      print TMPFILE "\n\n", "The following driver
             license update was received:", "  ";
58.      print TMPFILE "Date submitted:
             ",$FORM_DATA{'date'}, "\n";
59.      print TMPFILE "First Name:  ",
             $FORM_DATA{'fname'}, "\n";
60.      print TMPFILE "Middle Name:  ",
             $FORM_DATA{'mname'}, "\n";
61.      print TMPFILE "Last Name:  ",
             $FORM_DATA{'lname'}, "\n";
62.      print TMPFILE "Address:  ",
             $FORM_DATA{'address'}, "\n";
63.      print TMPFILE "City:  ", $FORM_DATA{'city'},
             "\n";
64.      print TMPFILE "State:  ", $FORM_DATA{'state'},
             "\n";
65.      print TMPFILE "Zip Code:  ",
             $FORM_DATA{'zip'}, "\n";
66.      print TMPFILE "Gender:  ", $FORM_DATA{'sex'},
             "\n";
67.      print TMPFILE "Hair:  ", $FORM_DATA{'hair'},
             "\n";
68.      print TMPFILE "Eyes:  ", $FORM_DATA{'eye'},
             "\n";
69.      print TMPFILE "Height:  ",
             $FORM_DATA{'hfeet'}, "' ",
             $FORM_DATA{'hinches'}, "\"", "\n";
```

```
70.      print TMPFILE "Weight:   ",
         $FORM_DATA{'weight'}, "\n";
71.      print TMPFILE "DOB:  ", $FORM_DATA{'dob'},
         "\n";
72.      print TMPFILE "Number:      ",
         $FORM_DATA{'number'}, "\n";
73.      print TMPFILE "Class:        ",
         $FORM_DATA{'class'}, "\n";
74.      print TMPFILE "Expiration:     ",
         $FORM_DATA{'expiration'}, "\n";
75.      print TMPFILE "Photo:     ", "\r\n",
         $FORM_DATA{'phrase'}, "\r\n\r\n";
76.      print TMPFILE "Signature:   ", "\r\n",
         $FORM_DATA{'signature'}, "\r\n\r\n";
77.      print TMPFILE "\r\n\r\n";
78.      close(TMPFILE);
79.  }
80.
81.  sub send_thank_you
82.  {
83.      local (*FORM_DATA) = @_;
84.
85.      print "Content-type: text/html\n\n";
86.
87.      print "<HTML>\n";
88.      print "<HEAD>\n";
89.      print "<TITLE>CGI Driver License
         Update</TITLE>\n";
90.      print "</HEAD>\n";
91.      print "<BODY><BR>\n";
92.      print "<H1>Thanks for Your Driver License
         Update</H1>\n";
93.      print "<PRE>\n";
94.      print "The information received was:  ";
95.      print "Date submitted: ",$FORM_DATA{'date'},
         "\n";
96.      print "First Name: ", $FORM_DATA{'fname'},
         "\n";
97.      print "Middle Name:  ", $FORM_DATA{'mname'},
         "\n";
```

```
98.     print "First Name:   ", $FORM_DATA{'lname'},
        "\n";
99.     print "Address:  ", $FORM_DATA{'address'},
        "\n";
100.    print "City:  ", $FORM_DATA{'city'}, "\n";
101.    print "State:  ", $FORM_DATA{'state'}, "\n";
102.    print "Zip Code:  ", $FORM_DATA{'zip'}, "\n";
103.    print "Gender:  ", $FORM_DATA{'sex'}, "\n";
104.    print "Hair:  ", $FORM_DATA{'hair'}, "\n";
105.    print "Eyes:  ", $FORM_DATA{'eye'}, "\n";
106.    print "Height:  ", $FORM_DATA{'hfeet'}, "' ",
        $FORM_DATA{'hinches'}, "\"", "\n";
107.    print "Weight:  ", $FORM_DATA{'weight'}, "\n";
108.    print "DOB:  ", $FORM_DATA{'dob'}, "\n";
109.    print "Number:      ", $FORM_DATA{'number'},
        "\n";
110.    print "Class:        ", $FORM_DATA{'class'},
        "\n";
111.    print "Expiration:      ",
        $FORM_DATA{'expiration'}, "\n";
112.    print "Photo:      ", "\r\n",
        $FORM_DATA{'phrase'}, "\r\n\r\n";
113.    print "Signature:   ", "\r\n",
        $FORM_DATA{'signature'}, "\r\n\r\n";
114.    print "\r\n\r\n";
115.    print "</PRE>\n";
116.    print "<HR>\n";
117.    print "<BR>\n";
118.    print "</BODY></HTML>\n";
119. }
120.
121. sub return_error
122. {
123.    local ($status, $errtype, $message) = @_;
124.
125.    print "Content-type: text/html\n";
126.    print "Status: ", $status, " ", $errtype,
        "\n\n";
127.    print "<HTML>\n";
128.    print "<HEAD>\n";
```

```
129.    print "<TITLE>CGI Program Error</TITLE>\n";
130.    print "</HEAD>\n";
131.    print "<BODY><BR>\n";
132.    print "<H1>This CGI program encountered a ",
        $errtype, "</H1>\n";
133.    print $message;
134.    print "<HR>\n";
135.    print "<BR>\n";
136.    print "</BODY></HTML>\n";
137.    exit(1);
138. }
```

The Example Script

Let's take a detailed look at our example script. Line one of our script is used to declare the location of the Perl interpreter to use when running this script. In a UNIX environment, this line looks something like this: #!/usr/local/bin/perl. It's all dependent on where the system's Perl application is located

```
1.    #!/usr/local/bin/perl
2.
3.    &parse_form_data(*FORM_DATA);
4.    &write_file();
5.    &send_thank_you();
6.    exit(0);
```

Lines three to six are the core of our script. They are three sub routines and the exit() routine. The first, parse_form_data(), gathers and decodes the information sent to us by the client. The second routine is write_file(). This routine creates a file on our server and writes the driver license submission information to it. When this is completed, the sub routine send_thank_you() returns an HTML thank you page to the client that submitted the information. Finally, the Perl script exits, returning a result code of zero. This signals that everything went without a problem.

The parse_form_data() Sub Routine

Now let's take a detailed look at our parse_form_data() sub routine. Line nine of our script is used to declare the following instructions are part of our parse_form_data() sub routine. Every instruction between the open curly bracket on line nine and the close curly bracket on line 44 is included in this routine. On line ten we call the Perl local routine to create a reference to the argument passed to the routine. Perl passes arguments to its routines through the @_ associative array. If this is unfamiliar to you, we've simply created a reference to the submitted form data that this sub routine and the main routine can share. On line 12 we create some more local space to store information we'll copy out of the submission.

```
8.      sub parse_form_data
9.      {
10.         local (*FORM_DATA) = @_;
11.
12.         local ( $request_method, $query_string,
            @key_value_pairs, $key_value, $key, $value);
```

The two most popular methods for submitting information to an HTTP server are POST and GET. Information sent to a server via the GET method is stored in the QUERY_STRING environment variable. If it's sent via a POST to the server, the data is placed in the STDIN buffer and its length is placed in the CONTENT_LENGTH environment variable. This architecture requires that we check for the method of submission in order to locate the form data. On line 14 we determine just how the information was sent to this script by calling the $ENV{} function and passing 'REQUEST_METHOD' as the parameter. This returns the submission method and stores it in the $request_method local variable. On line 16 we compare what's stored in $request_method with the string "GET". If they're equal, we again call $ENV{} but this time with 'QUERY_STRING' as the parameter. This stores the submission information in the local variable $query_string.

```
14.         $request_method = $ENV{'REQUEST_METHOD'};
15.
16.         if($request_method eq "GET")
17.         {
18.             $query_string = $ENV{'QUERY_STRING'};
19.         }
```

If what's stored in $request_method isn't equal to "GET", on line 20 we check to see if it's equal to "POST". If it is, we need to read the form data from the standard input buffer. We do this by calling the read() command. However, the read command requires three parameters. First it needs to know from where it is to read the information. Second, it needs to know where to put the information it reads, and third, how much information it's supposed to read. Invoking the read() command and passing it STDIN (the standard input buffer) provides the instruction as to where we want it to read from, and $query_string as to where to store the information read, while calling $ENV{'CONTENT_LENGTH'} retrieves the length of the data that should be read.

```
20.      elsif($request_method eq "POST")
21.      {
22.          read(STDIN, $query_string,
             $ENV{'CONTENT_LENGTH'});
23.      }
```

In case the $request_method isn't either GET or POST, we provide a catch-all that calls our return_error sub routine. This returns an HTML page informing the user we didn't know what to do with their request. It then exits the script without processing the submission.

```
24.      else
25.      {
26.          &return_error (500, "Server Error",
             "Server uses unsupported method");
27.      }
```

After we receive the information and properly store it in the $query_string local variable, our next task is to format and decode it. We know the HTTP protocol requires the client to separate each key/value pair with the ampersand character. Using this information, we can use the Perl split() command to store each key/value pair in an array. Line 29 accomplishes this by splitting the query string at each ampersand and storing it in the key_value_pairs array.

```
29.      @key_value_pairs = split(/&/,
         $query_string);
```

Once we have the key/value information in an array, we need to break it into its field and value components. The HTTP protocol requires each field and its value be separated by the "=" character. As we loop through each entry, line 31 splits the field name and its value and stores the two in the $key and $value local variables. Line 34 uses the Perl translate command to replace any "+" characters with a space. This is necessary because the client has done the reverse and replaced any space with "+" characters before transmitting the data to the server. Line 35 is another type of translation. Here we use the substitute command to revert all characters that have been converted to their hexadecimal equivalent back to their original ASCII values. The substitute command contains a regular expression that looks for a "%" followed by two characters. These two characters are stored in a variable $1. The expression then is evaluated by the e option, converting the value stored in $1 into its ASCII equivalent. Finally the "g" option searches the initial string and replaces all occurrences on the hexadecimal value with its ASCII equivalent.

We finally have our data in a state that we're ready to store. Line 37 checks for an existing entry for this field. If there is already an entry, we call the join command to append this value to the existing values in our array on line 39. If the field doesn't yet exist we add it and its value to the $FORM_DATA associative array on line 43.

```
31.        foreach $key_value (@key_value_pairs)
32.        {
33.            ($key, $value) = split (/=/,
               $key_value);
34.            $value =~ tr/+/ /;
35.            $value =~ s/%([\dA-Fa-f][\dA-Fa-f])/pack
               ("C", hex ($1))/eg;
36.
37.            if (defined($FORM_DATA{$key}))
38.            {
39.                $FORM_DATA{$key} = join ("\0",
                   $FORM_DATA{$key}, $value);
40.            }
41.            else
42.            {
43.                $FORM_DATA{$key} = $value;
44.            }
45.        }
46.    }
```

The entire purpose of the parse_form_data() sub routine is to format and decode the form submission data. At this point that task is accomplished.

The write_file() Sub Routine

The purpose of the write_file() sub routine is to format the submission and write it to a file on the server machine.

```
48.   sub write_file
49.   {
50.      local (*FORM_DATA) = @_;
51.
52.      $filepath = "C:\\license\\";
53.      $filepath .= $FORM_DATA{'number'};
54.      $filepath .= ".lic";
```

On line 48 we open the routine. On line 50 we declare a local reference to data from the main routine.

On lines 52-54 we assemble the path we'll use to create the file we'll use to store our submission. The path here is to a license directory located on our "C:\" drive. Be sure to create this directory on your server machine before you run the example. If you don't, the server will return an error instead of a confirmation page. The path we construct places a file in the "C:\license" directory. We add the number field retrieved from the form submission as the file's name. For our needs, we concatenate the ".lic" suffix to the file.

```
56.      open(TMPFILE, ">" . $filepath) or die
         "Couldn't create file: $!";
```

On line 56 we open a file using the path we placed in the $filepath variable. If for some reason the file cannot be opened, the die option is invoked and the script terminates.

```
57.      print TMPFILE "\n\n", "The following driver
         license update was received:", "   ";
58.      print TMPFILE "Date submitted:
         ",$FORM_DATA{'date'}, "\n";
59.      print TMPFILE "First Name:   ",
```

```
           $FORM_DATA{'fname'}, "\n";
60.    print TMPFILE "Middle Name:  ",
           $FORM_DATA{'mname'}, "\n";
61.    print TMPFILE "Last Name:  ",
           $FORM_DATA{'lname'}, "\n";
62.    print TMPFILE "Address:  ",
           $FORM_DATA{'address'}, "\n";
63.    print TMPFILE "City:  ", $FORM_DATA{'city'},
           "\n";
64.    print TMPFILE "State:  ", $FORM_DATA{'state'},
           "\n";
65.    print TMPFILE "Zip Code:  ",
           $FORM_DATA{'zip'}, "\n";
66.    print TMPFILE "Gender:  ", $FORM_DATA{'sex'},
           "\n";
67.    print TMPFILE "Hair:  ", $FORM_DATA{'hair'},
           "\n";
68.    print TMPFILE "Eyes:  ", $FORM_DATA{'eye'},
           "\n";
69.    print TMPFILE "Height:  ",
           $FORM_DATA{'hfeet'}, "' ",
           $FORM_DATA{'hinches'}, "\"", "\n";
70.    print TMPFILE "Weight:  ",
           $FORM_DATA{'weight'}, "\n";
71.    print TMPFILE "DOB:  ", $FORM_DATA{'dob'},
           "\n";
72.    print TMPFILE "Number:      ",
           $FORM_DATA{'number'}, "\n";
73.    print TMPFILE "Class:        ",
           $FORM_DATA{'class'}, "\n";
74.    print TMPFILE "Expiration:     ",
           $FORM_DATA{'expiration'}, "\n";
75.    print TMPFILE "Photo:      ", "\r\n",
           $FORM_DATA{'phrase'}, "\r\n\r\n";
76.    print TMPFILE "Signature:   ", "\r\n",
           $FORM_DATA{'signature'}, "\r\n\r\n";
77.    print TMPFILE "\r\n\r\n";
```

From line 57 to line 78 of the script, we print the value of each field in the submission. Each entry is printed to the TMPFILE we opened on our

server's hard drive. Each field of the form is retrieved from the local
$FORM_DATA reference.

```
78.    close(TMPFILE);
79.  }
```

Finally, on line 78 we close the temporary file and on line 79 the sub routine ends.

The send_thank_you() Sub Routine

Line 81 of our script is used to declare the following instructions are part of our send_thank_you() sub routine. On line 83 we call the Perl local command to create a reference to the array passed to this script's main routine. Again we create a reference to the submitted form data that this sub routine and the main routine can share. By the time we call this routine, we've formatted and decoded the information in the parse_form_data() sub routine.

On line 85 we use the print command to output a minimum HTTP response header. The line informs the client the file they're about to receive is of the "text/html" MIME type. The print command sends data to the standard output buffer (STDOUT). This is where the server looks for a response to send back to the client.

```
81.  sub send_thank_you
82.  {
83.    local (*FORM_DATA) = @_;
84.
85.    print "Content-type: text/html\n\n";
86.
87.    print "<HTML>\n";
88.    print "<HEAD>\n";
89.    print "<TITLE>CGI Driver License
       Update</TITLE>\n";
```

On lines 87-93 we begin printing HTML to STDOUT as our reply. On line 95 we include information from the array we prepared in the parse_form_data() sub routine. We start with some text and concatenate the value store in $FORM_DATA{'date'}. To this we concatenate the closing period for the sentence, and an HTML line break followed by a new line character. All this is then printed to STDOUT as part of our reply.

```
95.      print "Date submitted: ",$FORM_DATA{'date'},
         "\n";
```

On lines 96-117, we continue printing HTML combined with our $FORM_DATA to STDOUT as our reply. On line 118, we print the required closing HTML, and on line 119 the routine ends. Pretty simple!

```
96.      print "First Name:  ", $FORM_DATA{'fname'},
         "\n";
97.      print "Middle Name:  ", $FORM_DATA{'mname'},
         "\n";
98.      print "First Name:  ", $FORM_DATA{'lname'},
         "\n";
99.      print "Address:  ", $FORM_DATA{'address'},
         "\n";
100.     print "City:  ", $FORM_DATA{'city'}, "\n";
101.     print "State:  ", $FORM_DATA{'state'}, "\n";
102.     print "Zip Code:  ", $FORM_DATA{'zip'}, "\n";
103.     print "Gender:  ", $FORM_DATA{'sex'}, "\n";
104.     print "Hair:  ", $FORM_DATA{'hair'}, "\n";
105.     print "Eyes:  ", $FORM_DATA{'eye'}, "\n";
106.     print "Height:  ", $FORM_DATA{'hfeet'}, "' ",
         $FORM_DATA{'hinches'}, "\"", "\n";
107.     print "Weight:  ", $FORM_DATA{'weight'}, "\n";
108.     print "DOB:  ", $FORM_DATA{'dob'}, "\n";
109.     print "Number:     ", $FORM_DATA{'number'},
         "\n";
110.     print "Class:       ", $FORM_DATA{'class'},
         "\n";
111.     print "Expiration:    ",
         $FORM_DATA{'expiration'}, "\n";
112.     print "Photo:      ", "\r\n",
         $FORM_DATA{'phrase'}, "\r\n\r\n";
113.     print "Signature:   ", "\r\n",
         $FORM_DATA{'signature'}, "\r\n\r\n";
114.     print "\r\n\r\n";
```

```
115.    print "</PRE>\n";
116.    print "<HR>\n";
117.    print "<BR>\n";
118.    print "</BODY></HTML>\n";
119. }
```

The return_error() Sub Routine

Our return_error() sub routine is a very simple solution that sends an HTML response to the client advising them that an error occurred. Line 121 of our script is used to declare the instructions that follow are part of our send_thank_you() sub routine. On line 123 we call the Perl local command to create a local reference to the three parameters passed to this routine.

On line 125 we use the print command to output the content-type member of the HTTP response header. On line 126 we add the status to the header and append two new line characters signifying the response header's end. Lines 127-130 output the opening HTML needed to construct the reply. On lines 132 and 133 we combine the $errtype and $message into our response and then print the HTML required to complete the response file. In conclusion we call the Perl exit() command passing it "1" so the script will exit knowing an error has been encountered.

```
121. sub return_error
122. {
123.    local ($status, $errtype, $message) = @_;
124.
125.    print "Content-type: text/html\n";
126.    print "Status: ", $status, " ", $errtype,
        "\n\n";
127.    print "<HTML>\n";
128.    print "<HEAD>\n";
129.    print "<TITLE>CGI Program Error</TITLE>\n";
130.    print "</HEAD>\n";
131.    print "<BODY><BR>\n";
132.    print "<H1>This CGI program encountered a ",
        $errtype, "</H1>\n";
133.    print $message;
134.    print "<HR>\n";
```

```
135.     print "<BR>\n";
136.     print "</BODY></HTML>\n";
137.     exit(1);
138. }
```

Run The Example

To run the example, place the "d_license.pl" Perl script in your Netscape Server's "cgi-bin" directory. Place the "driver_license.pdf" file on your server in a directory that you can access through your browser.

Now enter the form's URL in your browser window. Enter some information into the form fields and click the submit button. An HTML page is returned, confirming the information you submitted. Be sure to check your server for the file the Perl script created to store the submission.

Employee Benefits

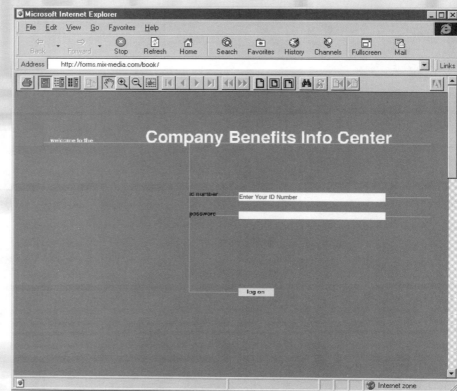

Overview

This example demonstrates how to construct a multi-page form application that allows a user to review company benefits programs. The information available is tailored to the specific user. As they log on to the site they are asked for their ID number (Social Security number) and password. A successful ID/password submission grants access to the individual's account and other general program information.

The account information available includes a brief description of current enrollment status, current claim status, and the next available date that changing plans is possible. An additional form is available to update account information such as change of name or address. This information is presented for medical, dental, and vision plans.

General information available includes programs' specifications and comparisons, a listing of frequently asked questions regarding the offered programs, and a current listing of approved health service providers.

This form application is intended for internal company use only. There are many security schemes possible but for simplicity we'll use a trivial database lookup. This will allow only users registered by the company's benefits administrator to access the benefits application.

Physical Requirements

The following list is a description of the setup used to create this example. The actual components are:

Windows NT Server version 4.0

Perl 5.0 for Win32

Netscape Enterprise Server 3.01

Oracle Workgroup Server version 7.3

Netscape Navigator 3.x or Netscape Communicator 4.04 or newer with Acrobat Plug-in or Microsoft Internet Explorer 4.0 or newer with Acrobat Plug-in

Adobe Acrobat Exchange 3.01 or newer with Adobe Forms Plug-in 3.5

Physical Setup the Example Uses

The example runs on Netscape Enterprise Server 3.0 running on a Windows NT 4.0 server. Perl 5.04 is installed on the Windows NT machine. During the installation the ".pl" file extension type was selected to be associated with Perl script files.

The Netscape server is set to use the Windows NT file extensions to determine which program to use to run this form application's CGI script. This requires that the example's Perl scripts reside in the "shell-cgi" directory in the root folder for our Web server.

We've added a "benefits" and a "claims" table to our Oracle database and configured it to accept connections from user "Adobe", password "book". The benefits table has thirty-nine fields that correspond to the fields of our employee information, retirement, medical, dental, and vision submission forms. They are:

fname	city
mname	state
lname	zip
address	ssnumber
dob	fnamed1
status	mnamed1
gender	lnamed1
hired	reld1
hours	genderd1
homephone	ssnumberd1
officephone	dobd1

fnamed2	lnamed3
mnamed2	reld3
lnamed2	genderd3
reld2	ssnumberd3
genderd2	dobd3
ssnumberd2	covtype
dobd2	covered
fnamed3	subdate
mnamed3	

A second table is used by the database to store health claim information. Every known claim is entered by the company benefits coordinator and accessible immediately. The table has eight fields. Six of these fields are displayed in HTML pages when a claim status request is made. The fields in the "claims" table are:

idnumber
type
patient
provider
dos
charged
planpay
patpay

For security reasons the benefits and claims tables are the only ones this user and password can access.

For this example we're using Oracle 7.3 running on a Windows NT machine.

To query the database and gather information about the connected employee we'll use Perl scripts. These scripts return information to our PDF forms and forward valid submissions back to Oracle.

We have installed Netscape Communicator 4.04 and Acrobat Reader 3.01 on our client machine. Additionally, Netscape Navigator has the Acrobat plug-in located in its plug_in directory. This allows PDF files to be viewed directly in the Navigator window.

The final piece of software we need to install is the Adobe FDF Active X server component. In this case the FdfAcX.dll and the Fdftk.dll are copied into our \winnt\system32\ directory. Any directory with execute permissions will do. If you're using an NTFS formatted hard drive, be sure the DLLs also have execute permission.

Once the files are copied, the FdfAcX.dll needs to be registered with the system. To do this, from the command line, cd into the directory containing the FdfAcX.dll. Then enter regsvr32 FdfAcX.dll. Be sure that FDF.pm is copied into the proper location in your Perl directory structure. With Perl 5.004 or newer, this is in the \lib\site\Acrobat directory.

Creating the Necessary Files

To get this complete example to work we need to put 24 document files on the server. The files are:

1 PDF file for the initial log on screen
1 PDF file for the current overview screen
1 PDF file for employee information updates and changes
1 Perl script for log on authentication and revieval of overview information
1 Perl script for retrieval of current employee information
1 Perl script for updating information

Health plan files

3 PDF files ,one for each category of coverage (Medical, Dental and Vision)
3 HTML files, one for each category FAQ (Frequently Asked Questions)
3 HTML files, one for each category approved service providers
3 Perl scripts for retrieval of health plan details
3 Perl scripts to generate current account activity

Two types of files will be generated dynamically. The health insurance claims forms and retirement account activity files are all created using Perl scripts to format information from the Oracle database.

The employee overview screen is a single PDF document. A successful log on retrieves user information and flows it into the PDF form fields.

One level below the overview page live four PDF files. The first is a PDF form that lets a user update their personal information. The second is the top of the retirement information branch. It provides an brief look at the employee's current retirement investment status. The remaining two PDF files are the top-level for each of our three medical categories. These give the user a starting point for browsing through each medical category.

The log on form requires one Perl script. The script queries the Oracle database to see if a user matches the submission information. If we have a match, the employee's information is looked up and returned to the browser so it can be flowed into the overview document.

Creating the Log-On PDF File

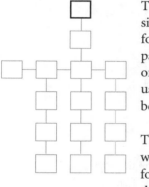

The PDF file the user first encounters to authenticate their log on is a single page PDF file. The next steps discuss creating this file. The log on form accepts an ID number (the user's social security number) and a password. When submitted, the log on sends information to a Perl script on the server that verifies the user exists and returns an overview of the user's benefits selections. The PDF form displays a field for an ID number and a password and a button for submitting the data to the server.

The designer used QuarkXPress to construct the original form. The file was then distilled into PDF format. The next steps discuss creating the form fields in Acrobat Exchange to handle the client side interaction of this transaction.

Step 1

The Form Field Names
The fields we want to display on this form are as follows:

idnumber
password
submit

Step 2

"idnumber" Field
The first field we'll create is the "idnumber" field. To create the field, choose the forms tool button on the Acrobat Exchange toolbar. The cursor changes to a crosshair. Click the mouse button and drag out a rectangle defining the area where you want the user to enter their idnumber. The

Field Properties dialog box appears asking for specifics about the text field we're creating.

Step 2: Field Properties Dialog-Appearance Tab

Enter "idnumber" as the field name and select Text as the field type. Leave the User Name field blank. Enter a value here only if you want to export a different field name with this field's value when the form is submitted to a server.

Activate the Appearance tab. Make sure the Border or Background Colors aren't selected. Select a color the text will display by clicking the Text Color chip. Select Helvetica as the Font and 12 as the Size.

Next activate the Options tab. Enter the default text to display in the field. Leave the limit on the number of characters and the password field unchecked for now.

Now activate the Format tab. The Format tab allows us to regulate the formatting of information entered into the field. Choose Special from the Category list and pick Social Security Number from the Special

Options list. This insures users only enter digits. If they try to enter letters, the system beeps and doesn't enter the character in the field. It also formats the entry, inserting hyphens after the first three digits and the first five digits.

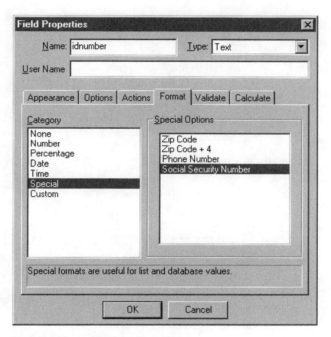

Step 2: Field Properties Dialog-Format Tab

Click the OK button. The dialog closes, adding the field to the document.

Step 3

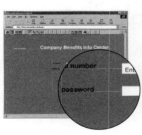

Password Field

Now we'll add the password field. This is a special text field where we gather the password to submit to the server.

With the Acrobat Exchange's forms tool, create the field where the password will be placed. The Field Properties dialog box appears, asking for specifics about the new field.

Step 3: Field Properties Dialog-Appearance Tab

Enter "password" as the field name and select Text as the field type. Again we leave the User Name field blank.

Activate the Appearance tab. We don't need to select a Border or Background Color due to our form's design. Make sure the text color is black. If it isn't, change it to black by clicking the Text Color chip. Select Helvetica as the Font and 12 as the Size.

Field Properties ☒

Name: password   Type: Text ▾

User Name

| Appearance | **Options** | Actions | Format | Validate | Calculate |

Default: password

Alignment: Left ▾

☐ Multi-line

☐ Limit of [   ] characters

☑ Password

OK   Cancel

Step 3: Field Properties Dialog-Options Tab

Now activate the Options tab. Here we'll enter the default text displayed in the field. Here we've entered "password". This will be custom tailored to the specific user by our back-end process. On this dialog tab be sure to select the Password checkbox. This option displays any entered text as asterisks, adding an extra level of security.

Once you've completed your choices, click the OK button. The dialog closes, adding the field to the document.

Step 4

Submit Button

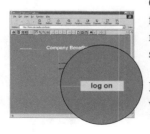

Our remaining field is the submit button. With the Acrobat Exchange's forms tool selected, drag out a rectangle defining the area where the submit button is located. The Field Properties dialog box appears asking for specifics about the field we're creating.

Enter "submit" as the field name and select Button as the field type. Again we leave the User Name field blank.

Field Properties   ☒

Name: submit   Type: Button ▼

User Name [   ]

Appearance | Options | Actions

Border
☐ Border Color ■   Width: Thin   ▼
☐ Background Color ■ Style: Solid   ▼

Text
Text Color: ■
Font: Helvetica   ▼ Size: 12 ▼

Common Properties
☐ Read Only   ☐ Hidden   ☐ Required   ☐ Don't Print

OK   Cancel

Step 4: Field Properties Dialog-Appearance Tab

Activate the Appearance tab. Again we don't need to select a Border or Background Color due to our form's design. The button's text color isn't important because we aren't displaying the button's title.

Step 4: Field Properties Dialog-Options Tab

The Options tab is where you select any special appearance options for the button. In this instance we set the Highlight option to Invert. The Layout option is set to Text only. Because we don't want any text to show over our buttons, the Text entry for the Button face attributes is left blank. The Button Face When option determines when the appearance we set up is invoked. Here we want it to Invert on a Mouse Up event.

Field Properties

Name: submit   Type: Button

User Name:

| Appearance | Options | **Actions** |

When this happens...   Do the following:

- ⦿ Mouse Up   Submit Form
- Mouse Down
- Mouse Enter
- Mouse Exit

Add...
Edit...
Delete

Up
Down

OK   Cancel

Step 4: Field Properties Dialog-Actions Tab

The Actions tab is where you select any action this field will invoke. Here we choose the Mouse up event. Click the Add button and choose Submit Form from the list of available action types.

Edit an Action

Action

Type: Submit Form

Submit all form fields to a World Wide Web "Universal Resource Locator"

Select the URL, export format and fields

Select URL...

OK   Cancel

Step 4: Edit an Action Dialog

Now we need to identify the URL that will process the form submission. Click the Select URL button and enter the URL we'll use to process this form.

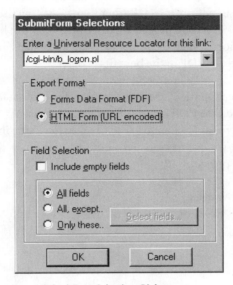

Step 4: SubmitForm Selections Dialog

Here we also choose to submit the data to the server in HTML format. We could submit in the FDF format but the Perl script we'll use to process the submission is set up to receive the data in HTML format. We also want to send all fields, even though we have the option to just send a subset of the fields from the form. Once the proper selections are made, click the OK buttons in the SubmitForm Selections, Edit an Action, and Field Properties dialogs.

Creating the Navigation Bar on all the Project PDF Files

Each PDF in this project uses a navigation bar on its left side to access the other files in the benefits project. Rather than revisiting the creation of this group of links on each page, we'll discuss its creation here and leave its implementation in each file to the user. The next steps discuss creating this portion of every PDF in the benefits project.

The designer used QuarkXPress to construct the original form. The file was then distilled into PDF format. The next steps discuss creating the form fields in Acrobat Exchange to handle the client side interaction of this transaction. The navigation area contains 14 buttons that link to other files in the project.

Step 1

The Form Field Names

The button fields we want to display on this form are as follows.

overview
empinfo
menroll
mclaim
mfaq
mlist
denroll
dclaim
dfaq
dlist
venroll
vclaim
vfaq
vlist

Step 2

Overview Button

Each form field on the navigation bar is really one of two kinds of buttons. The first type of button is the standard Submit Form button. These buttons submit information stored in two hidden fields on each PDF document. The hidden fields are used to store the user's idnumber and password. The other type of button uses the open file command to load another file in the browser window.

The first button we'll create is this second type of button. It loads the overview page the user saw when first logging on to the benefits application. With Acrobat Exchange's forms tool selected, drag out a rectangle defining the area where the overview button is located. The upper left corner of the navigation bar is where we'll place it. The Field Properties dialog box appears asking for specifics about the field we're creating.

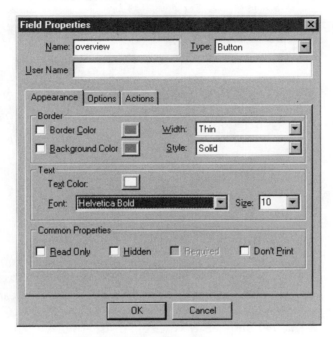

Step 2: Field Properties Dialog-Appearance Tab

Activate the Appearance tab. Again we don't need to select a Border or Background Color due to our form's design. The button's text color isn't important because we aren't displaying the button's title.

Enter "overview" as the field name and select Button as the field type. Again we leave the User Name field blank.

Step 2: Field Properties Dialog-Options Tab

The Options tab is where you select any special appearance options for the button. Is this instance we set the Highlight option to Invert. The Layout option is set to Text only. Because we don't want any text to show over our buttons, the Text entry for the Button Face Attributes is left blank. The Button Face When option determines when the appearance we set up is invoked. Here we want it to Invert on a Mouse Up event.

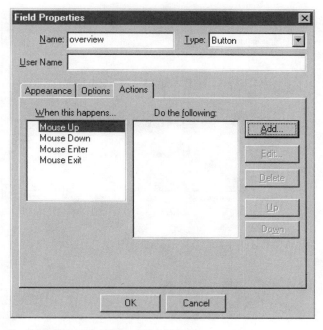

Step 2: Field Properties Dialog-Actions Tab

The Actions tab is where you select any action this field will invoke. Here we choose the Mouse Up event. Click the Add button and choose the Open File action from the list of available action types. The file dialog appears asking you to locate the file to open. Navigate to the overview.pdf file and select it.

Step 3

Info Record Button

The next button we'll create is the open file type of button. It launches a Perl script on the server that returns information and a reference to the employee information record "emp_info.pdf". We pass the contents of two hidden fields in the document to the script. The hidden fields are used to carry around the user's idnumber and password so we don't have to look them up each time there is a submission.

To create the field, select Acrobat Exchange's forms tool and drag out a rectangle defining the area where the button is located. The Field Properties dialog box appears asking for specifics about the field we're creating.

Step 3: Field Properties Dialog-Appearance Tab

Activate the Appearance tab. Again we don't need to select a Border or Background Color due to our form's design. The button's text color isn't important because we aren't displaying the button's title.

Enter "empinfo" as the field name and select Button as the field type. Again we leave the User Name field blank.

Step 3: Field Properties Dialog-Options Tab

The Options tab is where you select any special appearance options for the button. In this instance we set the Highlight option to Invert. The Layout option is set to Text only. Because we don't want any text to show over our buttons, the Text entry for the Button Face Attributes is left blank. The Button Face When option determines when the appearance we set up is invoked. Here we want it to Invert on a Mouse Up event.

Step 3: Field Properties Dialog-Actions Tab

The Actions tab is where you select any action this field will invoke. Here we choose the Mouse Up event. Click the Add button and choose Submit Form from the list of available action types.

Step 3: Edit an Action Dialog

Now we need to identify the URL that will process the form submission. Click the Select URL button and enter the URL we'll use to process this form.

Step 3: SubmitForm Selections Dialog

Here we also choose to submit the data to the server in HTML format. The Perl script we'll use to process the submission is set up to receive the data in HTML format. We also choose to send all fields even though we have the option to just send a subset of the fields from the form.

Once the proper selections are made click the OK buttons in the Submit Form Selections, Edit an Action, and Field Properties dialogs.

Step 4

Medical Plan Button

The next button is a submit type button. It launches a Perl script on the server that returns information and a reference to the selected medical plan "med_plan.pdf". We pass the contents of our two hidden fields in the document to the script.

To create the field, select Acrobat Exchange's forms tool and drag out a rectangle defining the area where the button is located. The Field Properties dialog box appears asking for specifics about the field we're creating.

Step 4: Field Properties Dialog-Appearance Tab

Activate the Appearance tab. Again we don't need to select a Border or Background Color due to our form's design. The button's text color isn't important because we aren't displaying the button's title.

Enter "menroll" as the field name and select Button as the field type. Again we leave the User Name field blank.

Field Properties

N̲ame: menroll   T̲ype: Button

U̲ser Name

Appearance | Options | Actions

Highlight: Invert   La̲yout: Text only

Button F̲ace When   Button Face Attributes

Up   Te̲xt:

Select Icon...

Clear

Advanced Layout...

OK   Cancel

Step 4: Field Properties Dialog-Options Tab

The Options tab is where you select any special appearance options for the button. In this instance we set the Highlight option to Invert. The Layout option is set to Text only. Because we don't want any text to show over our buttons, the Text entry for the Button Face Attributes is left blank. The Button Face When option determines when the appearance we set up is invoked. Here we want it to Invert on a Mouse Up event.

Step 4: Field Properties Dialog-Actions Tab

The Actions tab is where you select any action this field will invoke. Here we choose the Mouse Up event. Click the Add button and choose Submit Form from the list of available action types.

Step 4: Edit an Action Dialog

Now we need to identify the URL that will process the form submission. Click the Select URL button and enter the URL we'll use to process this form.

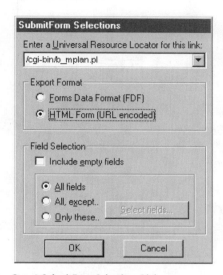

Step 4: SubmitForm Selections Dialog

Here we also choose to submit the data to the server in HTML format. The Perl script we'll use to process the submission is set up to receive the data in HTML format. We also choose to send all fields even though we have the option to just send a subset of the fields from the form.

Once the proper selections are made, click the OK buttons in the Submit Form Selections, Edit an Action, and Field Properties dialogs.

Step 5

Claim Status Button

The next button we'll create is the submit type of button. It launches a Perl script on the server that returns an HTML file detailing the user's current medical claims. Again, we pass the contents of all fields in the form but only two are important for now. The two hidden fields in the document we're concerned with are the "idnumber" and the "password" fields.

To create this button field, select Acrobat Exchange's forms tool and drag out a rectangle defining where to locate the button. The Field Properties dialog box appears asking for specifics about the field we're creating.

Step 5: Field Properties Dialog-Appearance Tab

Activate the Appearance tab. Don't select a Border or Background Color due to our form's design. The button's text color isn't important because we aren't displaying the button's title.

Enter "mclaim" as the field name and select Button as the field type. Again we leave the User Name field blank.

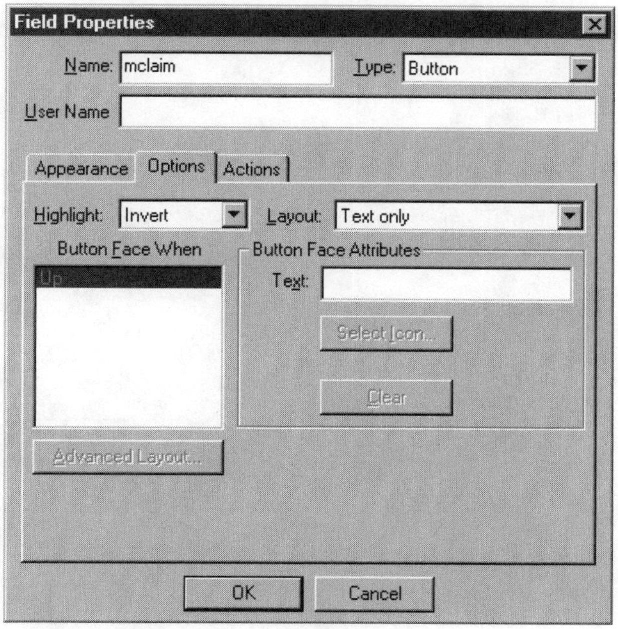

Field Properties

Name: mclaim   Type: Button

User Name

Appearance | Options | Actions

Highlight: Invert   Layout: Text only

Button Face When   Button Face Attributes

Up   Text:

Select Icon...

Clear

Advanced Layout...

OK   Cancel

Step 5: Field Properties Dialog-Options Tab

The Options tab is where you select any special appearance options for
the button. Is this instance we set the Highlight option to Invert. The
Layout option is set to Text only. Because we don't want any text to show
over our buttons, the Text entry for the Button Face Attributes is left
blank. The Button Face When option determines when the appearance
we set up is invoked. Here we want it to Invert on a Mouse Up event.

Step 5: Field Properties Dialog-Actions Tab

The Actions tab is where you select any action this field will invoke. Here we choose the Mouse Up event. Click the Add button and choose Submit Form from the list of available action types.

Step 5: Edit an Action Dialog

Now we need to identify the URL that will process the form submission. Click the Select URL button and enter the URL we'll use to process this form.

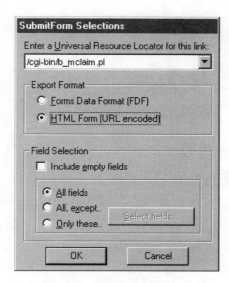

Step 5: SubmitForm Selections Dialog

Here we also choose to submit the data to the server in HTML format. The Perl script we'll use to process the submission is set up to receive the data in HTML format. We also choose to send all fields even though we have the option to just send a subset of the fields from the form.

Once the proper selections are made, click the OK buttons in the SubmitForm Selections, Edit an Action, and Field Properties dialogs.

Step 6

The Medical FAQ Button

The next field is an open file type button. It loads the Medical FAQ HTML file in the browser window. To create the field, with Exchange's forms tool selected, drag out a rectangle defining the area where the button is located. The Field Properties dialog box appears asking for specifics about the field we're creating.

Step 6: Field Properties Dialog-Appearance Tab

Activate the Appearance tab. Again we don't need to select a Border or Background Color due to our form's design. The button's text color isn't important because we aren't displaying the button's title.

Enter "mfaq" as the field name and select Button as the field type. Again we leave the User Name field blank.

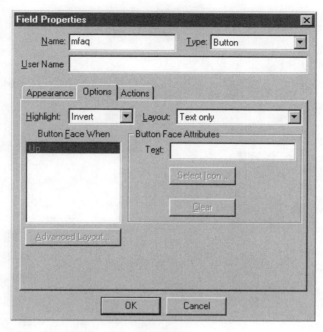

Step 6: Field Properties Dialog-Options Tab

The Options tab is where you select any special appearance options for the button. Here we set the Highlight option to Invert. The Layout option is set to Text only. Because we don't want any text to show over our buttons, the Text entry for the Button Face Attributes is left blank. The Button Face When option determines when the appearance we set up is invoked. Here we want it to Invert on a Mouse Up event.

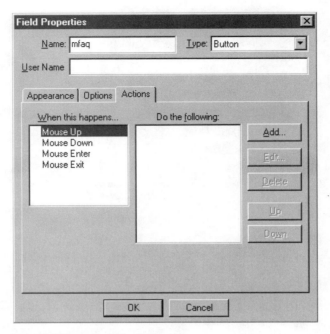

Step 6: Field Properties Dialog-Actions Tab

The Actions tab is where you select any action this field will invoke. Here we choose the Mouse Up event. Click the Add button and choose the Open File action from the list of available action types. The file dialog appears asking you to locate the file to open. Navigate to the med_faq.html file and select it. It will load into the browser window when the button is clicked.

Step 7

The Doctors List Button

The last field in this group is another open file type button. It loads the Doctors List HTML file in the browser window. To create the button, with Exchange's forms tool selected, drag out a rectangle defining the area where the button is located. The Field Properties dialog box appears asking for specifics about the field we're creating.

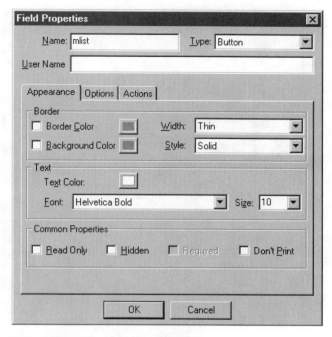

Step 7: Field Properties Dialog-Appearance Tab

Activate the Appearance tab. Again we don't need to select a Border or Background Color due to our form's design. The button's text color isn't important because we aren't displaying the button's title.

Enter "mlist" as the field name and select Button as the field type. Again we leave the User Name field blank.

Step 7: Field Properties Dialog-Options Tab

The Options tab is where you select any special appearance options for the button. Here we set the Highlight option to Invert. The Layout option is set to Text only. Because we don't want any text to show over our buttons, the Text entry for the Button Face Attributes is left blank. The Button Face When option determines when the appearance we set up is invoked. Here we want it to Invert on a Mouse Up event.

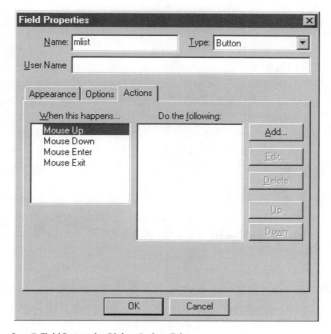

Step 7: Field Properties Dialog-Actions Tab

The Actions tab is where you select any action this field will invoke. Here we choose the Mouse Up event. Click the Add button and choose the Open File action from the list of available action types. The file dialog appears asking you to locate the file to open. Navigate to the med_faq.html file and select it. It will load into the browser window when the button is clicked.

Step 8

Repeating Button Creation for the Dental and Vision Files
The remaining vision and dental categories buttons require the same buttons created in steps 4-7. For each of these categories, repeat these steps to add buttons for the plan, claim status, FAQ and doctor list. The only differences are the location of the button on the page and the action the button invokes. Adjust each button's action according to the file you want to open or the Perl script you intend to run.

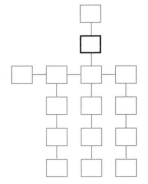

Creating the Benefits Overview PDF File

The overview PDF file is a single page PDF file. This application uses a PDF file as the starting point for browsing employee benefit information. This overview file allows a user to quickly review their current information. The PDF form displays a name, a social security number, medical, dental, vision, and retirement plan selections and their corresponding group numbers. This information is read only. If a user wants to update it or view additional information, they can do so by clicking one of the selections in the navigation bar on the left side of the page.

The designer used QuarkXPress to construct the original form. The file was then distilled into PDF format. The next steps discuss creating the form fields in Acrobat Exchange to handle the client side interaction of this transaction.

Step 1

The Form Field Names
The fields we want to display on this form are as follows:

name
ssnumber
medplan
medgroup
dentplan
dentgroup
vizplan
vizgroup
retplan
retgroup
idnumber
password

Step 2

Name Field
The first field we'll create is the name field. To create the field, choose the forms tool button on the Acrobat Exchange toolbar. The cursor changes to a crosshair. Click the mouse button and drag out a rectangle defining the area where you want the user to enter their name. The Field Properties dialog box appears asking for specifics about the text field we're creating.

Field Properties ☒

Name: `name`   Type: `Text` ▼

User Name `_____`

| Appearance | Options | Actions | Format | Validate | Calculate |

Border
☐ Border Color ▣   Width: `Thin` ▼
☐ Background Color ▣   Style: `Solid` ▼

Text
Text Color: ▣
Font: `Helvetica` ▼   Size: `Auto` ▼

Common Properties
☑ Read Only   ☐ Hidden   ☐ Required   ☐ Don't Print

`OK`   `Cancel`

Step 2: Field Properties Dialog-Appearance Tab

Enter "name" as the field name and select Text as the field type. Leave the User Name field blank. Enter a value here only if you want to export a different field name with this field's value when the form is submitted to a server.

Activate the Appearance tab. Here we're presented with options that affect the field's appearance. Our designer decided to create the fields as a graphic so we don't have a Border or Background Color selected. If the designer didn't add a field graphic, the Acrobat forms plug-in provides options to create a field with an outline or a background color. Select a color the text will display by clicking the Text Color chip. Select Helvetica as the Font and Auto as the Size. The text is sized to fit the box we've just drawn. Finally, check the Read Only checkbox.

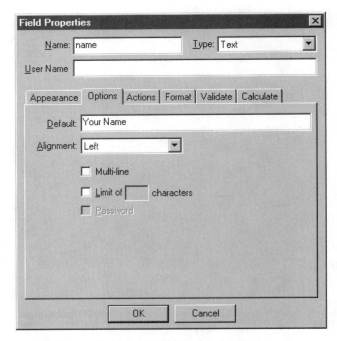

Step 2: Field Properties Dialog-Options Tab

Now activate the Options tab. Here we'll enter the default text displayed in the field. Here we've entered "Your Name". This is the default text that will appear if something goes wrong. Once the user has successfully logged on, the real information is received from the database and flowed into the form.

Once you've completed your choices click the OK button. The dialog closes, adding the field to the document.

Step 3

"ssnumber" Field

Now we'll add the "ssnumber" field. With Acrobat Exchange's forms tool selected, drag out a rectangle defining the area where you want to display the Social Security Number code. The Field Properties dialog box appears, asking for specifics about the field we're creating.

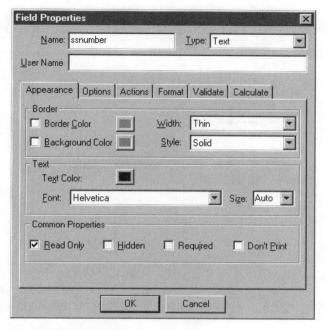

Step 3: Field Properties Dialog-Appearance Tab

Enter "ssnumber" as the field name and select Text as the field type. We left the User Name field blank because we want the field name to be "ssnumber" when the form is submitted.

Activate the Appearance tab. Make sure the Border or Background Colors aren't selected. Select a color the text will display by clicking the Text Color chip. Select Helvetica as the Font and Auto as the Size. Finally, check the Read Only checkbox.

Next activate the Options tab. Enter the default text to display in the field. Leave the limit on the number of characters and the password fields unchecked for now.

Now Activate the Format tab. The Format tab allows us to regulate the formatting of information entered into the field. Choose Special from the Category list and pick Social Security Number from the Special Options list. This insures users only enter digits. If they try to enter letters, the system beeps and doesn't enter the characters in the field. It also formats the entry, inserting hyphens after the first three digits and the first five digits.

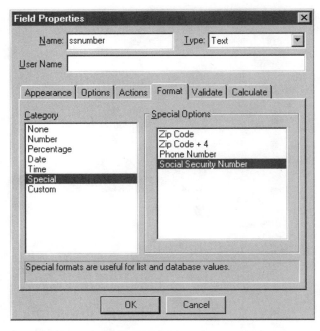

Step 3: Field Properties Dialog-Format Tab

Click the OK button. The dialog closes, adding the field to the document.

Step 4

Medical Plan Choice Field—Read Only

Next we'll create another read only field to hold the "medical plan cho-sen" text. To create the field, choose the forms tool button on the Acrobat Exchange toolbar. Click the mouse button and drag out a rectangle defining the area where you want the medical plan text to appear. The Field Properties dialog box appears, asking for specifics about the text field we're creating.

Step 4: Field Properties Dialog-Appearance Tab

Enter "medplan" as the field name and select Text as the field type. Leave the User Name field blank.

Activate the Appearance tab. Here we're presented with options that affect the field's appearance. Our designer decided to create the fields as a graphic so we don't have a Border or Background Color selected. If the designer didn't add a field graphic, the Acrobat forms plug-in provides options to create a field with an outline or a background color. Select a color the text will display by clicking the Text Color chip. Select Helvetica as the Font and Auto as the Size. The text is sized to fit the box we've just drawn. Finally check the Read Only checkbox.

Step 4: Field Properties Dialog-Options Tab

Now activate the Options tab. Here we'll enter the default text displayed in the field. Here we've entered "Your Medical Group". This will be custom tailored to the specific user by our back-end process.

Once you've completed your choices, click the OK button. The dialog closes, adding the field to the document.

Step 5

Medical Group Number Field

Now we'll add the medical group number field. This is a read only field where we display the group number. A group number is associated with the user's chosen medical plan. It's sent to the form by the back-end process but we'll create a placeholder for it here.

With Acrobat Exchange's forms tool, create the field where the number will be placed. The Field Properties dialog box appears, asking for specifics about the new number field.

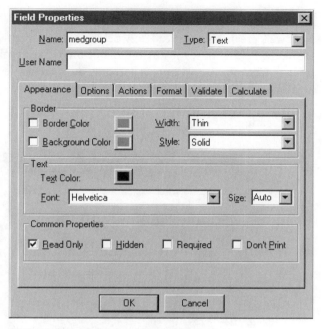

Step 5: Field Properties Dialog-Appearance Tab

Enter "medgroup" as the field name and select Text as the field type. Again we leave the User Name field blank.

Activate the Appearance tab. We don't need to select a Border or Background Color due to our form's design. Make sure the text color is black. If it isn't, change it to black by clicking the Text Color chip. Select Helvetica as the Font and Auto as the Size. Finally select the Read Only checkbox. This text box will hold and display text but it won't allow a user to enter any information.

Now Activate the Format tab. The Format tab allows us to regulate the formatting of information entered into the field. Choose Number from the category list and Decimal places to "0" from the Number Options List.

Now click the Field Properties dialog's OK button. The dialog closes, adding the field to the document.

Step 6

Dental Plan Choice Field—Read Only

Next we'll create another read only field to hold the dental plan text. To create the field, choose the forms tool button on the Acrobat Exchange toolbar. Click the mouse button and drag out a rectangle defining the area where you want to position the dental plan text. The Field Properties dialog box appears, asking for specifics about the text field we're creating.

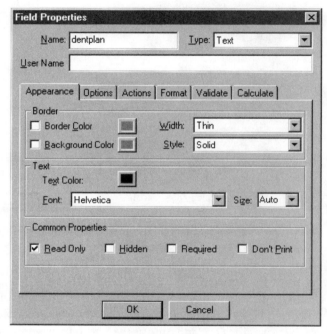

Step 6: Field Properties Dialog-Appearance Tab

Enter "dentplan" as the field name and select Text as the field type. Leave the User Name field blank.

Activate the Appearance tab. Here we're presented with options that affect the field's appearance. Our designer decided to create the field as a graphic so we don't have a Border or Background Color selected. If the designer didn't add a field graphic, the Acrobat forms plug-in provides options to create a field with an outline or a background color. Select a color the text will display by clicking the Text Color chip. Select Helvetica as the Font and Auto as the Size. The text is sized to fit the box we've just drawn. Finally check the Read Only checkbox.

Field Properties

Name: dentplan   Type: Text

User Name

Appearance | Options | Actions | Format | Validate | Calculate

Default: Your Dental Group

Alignment: Left

☐ Multi-line

☐ Limit of [____] characters

☐ Password

OK   Cancel

Step 6: Field Properties Dialog-Options Tab

Now activate the Options tab. Here we'll enter the default text displayed in the field. Here we've entered "Your Dental Group". This will be custom tailored to the specific user by our back-end process.

Once you've completed your choices click the OK button. The dialog closes, adding the field to the document.

Step 7

Dental Plan Group Number Field

Now we'll add the dental plan group number field. This is a read only field where we display the group number associated with the user's chosen dental plan. The actual information is sent to the form by the back-end process. We'll create a placeholder for it here.

With Acrobat Exchange's forms tool, create the field where the dental group number will be placed. The Field Properties dialog box appears, asking for specifics about the new number field.

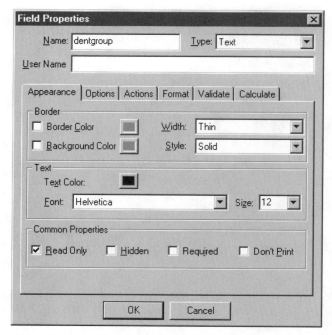

Step 7: Field Properties Dialog-Appearance Tab

Enter "dentgroup" as the field name and select Text as the field type. Again we leave the User Name field blank.

Activate the Appearance tab. We don't need to select a Border or Background Color due to our form's design. Make sure the text color is black. If it isn't, change it to black by clicking the Text Color chip. Select Helvetica as the Font and 12 as the Size. Finally select the Read Only checkbox. This text box will hold and display text but it won't allow a user to enter any information.

Now activate the Format tab. The Format tab allows us to regulate the formatting of information entered into the field. Choose Number from the category list and Decimal places to "0" from the Number Options List.

Now click the Field Properties dialog's OK button. The dialog closes, adding the field to the document.

Step 8

Vision Plan Choice Field—Read only

Next we'll create another read only field to hold the user's vision plan choice. To create the field, choose the forms tool button on the Acrobat Exchange toolbar. Click the mouse button and drag out a rectangle defining the area where you want to display the medical plan text. The Field Properties dialog box appears, asking for specifics about the text field we're creating.

Field Properties

Name: visplan   Type: Text

User Name:

Appearance | Options | Actions | Format | Validate | Calculate

Border
☐ Border Color   Width: Thin
☐ Background Color   Style: Solid

Text
Text Color:
Font: Helvetica   Size: Auto

Common Properties
☑ Read Only   ☐ Hidden   ☐ Required   ☐ Don't Print

OK   Cancel

Step 8: Field Properties Dialog-Appearance Tab

Enter "visplan" as the field name and select Text as the field type. Leave the User Name field blank.

Activate the Appearance tab. Here we're presented with options that affect the field's appearance. Our designer decided to create the fields as a graphic so we don't have a Border or Background Color selected. If the designer didn't add a field graphic, the Acrobat forms plug-in provides options to create a field with an outline or a background color. Select a color the text will display by clicking the Text Color chip. Select Helvetica as the Font and Auto as the Size. The text is sized to fit the box we've just drawn. Finally check the Read Only checkbox.

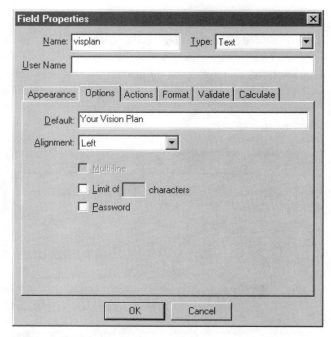

Step 8: Field Properties Dialog-Options Tab

Now activate the Options tab. Here we'll enter the default text displayed in the field. Here we've entered "Your Vision Plan". This will be custom tailored to the specific user by our back-end process.

Once you've completed your choices click the OK button. The dialog closes, adding the field to the document.

Step 9

Vision Plan Group Number Field

Now we'll add the vision plan group number field. This is a read only field where we display the group number associated with the user's chosen vision plan. It's sent to the form by the back-end process, but we'll create a placeholder for it here.

With Acrobat Exchange's forms tool, create the field where the vision group number will be placed. The Field Properties dialog box appears, asking for specifics about the new number field.

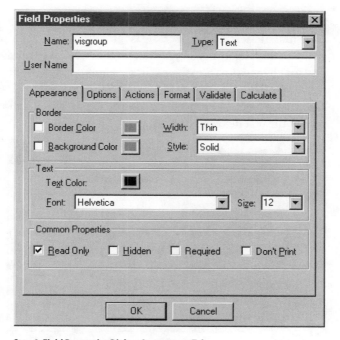

Step 9: Field Properties Dialog-Appearance Tab

Enter "visgroup" as the field name and select Text as the field type. Again we leave the User Name field blank.

Activate the Appearance tab. We don't need to select a Border or Background Color due to our form's design. Make sure the text color is black. If it isn't, change it to black by clicking the Text Color chip. Select Helvetica as the Font and 12 as the Size. Finally select the Read Only checkbox. This text box will hold and display text but it won't allow a user to enter any information.

Now activate the Format tab. The Format tab allows us to regulate the formatting of information entered into the field. Choose Number from the category list and Decimal places to "0" from the Number Options List.

Now click the Field Properties dialog's OK button. The dialog closes, adding the field to the document.

Step 10

"idnumber" Field—Hidden Text

The first hidden field we'll create is the "idnumber" field. To create the field choose the forms tool button on the Acrobat Exchange toolbar. The cursor changes to a crosshair. Click the mouse button and drag out a rectangle defining the area where you want the user to enter their id-number. The Field Properties dialog box appears asking for specifics about the text field we're creating.

Step 10: Field Properties Dialog-Appearance Tab

Enter "idnumber" as the field name and select Text as the field type. Leave the User Name field blank. Enter a value here only if you want to export a different field name with this field's value when the form is submitted to a server.

Activate the Appearance tab. Make sure the Border or Background Colors aren't selected. Select a color the text will display by clicking the Text Color chip. Select Helvetica as the Font and 12 as the Size. On this dialog tab, be sure to select the Hidden and Read Only checkboxes. Selecting the Read Only checkbox insures the user won't enter any information in this field. The Hidden option makes this field invisible.

Finally, activate the Validate tab. The Validate tab lets us set up a field to validate the value of this field. Click the custom validate script radio button and then click the Edit button. The Acrobat Javascript editing window appears. Type in the following code.

```
1. var f = this.getField("idnumber");
2. global.idnumber = f.value;
```

This simple script grabs the value of our idnumber field and stores it in the global JavaScript object. The first line of this script gets a reference to the idnumber field and stores it in the variable "f". The second line accesses the "value" member of "f" and copies it to the global object in a field we can reference later. The global JavaScript object exists inside Acrobat and can be used to share information between documents. We can access this value later by simply referencing it as global.idnumber.

Step 11

Password Field—Hidden Text

Now we'll add the password field. This is a special text field where we store the user's password to submit to the server.

With the Acrobat Exchange's forms tool, create the field where the password will be placed. The Field Properties dialog box appears asking for specifics about the new field.

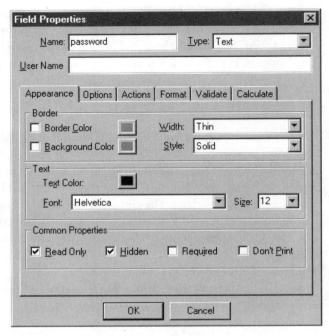

Step 11: Field Properties Dialog-Appearance Tab

Enter "password" as the field name and select Text as the field type. Again we leave the User Name field blank.

Activate the Appearance tab. We don't need to select a Border or Background Color due to our form's design. Make sure the text color is black. If it isn't, change it to black by clicking the Text Color chip. Select Helvetica as the Font and 12 as the Size. Be sure to select the Hidden and Read Only checkboxes. We don't want the user to enter any information in this field. Clicking the Read Only checkbox insures the user won't. The Hidden option makes this field invisible.

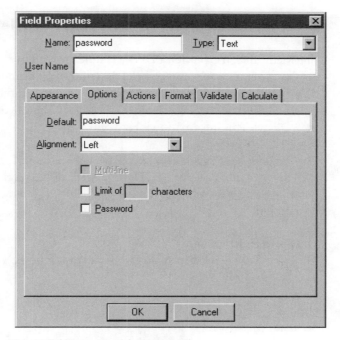

Step 11: Field Properties Dialog-Options Tab

Now activate the Options tab. Here we'll enter the default text displayed in the field. Here we've entered "password". This will be custom tailored to the specific user by our back-end process. You can select the Password checkbox but remember the field is hidden so the user won't see it.

Once you've completed your choices, click the OK button. The dialog closes, adding the field to the document.

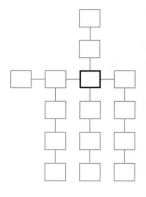

Creating the Medical Plan Overview PDF File

The Medical Plan Overview PDF is a simple file with five fields we use to display the employee's name, a brief description of the medical plan they've subscribed to, the next opportunity to enroll, choices of coverage type, and the date coverage changes. The following steps discuss creating the PDF file. This information is read only.

The designer used PageMaker to construct the original form. The file was then distilled into PDF format. The next steps discuss creating the form fields in Acrobat Exchange to handle the client side interaction of this transaction.

Step 1

The Form Field Names
The fields we want to display on this form are as follows:

name
plandesc
nextdate
covtype
subdate
idnumber
password

Step 2

Name Field
The first field we'll create is the name field. To create the field, choose the forms tool button on the Acrobat Exchange toolbar. The cursor changes to a crosshair. Click the mouse button and drag out a rectangle defining the area where you want the user's name to display. The Field Properties dialog box appears, asking for specifics about the text field we're creating.

Step 2: Field Properties Dialog-Appearance Tab

Enter "name" as the field name and select Text as the field type. Leave the User Name field blank. Enter a value here only if you want to export a different field name with this field's value when the form is submitted to a server.

Activate the Appearance tab. Here we're presented with options that affect the field's appearance. Our designer decided to create the fields as a graphic so we don't have a Border or Background Color selected. If the designer didn't add a field graphic, the Acrobat forms plug-in provides options to create a field with an outline or a background color. Select a color the text will display by clicking the Text Color chip. Select Helvetica as the Font and Auto as the Size. The text is sized to fit the box we've just drawn. Finally check the Read Only checkbox.

Field Properties ☒

Name: name   Type: Text ▼

User Name [   ]

| Appearance | Options | Actions | Format | Validate | Calculate |

Default: Your Name

Alignment: Left ▼

☐ Multi-line

☐ Limit of [   ] characters

☐ Password

[OK]   [Cancel]

Step 2: Field Properties Dialog-Options Tab

Now activate the Options tab. Here we'll enter the default text displayed in the field. Here we've entered "Your Name". This is the default text that will appear if something goes wrong. Once the user has successfully logged on, the real information is received from the database and flowed into the form.

Once you've completed your choices click the OK button. The dialog closes, adding the field to the document.

Step 3

"plandesc" Field

Now we'll add the "plandesc" field. With Acrobat Exchange's forms tool selected, drag out a rectangle defining the area where you want to display the medical plan's description. The Field Properties dialog box appears, asking for specifics about the field we're creating.

Step 3: Field Properties Dialog-Appearance Tab

Enter "plandesc" as the field name and select Text as the field type. We left the User Name field blank because we want the field name to be "plandesc" when information is returned to the form.

Activate the Appearance tab. Make sure the Border or Background Colors aren't selected. Select a color the text will display by clicking the Text Color chip. Select Helvetica as the Font and 12 as the Size. Finally, check the Read Only checkbox.

Next activate the Options tab. Enter the default text to display in the field. Check the multi-line option. This allows us to flow in up to 32,756 characters. Leave the limit on the number of characters and the password fields unchecked for now.

Click the OK button. The dialog closes, adding the field to the document.

Step 4

Date Field
Now we'll add a date field. This field enters a date and formats it in the way we specify. Error checking is performed and the user is warned if

they try to enter information that can't be converted into a date. With Acrobat Exchange's forms tool, define the area where the user will enter the date. The Field Properties dialog box appears, asking for specifics about the field we're creating.

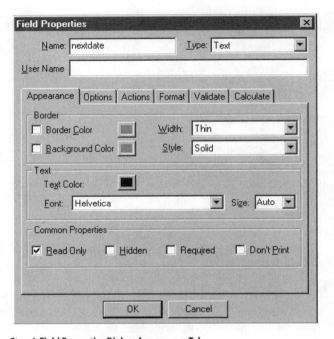

Step 4: Field Properties Dialog-Appearance Tab

Enter "nextdate" as the field name and select Text as the field type. Leave the User Name field blank.

Activate the Appearance tab. We don't need a Border or Background Color. Select a color the text will display by clicking the Text Color chip. Select Helvetica as the Font and Auto as the Size. Finally, select the Read Only checkbox.

Now activate the Format tab. The Format tab allows us to regulate the formatting of information entered into the field. Choose Date from the Category list and pick a date format from the Date Options list.

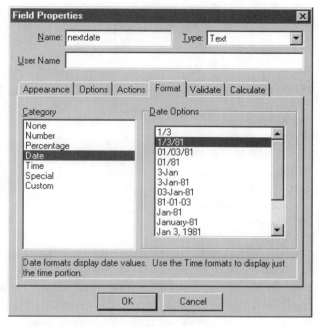

Step 4: Field Properties Dialog-Format Tab

Click the OK button. The dialog closes, adding the field to the document.

Step 5

Coverage Type Field—Combo Box

Now we'll add the 'covtype' field. With Acrobat Exchange's forms tool selected, drag out a rectangle defining the area where you want to display the medical plan's description. The Field Properties dialog box appears, asking for specifics about the field we're creating.

Enter "covtype" as the field name and select Combo Box as the field type. Again leave the User Name field blank. We want this field's name to be exported as "class" and not anything else when the form is submitted.

Activate the Appearance tab. Select a Border and a Background Color. Try black as the border and white as the background color. Select black as the text color by clicking the Text Color chip. Select Helvetica as the Font and 12 as the Size. Finally check the Required checkbox.

Now activate the Options tab. Here we'll enter the items to display in our combo box. We want the drop down list to contain four items. The types of coverage we'll allow are:

Item	Export Value
I decline coverage	0
PPO-Self	1
PPO-Self and spouse	2
PPO-Self and child(ren)	3
PPO-Family	4
HMO-Self	5
HMO-Self and spouse	6
HMO-Self and child(ren)	7
HMO-Family	8

Enter each item and its corresponding export value that the form sends to the server and click the Add button. If you enter the items out of order, you can move them around in the list by selecting an item and clicking the up or down button. Choose the combo box's default value by selecting it. When the four values are entered, select "I decline coverage" as the default value and click the OK button to save the field to the document.

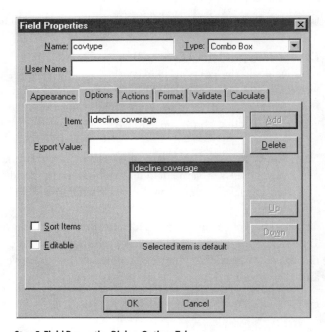

Step 5: Field Properties Dialog-Options Tab

Step 6

Current Date Field

Now we'll add a current date field. This is a read only field that we insert for the current date of the submission. With Acrobat Exchange's forms tool, create a rectangle defining the area where you want to display the date. The Field Properties dialog box appears.

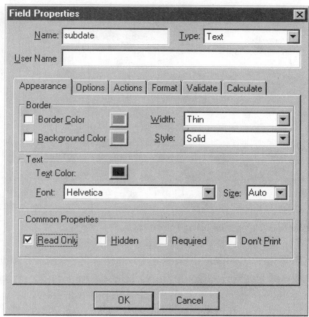

Step 6: Field Properties Dialog-Appearance Tab

Enter "subdate" as the field name and select Text as the field type. We left the User Name field blank. It's used if we want to have a different field name exported with this field's value when the form is submitted.

Activate the Appearance tab. We don't want a Border or Background Color so make sure they're not selected. Select a color the text will display by clicking the Text Color chip. Select Helvetica as the Font and Auto as the Size. Finally, select the Read Only checkbox. This text box will hold and display text but it won't allow a user to enter any information.

Now activate the Format tab. The Format tab allows us to regulate the formatting of information entered into the field. Choose Date from the Category list and pick a date format from the Date Options list.

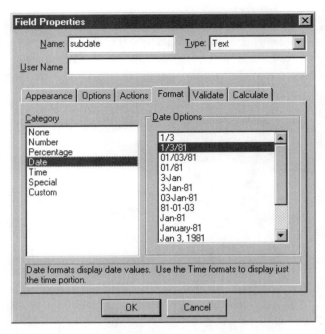

Step 6: Field Properties Dialog-Format Tab

Right now we have a date field, but to make it useful we'll need to attach a bit of JavaScript. To do this, while still in the Format tab, select the Custom Category and click the Edit button. The Acrobat JavaScript editing window appears. Type in the following code:

```
1.    var d = new Date();
2.    d.setDate(d.getDate());
3.    event.value = util.printd("mm/dd/yy", d);
```

This script gets today's date and sets the current field's value to the date. The first line of this script creates a new date value. A reference to this date is stored in the variable "d". The second line of this script uses two member functions of the date object. The second line calls the setDate member function to actually set the numeric value of the date. The parameter passed into the function is the result of the getDate member function. In short, we're setting the date to the value returned by getDate. This value is today's date. The third line of this script formats and prints the value in our "d" variable. We've formatted it as "mm/dd/yy", two digits for month, two digits for day, and two digits for year. This formatted string is stored in the event.value field of the current event. In this case, the script is called whenever the field is asked to format its contents.

Click the OK button. The dialog closes, adding the field to the document.

Step 7

"idnumber" Field—Hidden Text

The first hidden field we'll create is the "idnumber" field. To create the field, choose the forms tool button on the Acrobat Exchange toolbar. The cursor changes to a crosshair. Click the mouse button and drag out a rectangle defining the area where you want the user to enter their idnumber. The Field Properties dialog box appears asking for specifics about the text field we're creating.

Step 7: Field Properties Dialog-Appearance Tab

Enter "idnumber" as the field name and select Text as the field type. Leave the User Name field blank. Enter a value here only if you want to export a different field name with this field's value when the form is submitted to a server.

Activate the Appearance tab. Make sure the Border or Background Colors aren't selected. Select a color the text will display by clicking the Text Color chip. Select Helvetica as the Font and 12 as the Size. On this dialog tab, be sure to select the Hidden and Read Only checkboxes. Selecting the Read Only checkbox insures the user won't enter any information in this field. The Hidden option makes this field invisible.

Finally, activate the Validate tab. The Validate tab lets us set up a field to validate the value of this field. Click the custom validate script radio button and then click the Edit button. The Acrobat JavaScript editing window appears. Type in the following code.

```
1.  var f = this.getField("idnumber");
2.  global.idnumber = f.value;
```

This simple script grabs the value of our idnumber field and stores it in the global JavaScript object. The first line of this script gets a reference to the idnumber field and stores it in the variable "f". The second line accesses the "value" member of "f" and copies it to the global object in a field we can reference later. The global JavaScript object exists inside Acrobat and can be used to share information between documents. We can access this value later by simply referencing it as global.idnumber.

Step 8

Password Field—Hidden Text
Now we'll add the password field. This is a special text field where we store the user's password to submit to the server.

With the Acrobat Exchange's forms tool, create the field where the password will be placed. The Field Properties dialog box appears asking for specifics about the new field.

Step 8: Field Properties Dialog-Appearance Tab

Enter "password" as the field name and select Text as the field type. Again we leave the User Name field blank.

Activate the Appearance tab. We don't need to select a Border or Background Color due to our form's design. Make sure the text color is black. If it isn't, change it to black by clicking the Text Color chip. Select Helvetica as the Font and 12 as the Size. Be sure to select the Hidden and Read Only checkboxes. We don't want the user to enter any information in this field. Clicking the Read Only checkbox insures the user won't. The Hidden option makes this field invisible.

Step 8: Field Properties Dialog-Options Tab

Now activate the options tab. Here we'll enter the default text displayed in the field. Here we've entered "password". This will be custom tailored to the specific user by our back-end process. You can select the Password checkbox, but remember the field is hidden so the user won't see it anyway.

Once you've completed your choices, click the OK button. The dialog closes, adding the field to the document.

Creating the Claims HTML Files

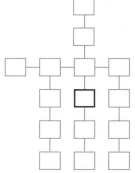

The HTML claims files for this application are generated dynamically by a Perl script on the server machine. Each type of claim is sent to the server and the database is queried for matching records. If any are found an HTML page is constructed dymanically and forwarded to the user. The creation of these files is discussed in the code examples section of this project.

Creating the Medical FAQ HTML File

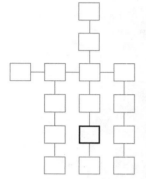

The Medical FAQ file is an HTML document we use to display a list of frequently asked questions and answers regarding the available medical plan. The following steps discuss creating the static HTML file used to display this information.

Create the HTML page

This file was visually created using Claris HomePage. Using a WSIWYG application to create HTML pages is becoming more popular, but the HTML created by these editors varies greatly. It is common to use visual editors to prototype pages but it is almost always necessary to edit the HTML using a text editor to guarantee its consistency. The following example details the HTML used to create the static HTML page. Actually, any page would do, but we'll briefly touch on the structure calling out several useful HTML tags.

```
1.   <HTML>
2.   <HEAD>
3.     <TITLE>Medical FAQ's</TITLE>
4.   </HEAD>
5.   <BODY BGCOLOR="#FFFFFF">
6.   <P><TABLE BORDER=0 CELLPADDING=6 WIDTH=640
     HEIGHT=100>
7.     <TR>
8.       <TD VALIGN=bottom bgcolor="#3F4CFF">
9.       <H3><B><FONT SIZE="+4" FACE="Helvetica"
     COLOR="#FFFFFF">Insurance Plan
     FAQ's</FONT></B></H3>
10.      </TD></TR>
11.  </TABLE><TABLE BORDER=0 WIDTH=640>
12.    <TR>
13.      <TD WIDTH="33%">
14.        <P>
15.      </TD><TD COLSPAN=2>
16.        <P><B><FONT FACE="Helvetica">1. how long
     does it take for my claim to be
     processed? </FONT></B>
17.  </TD></TR>
18.    <TR>
```

```
19.        <TD COLSPAN=3>
20.          <P><FONT FACE="Helvetica">We enter all
claims within 72 hours of receipt. Once a claim is
entered, every effort is made to complete the pro-
cessing and mail payment, if any, within three
weeks. </FONT></P>
21.          <P>
22.        </TD></TR>
23.    <TR>
24.      <TD WIDTH="33%">
25.          <P>
26.        </TD><TD COLSPAN=2>
27.          <P><B><FONT FACE="Helvetica">2. what's an
          eob?</FONT></B> 
          </TD></TR>
28.    <TR>
29.      <TD COLSPAN=3>
30.          <P><FONT FACE="Helvetica">"EOB" stands for
"Explanation of Benefits". Every claim contains
EOB information, detailing coverage, costs, and
any remarks related to its processing. If you have
questions about any information contained within
an EOB, please call customer service. The repre-
sentative will need your name, social security
number, doctor's name and service date to answer
your questions. </FONT></P>
31.          <P>
32.        </TD></TR>
33.    <TR>
34.      <TD WIDTH="33%">
35.          <P>
36.        </TD><TD COLSPAN=2>
37.          <P><B><FONT FACE="Helvetica">3. how can i
tell if my doctor is part of the
network?</FONT></B>
38.        </TD></TR>
39.    <TR>
40.      <TD COLSPAN=3>
41.          <P><FONT FACE="Helvetica">A Network
Directory of Providers for your company's region
```

is distributed to each individualupon enrollment
into the plan. Participating doctors for each
region are outlined by specialty. The Directory
is updated annually, so do not assume that all
listings are current. To verify if a doctor is
currently participating in the plan, go to the
Network Doctor site or call customer
service. </FONT></P>

```
42.          <P>
43.        </TD></TR>
44.      <TR>
45.        <TD WIDTH="33%">
46.          <P>
47.        </TD><TD COLSPAN=2>
48.          <P><B><FONT FACE="Helvetica">4. how do i
add a dependent?</FONT></B>
49.        </TD></TR>
50.      <TR>
51.        <TD COLSPAN=3>
52.          <P><FONT FACE="Helvetica">Dependents may
only be added or deleted if one of the following
"life events" occurs: Marriage, birth/adoption of
a child, death or divorce.</FONT></P>
53.          <P><FONT FACE="Helvetica">Participants
have 30 days from the date of the event to make
changes in their coverage. If this window of
opportunity is missed, the next occasion to make
changes will be the plan's Open Enrollment date.
Contact your company's Plan Administrator for more
details.</FONT></P>
54.          <P>
55.        </TD></TR>
56.      <TR>
57.        <TD WIDTH="33%">
58.          <P>
59.        </TD><TD COLSPAN=2>
60.          <P><B><FONT FACE="Helvetica">5. where can
i find detailed benefit information on the
plan?</FONT></B>
61.        </TD></TR>
```

```
62.      <TR>
63.        <TD COLSPAN=3>
64.          <P><FONT FACE="Helvetica">All participants
are furnished with both a comprehensive plan
document and a condensed plan summary sheet upon
enrollment. The information is also located on the
Plan Summary page of your Benefit Information
site. Customer service can also answer questions
and explain how benefits work.</FONT></P>
65.      <P>
66.      </TD></TR>
67.      </TABLE></P>
68.      </BODY>
69.      </HTML>
```

Examining the HTML Code

Lines one through five are standard opening HTML and line seven is where things begin to get interesting.

On line six we create a table using the <TABLE> tag. The <TABLE> tag is a diatomic tag, meaning it requires a closing tag. The table is opened on line seven, but not closed until line 11. For large tables, it is wise to break the data into several smaller tables. This strategy doesn't change the layout or look of a file, but it does allow the browser to display data received while it waits to download the file's remaining tables.

The items contained in the table are questions followed by their answers. Line 12 starts the row that contains our first question. Each row in a table is contained within the diatomic <TR></TR> tags. To divide a row further, each row can contain details, or cells. The first detail is added on line 13. It is to occupy 33% of the browser window in width. This detail is just a placeholder, so only the paragraph tag is placed in it. Empty details are an excellent way to control placement of text and graphics. Their sole purpose is to adjust the placement of the next detail cell. On line 15 we add the cell that contains our question. We also set the font to bold and ask the browser to use Helvetica if it's available. On line 17 we close the detail. Lines 19 through 22 are where we add the question's answer.

```
12.      <TR>
13.        <TD WIDTH="33%">
14.          <P>
```

```
15.        </TD><TD COLSPAN=2>
16.          <P><B><FONT FACE="Helvetica">1. how long
   does it take for my claim to be
   processed? </FONT></B>
17.        </TD></TR>
```

Finally, the table containing our questions and answers is closed on line 67. The body of the document is closed on line 68 and the HTML document is closed on line 69.

```
67.      </TABLE></P>
68.      </BODY>
69.      </HTML>
```

No matter what method you decide to use to create this file, be sure the HTML resembles the above example. Maintaining a consistent approach to HTML creation makes a world of difference when you have to go back and fix display or downloading problems.

Creating the Doctors List HTML File

The Medical Doctors List file is another static HTML document used to display a list of approved medical plan doctors. The following steps discuss creating the static HTML file used to display this information.

The designer used Adobe PageMill to construct the HTML document. The HTML code was then reviewed using a text editor to verify its consistency. The next steps discuss creating the form fields in Acrobat Exchange to handle the client side interaction of this transaction.

This file was visually created using Adobe PageMill. As noted earlier, using a WSIWYG application to create HTML pages is popular but the HTML created by these editors varies greatly. The following example illustrates the HTML used to create the static document.

```
1.      <HTML>
2.      <HEAD>
3.        <TITLE>Doctor's Directory</TITLE>
4.      </HEAD>
```

```
5.    <BODY BGCOLOR="#FFFFFF">
6.     <TABLE BORDER=0 CELLPADDING=6 WIDTH=640
      HEIGHT=100>
7.       <TR>
8.         <TD VALIGN=bottom bgcolor="#3F4CFF">
9.           <H3><B><FONT SIZE="+4" FACE="Helvetica"
      COLOR="#FFFFFF">Doctor's Directory</FONT></B></H3>
10.        </TD></TR>
11.    </TABLE>   <TABLE BORDER=0 WIDTH=640>
12.      <TR>
13.        <TD WIDTH="33%" VALIGN=MIDDLE>
14.          <P> 
15.        </TD><TD VALIGN=top COLSPAN=2 WIDTH="66%">
16.          <P><B><FONT FACE="Helvetica">directory of
             participating health care
             providers</FONT></B></P>
17.          <P> 
18.        </TD></TR>
19.      <TR>
20.        <TD WIDTH="33%">
21.          <P>
22.        </TD><TD WIDTH="33%">
23.          <P>
24.        </TD><TD WIDTH="33%">
25.          <P>
26.        </TD></TR>
27.      <TR>
28.        <TD WIDTH="33%">
29.          <P>
30.        </TD><TD VALIGN=top WIDTH="33%">
31.          <P><B><FONT FACE="Helvetica">
             Allergy &amp; Immunology</FONT></B>
32.        </TD><TD WIDTH="33%">
33.          <P><B><FONT FACE="Helvetica">
             Family Practice</FONT></B>
34.        </TD></TR>
35.      <TR>
36.        <TD WIDTH="33%">
37.          <P>
38.        </TD><TD VALIGN=top WIDTH="33%">
39.          <P><FONT FACE="Helvetica">Jane Keys<BR>
             10 Vista View<BR>
```

```
40.              Berkeley, CA 90009</FONT></P>
41.              <P><FONT FACE="Helvetica">Joe Bickler<BR>
42.              6666 Skyline Rd.<BR>
43.              San Francisco, CA 94111</FONT>
44.          </TD><TD VALIGN=top WIDTH="33%">
45.              <P><FONT FACE="Helvetica">Chuck Szabo<BR>
46.              444 Army St.<BR>
47.              San Francisco, CA 90089</FONT></P>
48.               <P><FONT FACE="Helvetica">David Lewis<BR>
49.              6500 Geary Blvd.<BR>
50.              San Francisco, CA 97787</FONT></P>
51.              <P> 
52.          </TD></TR>
53.      <TR>
54.          <TD WIDTH="33%">
55.              <P>
56.          </TD><TD WIDTH="33%">
57.              <P><B><FONT FACE="Helvetica">
                 Internal Medicine</FONT></B>
58.          </TD><TD WIDTH="33%">
59.              <P><B><FONT FACE="Helvetica">
60.              Obstetrics</FONT></B>
             </TD></TR>
61.      <TR>
62.          <TD WIDTH="33%">
63.               <P>
64.          </TD><TD VALIGN=top WIDTH="33%">
65.              <P><FONT FACE="Helvetica">
                 Madeleine O'Hara<BR>
66.              50 First St.<BR>
67.              Oakland, CA 90089</FONT></P>
68.              <P><FONT FACE="Helvetica">Alvin Poster<BR>
69.              4443 S. Main St.<BR>
70.              Emeryville, CA 99999</FONT></P>
71.              <P> 
72.          </TD><TD VALIGN=top WIDTH="33%">
73.              <P><FONT FACE="Helvetica">Lucy Conner<BR>
74.              444 Stanyan St.<BR>

75.              San Francisco, CA 90008</FONT></P>
```

```
76.        <P><FONT FACE="Helvetica">
           Samuel Noonan<BR>
77.        200 Bush St., Suite 600<BR>
78.        San Francisco, CA 98990</FONT></P>
79.        <P> 
80.      </TD></TR>
81.    <TR>
82.      <TD WIDTH="33%">
83.        <P>
84.      </TD><TD WIDTH="33%">
85.        <P><B><FONT FACE="Helvetica">
           Orthopedic Surgery</FONT></B>
86.      </TD><TD WIDTH="33%">
87.        <P><B><FONT FACE="Helvetica">
           Pediatrics</FONT></B>
88.      </TD></TR>
89.    <TR>
90.      <TD WIDTH="33%">
91.        <P>
92.      </TD><TD VALIGN=top WIDTH="33%">
93.        <P><FONT FACE="Helvetica">Jane Keys<BR>
94.        10 Vista View<BR>
95.        Berkeley, CA 90009</FONT></P>
96.        <P><FONT FACE="Helvetica">Joe Bickler<BR>
97.        6666 Skyline Rd.<BR>
98.        San Francisco, CA 94111</FONT>
99.      </TD><TD VALIGN=top WIDTH="33%">
100.       <P><FONT FACE="Helvetica">Lucy Conner<BR>
101.       444 Stanyan St.<BR>
102.       San Francisco, CA 90008</FONT></P>
103.       <P><FONT FACE="Helvetica">Samuel Noonan<BR>
104.       200 Bush St., Suite 600<BR>
105.       San Francisco, CA 98990</FONT></P>
106.       <P> 
107.     </TD></TR>
108.   <TR>
109.     <TD WIDTH="33%">
110.       <P>
111.     </TD><TD VALIGN=top WIDTH="33%">
112.       <P><B><FONT FACE="Helvetica">Sports
```

```
113.  Medicine</FONT></B>
         </TD><TD VALIGN=top WIDTH="33%">
114.        <P><B><FONT FACE="Helvetica">
            Thoracic Surgery</FONT></B>
115.     </TD></TR>
116.    <TR>
117.     <TD WIDTH="33%">
118.        <P>
119.     </TD><TD WIDTH="33%">
120.        <P><FONT FACE="Helvetica">
            Madeleine O'Hara<BR>
121.        50 First St.<BR>
122.        Oakland, CA 90089</FONT></P>
123.        <P><FONT FACE="Helvetica">Alvin Poster<BR>
124.        4443 S. Main St.<BR>
125.        Emeryville, CA 99999</FONT></P>
126.        <P> 
127.     </TD><TD WIDTH="33%">
128.        <P><FONT FACE="Helvetica">Chuck Szabo<BR>
129.        444 Army St.<BR>
130.        San Francisco, CA90089</FONT></P>
131.        <P><FONT FACE="Helvetica">David Lewis<BR>
132.        6500 Geary Blvd.<BR>
133.        San Francisco, CA 97787</FONT></P>
134.        <P> 
135.     </TD></TR>
136.  </TABLE>
137.  </BODY>
138.  </HTML>
```

Examining the HTML Code

Line one is the tag that indicates the beginning of the HTML file. Lines two, three, and four define our file's head. The head can contain scripts, meta information, and other tags, but this bare bones head contains only the document title that is displayed in the browser's window. Line five declares the document's body opens here and sets the document's background color to white.

On line six we create a table using the <TABLE> tag. For large tables, it is advisable to break them into several smaller tables. Browsers will display a table once it is completely downloaded even though there is still more information needed to display the whole file. The table definition includes three parameters that instruct the browser about how the table is to be constructed. This table sets the CELLPADDING=6, BORDER=0, HEIGHT=100 and WIDTH=640. There is no extra space in between cells and there is no width on this table's border. The table width is set to 640. This tells the browser to construct the table using 640 pixels as the table width.

Tables are easy to construct. Once we've opened a table with the <TABLE> tag, we add rows to it using the <TR></TR> tags. Inside the table row tags we place <TD></TD> tags that contain table data. These tags indicate how many cells are in the row. Two <TD> tag pairs mean the row contains two cells of information. This is how we construct the first row of our table. On line 12 we open a row. On line 13 we add a cell of table data that has a width of 33% of the table. The vertical alignment or VALIGN is set to middle. This centers the text in the middle of the cell. The data in these cells is just a non-breaking space. It's inserted to put something in the cell. We could do without the cell altogether but it's useful to construct blank table cells to control the spacing of other table cells. The table row is closed on line 18.

```
11.   </TABLE>   <TABLE BORDER=0 WIDTH=640>
12.      <TR>
13.        <TD WIDTH="33%" VALIGN=MIDDLE>
14.          <P> 
15.        </TD><TD VALIGN=top COLSPAN=2 WIDTH="66%">
16.        <P><B><FONT FACE="Helvetica">directory of
participating health care providers</FONT></B></P>
17.          <P> 
18.        </TD></TR>
```

We add another row to the table on line 27. Inside the row tags we place two <TD> tag pairs that contain data. The two cells in this row contain the type of doctor that will be displayed below it. Lines 31 inserts the type Family Practice. We use the <B> tag to make the text bold and the <FONT FACE="Helvetica"> tag and attribute to try and force a font choice.

```
33.          <P><B><FONT FACE="Helvetica">
             Family Practice</FONT></B>
34.        </TD></TR>
```

We add another row to the table on line 35. Inside the row tags we place two <TD> tag pairs that contain data. The three cells in this row contain the doctor's information that relates to the row we created above it. Lines 39 through 41 and 42 through 44 insert the doctor's name and address.

```
35.      <TR>
36.        <TD WIDTH="33%">
37.          <P>
38.        </TD><TD VALIGN=top WIDTH="33%">
39.          <P><FONT FACE="Helvetica">Jane Keys<BR>
             10 Vista View<BR>
40.          Berkeley, CA 90009</FONT></P>
41.          <P><FONT FACE="Helvetica">Joe Bickler<BR>
42.          6666 Skyline Rd.<BR>
43.          San Francisco, CA 94111</FONT>
44.        </TD><TD VALIGN=top WIDTH="33%">
45.          <P><FONT FACE="Helvetica">Chuck Szabo<BR>
46.          444 Army St.<BR>
47.          San Francisco, CA 90089</FONT></P>
48.           <P><FONT FACE="Helvetica">David Lewis<BR>
49.          6500 Geary Blvd.<BR>
50.          San Francisco, CA 97787</FONT></P>
51.          <P> 
52.        </TD></TR>
```

This procedure of adding rows and cells to the table is repeated for each type and doctor we want to add to the table.

```
136.     </TABLE>
137.     </BODY>
138.     </HTML>
```

Finally, on line 136 we close the table. On lines 137 and 138 we close the document's body and then the HTML document itself.

Since this file is static, it can be created using a number of methods. Definition lists and tables are two common approaches. If you construct this page using tables, open the file you'll use with a text editor and be sure the HTML resembles the above example.

Creating the Employee Information PDF File

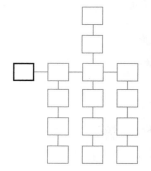

This PDF form displays a name, a social security number, date of birth, address, city, state, ZIP code, home telephone, marital status, gender, date of hire, hours worked per week, company telephone, and information for a variable number of dependents. This information is editable.

The designer used Adobe Illustrator to construct the original form. The file was then distilled into PDF format. The next steps discuss creating the form fields in Acrobat Exchange to handle the client side interaction of this transaction.

Step 1

The Form Field Names
The fields we want to display on this form are as follows.

name	named1
ssnumber	reld1
dob	genderd1
address	ssnumberd1
city	dobd1
state	named2
zip	reld2
homephone	genderd2
status	ssnumberd2
gender	dobd2
hired	idnumber
hours	password
officephone	

Step 2

Name Field
The first field we'll create is the name field. To create the field, choose the forms tool button on the Acrobat Exchange toolbar. The cursor changes to a crosshair. Click the mouse button and drag out a rectangle defining the area where you want the user to enter their name. The Field Properties dialog box appears, asking for specifics about the text field we're creating.

Step 2: Field Properties Dialog-Appearance Tab

Enter "name" as the field name and select Text as the field type. Leave the User Name field blank. Enter a value here only if you want to export a different field name with this field's value when the form is submitted to a server.

Activate the Appearance tab. Here we're presented with options that affect the field's appearance. Our designer decided to create the fields as a graphic so we don't have a Border or Background Color selected. If the designer didn't add a field graphic, the Acrobat forms plug-in provides options to create a field with an outline or a background color. Select a color the text will display by clicking the Text Color chip. Select Helvetica as the Font and Auto as the Size. The text is sized to fit the box we've just drawn. Finally check the Required checkbox.

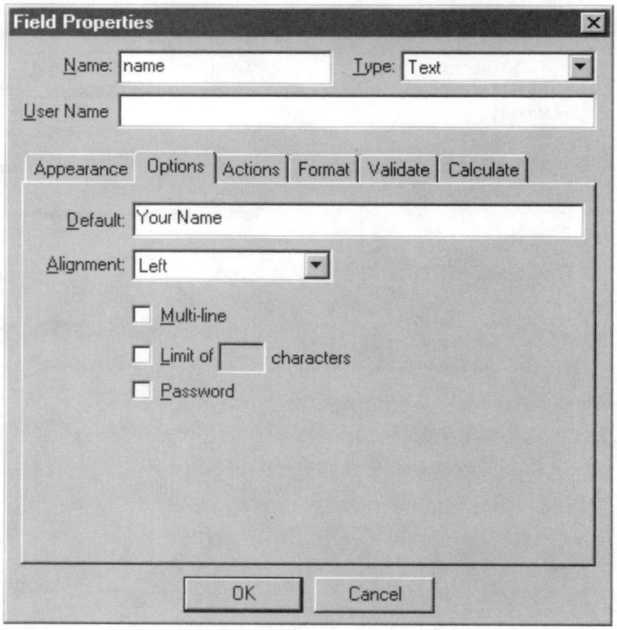

Step 2: Field Properties Dialog-Options Tab

Now activate the Options tab. Here we'll enter the default text displayed in the field. Here we've entered "Your Name". This is the default text that will appear if something goes wrong. Once the user has successfully logged on, the real information is received from the database and flowed into the form.

Once you've completed your choices, click the OK button. The dialog closes, adding the field to the document.

Step 3

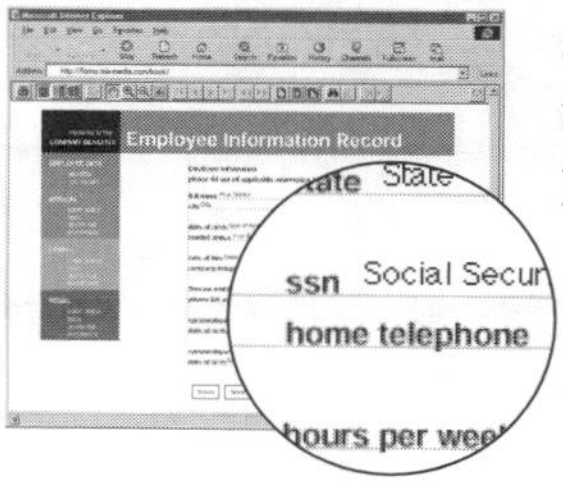

"ssnumber" Field

Now we'll add the "ssnumber" field. With Acrobat Exchange's forms tool selected, drag out a rectangle defining the area where you want to display the Social Security Number code. The Field Properties dialog box appears, asking for specifics about the field we're creating.

Step 3: Field Properties Dialog-Appearance Tab

Enter "ssnumber" as the field name and select Text as the field type. We left the User Name field blank because we want the field name to be "ssnumber" when the form is submitted.

Activate the Appearance tab. Make sure the Border or Background Colors aren't selected. Select a color the text will display by clicking the Text Color chip. Select Helvetica as the Font and 12 as the Size.

Next activate the Options tab. Enter the default text to display in the field. Leave the limit on the number of characters and the password fields unchecked for now.

Now Activate the Format tab. The Format tab allows us to regulate the formatting of information entered into the field. Choose Special from the Category list and pick Social Security Number from the Special Options list. This insures users only enter digits. If they try to enter letters, the system beeps and doesn't enter the character in the field. It also formats the entry, inserting hyphens after the first three digits and the first five digits.

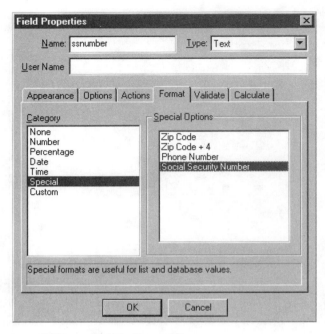

Step 3: Field Properties Dialog-Format Tab

Click the OK button. The dialog closes, adding the field to the document.

Step 4

Date Field

Now we'll add a date field used to store the date of birth. This field allows a user to enter a date and formats it in the way we specify. Error checking is performed and the user is warned if they try to enter information that can't be converted into a date. With Acrobat Exchange's forms tool, define the area where the user will enter the date. The Field Properties dialog box appears, asking for specifics about the field we're creating.

Step 4: Field Properties Dialog-Appearance Tab

Enter "dob" as the field name and select Text as the field type. Leave the User Name field blank.

Activate the Appearance tab. We don't need a Border or Background Color. Select a color the text will display by clicking the Text Color chip. Select Helvetica as the Font and Auto as the Size.

Now activate the Format tab. The Format tab allows us to regulate the formatting of information entered into the field. Choose Date from the Category list and pick a date format from the Date Options list.

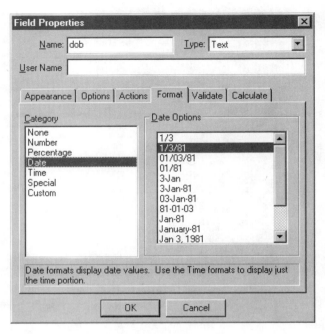

Step 4: Field Properties Dialog-Format Tab

Click the OK button. The dialog closes, adding the field to the document.

Step 5

Address, City, and State Fields

Now we'll create the address, city, and state fields. To create these fields we'll repeat step two for each field. The Field Properties dialog box appears each time we create a field, asking for specifics about the text field we're creating.

As you create each field, activate the Appearance tab, enter the field name and be sure to select Text as the field type. Select Helvetica as the Font and 12 as the Size. Finally check the Required checkbox. The user will be warned if they don't fill out this field before submitting the form to the server.

For each field we add, activate the Options tab. Here we'll enter the default text displayed in the field. Enter some unique identifier, giving the user a hint about what to enter. Leave the limit on the number of characters and the password fields unchecked for now.

For each field, click the OK button, closing the dialog and adding the field to the document.

Step 6

ZIP code Field

Now we'll add a ZIP code field. With Acrobat Exchange's forms tool selected, drag out a rectangle defining the area where you want to display the ZIP code. The Field Properties dialog box appears, asking for specifics about the field we're creating.

Field Properties

Name: zip   Type: Text

User Name

Appearance | Options | Actions | Format | Validate | Calculate

Border
☐ Border Color   Width: Thin
☐ Background Color   Style: Solid

Text
Text Color:
Font: Helvetica   Size: 12

Common Properties
☐ Read Only   ☐ Hidden   ☑ Required   ☐ Don't Print

OK   Cancel

Step 6: Field Properties Dialog-Appearance Tab

Enter "zip" as the field name and select Text as the field type. We left the User Name field blank because we want the field name to be "zip" when the form is submitted.

Activate the Appearance tab. Make sure the Border or Background Colors aren't selected. Select a color the text will display by clicking the Text Color chip. Select Helvetica as the Font and 12 as the Size.

Next activate the Options tab. Enter the default text to display in the field. Leave the limit on the number of characters and the password fields unchecked for now.

Now Activate the Format tab. The Format tab allows us to regulate the formatting of information entered into the field. Choose Special from the category list and pick ZIP code from the Special Options List. This insures users only enter five digits. If they try to enter letters, the system beeps and doesn't enter the characters in the field.

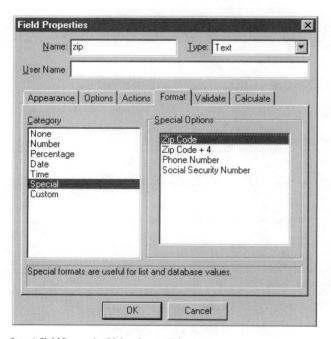

Step 6: Field Properties Dialog-Format Tab

Click the OK button. The dialog closes, adding the field to the document.

Step 7

Telephone Field

Now we'll add a telephone field. With Acrobat Exchange's forms tool selected, drag out a rectangle defining the area where you want to display the telephone number. The Field Properties dialog box appears, asking for specifics about the field we're creating.

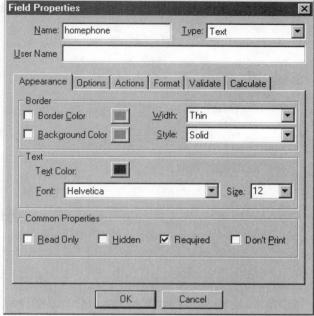

Step 7: Field Properties Dialog-Appearance Tab

Enter "homephone" as the field name and select Text as the field type. We left the User Name field blank because we want the field name to be "homephone" when the form is submitted.

Activate the Appearance tab. Make sure the Border or Background Colors aren't selected. Select a color the text will display by clicking the Text Color chip. Select Helvetica as the Font and 12 as the Size.

Next activate the Options tab. Enter the default text to display in the field. Leave the limit on the number of characters and the password fields unchecked for now.

Now Activate the Format tab. The Format tab allows us to regulate the formatting of information entered into the field. Choose Special from the Category list and pick Phone Number from the Special Options list. This insures users only enter digits. If they try to enter letters, the system beeps and doesn't enter the characters in the field.

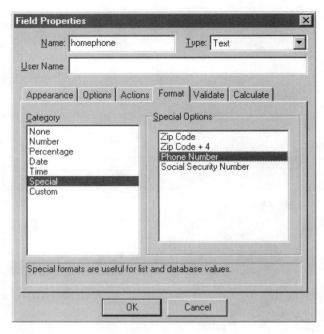

Step 7: Field Properties Dialog-Format Tab

Click the OK button. The dialog closes, adding the field to the document.

Step 8

Marital Status Text Field—Read only

Next we'll create another read only field to hold the Marital Status text. To create the field, choose the forms tool button on the Acrobat Exchange toolbar. Click the mouse button and drag out a rectangle defining the area where you want to position the marital status text. The Field Properties dialog box appears, asking for specifics about the text field we're creating.

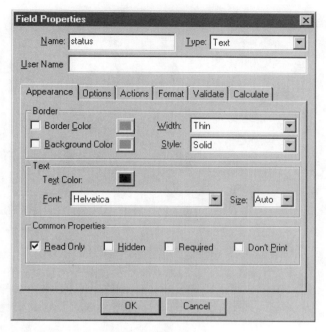

Step 8: Field Properties Dialog-Appearance Tab

Enter "status" as the field name and select Text as the field type. Leave the User Name field blank.

Activate the Appearance tab. Here we're presented with options that affect the field's appearance. Our designer decided to create the fields as a graphic, so we don't have a Border or Background Color selected. Select a color the text will display by clicking the Text Color chip. Select Helvetica as the Font and Auto as the Size. The text is sized to fit the box we've just drawn. Finally check the Read Only checkbox.

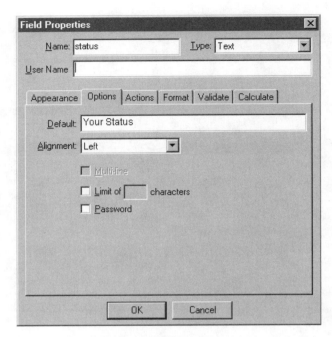

Step 8: Field Properties Dialog-Options Tab

Now activate the Options tab. Here we'll enter the default text displayed in the field. Here we've entered "Your Status". This will be custom tailored to the specific user by our back-end process.

Once you've completed your choices, click the OK button. The dialog closes, adding the field to the document.

Step 9

Gender Text Field—Read Only

Next we'll create another read only field to hold the gender text. To create the field, choose the forms tool button on the Acrobat Exchange toolbar. Click the mouse button and drag out a rectangle defining the area where you want to position the dental plan text. The Field Properties dialog box appears, asking for specifics about the text field we're creating.

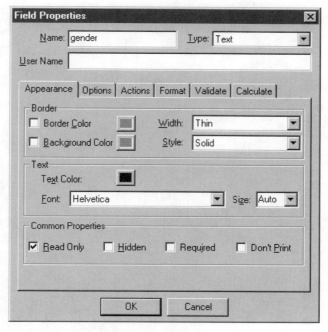

Step 9: Field Properties Dialog-Appearance Tab

Enter "gender" as the field name and select Text as the field type. Leave the User Name field blank.

Activate the Appearance tab. Here we're presented with options that affect the field's appearance. Our designer decided to create the fields as a graphic, so we don't have a Border or Background Color selected. If the designer didn't add a field graphic, the Acrobat forms plug-in provides options to create a field with an outline or a background color. Select a color the text will display by clicking the Text Color chip. Select Helvetica as the Font and Auto as the Size. The text is sized to fit the box we've just drawn. Finally check the Read Only checkbox.

Step 9: Field Properties Dialog-Options Tab

Now activate the Options tab. Here we'll enter the default text displayed in the field. Here we've entered "Your Gender". This will be custom tailored to the specific user by our back-end process.

Once you've completed your choices, click the OK button. The dialog closes, adding the field to the document.

Step 10

Hired Date Field

Now we'll add a hired date field. This field allows a user to enter a date and formats it in the way we specify. Error checking is performed and the user is warned if they try to enter information that can't be converted into a date. With Acrobat Exchange's forms tool, define the area where the user will enter the date. The Field Properties dialog box appears, asking for specifics about the field we're creating.

Step 10: Field Properties Dialog-Appearance Tab

Enter "hired" as the field name and select Text as the field type. Leave the User Name field blank.

Activate the Appearance tab. We don't need a Border or Background Color. Select a color the text will display by clicking the Text Color chip. Select Helvetica as the Font and Auto as the Size. Be sure to check the Read Only checkbox.

Now Activate the Format tab. The Format tab allows us to regulate the formatting of information entered into the field. Choose Date from the Category list and pick a date format from the Date Options list.

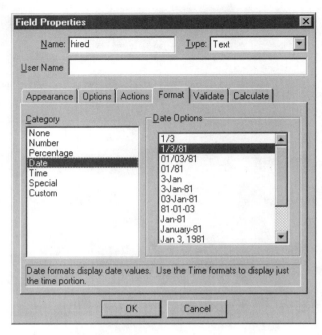

Step 10: Field Properties Dialog-Format Tab

Click the OK button. The dialog closes, adding the field to the document.

Step 11

Hours Worked Per Week Field—Read Only
Now we'll add the hours per week field. This is a read only field where we display the hours worked per week. It's sent to the form by the back-end process but we'll create a placeholder for it here.

With Acrobat Exchange's forms tool, create the field where the number will be placed. The Field Properties dialog box appears, asking for specifics about the new number field.

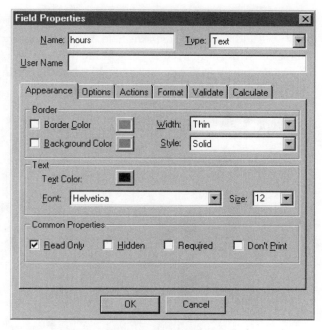

Step 11: Field Properties Dialog-Appearance Tab

Enter "hours" as the field name and select Text as the field type. Again we leave the User Name field blank.

Activate the Appearance tab. We don't need to select a Border or Background Color due to our form's design. Make sure the text color is black. If it isn't, change it to black by clicking the Text Color chip. Select Courier Bold as the Font and 12 as the Size. Finally select the Read Only checkbox. This text box will hold and display text but it won't allow a user to enter any information.

Now activate the Format tab. The Format tab allows us to regulate the formatting of information entered into the field. Choose Number from the Category list and Decimal places to "0" from the Number Options list.

Now click the Field Properties dialog's OK button. The dialog closes, adding the field to the document.

Step 12

Office Telephone Field

Now we'll add an office telephone field. With Acrobat Exchange's forms tool selected, drag out a rectangle defining the area where you want to display the telephone number. The Field Properties dialog box appears, asking for specifics about the field we're creating.

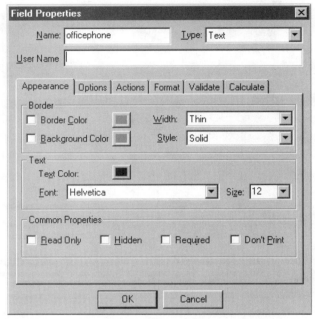

Step 12: Field Properties Dialog-Appearance Tab

Enter "officephone" as the field name and select Text as the field type. We left the User Name field blank because we want the field name to be "telephone" when the form is submitted.

Activate the Appearance tab. Make sure the Border or Background Colors aren't selected. Select a color the text will display by clicking the Text Color chip. Select Helvetica as the Font and 12 as the Size.

Next activate the Options tab. Enter the default text to display in the field. Leave the limit on the number of characters and the password fields unchecked for now.

Now activate the Format tab. The Format tab allows us to regulate the formatting of information entered into the field. Choose Special from the Category list and pick a Phone Number from the Special Options list. This insures users only enter digits. If they try to enter letters, the system beeps and doesn't enter the character in the field.

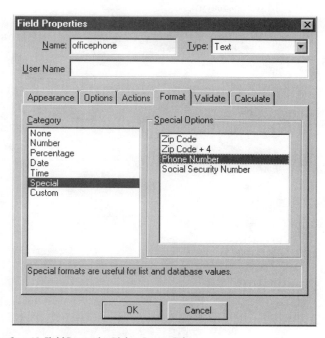

Step 12: Field Properties Dialog-Format Tab

Click the OK button. The dialog closes, adding the field to the document.

Step 13

Employee's Dependent Information Fields

Next we'll add the employee's dependent information. The form we've created displays information for up to two dependents. For each dependent we show their name, relation, gender, social security number, and date of birth. These are Required fields we use to display the information. We'll walk through the creation of the five fields for the first dependent. We can then select these five fields and, by holding down the control key for Windows or the option key for Mac, copy-drag them, creating a duplicate line below.

The first field we'll create is the dependent's name field. To create the field, choose the forms tool button on the Acrobat Exchange toolbar. The cursor changes to a crosshair. Click the mouse button and drag out a rectangle defining the area where you want the user to enter their name. The Field Properties dialog box appears, asking for specifics about the text field we're creating.

Step 13: Field Properties Dialog-Appearance Tab

Enter "named1" as the field name and select Text as the field type. Leave the User Name field blank. Enter a value here only if you want to export a different field name with this field's value when the form is submitted to a server.

Activate the Appearance tab. Here we're presented with options that affect the field's appearance. Our designer decided to create the fields as a graphic so we don't have a Border or Background Color selected. If the designer didn't add a field graphic, the Acrobat forms plug-in provides options to create a field with an outline or a background color. Select a color the text will display by clicking the Text Color chip. Select Helvetica as the Font and Auto as the Size. The text is sized to fit the box we've just drawn. Finally check the Required checkbox.

Field Properties

Name: named1   Type: Text

User Name:

| Appearance | **Options** | Actions | Format | Validate | Calculate |

Default: Dependent Name

Alignment: Left

☐ Multi-line

☐ Limit of [   ] characters

☐ Password

[OK]   [Cancel]

Step 13: Field Properties Dialog-Options Tab

Now activate the Options tab. Here we'll enter the default text displayed in the field. Here we've entered "Dependent Name". This is the default text that will appear if something goes wrong. Once the user has successfully logged on, the real information is received from the database and flowed into the form.

Once you've completed your choices, click the OK button. The dialog closes, adding the field to the document.

Next we'll create another Required field to hold the dependent's relationship. To create the field, choose the forms tool button on the Acrobat Exchange toolbar. Click the mouse button and drag out a rectangle defining the area where you want to position the dependent's relationship text. The Field Properties dialog box appears, asking for specifics about the text field we're creating.

Step 13: Field Properties Dialog-Appearance Tab

Enter "reld1" as the field name and select Text as the field type. Leave the User Name field blank.

Activate the Appearance tab. Here we're presented with options that affect the field's appearance. Our designer decided to create the fields as a graphic so we don't have a Border or Background Color selected. If the designer didn't add a field graphic, the Acrobat forms plug-in provides options to create a field with an outline or a background color. Select a color the text will display by clicking the Text Color chip. Select Helvetica as the Font and Auto as the Size. The text is sized to fit the box we've just drawn. Finally, check the Required checkbox.

Field Properties

Name: reld1   Type: Text

User Name: |

Appearance | **Options** | Actions | Format | Validate | Calculate

Default: Relation

Alignment: Left

☐ Multi-line

☐ Limit of ____ characters

☐ Password

OK   Cancel

Step 13: Field Properties Dialog-Options Tab

Now activate the Options tab. Here we'll enter the default text displayed in the field. Here we've entered "Relation". This will be custom tailored to the specific user by our back-end process.

Once you've completed your choices, click the OK button. The dialog closes, adding the field to the document.

Next we'll create another Required field to hold the dependent's gender. To create the field, choose the forms tool button on the Acrobat Exchange toolbar. Click the mouse button and drag out a rectangle defining the area where you want to position the dependent's gender text. The Field Properties dialog box appears, asking for specifics about the text field we're creating.

Step 13: Field Properties Dialog-Appearance Tab

Enter "genderd1" as the field name and select Text as the field type. Leave the User Name field blank.

Activate the Appearance tab. Here we're presented with options that affect the field's appearance. Our designer decided to create the fields as a graphic so we don't have a Border or Background Color selected. If the designer didn't add a field graphic, the Acrobat forms plug-in provides options to create a field with an outline or a background color. Select a color the text will display by clicking the Text Color chip. Select Helvetica as the Font and Auto as the Size. The text is sized to fit the box we've just drawn. Finally check the Required checkbox.

Step 13: Field Properties Dialog-Options Tab

Now activate the Options tab. Here we'll enter the default text displayed in the field. Here we've entered "Your Gender". This will be custom tailored to the specific user by our back-end process.

Once you've completed your choices, click the OK button. The dialog closes, adding the field to the document.

Now we'll add the "ssnumberd1" field. With Acrobat Exchange's forms tool selected, drag out a rectangle defining the area where you want to display the Social Security Number. The Field Properties dialog box appears, asking for specifics about the field we're creating.

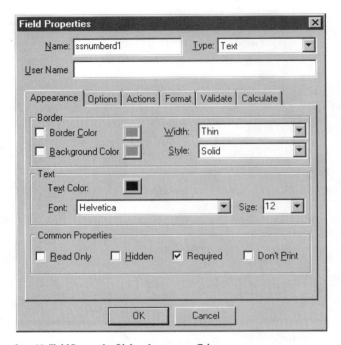

Step 13: Field Properties Dialog-Appearance Tab

Enter "ssnumberd1" as the field name and select Text as the field type. We left the User Name field blank because we want the field name to be "ssnumberd1" when the form is submitted.

Activate the Appearance tab. Make sure the Border or Background Colors aren't selected. Select a color the text will display by clicking the Text Color chip. Select Helvetica as the Font and 12 as the Size.

Next activate the Options tab. Enter the default text to display in the field. Leave the limit on the number of characters and the password fields unchecked for now.

Now activate the Format tab. The Format tab allows us to regulate the formatting of information entered into the field. Choose Special from the Category list and pick Social Security Number from the Special Options list. This insures users only enter digits. If they try to enter letters, the system beeps and doesn't enter the characters in the field. It also formats the entry, inserting hyphens after the first three digits and the first five digits.

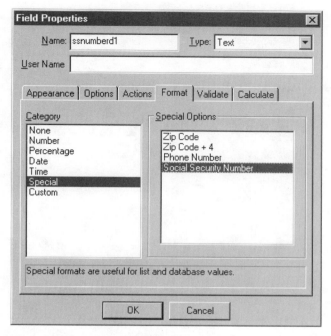

Step 13: Field Properties Dialog-Format Tab

Click the OK button. The dialog closes, adding the field to the document.

Now we'll add a date of birth field. This field allows a user to enter a date and formats it in the way we specify. Error checking is performed and the user is warned if they try to enter information that can't be converted into a date. With Acrobat Exchange's forms tool, define the area where the user will enter the date. The Field Properties dialog box appears, asking for specifics about the field we're creating.

Step 13: Field Properties Dialog-Appearance Tab

Enter "dobd1" as the field name and select Text as the field type. Leave the User Name field blank.

Activate the Appearance tab. We don't need a Border or Background Color. Select a color the text will display by clicking the Text Color chip. Select Helvetica as the Font and Auto as the Size. Be sure to check the Required checkbox.

Now Activate the Format tab. The Format tab allows us to regulate the formatting of information entered into the field. Choose Date from the Category list and pick a date format from the Date Options list.

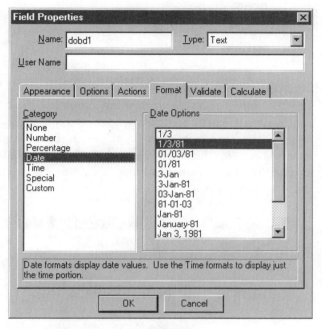

Step 13: Field Properties Dialog-Format Tab

Click the OK button. The dialog closes, adding the field to the document.

Congratulations, you've completed the first row of dependent information. Now, in Acrobat Exchange, click to select the dependent name field you just created. Hold down the shift key and click the relation, the gender, the social security, and date of birth fields. The selection extends, including each field you've clicked. Now with no key pressed, click on one of the selected fields and hold the mouse down. Click the control key on Windows or the Option key on the Mac and drag the mouse to a new location where you want the duplicate fields to appear. Release the mouse button and you should see a duplicate row of fields. Double click each field and rename them, incrementing the number on the end of the file name to match the row number of the dependent information you're creating.

If this process seems confusing, just repeat these steps to create fields for each row of dependent information. Each row's fields should end with a number corresponding to its row. For instance, the second row of dependent information should be labeled with the names named2, reld2, genderd2, ssnumberd2, and dobd2. The third row's fields should be named3, reld3, genderd3, ssnumberd3, and dobd3. Repeat this for as many rows as you feel you need.

Step 14

"idnumber" Field—Hidden Text

The first hidden field we'll create is the "idnumber" field. To create the field, choose the forms tool button on the Acrobat Exchange toolbar. The cursor changes to a crosshair. Click the mouse button and drag out a rectangle defining the area where you want the user to enter their idnumber. The Field Properties dialog box appears asking for specifics about the text field we're creating.

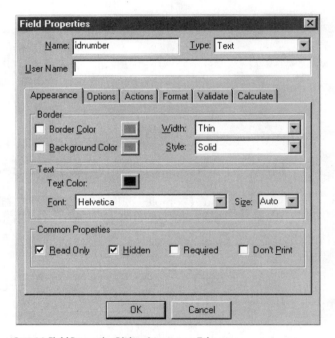

Step 14: Field Properties Dialog-Appearance Tab

Enter "idnumber" as the field name and select Text as the field type. Leave the User Name field blank. Enter a value here only if you want to export a different field name with this field's value when the form is submitted to a server.

Activate the Appearance tab. Make sure the Border or Background Colors aren't selected. Select a color the text will display by clicking the

Text Color chip. Select Helvetica as the Font and 12 as the Size. On this dialog tab, be sure to select the Hidden and Read Only checkboxes. Selecting the Read Only checkbox insures the user won't enter any information in this field. The Hidden option makes this field invisible.

Finally activate the Validate tab. The Validate tab lets us set up a field to validate the value of this field. Click the custom validate script radio button and then click the Edit button. The Acrobat Javascript editing window appears. Type in the following code.

```
1.  var f = this.getField("idnumber");
2.  global.idnumber = f.value;
```

This simple script grabs the value of our idnumber field and stores it in the global JavaScript object. The first line of this script gets a reference to the idnumber field and stores it in the variable "f". The second line accesses the "value" member of "f" and copies it to the global object in a field we can reference later. The global JavaScript object exists inside Acrobat and can be used to share information between documents. We can access this value later by simply referencing it as global.idnumber.

Step 15

Password Field—Hidden Text
Now we'll add the password field. This is a special text field where we store the user's password to submit to the server.

With Acrobat Exchange's forms tool, create the field where the password will be placed. The Field Properties dialog box appears asking for specifics about the new field.

Step 15: Field Properties Dialog-Appearance Tab

Enter "password" as the field name and select Text as the field type. Again we leave the User Name field blank.

Activate the Appearance tab. We don't need to select a Border or Background Color due to our form's design. Make sure the text color is black. If it isn't, change it to black by clicking the Text Color chip. Select Courier Bold as the Font and 12 as the Size. Be sure to select the Hidden and Read Only checkboxes. We don't want the user to enter any information in this field. Clicking the Read Only checkbox insures the user won't. The Hidden option makes this field invisible.

Field Properties

Name: password   Type: Text

User Name:

Appearance | Options | Actions | Format | Validate | Calculate

Default:

Alignment: Left

☐ Multiline

☐ Limit of ___ characters

☑ Password

OK   Cancel

Step 15: Field Properties Dialog-Options Tab

Now activate the Options tab. Here we'll enter the default text displayed in the field. Here we've entered "password". This will be custom tailored to the specific user by our back-end process. You can select the Password checkbox, but remember the field is hidden, so the user won't see it.

Once you've completed your choices click the OK button. The dialog closes, adding the field to the document.

Step 16

Submit button

Our two remaining fields correspond to the submit and reset buttons. First we'll create the submit button. With Acrobat Exchange's forms tool selected, drag out a rectangle defining the area where the submit button is located. The Field Properties dialog box appears, asking for specifics about the field we're creating.

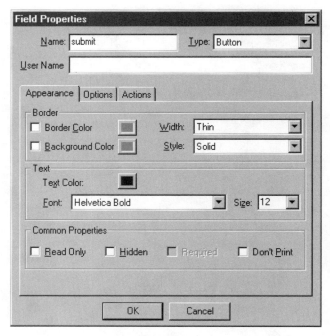

Step 16: Field Properties Dialog-Appearance Tab

Activate the Appearance tab. Again we don't need to select a Border or Background Color due to our form's design. The button's text color isn't important because we aren't displaying the button's title.

Step 16: Field Properties Dialog-Options Tab

The Options tab is where you select any special appearance options for
the button. In this instance we set the Highlight option to Invert. The
Layout option is set to Text only. Because we don't want any text to show
over our buttons, the Text entry for the Button Face Attributes is left
blank. The Button Face When option determines when the appearance
we set up is invoked. Here we want it to Invert on a Mouse up event.

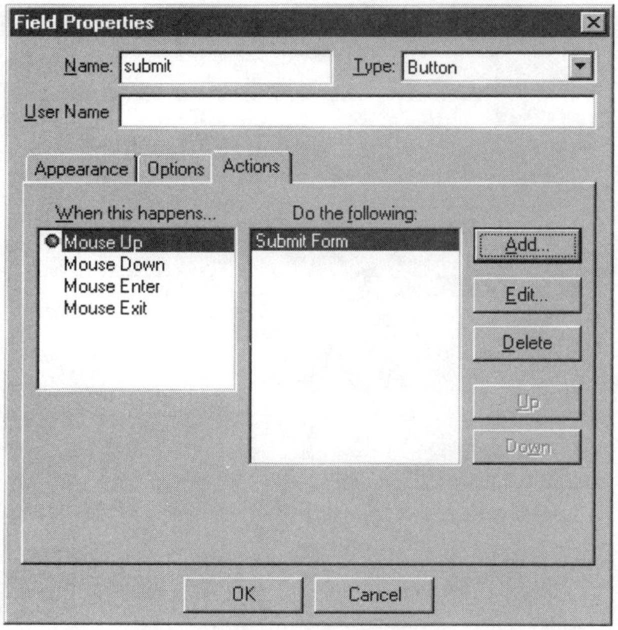

Field Properties

Name: submit   Type: Button

User Name:

| Appearance | Options | Actions |

When this happens...   Do the following:

- Mouse Up
- Mouse Down
- Mouse Enter
- Mouse Exit

Submit Form

Add...

Edit...

Delete

Up

Down

OK   Cancel

Step 16: Field Properties Dialog-Actions Tab

The Actions tab is where you select any action this field will invoke. Here we choose the Mouse up event. Click the Add button and choose Submit Form from the list of available action types.

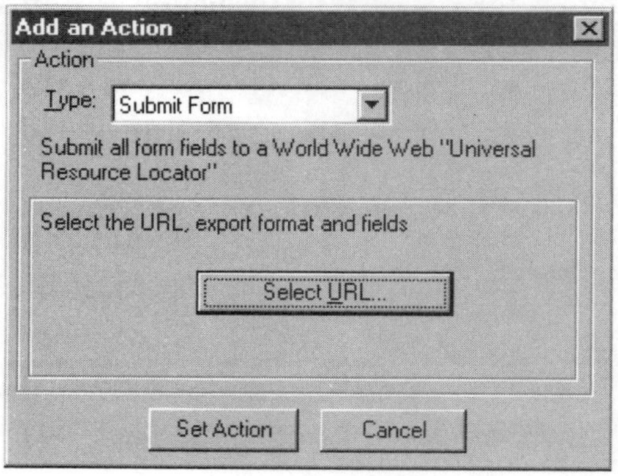

Add an Action

Action

Type: Submit Form

Submit all form fields to a World Wide Web "Universal Resource Locator"

Select the URL, export format and fields

Select URL...

Set Action   Cancel

Step 16: Add an Action Dialog

Now we need to identify the URL that will process the form submission. Click the Select URL button and enter the URL we'll use to process this form.

SubmitForm Selections

Enter a Universal Resource Locator for this link:

/shell-cgi/b_empupd.pl

Export Format
- ○ Forms Data Format (FDF)
- ● HTML Form (URL encoded)

Field Selection
- ☐ Include empty fields
- ● All fields
- ○ All, except..   Select fields...
- ○ Only these..

OK   Cancel

Step 16: SubmitForm Selections Dialog

Here we also choose to submit the data to the server in HTML format. We could submit in the FDF format but the Perl script we'll use to process the submission is set up to receive the data in HTML format. We also want to send all fields even though we have the option to just send a subset of the fields from the form. Once the proper selections are made, click the OK buttons in the Submit Form Selections, Edit an Action, and Field Properties dialogs.

Step 17

Reset button

Our final field is the reset button. With Acrobat Exchange's forms tool selected, drag out a rectangle defining the area where the reset button is located. The Field Properties dialog box appears, asking for specifics about the field we're creating.

Step 17: Field Properties Dialog-Appearance Tab

Activate the Appearance tab. Again we don't need to select a Border or Background Color due to our form's design. The button's text color isn't important because we aren't displaying the button's title.

Step 17: Field Properties Dialog-Options Tab

The Options tab is where you select any special appearance options for the button. In this instance we set the Highlight option to Invert. The Layout option is set to Text only. Because we don't want any text to show over our buttons, the Text entry for the Button Face Attributes is left blank. The Button Face When option determines when the appearance we set up is invoked. Here we want it to Invert on a Mouse up event.

Step 17: Field Properties Dialog-ActionsTab

The Actions tab is where you select any action this field will invoke. Here we choose the Mouse up event. Click the Add button and choose Reset Form from the list of available action types.

Step 17: Edit an Action Dialog

Here we can choose the fields we want to reset. All fields is the default. Once the proper selections are made click the OK buttons in the Edit an Action and Field Properties dialogs.

We're ready to discuss setting up the back end of the process to receive information from this form.

Creating the Perl Scripts

This example uses nine Perl scripts on the server side to perform these transactions. The "b_logon.pl" script validates a user and processes the request for an overview of employee benefit information. The response is returned as FDF data that is flowed into a PDF file in a user's browser window. The "b_empinfo.pl" script returns FDF data that is flowed into a PDF form file used to display and "b_empupd.pl" updates important employee information. The "b_mplan.pl", "b_dplan.pl", and "b_vplan" scripts retrieve specific information regarding their specific benefit package and return FDF data for display in a PDF form.

Three scripts generate claim status information for current health issues. These scripts are, "b_mclaim.pl", "b_dclaim.pl", and "b_vclaim.pl".

Creating the b_logon.pl Script

The first script is "b_logon.pl". For this example to work, the script must exist as a file named "b_logon.pl". This file is placed in the "shell-cgi" directory in Netscape Enterprise Server's root directory. The Netscape Server's root directory and shell-cgi directory were created automatically when we installed the Web server on our Windows NT machine.

Code Example: b_logon.pl

```perl
1.   #!/usr/local/bin/perl
2.
3.   use CGI;
4.   use Win32::ODBC;
5.   use Acrobat::FDF;
6.
7.   # Create a new instance of CGI
8.   my $q = new CGI;
9.   my $d = new
     Win32::ODBC("DSN=Adobe;UID=Adobe;PWD=book");
10.  my $theFdf = Acrobat::FDF::new( );
11.
12.  my $notfound = "Value not found.";
13.  my $filename = "c:\\temp\\a" . (int( rand( 1000000
     ) ) + 1) . ".fdf";
14.  my $id = $q->param('idnumber');
15.  my $pw = $q->param('password');
16.  my $verified = 'false';
17.
18.  $id =~ s/[^0-9]//g;
19.
20.  if(! $d->Sql("SELECT * FROM BENEFITS WHERE
     SSNUMBER = " . "\'" . $id . "\'") )
21.  {
22.    if($d->FetchRow()){
23.      %hash = $d->DataHash;
24.      $verified = "true";
25.    }
26.  }
27.  if($verified eq "true")
28.  {
29.    &create_fdf( $theFdf, $filename );
30.
31.    print $q->header('application/vnd.fdf');
32.
33.    open( IN, $filename ) || die "cannot open
     $filename for reading";
34.    binmode IN;
```

```
35.    binmode STDOUT;
36.    while( <IN> ){
37.      print $_;
38.    }
39.    close( IN );
40.    unlink( $filename );
41.  }
42.  else{
43.    &return_error( $q, 404, "Access Denied!", "User
       could not be authenticated.");
44.  }
45.  $d->Close();
46.  exit(0);
47.
48.  sub create_fdf
49.  {
50.    my $theFdf = shift;
51.    my $filename = shift;
52.
53.    $theFdf->SetValue( "name", $hash{'FNAME'}. " " .
       $hash{'MNAME'}.". ".$hash{'LNAME'}, False );
54.    $theFdf->SetValue( "ssnumber", $q->param
       ('idnumber'), False );
55.    $theFdf->SetValue( "medplan", $hash{'COVTYPE'},
       False );
56.    $theFdf->SetValue( "medgroup",
       $q->param('idnumber'), False );
57.    $theFdf->SetValue( "dentplan",
       $hash{'COVERED'}, False );
58.    $theFdf->SetValue( "dentgroup",
       $q->param('idnumber'), False );
59.    $theFdf->SetValue( "vizplan", $hash{'COVTYPE'},
       False );
60.    $theFdf->SetValue( "vizgroup",
       $q->param('idnumber'), False );
61.    $theFdf->SetValue( "retplan", $hash{'COVERED'},
       False );
62.    $theFdf->SetValue( "retgroup",
       $q->param('idnumber'), False );
63.
```

```
64.      $theFdf->SetFile( "http://home.mix-
         media.com/book/benefits/overview.pdf" );
65.      $theFdf->Save( $filename );
66.   }
67.
68.   sub return_error
69.   {
70.      my $q = shift;
71.      local ( $status, $errtype, $message ) = @_;
72.
73.      print $q->header( -status=>$status . ' ' .
         $errtype);
74.      print $q->start_html('CGI Program Error', 0, 0,
         'BGCOLOR="#FFFFFF"');
75.      print $q->h1( "This CGI program encountered an
         error: ", $errtype );
76.      print $message;
77.      print $q->hr;
78.      print $q->end_html();
79.      exit(1);
80.   }
```

Let's take a detailed look at our "b_logon.pl" script. Line one of our script is used to declare the location of the Perl interpreter to use when running this script. In a UNIX environment, this line would look something like this: #!/usr/local/bin/perl. Windows NT keeps track of which programs run which type of files, so it isn't necessary to point out the path of the Perl interpreter to use.

```
1.   #!/usr/local/bin/perl
2.
3.   use CGI;
4.   use Win32::ODBC;
5.   use Acrobat::FDF;
```

Lines three, four and five tell the Perl interpreter to include the CGI, Win32:ODBC, and Acrobat::FDF modules. A Perl module is a library of Perl routines stored in a file where the Perl executable can access it. The Acrobat::FDF module is a set of Perl routines that make it easier to send FDF replies. The CGI module makes it easy to decode form submission and output HTML. The ODBC module aids in connecting to databases.

```
7.    # Create a new instance of CGI
8.    my $q = new CGI;
9.    my $d = new
      Win32::ODBC("DSN=Adobe;UID=Adobe;PWD=book");
10.   my $theFdf = Acrobat::FDF::new( );
```

This part of our script is used to initialize variables. Lines eight, nine and ten create references to the modules we used earlier in the script. This is Perl's way of allowing object-oriented programming. Now that we've declared a new reference to a module, we can access it's member functions using notation.

```
12.   my $notfound = "Value not found.";
13.   my $filename = "c:\\temp\\a" . (int( rand( 1000000
      ) ) + 1) . ".fdf";
14.   my $id = $q->param('idnumber');
15.   my $pw = $q->param('password');
16.   my $verified = 'false';
```

Lines 12-16 are used to initialize locally scoped variables. On line 13 we create a temporary path we'll use to store the FDF data before we send it back to the user. On lines 14 and 15 we use the param() member function of the CGI module to retrieve field information from the client's submission. We store the id number and password for use later in the script.

```
18.   $id =~ s/[^0-9]//g;
```

Line 18 is a safety catch. If the user submits any information that isn't a number 0-9 it's removed here. The Perl search command is used and if it finds anything other than 0-9 it replaces it with nothing. The "g" parameter tells search to repeat as many times as needed.

```
20.   if(! $d->Sql("SELECT * FROM BENEFITS WHERE
      SSNUMBER = " . "\'" . $id . "\'") )
21.   {
22.     if($d->FetchRow()){
23.       %hash = $d->DataHash;
24.       $verified = "true";
25.     }
26.   }
```

Here's where we query the database. On line 20 we assemble the SQL string we send to the database for execution. We want to select every match "*" from the benefits table where the ss number field matches the $id. variable. On line 22 we see if we can fetch a row from the result. If we can, we store it in a host variable and set the $verified to true. Hashes are great for sorting.

```
27.    if($verified eq "true")
28.    {
29.       &create_fdf( $theFdf, $filename );
30.
31.       print $q->header('application/vnd.fdf');
32.
33.       open( IN, $filename ) || die "cannot open
          $filename for reading";
34.       binmode IN;
35.       binmode STDOUT;
36.       while( <IN> ){
37.          print $_;
38.       }
39.       close( IN );
40.       unlink( $filename );
41.    }
```

If we found a match and set $verified to true, we branch into the code block starting on line 27. On line 29 we call the create_fdf() sub routine. If all goes well, we print our header to standard output and prepare to return the contents of our FDF temporary file. On line 33 we open our file and associate the IN filehandle with it. In lines 34 and 35 we change the mode of files to binary. PDF and FDF files contain binary information. If we try to read or write to them in ASCII mode, data corruption can occur. Lines 36-38 are a simple while loop that reads the contents from the IN filehandle we created and prints it to STDOUT. On line 39 we close the file and on line 40 the unlink() function removes our temporary file.

```
42.    else{
43.       &return_error( $q, 404, "Access Denied!", "User
          could not be authenticated.");
```

```
44.   }
45.   $d->Close();
46.   exit(0);
```

If the database query couldn't find a match, we branch into the else block on line 42 and call the return_error() sub routine, returning an HTML error page describing the error encountered. Finally, the script exits on line 46, returning zero, signifying no error occurred.

The create_fdf() Sub Routine

Now let's take a look at the create_fdf() sub routine. Our sub opens by declaring two local variables and using shift to assign values to them passed to the sub routine. Now we can safely access them.

```
48.   sub create_fdf
49.   {
50.     my $theFdf = shift;
51.     my $filename = shift;
```

On lines 53 to 62 we assign values to the FDF object we're creating. The values are retrieved from the hash object initialized by our call to the database. We access the setvalue() member function of our FDF object, passing it the name of the field to set the value to set and whether or not we want the value created as a FDF name object. We don't want name objects here, so pass false.

```
64.     $theFdf->SetFile( "http://home.mix-
        media.com/book/benefits/overview.pdf" );
65.     $theFdf->Save( $filename );
66.   }
```

The sub routine draws to a close by initializing the FDF's file value and saving the file to disk. On line 64 the setfile() member function is called passing the URL of the file we want to import the form data. On line 65 we access the save() member function with our temporary file path to save the file to disk. On line 66 the routine ends.

The return_error() Sub Routine

The return_error() sub routine is another simple solution that sends an HTML response to the client if an error occurs.

On line 71 we call the Perl local operator to create local references to the four parameters passed to this routine.

```
68.   sub return_error
69.   {
70.      my $q = shift;
71.      local ( $status, $errtype, $message ) = @_;
72.
73.      print $q->header( -status=>$status . ' ' .
         $errtype);
74.      print $q->start_html('CGI Program Error', 0, 0,
         'BGCOLOR="#FFFFFF"');
75.      print $q->h1( "This CGI program encountered an
         error: ", $errtype );
76.      print $message;
77.      print $q->hr;
78.      print $q->end_html();
79.      exit(1);
80.   }
```

Line 73 prints the result of the CGI module's header member function. To this function we pass a status parameter containing the error code status, followed by a space and the description of the error that occurred.

On line 75 we add a level one header informing the user an error occurred. The type of error is concatenated to the string to further identify the problem. Line 76 adds the message passed to the sub routine. This should be text that will help the user track down the source of their problem. Line 77 outputs a horizontal rule HTML tag and line 78 completes the file by outputting the required close body and HTML tags.

On line 79 we call the Perl exit() function, passing it a value of one to inform the interpreter an error has occurred. Finally, on line 80 the sub routine ends.

Creating the b_mplan.pl Perl Script

This script gathers information from the Oracle database and flows it into the medical plan PDF file. Let's take a detailed look at this script. The first 46 lines of this script are similar to the b_logon.pl script.

Code Example: b_mplan.pl

```
1.    #!/usr/local/bin/perl
2.
3.    use CGI;
4.    use Win32::ODBC;
5.    use Acrobat::FDF;
6.
7.    # Create a new instance of CGI
8.    my $q = new CGI;
9.    my $d = new
      Win32::ODBC("DSN=Adobe;UID=Adobe;PWD=book");
10.   my $theFdf = Acrobat::FDF::new( );
11.
12.   my $notfound = "Value not found.";
13.   my $filename = "c:\\temp\\a" . (int( rand( 1000000
      ) ) + 1) . ".fdf";
14.   my $id = $q->param('idnumber');
15.   my $pw = $q->param('password');
16.   my $verified = 'false';
17.   my $desc;
18.
19.   $id =~ s/[^0-9]//g;
20.
21.   if(! $d->Sql("SELECT * FROM BENEFITS WHERE
      SSNUMBER = " . "\'" . $id . "\'") )
22.   {
23.     if($d->FetchRow()){
24.       %hash = $d->DataHash;
25.       $verified = "true";
26.     }
27.   }
28.   if($verified eq "true")
29.   {
```

```
30.     if( $hash{'COVTYPE'} eq "HMO" ){
31.       $desc = "You\'ve chosen the best plan in the
          whole world. \r\nYou have nothing to fear."
32.     }
33.     else{
34.       $desc = "You\'ve chosen a good plan. You\'ll
          save money this year."
35.     }
36.
37.     &create_fdf( $theFdf, $filename );
38.
39.     print $q->header('application/vnd.fdf');
40.
41.     open( IN, $filename ) || die "cannot open
          $filename for reading";
42.     binmode IN;
43.     binmode STDOUT;
44.     while( <IN> ){
45.       print $_;
46.     }
47.     close( IN );
48.     unlink( $filename );
49.   }
50.   else{
51.     &return_error( $q, 404, "Access Denied!", "User
          could not be authenticated.");
52.   }
53.   $d->Close();
54.   exit(0);
55.
56.   sub create_fdf
57.   {
58.     my $theFdf = shift;
59.     my $filename = shift;
60.
61.     $theFdf->SetValue( "name", $hash{'FNAME'}. " " .
          $hash{'MNAME'}.". ".$hash{'LNAME'}, False );
62.     $theFdf->SetValue( "plandesc", $desc, False );
63.     $theFdf->SetValue( "nextdate", "01\/01\/98",
          False );
```

```
64.     $theFdf->SetValue( "covtype", $hash{'COVTYPE'},
        False );
65.     $theFdf->SetValue( "subdate", "01\/01\/97",
        False );
66.
67.     $theFdf->SetFile( "http://home.mix-
        media.com/book/benefits/med_plan.pdf" );
68.     $theFdf->Save( $filename );
69.   }
70.
71.   sub return_error
72.   {
73.     my $q = shift;
74.     local ( $status, $errtype, $message ) = @_;
75.
76.     print $q->header( -status=>$status . ' ' .
        $errtype);
77.     print $q->start_html('CGI Program Error', 0, 0,
        'BGCOLOR="#FFFFFF"');
78.     print $q->h1( "This CGI program encountered an
        error: ", $errtype );
79.     print $message;
80.     print $q->hr;
81.     print $q->end_html();
82.     exit(1);
83.   }
```

Line one is used to declare the location of the Perl interpreter to use when running this script. Windows NT keeps track of which programs run which type of files, so it isn't necessary to point out the path of the Perl interpreter to use. The line is included in case we decide to later transfer the script to a UNIX machine but all that's required is #!/usr/local/bin/perl

```
3.    use CGI;
4.    use Win32::ODBC;
5.    use Acrobat::FDF;
```

Lines three, four and five tell the Perl Interpreter to include the CGI, Win32:ODBC, and Acrobat::FDF modules. A Perl module is a library of Perl routines stored in a file where the Perl executable can access it. The

Acrobat::FDF module is a set of Perl functions that make it easy to send FDF replies to the client. The CGI module makes it easy to decode form submission and output HTML. The ODBC module manages the database connection .

```
7.    # Create a new instance of CGI
8.    my $q = new CGI;
9.    my $d = new
      Win32::ODBC("DSN=Adobe;UID=Adobe;PWD=book");
10.   my $theFdf = Acrobat::FDF::new( );
```

Lines eight, nine and ten create references to the modules we used earlier in the script. This is Perl's attempt at object-oriented programming. Once we declare a new reference to a module, we can access it's member functions using -> notation.

```
12.   my $notfound = "Value not found.";
13.   my $filename = "c:\\temp\\a" . (int( rand( 1000000
      ) ) + 1) . ".fdf";
14.   my $id = $q->param('idnumber');
15.   my $pw = $q->param('password');
16.   my $verified = 'false';
17.   my $desc;
```

Lines 12-17 initialize locally scoped variables. On line 13 we create a temporary path we'll use to store the FDF data before we send it back to the user. On lines 14 and 15 we use the param() member function of the CGI module to retrieve field information from the client's submission. We store the id number and password for use later in the script.

```
19.   $id =~ s/[^0-9]//g;
```

On line 19, if the user submits any information that isn't a number from 0-9, it's removed here. The Perl search command looks through the $id string for anything other than 0-9. If it finds any errant characters, it replaces them with nothing. The "g" parameter tells search to repeat as many times as needed.

```
21.   if(! $d->Sql("SELECT * FROM BENEFITS WHERE
      SSNUMBER = " . "\'" . $id . "\'") )
22.   {
23.     if($d->FetchRow()){
24.       %hash = $d->DataHash;
25.       $verified = "true";
26.     }
27.   }
```

On line 21 we query the database. We want to select every match "*" from the benefits table where the ssnumber field matches the $id variable. On line 23 we see if we can fetch a row from the result. If we can, we store it in a host variable and set $verified to true. Hashes are associative arrays. each member of the array has two parts a key and a value. Here the keys are the field names and the values are the values stored in the fields.

If we found a match and set $verified to true, we branch into the code block starting on line 28. On line 30 through 35 we check for a coverage type and place a message in the $desc variable depending on what we found.

```
28.   if($verified eq "true")
29.   {
30.     if( $hash{'COVTYPE'} eq "HMO" ){
31.       $desc = "You\'ve chosen the best plan in the
            whole world. \r\nYou have nothing to fear."
32.     }
33.     else{
34.       $desc = "You\'ve chosen a good plan. You\'ll
            save money this year."
35.     }
```

On line 37 we call the create_fdf() sub routine. We'll discuss the specifics of this routine below. On line 39, if all goes well, we print our header to standard output and prepare to return the contents of our FDF temporary file. On line 41 we open our file and associate the IN filehandle with it. Lines 42 and 43 change the mode of the files to binary. If we try to read or write PDF and FDF using ASCII mode, corruption of binary data they contain can occur.

```
44.    while( <IN> ){
45.      print $_;
46.    }
47.    close( IN );
48.    unlink( $filename );
```

Lines 44-48 are a while loop that reads the contents from the IN filehandle we created and prints it to STDOUT. On line 47 we close the file and on line 48 we call the Perl unlink() function to remove our temporary file.

```
50.    else{
51.      &return_error( $q, 404, "Access Denied!", "User
         could not be authenticated.");
52.    }
53.    $d->Close();
54.    exit(0);
```

If the database query didn't find a match, we branch into the else block on line 50 and call the return_error() sub routine. This sub routine returns an HTML error page describing the error encountered. On line 53 the database connection is closed. Finally, the script exits on line 54, returning zero, signifying no error occurred.

The create_fdf() Sub Routine
Now let's look at this script's create_fdf() sub routine. Our sub routine begins by declaring two local variables and using shift to assign values to them passed to the sub routine. Now we can safely access them.

```
56.    sub create_fdf
57.    {
58.      my $theFdf = shift;
59.      my $filename = shift;
```

On lines 61 to 65 we assign values to the FDF object we're creating. The values are retrieved from the hash object initialized by our call to the database.

```
61.    $theFdf->SetValue( "name", $hash{'FNAME'}. " " .
       $hash{'MNAME'}.". ".$hash{'LNAME'}, False );
```

```
62.     $theFdf->SetValue( "plandesc", $desc, False );
63.     $theFdf->SetValue( "nextdate", "01\/01\/98",
        False );
64.     $theFdf->SetValue( "covtype", $hash{'COVTYPE'},
        False );
65.     $theFdf->SetValue( "subdate", "01\/01\/97",
        False );
```

We access the setvalue() member function of our FDF object, passing it the name of the field to set, the value to set, and whether or not we want the value created as a FDF name object. Pass in each field's name as a string for the first parameter. The second parameter is also a string. It is either one of two values. On line 64 the value for the COVTYPE key is retrieved and passed to the function. The final parameter of the function indicates if we want to create a PDF name object from the value. We don't want name objects here, so pass false.

```
67.     $theFdf->SetFile( "http://home.mix-
        media.com/book/benefits/overview.pdf" );
68.     $theFdf->Save( $filename );
69.  }
```

The sub routine closes by initializing the FDF's file value and saving the file to disk. On line 67 the setfile() member function is called, passing the URL of the file we want to import the form data. On line 68 we access the save() member function with our temporary file path to save the file to disk.

The return_error() Sub Routine

This sub routine is our standard method for returning errors. It's used in several of our scripts and its explanation is included with the b_logon.pl script.

Creating the b_mclaim.pl Perl Script

This script is used to retrieve current claim information and return it formatted as an HTML page.

Code Example: b_mclaim.pl

```
1.    #!/usr/local/bin/perl
2.
3.    use CGI;
4.    use Win32::ODBC;
5.
6.    # Create a new instance of CGI
7.    my $q = new CGI;
8.    my $d = new
      Win32::ODBC("DSN=Adobe;UID=Adobe;PWD=book");
9.    my $id = $q->param('idnumber');
10.
11.   $id =~ s/[^0-9]//g;
12.
13.   print $q->header;
14.   print <<"TOP";
15.   <P>  <TABLE BORDER=0 CELLPADDING=6 WIDTH=640
      HEIGHT=100>
16.      <TR>
17.        <TD VALIGN=bottom bgcolor="#3F4CFF">
18.          <H3><B><FONT SIZE="+4" FACE="Helvetica"
             COLOR="#FFFFFF">Claim
19.          Status</FONT></B></H3>
20.        </TD></TR>
21.   </TABLE>   <TABLE BORDER=0 WIDTH=640>
22.      <TR>
23.        <TD COLSPAN=3 WIDTH="86%">
24.          <P><B><FONT SIZE="+1"
      FACE="Helvetica">claims processed
25.   from </FONT></B><FONT
26.          FACE="Helvetica">10-01-97</FONT><B><FONT
      SIZE="+1"
27.          FACE="Helvetica"> to </FONT></B> 12-31-97
28.        </TD></TR>
```

```
29.       <TR>
30.         <TD WIDTH="20%">
31.           <P>
32.         </TD><TD WIDTH="33%">
33.           <P>
34.         </TD><TD WIDTH="33%">
35.           <P>
36.         </TD></TR>
37.       <TR>
38.         <TD WIDTH="20%">
39.           <P>
40.         </TD><TD VALIGN=top COLSPAN=2 WIDTH="66%">
41.           <P><FONT SIZE="+1" FACE="Helvetica">To
    review the status of
42.    your dependent's claim, carefully complete all
43.    applicable fields. Claims take up to 72 hours from
44.    the date of receipt by insurance company to be en-
45.    tered into the system. If you receive a "No Claim
       Found" message in the "Remark" field, either call
46.    customer service at 800/852-8000, or try again in
47.    a day or two.</FONT> 
48.           </TD></TR>
49. </TABLE> <FONT SIZE="+1"> </FONT> <TABLE
    BORDER=0 WIDTH=640>
50.      <TR>
51.        <TD VALIGN=bottom bgcolor="#000000"
    WIDTH="22%">
52.          <P><B><FONT FACE="Helvetica"
53.          COLOR="#FFFFFF">patient/</FONT></B><BR>
54.
55.          <B><FONT FACE="Helvetica"
56. COLOR="#FFFFFF">dependant</FONT></B> 
57.        </TD><TD VALIGN=bottom bgcolor="#000000"
    WIDTH="20%">
58.          <P><B><FONT FACE="Helvetica"
59.          COLOR="#FFFFFF">provider</FONT></B> 
60.        </TD><TD VALIGN=bottom bgcolor="#000000"
    WIDTH="15%">
61.          <P><B><FONT FACE="Helvetica"
    COLOR="#FFFFFF">service
```

```
62.              date</FONT></B>
63.          </TD><TD VALIGN=bottom bgcolor="#000000"
      WIDTH="15%">
64.              <P><B><FONT FACE="Helvetica"
65.              COLOR="#FFFFFF">charged</FONT></B>  
66.          </TD><TD VALIGN=bottom bgcolor="#000000"
      WIDTH="15%">
67.              <P><B><FONT FACE="Helvetica"
      COLOR="#FFFFFF">plan
68.     pays</FONT></B> 
69.          </TD><TD VALIGN=bottom bgcolor="#000000"
      WIDTH="15%">
70.              <P><B><FONT FACE="Helvetica"
      COLOR="#FFFFFF">patient
71.     pays</FONT></B>  
72.          </TD><TD WIDTH="15%">
73.              <P>
74.          </TD></TR>
75.     TOP
76.
77.     if(! $d->Sql("SELECT * FROM CLAIMS WHERE IDNUMBER
      = " . "\'" . $id . "\'") )
78.     {
79.       while($d->FetchRow())
80.       {
81.         %hash = $d->DataHash;
82.         print <<"BODY";
83.       <TR>
84.         <TD bgcolor="#DEDEDE" WIDTH="22%">
85.            <P><FONT
      FACE="Helvetica">$hash{'PATIENT'}</FONT> 
86.         </TD><TD bgcolor="#DEDEDE" WIDTH="20%">
87.            <P><FONT
      FACE="Helvetica">$hash{'POVIDER'}</FONT> 
88.         </TD><TD bgcolor="#DEDEDE" WIDTH="15%">
89.            <P><FONT
      FACE="Helvetica">$hash{'SERVDATE'}</FONT> 
90.         </TD><TD bgcolor="#DEDEDE" WIDTH="15%">
91.            <P><FONT
      FACE="Helvetica">$hash{'CHARGED'}</FONT> 
92.         </TD><TD bgcolor="#DEDEDE" WIDTH="15%">
```

```
93.              <P><FONT
     FACE="Helvetica">$hash{'PLANPAYS'}</FONT> 
94.       </TD><TD bgcolor="#DEDEDE" WIDTH="15%">
95.              <P><FONT
     FACE="Helvetica">$hash{'PATPAYS'}</FONT> 
96.       </TD><TD WIDTH="15%">
97.              <P>
98.       </TD></TR>
99.  BODY
100.
101.    }
102. }
103. $d->Close();
104. print "</TABLE>";
105. print $q->end_html();
106. exit(0);
107.
108. sub return_error
109. {
110.    my $q = shift;
111.    local ( $status, $errtype, $message ) = @_;
112.
113.    print $q->header( -status=>$status . ' ' .
     $errtype);
114.    print $q->start_html('CGI Program Error', 0, 0,
     'BGCOLOR="#FFFFFF"');
115.    print $q->h1( "This CGI program encountered an
     error: ", $errtype );
116.    print $message;
117.    print $q->hr;
118.    print $q->end_html();
119.    exit(1);
120. }
```

This script doesn't generate any FDF data so we don't need to use the FDF Perl module. Line one of our script identifies the path to our Perl interpreter. The third and fourth lines of our script invoke the use declaration. Use lets the script import declarations from another module. These declarations are imported into the script's own namespace. Here we use the CGI and Win32::ODBC modules.

```
1.      #!/usr/local/bin/perl
2.
3.      use CGI;
4.      use Win32::ODBC;
5.
```

On lines seven, eight and nine we create locally scoped variables to use in our script. On line seven we create an instance of the CGI module and assign it to the $q variable. Line eight creates an instance of the Win32::ODBC module. We're connecting to the Adobe DSN as Adobe and useing the book password. On line nine we access the param()member function of the $q variable. Remember that it's really a reference to the CGI module. We retrieve the idnumber from the form submission and store it in the $ id variable. To be safe, we remove any non-numeric values in the idnumber on line 11.

```
7.      my $q = new CGI;
8.      my $d = new
        Win32::ODBC("DSN=Adobe;UID=Adobe;PWD=book");
9.      my $id = $q->param('idnumber');
10.
11.     $id =~ s/[^0-9]//g;
```

On line 13 we print the required header using the header() member function of the CGI module. This one line outputs all the required information to construct a valid response header. On line 13 we set up the print function to print multiple lines of text. The print function usually prints a comma-separated list of strings. On line 14 we call print using the line-oriented quoting. This is done with the "<<". It works like this: any value from right after the "<<" to the following semi-colon to the next instance of the identifier is printed. On line 14 we also set print to print all text to the "TOP" identifier. It can be found on line 75.

```
13.     print $q->header;
14.     print <<"TOP";
15.     <P>  <TABLE BORDER=0 CELLPADDING=6 WIDTH=640
        HEIGHT=100>
16.        <TR>
17.           <TD VALIGN=bottom bgcolor="#3F4CFF">
```

```
18.                <H3><B><FONT SIZE="+4" FACE="Helvetica"
               COLOR="#FFFFFF">Claim
19.            Status</FONT></B></H3>
20.        </TD></TR>
21.    </TABLE>   <TABLE BORDER=0 WIDTH=640>
22.      <TR>
23.        <TD COLSPAN=3 WIDTH="86%">
24.            <P><B><FONT SIZE="+1"
     FACE="Helvetica">claims processed
25.  from </FONT></B><FONT
26.            FACE="Helvetica">10-01-97</FONT><B><FONT
     SIZE="+1"
27.            FACE="Helvetica"> to </FONT></B> 12-31-97
28.        </TD></TR>
29.      <TR>
30.        <TD WIDTH="20%">
31.          <P>
32.        </TD><TD WIDTH="33%">
33.          <P>
34.        </TD><TD WIDTH="33%">
35.          <P>
36.        </TD></TR>
37.      <TR>
38.        <TD WIDTH="20%">
39.          <P>
40.        </TD><TD VALIGN=top COLSPAN=2 WIDTH="66%">
41.            <P><FONT SIZE="+1" FACE="Helvetica">To
     review the status of
42.  your dependent's claim, carefully complete all
43.  applicable fields. Claims take up to 72 hours from
44.  the date of receipt by insurance company to be en-
45.  tered into the system. If you receive a "No Claim
     Found" message in the "Remark" field, either call
46.  customer service at 800/852-8000, or try again in
47.  a day or two.</FONT> 
48.        </TD></TR>
49.    </TABLE> <FONT SIZE="+1"> </FONT> <TABLE
     BORDER=0 WIDTH=640>
50.      <TR>
51.        <TD VALIGN=bottom bgcolor="#000000"
     WIDTH="22%">
```

```
52.              <P><B><FONT FACE="Helvetica"
53.              COLOR="#FFFFFF">patient/</FONT></B><BR>
54.
55.              <B><FONT FACE="Helvetica"
56.      COLOR="#FFFFFF">dependant</FONT></B> 
57.         </TD><TD VALIGN=bottom bgcolor="#000000"
         WIDTH="20%">
58.              <P><B><FONT FACE="Helvetica"
59.              COLOR="#FFFFFF">provider</FONT></B> 
60.         </TD><TD VALIGN=bottom bgcolor="#000000"
         WIDTH="15%">
61.              <P><B><FONT FACE="Helvetica"
         COLOR="#FFFFFF">service
62.              date</FONT></B>
63.         </TD><TD VALIGN=bottom bgcolor="#000000"
         WIDTH="15%">
64.              <P><B><FONT FACE="Helvetica"
65.              COLOR="#FFFFFF">charged</FONT></B>  
66.         </TD><TD VALIGN=bottom bgcolor="#000000"
         WIDTH="15%">
67.              <P><B><FONT FACE="Helvetica"
         COLOR="#FFFFFF">plan
68.      pays</FONT></B> 
69.         </TD><TD VALIGN=bottom bgcolor="#000000"
         WIDTH="15%">
70.              <P><B><FONT FACE="Helvetica"
         COLOR="#FFFFFF">patient
71.      pays</FONT></B>  
72.         </TD><TD WIDTH="15%">
73.            <P>
74.         </TD></TR>
75.    TOP
```

After printing all that HTML to STDOUT, we need to contact the database and retrieve the actual claim information. On line 76 we execute an SQL statement selecting all entries in the claims table where the idnumber field matches the idnumber in the form.

```
77.    if(! $d->Sql("SELECT * FROM CLAIMS WHERE IDNUMBER
       = " . "\'" . $id . "\'") )
78.    {
```

```
79.      while($d->FetchRow())
80.      {
81.        %hash = $d->DataHash;
```

On line 79 we fetch the results of our query. If there are results, we retrieve them in an associative array or hash on line 80. On line 82 we call print using the "<<" once again. This time we use the "BODY" identifier. The information we retrieve:

```
82.        print <<"BODY";
83.      <TR>
84.        <TD bgcolor="#DEDEDE" WIDTH="22%">
85.          <P><FONT
    FACE="Helvetica">$hash{'PATIENT'}</FONT> 
86.        </TD><TD bgcolor="#DEDEDE" WIDTH="20%">
87.          <P><FONT
    FACE="Helvetica">$hash{'POVIDER'}</FONT> 
88.        </TD><TD bgcolor="#DEDEDE" WIDTH="15%">
89.          <P><FONT
    FACE="Helvetica">$hash{'SERVDATE'}</FONT> 
90.        </TD><TD bgcolor="#DEDEDE" WIDTH="15%">
91.          <P><FONT
    FACE="Helvetica">$hash{'CHARGED'}</FONT> 
92.        </TD><TD bgcolor="#DEDEDE" WIDTH="15%">
93.          <P><FONT
    FACE="Helvetica">$hash{'PLANPAYS'}</FONT> 
94.        </TD><TD bgcolor="#DEDEDE" WIDTH="15%">
95.          <P><FONT
    FACE="Helvetica">$hash{'PATPAYS'}</FONT> 
96.        </TD><TD WIDTH="15%">
97.          <P>
98.        </TD></TR>
99.    BODY
100.
101.    }
102. }
```

is neatly formatted in a table row. Each table detail <TD></TD> contains the appropriate data. It's accessed through the hash table. The patient value is accessed on line 85 of the script. The print statement ends on line 99 with the BODY tag.

After we output the row information we continue looping in our while loop until all returned rows are retrieved.

```
103.   $d->Close();
104.   print "</TABLE>";
105.   print $q->end_html();
106.   exit(0);
```

On line 103 we close the connection to the datbase and on line 104 the close table HTML tag is printed to our response. On line 105 we access the end_html() member variable of our CGI library. On line 106 the script exits, returning a result code of zero.

The return_error() Sub Routine

This sub routine is our standard method for returning errors. It's used in several of our scripts and its explanation is included with the b_logon.pl script.

Creating the b_empinfo.pl Perl Script

This script retrieves information from the Oracle database and flows it into the employee information PDF file.

Code Example: b_empinfo.pl

```
1.    #!/usr/local/bin/perl
2.
3.    use CGI;
4.    use Win32::ODBC;
5.    use Acrobat::FDF;
6.
7.    ## Create a new instance of CGI
8.    my $q = new CGI;
9.    my $theFdf = Acrobat::FDF::new( );
10.   my $d = new
      Win32::ODBC("DSN=Adobe;UID=Adobe;PWD=book");
11.
12.   my $verified = 'false';
13.   my $notfound = "Value not found.";
```

```perl
14.   my $filename = "c:\\temp\\a" . (int( rand( 1000000
      ) ) + 1) . ".fdf";
15.   my $id = $q->param('idnumber');
16.   my $pw = $q->param('password');
17.
18.   $id =~ s/[^0-9]//g;
19.
20.   if(! $d->Sql("SELECT * FROM BENEFITS WHERE
      SSNUMBER = " .  $id ) )
21.   {
22.     while($d->FetchRow()){
23.       %hash = $d->DataHash;
24.       $verified = "true";
25.     }
26.   }
27.   if($verified eq "true")
28.   {
29.     &create_fdf( $theFdf, $filename );
30.
31.     print $q->header('application/vnd.fdf');
32.
33.     open( IN, $filename ) || die "cannot open
      $filename for reading";
34.     binmode IN;
35.     binmode STDOUT;
36.     while( <IN> ){
37.       print $_;
38.     }
39.     close( IN );
40.     unlink( $filename );
41.   }
42.   else{
43.     &return_error( $q, 404, "Access Denied!", "User
      could not be authenticated.");
44.   }
45.   $d->Close();
46.   exit(0);
47.
48.   sub create_fdf
49.   {
```

```
50.     my $theFdf = shift;
51.     my $filename = shift;
52.
53.     $theFdf->SetValue( "name", $hash{'FNAME'}. " " .
        $hash{'MNAME'}.". ".$hash{'LNAME'}, False );
54.     $theFdf->SetValue( "address", $hash{'ADDRESS'},
        False );
55.     $theFdf->SetValue( "city", $hash{'CITY'},
        False );
56.     $theFdf->SetValue( "state", $hash{'STATE'},
        False );
57.     $theFdf->SetValue( "zip", $hash{'ZIP'}, False );
58.     $theFdf->SetValue( "dob", $hash{'DOB'}, False );
59.     $theFdf->SetValue( "ssnumber",
        $q->param('idnumber'), False );
60.     $theFdf->SetValue( "gender", $hash{'GENDER'},
        False );
61.     $theFdf->SetValue( "status", $hash{'STATUS'},
        False );
62.     $theFdf->SetValue( "homephone",
        $hash{'HOMEPHONE'}, False );
63.     $theFdf->SetValue( "hired", $hash{'HIRED'},
        False );
64.     $theFdf->SetValue( "hours", $hash{'HOURS'},
        False );
65.     $theFdf->SetValue( "officephone",
        $hash{'OFFICEPHONE'}, False );
66.
67.     $theFdf->SetValue( "named1", $hash{'FNAMED1'}.
        " " . $hash{'MNAMED1'}.". ".$hash{'LNAMED1'},
        False );
68.     $theFdf->SetValue( "genderd1",
        $hash{'GENDERD1'}, False );
69.     $theFdf->SetValue( "dobd1", $hash{'DOBD1'},
        False );
70.     $theFdf->SetValue( "ssnumberd1",
        $hash{'SSNUMBERD1'}, False );
71.     $theFdf->SetValue( "reld1", $hash{'RELD1'},
        False );
72.
```

```
73.    $theFdf->SetValue( "named2", $hash{'FNAMED2'}.
       " " . $hash{'MNAMED2'}.". ".$hash{'LNAMED2'},
       False );
74.    $theFdf->SetValue( "genderd2",
       $hash{'GENDERD2'}, False );
75.    $theFdf->SetValue( "dobd2", $hash{'DOBD2'},
       False );
76.    $theFdf->SetValue( "ssnumberd2",
       $hash{'SSNUMBERD2'}, False );
77.    $theFdf->SetValue( "reld2", $hash{'RELD2'},
       False );
78.
79.    $theFdf->SetFile( "http://home.mix-
       media.com/book/benefits/emp_info.pdf" );
80.    $theFdf->Save( $filename );
81. }
82.
83. sub return_error
84. {
85.    my $q = shift;
86.    local ( $status, $errtype, $message ) = @_;
87.
88.    print $q->header( -status=>$status . ' ' .
       $errtype);
89.    print $q->start_html('CGI Program Error', 0, 0,
       'BGCOLOR="#FFFFFF"');
90.    print $q->h1( "This CGI program encountered an
       error: ", $errtype );
91.    print $message;
92.    print $q->hr;
93.    print $q->end_html();
94.    exit(1);
95. }
```

Let's take a detailed look at our script. The first 46 lines of this script are identical to the b_logon.pl script. We'll discuss it again here for the sake of completeness. Line one is used to declare the location of the Perl interpreter to use when running this script. Windows NT keeps track of which programs run which type of files, so it isn't necessary to point out the path of the Perl interpreter to use. The line is included in case we decide to later transfer the script to a UNIX machine but all that's required is "#!". This character combination is pronounced, "shh bang". It confirms to the interpreter that this is a Perl script.

```
1.    #!/usr/local/bin/perl
2.
3.    use CGI;
4.    use Win32::ODBC;
5.    use Acrobat::FDF;
```

Lines three, four, and five tell the Perl Interpreter to include the CGI, Win32:ODBC, and Acrobat::FDF modules. A Perl module is a library of Perl routines stored in a file where the Perl executable can access it. The Acrobat::FDF module is a set of Perl functions that make it easy to send FDF replies to the client. The CGI module makes it easy to decode form submission and output HTML. The ODBC module manages the database connection .

```
7.    # Create a new instance of CGI
8.    my $q = new CGI;
9.    my $theFdf = Acrobat::FDF::new( );
10.   my $d = new
      Win32::ODBC("DSN=Adobe;UID=Adobe;PWD=book");
```

This part of our script is used to initialize variables. Lines eight, nine and ten create references to the modules we used earlier in the script. This is Perl's attempt at object-oriented programming. Once we declare a new reference to a module, we can access its member functions using "->" notation.

```
12.   my $verified = 'false';
13.   my $notfound = "Value not found.";
14.   my $filename = "c:\\temp\\a" . (int( rand( 1000000
      ) ) + 1) . ".fdf";
15.   my $id = $q->param('idnumber');
16.   my $pw = $q->param('password');
```

Lines 12-16 are used to initialize locally scoped variables. On line 14 we create a temporary path we'll use to store the FDF data before we send it back to the user. On lines 15 and 16 we use the param() member function of the CGI module to retrieve field information from the client's submission. We store the id number and password for use later in the script.

```
18.    $id =~ s/[^0-9]//g;
```

On line 18, if the user submits any information that isn't a number from 0-9, it's removed here. The Perl search command is used to look for anything other than 0-9, which it replaces with nothing. The "g" parameter tells search to repeat as many times as needed.

```
20.    if(! $d->Sql("SELECT * FROM BENEFITS WHERE
       SSNUMBER = " . "\'" . $id . "\'") )
21.    {
22.      if($d->FetchRow()){
23.        %hash = $d->DataHash;
24.        $verified = "true";
25.      }
26.    }
```

Here's where we query the database. On line 20 we assemble the SQL string to send the database for execution. We want to select every match "*" from the benefits table where the ssnumber field matches the $id variable. On line 22 we see if we can fetch a row from the result. If we can, we store it in a host variable and set the $verified to true. Hashes are great for sorting.

```
27.    if($verified eq "true")
28.    {
29.      &create_fdf( $theFdf, $filename );
30.
31.      print $q->header('application/vnd.fdf');
32.
33.      open( IN, $filename ) || die "cannot open
       $filename for reading";
34.      binmode IN;
35.      binmode STDOUT;
36.      while( <IN> ){
37.        print $_;
38.      }
```

```
39.    close( IN );
40.    unlink( $filename );
41.  }
```

If we found a match and set $verified to true, we branch into the code block starting on line 27. On line 29 we call the create_fdf() sub routine. Next, if all goes well, we print our header to standard output and prepare to return the contents of our FDF temporary file. On line 33 we open our file and associate the IN filehandle with it. Lines 34 and 35 change the mode of the files to binary. If we try to read or write PDF and FDF using ASCII mode, corruption of binary data they contain can occur.

Lines 36-38 are a while loop that reads the contents from the IN filehandle we created and prints it to STDOUT. On line 39 we close the file and on line 40 we call the Perl unlink() function to remove our temporary file.

```
42.  else{
43.    &return_error( $q, 404, "Access Denied!", "User
       could not be authenticated.");
44.  }
45.  $d->Close();
46.  exit(0);
```

If the database query couldn't find a match, we branch into the else block on line 42 and call the return_error() sub routine, returning an HTML error page describing the error encountered. Finally, the script exits on line 46 returning zero, signifying no error occurred.

The create_fdf() Sub Routine

Now let's take a look at this script's create_fdf() sub routine. This is where the script begins to differ from the b_logon.pl script. Our sub opens by declaring two local variables and using shift to assign values to them passed to the sub routine. Now we can safely access them.

```
48.  sub create_fdf
49.  {
50.    my $theFdf = shift;
51.    my $filename = shift;
```

On lines 52 to 61 we assign values to the FDF object we're creating. The values are retrieved from the hash object initialized by our call to the database.

```
53.    $theFdf->SetValue( "name", $hash{'FNAME'}. " " .
       $hash{'MNAME'}.". ".$hash{'LNAME'}, False );
54.    $theFdf->SetValue( "address", $hash{'ADDRESS'},
       False );
55.    $theFdf->SetValue( "city", $hash{'CITY'},
       False );
56.    $theFdf->SetValue( "state", $hash{'STATE'},
       False );
57.    $theFdf->SetValue( "zip", $hash{'ZIP'}, False );
58.    $theFdf->SetValue( "dob", $hash{'DOB'}, False );
59.    $theFdf->SetValue( "ssnumber",
       $q->param('idnumber'), False );
60.    $theFdf->SetValue( "gender", $hash{'GENDER'},
       False );
61.    $theFdf->SetValue( "status", $hash{'STATUS'},
       False );
62.    $theFdf->SetValue( "homephone",
       $hash{'HOMEPHONE'}, False );
63.    $theFdf->SetValue( "hired", $hash{'HIRED'},
       False );
64.    $theFdf->SetValue( "hours", $hash{'HOURS'},
       False );
65.    $theFdf->SetValue( "officephone",
       $hash{'OFFICEPHONE'}, False );
66.
67.    $theFdf->SetValue( "named1", $hash{'FNAMED1'}.
       " " . $hash{'MNAMED1'}.". ".$hash{'LNAMED1'},
       False );
68.    $theFdf->SetValue( "genderd1",
       $hash{'GENDERD1'}, False );
69.    $theFdf->SetValue( "dobd1", $hash{'DOBD1'},
       False );
70.    $theFdf->SetValue( "ssnumberd1",
       $hash{'SSNUMBERD1'}, False );
71.    $theFdf->SetValue( "reld1", $hash{'RELD1'},
       False );
```

```
72.
73.      $theFdf->SetValue( "named2", $hash{'FNAMED2'}.
         " " . $hash{'MNAMED2'}.". ".$hash{'LNAMED2'},
         False );
74.      $theFdf->SetValue( "genderd2",
         $hash{'GENDERD2'}, False );
75.      $theFdf->SetValue( "dobd2", $hash{'DOBD2'},
         False );
76.      $theFdf->SetValue( "ssnumberd2",
         $hash{'SSNUMBERD2'}, False );
77.      $theFdf->SetValue( "reld2", $hash{'RELD2'},
         False );
78.
```

On lines 53-80 we access the setvalue() member function of our FDF object, passing it the name of the field to set, the value to set, and whether or not we want the value created as a FDF name object. Pass in each field's name as a string for the first parameter. The second parameter is also a string. It is either one of two values. On line 63 the value for the HIRED key is retrieved and passed to the function. On line 59 the value passed to the SetValue() function is retrieved by calling the param() funcion of the CGI module. The final parameter of the function indicates if we want to create a PDF name object from the value. We don't want name objects here so pass false.

```
79.      $theFdf->SetFile( "http://home.mix-
         media.com/book/benefits/overview.pdf" );
80.      $theFdf->Save( $filename );
81.    }
```

The sub routine draws to a close by initializing the FDF's file value and saving the file to disk. On line 79 the setfile() member function is called, passing the URL of the file we want to import the form data. On line 80 we access the save() member function with our temporary file path to save the file to disk. On line 81 the routine ends.

The return_error() Sub Routine
This sub routine is our standard method for returning errors. It's used in several of our scripts and its explanation is included with the b_logon.pl script.

Creating the b_empupd.pl Perl Script

This script is used by the employee information form to make an update to the employee database record.

Code example: b_empupd.pl

```perl
1.    #!/usr/local/bin/perl
2.
3.    use CGI;
4.    use Win32::ODBC;
5.    use Acrobat::FDF;
6.
7.    ## Create a new instance of CGI
8.    my $q = new CGI;
9.    my $theFdf = Acrobat::FDF::new( );
10.   my $d = new
      Win32::ODBC("DSN=Adobe;UID=Adobe;PWD=book");
11.
12.   my $verified = 'false';
13.   my $notfound = "Value not found.";
14.   my $filename = "c:\\temp\\a" . (int( rand( 1000000
      ) ) + 1) . ".fdf";
15.   my $id = $q->param('idnumber');
16.   my $pw = $q->param('password');
17.
18.   $id =~ s/[^0-9]//g;
19.   $sqlstr = "update benefits set address = \'" .
      $q->param('address') .
20.   "\', city = \'" . $q->param('city') .
21.   "\', state = \'" . $q->param('state') .
22.   "\', zip = \'" . $q->param('zip') .
23.   "\', gender = \'" . $q->param('gender') .
24.   "\', status = \'" . $q->param('status') .
25.   "\', homephone = \'" . $q->param('homephone') .
26.   "\', hours = \'" . $q->param('hours') .
27.   "\', officephone = \'" . $q->param('officephone')
      .
28.   "\' where ssnumber = \'" . $id . "\'";
29.
```

```
30.    if(! $d->Sql( $sqlstr ) ){
31.         $verified = "true";
32.    }
33.    if($verified eq "true")
34.    {
35.
36.         print $q->header;
37.         print $q->start_html('Thank You', 0, 0,
            'BGCOLOR="#FFFFFF"');
38.         print $q->h1( "Thanks for your
            update.<BR><BR>" );
39.         print $q->hr;
40.         print "Your new information will be recorded
            as soon as humanly possible.<BR>\r\n";
41.         print $q->hr;
42.         print $q->end_html();
43.
44.    }
45.    else{
46.         &return_error( $q, 404, "Update Denied!",
            "Information could not be updated. Try again
            later.");
47.    }
48.    $d->Close();
49.    exit(0);
50.
51.    sub return_error
52.    {
53.         my $q = shift;
54.         local ( $status, $errtype, $message ) = @_;
55.
56.         print $q->header( -status=>$status . ' ' .
            $errtype);
57.         print $q->start_html('CGI Program Error', 0,
            0, 'BGCOLOR="#FFFFFF"');
58.         print $q->h1( "This CGI program encountered
            an error: ", $errtype );
59.         print $message;
60.         print $q->hr;
61.         print $q->end_html();
```

```
62.          exit(1);
63.     }
```

Line one of our script is used to declare the location of the Perl interpreter to use when running this script. In a UNIX environment, this line would look something like this: #!/usr/local/bin/perl. Windows NT keeps track of which programs run which type of files, so it isn't necessary to point out the path of the Perl interpreter to use.

```
1.    #!/usr/local/bin/perl
2.
3.    use CGI;
4.    use Win32::ODBC;
5.    use Acrobat::FDF;
```

Lines three, four, and five tell the Perl interpreter to include the CGI, Win32:ODBC, and Acrobat::FDF modules. A Perl module is a library of Perl routines stored in a file where the Perl executable can access it. The Acrobat::FDF module is a set of Perl routines that make it easier to send FDF replies. The CGI module makes it easy to decode form submission and output HTML. The ODBC module aids in connecting to databases.

```
7.    # Create a new instance of CGI
8.    my $q = new CGI;
9.    my $theFdf = Acrobat::FDF::new( );
10.   my $d = new
      Win32::ODBC("DSN=Adobe;UID=Adobe;PWD=book");
```

This part of our script is used to initialize variables. Lines eight, nine and ten create references to the modules we used earlier in the script. This is Perl's way of allowing object-oriented programming. Now that we've declared a new reference to a module, we can access its member functions using notation.

```
12.   my $verified = 'false';
13.   my $notfound = "Value not found.";
14.   my $filename = "c:\\temp\\a" . (int( rand( 1000000
      ) ) + 1) . ".fdf";
15.   my $id = $q->param('idnumber');
```

```
16.    my $pw = $q->param('password');
```

Lines 12-16 are used to initialize locally scoped variables. On line 13 we create a temporary path we'll use to store the FDF data before we send it back to the user. On lines 15 and 16 we use the param() member function of the CGI module to retrieve field information from the client's submission. We store the id number and password for use later in the script.

```
18.    $id =~ s/[^0-9]//g;
```

Line 18 is a safety catch. If the user submits any information that isn't a number 0-9 it's removed here. The Perl search command is used and if it finds anything other than 0-9 it replaces it with nothing. The "g" parameter tells search to repeat as many times as needed.

```
19.    $sqlstr = "update benefits set address = \'" .
       $q->param('address') .
20.    "\', city = \'" . $q->param('city') .
21.    "\', state = \'" . $q->param('state') .
22.    "\', zip = \'" . $q->param('zip') .
23.    "\', gender = \'" . $q->param('gender') .
24.    "\', status = \'" . $q->param('status') .
25.    "\', homephone = \'" . $q->param('homephone') .
26.    "\', hours = \'" . $q->param('hours') .
27.    "\', officephone = \'" . $q->param('officephone')
       .
28.    "\' where ssnumber = \'" . $id . "\'";
```

On line 19 we begin assembling the SQL code we'll use to update the database. We do this by retrieving these fields from the emp_info.pdf's submission. These values are concatenated to form one long string. The SQL string we construct looks something like the following example:

```
update benefits set address    = 'IIII
                                   Pennsylvania'
   city  = 'Washington'
   state = 'DC'
   zip = '02134'
   gender  = 'male'
   status  = 'single'
   home phone= '555-555-1222'
```

```
hours = '32'
office phone = '555-555-1223'
where ss number = '123-45-678'
```

This SQL statement updates the existing fields in the database. It sets the fields in the database we identify to the values we pass to it. This is done only to the record where the database's ss number field matches the id number submitted to the form.

```
30.    if(! $d->Sql( $sqlstr ) ){
31.        $verified = "true";
32.    }
```

Once assembled, we send the SQL command to the server execution. We do this on line 30 by calling the Sql() member function at the Win32::ODBC module. If the SQL method succeeds, we get the $verified variable to "true" on line 31.

```
33.    if($verified eq "true")
34.    {
35.
```

If it's verified that the SQL statement executed, we branch into the code block that starts on line 33. If we're successful, we want to return to the HTML page confirming the user's update. On line 36 we print the required header using the CGI module's header() function. On line 37 we add the HTML to open the file construct the <HEAD></HEAD>, and open the <BODY> tag. On line 38 we add level one header using the h1() function . Two <BR> tags are added here to give a little space between the header and the body text. On line 39 we add an HTML horizontal rule and on line 40 we print a brief message assuring the user their submission is being processed. On line 41 another horizontal rule is added. On line 42 the necessary closing tags are added through the end_html() member function of the CGI module.

```
45.    else{
46.        &return_error( $q, 404, "Update Denied!",
           "Information could not be updated. Try again
           later.");
47.    }
```

If the update wasn't verified we enter the else block starting on line 45. If we reach this block we want to return an HTML error page. This is accomplished by calling the return_error() sub routine.

```
48.    $d->Close();
49.    exit(0);
```

On line 48 we close the connection to the database and on line 49 the exit() function is called, passing a value of zero signifying no error occurred .

The return_error() Sub Routine

The sub routine is our standard error return method. The benefits example uses it in several different scripts. Its explanation is included with the b_logon.pl script.

Run the Example

To run the example, place the nine Perl scripts in you Netscape Server's "shell-cgi" directory. Place all the remaining project PDF and HTML files in a single directory in your Web server's root directory. You might create a "benefits" directory and place your documents in it. Don't forget to create your datasource, database and tables.

Now enter the log on PDF file's URL and walk through the example.

Stock Photo Library

Overview

This example demonstrates how to construct a multi-page form application that allows a user to browse and select an image file from a library of image files. The user can select images from three categories and then browse through all related images under that category. Upon locating a desirable image, the user can then submit a request for a download, along with a method of payment. Upon credit approval, the image file is returned to the user. Transactions are logged to a database for future reference.

Physical Requirements

The following list is a description of the setup used to create this example. The actual components are:

Windows NT Server version 4.0
Perl 5.0 for Win 32
Microsoft IIS 4.0
Netscape Navigator 3.x or Netscape Communicator 4.04 or newer with Acrobat Plug-in or Microsoft Internet Explorer 4.0 or newer with Acrobat Plug-in
Adobe Acrobat Exchange 3.1 or newer with Adobe Forms Plug-in 3.5

Physical Setup the Example Uses

The example runs on Microsoft IIS 4.0 running on a Windows NT 4.0 Server. Perl 5.004 is installed on the Windows NT machine. During the installation the ".pl" file extension type was selected to be associated with Perl script files.

IIS 4.0 is set to use the operating system file extensions associations to recognize the program with which to run the CGI script used by this form. This requires that the example script "i_library.pl" resides in the "scripts" directory in the root folder for our Web server.

We have installed Netscape Communicator 4.04 and Acrobat Reader 3.01 on our client machine. Additionally, Netscape Communicator has the Acrobat plug-in located in its plug_in directory. This allows PDF files to be viewed directly in the Navigator window. Any browser can be used, as long as the Acrobat plug-in is in the browser's plug-in directory.

Creating the Necessary Files

To get this example to work we need to put eight files on the server. The files are:

2 HTML files to create the frameset
1 HTML file for the initial welcome screen
3 PDF files, one for each photo category's initial page
1 PDF file containing 9 pages of low-resolution images
1 Perl script, which returns these pages to the browser

Our HTML welcome screen is actually a two-frame document. It is constructed from three separate HTML files and sets up the frameset used by our PDF document. The first PDF file is the top level file for each of our three categories. It gives the user a starting point for browsing through the photos. Our PDF file containing nine pages houses the information we'll send back to the user when they hit the next button on the PDF page. We could save these images as individual files just as easily but they're combined here to show you it's possible to retrieve a single page from a PDF document.

This form application requires one Perl script. The script identifies the image being viewed, and in response to a click on the next button, returns the appropriate information. If the submit button is pressed it processes the submission and returns an HTML confirmation to the user. A real world application might validate the credit card information and upon approval return a high-resolution image to the user.

Creating the HTML Files

This example uses an HTML file as its welcome screen. The index.html file is the point of contact for the user. It's a simple nine line file that defines the frameset the form application uses.

```
1.    <HTML>
2.    <HEAD>
```

```
3.      <TITLE>Photo Image Library</TITLE>
4.      </HEAD>
5.      <FRAMESET  COLS="100,*" BORDER=0>
6.        <FRAME SRC="toc.html" NAME="toc" SCROLLING=AUTO
          MARGINHEIGHT=5 MARGINWIDTH=5 NORESIZE>
7.        <FRAME SRC="welcome.html" NAME="content"
          SCROLLING=AUTO MARGINHEIGHT=5 MARGINWIDTH=5
          NORESIZE>
8.      </FRAMESET>
9.      </HTML>
```

Lines one through four are standard HTML, but line five is where things begin to get interesting. On line five we define a two-frame document. The frameset has two columns. One is 100 pixels in width and the other uses the "*", meaning extend it to the end of the client's browser window no matter what size it is. Lines six and seven indicate which files to load in the frames, and actually give names to each of the frames. Our first 100 pixel frame is named "toc", and our frame that extends to the edge of the browser window is named "content". We'll use these names to direct any new pages. Line eight closes the frameset.

Let's take a closer look at our "toc" frame. The HTML file that fills the "toc" frame contains four images. Three of the HREF tags let us jump to the starting point of each image category by placing a PDF file in the "content" frame. The fourth image allows us to jump back to our welcome page, and reloads our frameset from scratch. It's sort of a reset button in case events seem to be going the wrong way. The HTML is very simple.

```
1.      <HTML>
2.      <HEAD>
3.        <TITLE>Stock Photo Library Navigation</TITLE>
4.      </HEAD>
5.      <BODY BGCOLOR="#FFFFFF">
6.      <A HREF="/book/photo/index.html"
        TARGET="_top">
7.      <IMG SRC="/images/home.gif" WIDTH=70 HEIGHT=70
        BORDER=0 ALIGN=bottom></A>
8.      <BR>
9.      <A HREF="/book/photo/things.pdf" TARGET="content">
```

```
10.   <IMG SRC="/images/things.gif" WIDTH=70 HEIGHT=70
      BORDER=0 ALIGN=bottom></A>
11.   <BR>
12.   <A HREF="/book/photo/places.pdf" TARGET="content">
13.   <IMG SRC="/images/places.gif" WIDTH=70 HEIGHT=70
      BORDER=0 ALIGN=bottom></A>
14.   <BR>
15.   <A HREF="/book/photo/people.pdf" TARGET="content">
16.   <IMG SRC="/images/people.gif" WIDTH=70 HEIGHT=70
      BORDER=0 ALIGN=bottom></A>
17.   <BR>
18.   </BODY>
19.   </HTML>
```

Again, lines one through five are standard opening HTML, and line six is where things begin to get interesting. On line six we define a HREF to our index.html file and target it to "_top". This tells the browser to blow away any frameset it might be using and load the indicated HREF in the top frame. Browsers define "_top" as a special root-level frame.

On lines 9, 12, and 15, we've created HREFs that target the "content" frame. Clicking any of these HREFs will load the indicated file in the "content" frame. Remember the "content" frame is the one that starts 100 pixels over and extends to the right edge of the browser window. Since there is an image definition tag between the <A> and </A> HTML tags, these HREFs will be displayed as clickable images. Lines 10, 13, and 16 define image attributes for these images. The name to display when the mouse is positioned over the image, the path to the image file to use, and alternate text to display if the image file cannot be retrieved are defined. Finally the document closes as a standard-issue HTML file.

The HTML file that defines the welcome text in the "content" frame is the simplest yet. The file contains a title and two lines of text. The first is set to heading level one using the <H1> tag. To be fancy, we've also included the <FONT> tag and indicated that Arial or Helvetica should be used if they are available. The second line of text, on line seven, is plain body copy.

```
1.    <HTML>
2.    <HEAD>
3.      <TITLE>Photo Image Library</TITLE>
4.    </HEAD>
5.    <BODY BGCOLOR="#FFFFFF">
6.    <H1><FONT FACE="Arial">Welcome to the Flippox
      Photo Image Library</FONT></H1>
7.    <P>Click on a category to the left to begin brows-
      ing.</P>
8.    </BODY>
9.    </HTML>
```

When the index.html file is loaded into a browser window, it will create a document that looks like the following screen capture.

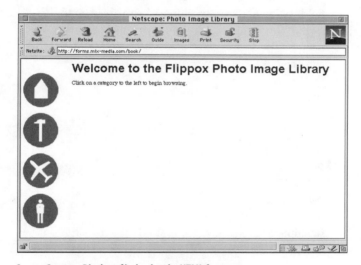

Screen Capture: Display of index.html – HTML frameset

Creating the PDF Category Files

This example uses one PDF file as the starting point for browsing the images. The file allows a user to enter information and submit a request to download a selected image. The PDF form takes a name, company, address, city, state, ZIP code, telephone, payment method, and account number. This information can be submitted to a server for approval, or the next image in the category can be requested. In addition the form displays location, image number, description and cost fields for each image it displays. We'll walk through creating the "people.pdf" file and leave creating the nearly identical, "places.pdf" and "things.pdf" files to the user.

Adobe Illustrator was used to construct the original form. The file was then distilled into PDF format. The next steps discuss creating the form fields in Acrobat Exchange to handle the client side interaction of this transaction.

Step 1

The Form Field Names

Before we begin, we need to identify the fields we will create on the form document. On this form we not only need to gather information from the user, but we need to send information back depending on what image they want to view. Realizing this, we need to add the following form fields using Acrobat Exchange's form creation tool:

name
company
address
city
state
zip
telephone
payment
account
place
image
description
cost

Step 2

Name Field

The first field we'll create is the name field. To create the field, choose the forms tool button on the Acrobat Exchange toolbar. The cursor changes to a crosshair. Click the mouse button and drag out a rectangle defining the area where you want the user to enter their name. The Field Properties dialog box appears asking for specifics about the text field we're creating.

Step 2: Field Properties Dialog-Appearance Tab

Enter "name" as the field name and select Text as the field type. Leave the User Name field blank. It's only used to export a different field name with this field's value when the form is submitted.

Activate the Appearance tab. Here we're presented with options that affect the field's appearance. Our designer decided to create the fields as a graphic, so we don't have a Border or Background Color selected. If there isn't a field graphic, the Acrobat forms plug-in provides options to create a field with an outline or a background color. Select a color the text will display by clicking the Text Color chip. Select Helvetica as the Font and Auto as the Size. The text is sized to fit the box we've just drawn. Finally check the Required checkbox. The user will be warned if they don't fill out this field before submitting the form to the server.

```
┌─────────────────────────────────────────────────┐
│              Field Properties                      │
├─────────────────────────────────────────────────┤
│ Name:    [name        ]    Type: [ Text      ▼ ]  │
│ User name: [           ]                           │
│ ╱Appearance╲ Options ╲Actions╲ Format ╲Validate╲Calculate╲ │
│                                                    │
│   Default: [Enter Your Name              ]         │
│                                                    │
│   Alignment: [ Left    ▼ ]                         │
│                                                    │
│      □ Multi-line                                  │
│      □ Limit of [    ] characters                  │
│      □ Password                                    │
│                                                    │
│                    [ Cancel ]   [   OK   ]         │
└─────────────────────────────────────────────────┘
```

Step 2: Field Properties Dialog-Options Tab

Now activate the Options tab. Here we'll enter the default text displayed in the field. Here we've entered "Enter Your Name". This gives the user a little hint to guide them in their entry. We could also limit the number of characters or change this to a password field if we desired. Leave them blank for now.

Once you've completed your choices, click the OK button. The dialog closes, adding the field to the document.

Step 3

Company Field

Now we'll create the company field. To create the field, choose the forms tool button on the Acrobat Exchange toolbar. The cursor changes to a crosshair. Click the mouse button and drag out a rectangle defining the area where you want the user to enter their company name. The Field Properties dialog box appears asking for specifics about the text field we're creating.

Step 3: Field Properties Dialog-Appearance Tab

Enter "company" as the field name and select Text as the field type. Leave the User Name field blank. It's only used to export a different field name with this field's value when the form is submitted.

Activate the Appearance tab. Here we're presented with options that affect the field's appearance. Our designer decided to create the fields as a graphic so we don't have a Border or Background Color selected. Select Helvetica as the Font and Auto as the Size. The text is sized to fit the box we've just drawn. Finally check the Required checkbox. The user will be warned if they don't fill out this field before submitting the form to the server.

```
┌─────────────────────────────────────────────────────┐
│                    Field Properties                   │
├───────────────────────────────────────────────────────┤
│  Name:     │ company           │   Type: │ Text    ▼ │ │
│  User name:│                   │                       │
│ ╱Appearance╲Options╲Actions╲Format╲Validate╲Calculate╲ │
│ ┌─────────────────────────────────────────────────┐   │
│ │                                                   │   │
│ │   Default:  │ Enter Company Name              │   │   │
│ │                                                   │   │
│ │   Alignment:  │ Left     ▼ │                     │   │
│ │                                                   │   │
│ │     ☐ Multi-line                                  │   │
│ │     ☐ Limit of │    │ characters                  │   │
│ │     ☐ Password                                    │   │
│ │                                                   │   │
│ │                        ┌────────┐  ┌──────────┐   │   │
│ │                        │ Cancel │  │    OK    │   │   │
│ │                        └────────┘  └──────────┘   │   │
│ └─────────────────────────────────────────────────┘   │
└───────────────────────────────────────────────────────┘
```

Step 3: Field Properties Dialog-Options Tab

Now activate the Options tab, where we'll enter the default text displayed in the field. Here we've entered "Enter Company Name". This gives the user a little hint to guide them in their entry. We could also limit the number of characters or change this to a password field if we desired.

Complete your choices, then click the OK button. The dialog closes adding the field to the document.

Step 4

Address, City, and State Fields

Now we'll create the address, city, and state fields. To create these fields, we'll repeat step two for each field. The Field Properties dialog box appears each time we create a field, asking for specifics about the text field we're creating.

As you create each field, activate the Appearance tab and enter its name, and be sure to select Text as the field type. Select Helvetica as the Font and Auto as the Size. Finally check the Required checkbox. The user will be warned if they don't fill out this field before submitting the form to the server.

For each field we add, activate the Options tab. Here we'll enter the default text displayed in the field. Enter some unique identifier that gives the user a hint about what to enter. Leave the limit on the number of characters and the password field unchecked for now.

For each field, click the OK button, closing the dialog, and adding the field to the document.

Step 5

ZIP Code Field

Now we'll add a ZIP code field. With Acrobat Exchange's forms tool selected, drag out a rectangle defining the area where you want to display the ZIP code. The Field Properties dialog box appears asking for specifics about the field we're creating.

Field Properties

Name: zip   Type: Text

User name:

Appearance | Options | Actions | Format | Validate | Calculate

Border :
☐ Border Color   Width: Thin
☐ Background Color   Style: Solid

Text :
Font: Helvetica   Size: Auto

☐ Read Only ☐ Hidden ☐ Required ☐ Don't Print

Cancel   OK

Step 5: Field Properties Dialog-Appearance Tab

Enter "zip" as the field name and select Text as the field type. We left the User Name field blank because we want the field name to be "zip" when the form is submitted.

Activate the Appearance tab. Make sure the Border or Background Colors aren't selected. Select a color the text will display by clicking the Text Color chip. Select Helvetica as the Font and Auto as the Size.

Next activate the Options tab. Enter the default text to display in the field. Leave the limit on the number of characters and the password field unchecked for now.

Now activate the Format tab. The Format tab allows us to regulate the formatting of information entered into the field. Choose Special from the Category list and pick ZIP Code from the Category Options list. This insures users only enter five digits. If they try to enter letters, the system beeps and doesn't enter the character in the field.

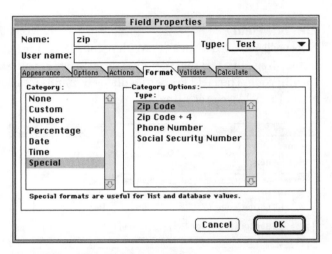

Step 5: Field Properties Dialog-Format Tab

Click the OK button. The dialog closes, adding the field to the document.

Step 6

Telephone Number Field

Now we'll add a telephone number field. With Acrobat Exchange's forms tool selected, drag out a rectangle defining the area where you want to display the telephone number. The Field Properties dialog box appears asking for specifics about the field we're creating.

```
╔═══════════════════════════════════════════════════╗
║                 Field Properties                   ║
╠═══════════════════════════════════════════════════╣
║  Name:     [telephone          ]                    ║
║                              Type: [ Text      ▼]   ║
║  User name: [|                ]                     ║
║                                                     ║
║ ┌Appearance┐ Options  Actions  Format  Validate  Calculate ║
║  ┌─Border :──────────────────────────────────────┐ ║
║  │  ☐ Border Color    [▩]   Width: [ Thin    ▼]  │ ║
║  │                                                │ ║
║  │  ☐ Background Color [▩]  Style: [ Solid   ▼]  │ ║
║  └────────────────────────────────────────────────┘ ║
║  ┌─Text :────────────────────────────────────────┐ ║
║  │                             [■]                │ ║
║  │  Font: [ Helvetica      ▼]                     │ ║
║  │                        Size: [Auto ▼]          │ ║
║  └────────────────────────────────────────────────┘ ║
║                                                     ║
║   ☐ Read Only   ☐ Hidden   ☐ Required   ☐ Don't Print ║
║                                                     ║
║                         ( Cancel )  (( OK ))        ║
╚═══════════════════════════════════════════════════╝
```

Step 6: Field Properties Dialog-Appearance Tab

Enter "telephone" as the field name and select Text as the field type. We left the User Name field blank because we want the field name to be "telephone" when the form is submitted.

Activate the Appearance tab. Make sure the Border or Background Colors aren't selected. Select a color the text will display by clicking the Text Color chip. Select Helvetica as the Font and Auto as the Size.

Next activate the Options tab. Enter the default text to display in the field. Leave the limit on the number of characters and the password field unchecked for now.

Now activate the Format tab. The Format tab allows us to regulate the formatting of information entered into the field. Choose Special from the Category list and pick Phone Number from the Category Options list. This insures users only enter digits. If they try to enter letters, the system beeps and won't enter the character in the field.

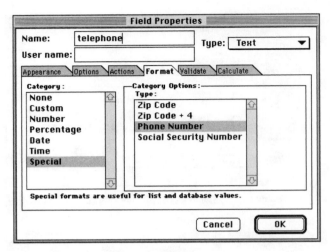

Step 6: Field Properties Dialog-Format Tab

Click the OK button. The dialog closes, adding the field to the document.

Step 7

Visa, MasterCard, and American Express Radio Buttons

In this step we'll add Visa, MasterCard, and American Express radio buttons to our document. These radio buttons are in a group, meaning only one of them can be selected at a time. This is accomplished in HTML by naming the buttons the same. But the value they export when selected is different. The same is true for PDF radio buttons. In this step we'll add one of three radio buttons that allow the user to indicate their preferred method of payment.

With the Acrobat Exchange forms tool selected, drag out a rectangle defining the area where you want the radio button to appear. The Field Properties dialog box appears asking for specifics about the field we're creating.

```
┌─────────────────────────────────────────────────────┐
│              ▓▓▓▓▓ Field Properties ▓▓▓▓▓             │
│ ┌───────────────────────────────────────────────────┐│
│ │ Name:      [ payment          ]                   ││
│ │                              Type: [ Radio Button ▼]││
│ │ User name: [                  ]                   ││
│ │ ┌─Appearance─┐ Options \ Actions \                ││
│ │ │ ┌─Border :─────────────────────────────────────┐││
│ │ │ │  ☒ Border Color      [█]   Width: [ Thin    ▼]│││
│ │ │ │  ☒ Background Color  [ ]   Style: [ Solid   ▼]│││
│ │ │ └──────────────────────────────────────────────┘││
│ │ │ ┌─Text :───────────────────────────────────────┐││
│ │ │ │                              [█]             │││
│ │ │ │  Font: [ Zapf Dingbats    ▼]                 │││
│ │ │ │                      Size: [    ▼]           │││
│ │ │ └──────────────────────────────────────────────┘││
│ │ │  ☐ Read Only  ☐ Hidden  ☒ Required  ☐ Don't Print││
│ │ └───────────────────────────────────────────────────┘│
│ │                          [ Cancel ] (( OK ))      ││
│ └───────────────────────────────────────────────────┘│
└─────────────────────────────────────────────────────┘
```

Step 7: Field Properties Dialog-Appearance Tab

Enter "payment" as the field name and select Radio Button as the field type. Leave the User Name field blank. We want this field's name to be exported as "payment" when the form is submitted.

Activate the Appearance tab. Select the Border Color checkbox and choose a color for the outline of the radio button by clicking the color chip next to the Border Color checkbox. Select black or any dark color so we'll be able to see it. Now select the Background Color checkbox and choose a background color for the radio button by clicking the color chip next to it. Select white or any light color so we'll be able to see when the radio button is chosen. You can play with combinations of the Width and Style options to produce radio buttons with different looks. Our example uses the Thin Width and Solid Style options. Font selection is disabled for radio buttons but you might see Zapf Dingbats as the disabled selection. Finally check the Required checkbox.

Now activate the Options tab. Here we choose the look of the radio button we'll create, identify the value to export if this radio button is selected, and indicate if this button is selected as the default. Choose the list's default value by selecting it.

The Radio Style option presents us with half a dozen different options for radio button styles. Let's stick to the basics and select "Circle". Enter "visa" as the export value and select the Default is Checked checkbox. When the form is initially opened, the "visa" radio button will now be selected.

```
╔═══════════════════════════════════════════════════╗
║                   Field Properties                 ║
╟───────────────────────────────────────────────────╢
║  Name:       payment          Type: [ Radio Button ▼ ] ║
║  User name:  [            ]                         ║
║  ┌Appearance─┐Options─┐Actions┐                    ║
║  │                                             │   ║
║  │                                             │   ║
║  │    Radio Style:  [ Circle      ▼ ]          │   ║
║  │                                             │   ║
║  │    Export Value: [visa               ]      │   ║
║  │                                             │   ║
║  │    ⊠ Default is Checked                      │   ║
║  │                                             │   ║
║  └─────────────────────────────────────────────┘   ║
║                         [ Cancel ]   ( OK )         ║
╚═══════════════════════════════════════════════════╝
```

Step 7: Field Properties Dialog-Options Tab

We've finished the first of three Radio Buttons, so click the OK button, closing the dialog and adding our work to the document.

Now we need to add another payment radio button to our document. With the Acrobat Exchange forms tool selected, drag out a rectangle defining the area where you want the MasterCard radio button to appear. The Field Properties dialog box appears.

```
┌────────────────────────────────────────────────────┐
│≡≡≡≡≡≡≡≡≡≡≡≡≡≡≡≡  Field Properties  ≡≡≡≡≡≡≡≡≡≡≡≡≡≡≡≡│
│                                                      │
│   Name:     │ payment        │    Type: │ Radio Button ▼ │
│   User name:│                │                        │
│  ┌─Appearance─┐ Options ╲ Actions ╲                   │
│  │ ┌─Border :───────────────────────────────────┐    │
│  │ │ ⊠ Border Color      ■    Width: │ Thin   ▼ │    │
│  │ │ ⊠ Background Color   □   Style: │ Solid  ▼ │    │
│  │ └───────────────────────────────────────────┘    │
│  │ ┌─Text :─────────────────────────────────────┐   │
│  │ │                              ■              │   │
│  │ │ Font: │ Zapf Dingbats    ▼ │               │   │
│  │ │                         Size: │ ▼ │         │   │
│  │ └─────────────────────────────────────────────┘   │
│                                                      │
│   □ Read Only   □ Hidden   ⊠ Required   □ Don't Print │
│                                                      │
│                          ( Cancel )  (( OK ))         │
└────────────────────────────────────────────────────┘
```

Step 7: Field Properties Dialog-Appearance Tab

Enter "payment" as the field name and select Radio Button as the field type. Leave the User Name field blank. We want this field's name to be exported as "payment" when the form is submitted.

Activate the Appearance tab. Make sure to select the Border Color checkbox. In addition choose a color for the outline of the radio button by clicking the color chip next to the Border Color checkbox. Select black or any dark color so we'll be able to see it. Now select the Background Color checkbox and choose a background color for the radio button by clicking the color chip next to it. Select white or any light color so we'll be able to see when the radio button is chosen.

Up to this point does everything look the same? If it doesn't, go back and walk through the steps for the radio buttons again.

Activate the Options tab and select "Circle" as the Radio Style. Enter "mastercard" as the export value. Be sure the Default is Checked checkbox is not selected. If this radio button is selected when the form is submitted, the payment field will have the value "mastercard".

Now we need to add the third payment radio button to our document. With the Acrobat Exchange forms tool selected, drag out a rectangle defining the area where you want the American Express radio button to appear. The Field Properties dialog box appears.

Enter "payment" as the field name and select Radio Button as the field type. We want this field's name to be exported as "payment" when the form is submitted.

Activate the Appearance tab. Make sure to select the Border Color checkbox. In addition, choose a color for the outline of the radio button by clicking the color chip next to the Border Color checkbox. Select black or any dark color so we'll be able to see it. Now select the Background Color checkbox and choose a background color for the radio button by clicking the color chip next to it. Select white or any light color so we'll be able to see when the radio button is chosen.

Now activate the Options tab and select "Circle" as the Radio Style. Enter "amex" as the export value. Be sure the Default is Checked checkbox is not selected. If this radio button is selected when the form is submitted, the payment field will have the value "amex".

We've finished this group of Radio buttons, so click the OK button closing the dialog and adding our work to the document. This is a good time to test if the buttons are working. To do this, choose the Hand tool on the Acrobat toolbar and click on the radio buttons. Initially the "visa" button should be selected. When you click on the "amex" radio button, the "visa" button should deselect.

Step 8

Account Number Field

Now we'll add an account number field. With Acrobat Exchange's forms tool selected, drag out a rectangle defining the area where you want to display the telephone number. The Field Properties dialog box appears asking for specifics about the field we're creating.

```
┌──────────────────────────────────────────────────────┐
│                    Field Properties                    │
│ ┌──────────────────────────────────────────────────┐  │
│   Name:     │account          │   Type: │ Text    ▼│   │
│   User name:│                 │                       │
│  ┌Appearance╲Options╲Actions╲Format╲Validate╲Calculate╲ │
│   ┌─Border:──────────────────────────────────────┐    │
│   │  ☐ Border Color      ▓    Width: │ Thin    ▼│ │    │
│   │  ☐ Background Color  ▓    Style: │ Solid   ▼│ │    │
│   └──────────────────────────────────────────────┘    │
│   ┌─Text:────────────────────────────────────────┐    │
│   │                              ▓                 │    │
│   │  Font: │ Helvetica      ▼│                     │    │
│   │                      Size: │Auto│▼│            │    │
│   └──────────────────────────────────────────────┘    │
│   ☐ Read Only   ☐ Hidden   ☐ Required   ☐ Don't Print │
│                            ( Cancel )  (  OK  )        │
└──────────────────────────────────────────────────────┘
```

Step 8: Field Properties Dialog-Appearance Tab

Enter "account" as the field name and select Text as the field type. We left the User Name field blank because we want the field name to be "account" when the form is submitted.

Activate the Appearance tab. Make sure the Border or Background Colors aren't selected. Select a color the text will display by clicking the Text Color chip. Select Helvetica as the Font and Auto as the Size.

Next activate the Options tab. Enter the default text to display in the field. Leave the limit on the number of characters and the password field unchecked for now.

Now activate the Format tab. Choose Number from the Category list and pick "0" for the number of decimal places and choose "none" for the currency symbol. This is a basic method of authentication that insures users only enter digits. We'll do a more detailed check on the server side of the transaction.

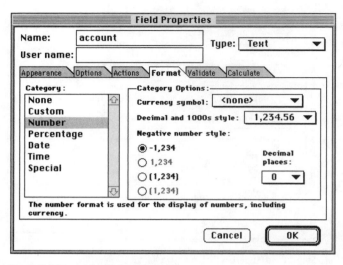

Step 8: Field Properties Dialog-Format Tab

Click the OK button. The dialog closes, adding the field to the document.

Step 9

Photo Image Button

The next field is a button. It's the field we'll use to hold the photo image. PDF buttons have a set of appearances we can alter. This is how we'll send the next photo and have it replace the existing photo image.

To start, select the Acrobat Exchange forms tool, and define a rectangle where the photo button is located. The Field Properties dialog box appears asking for specifics about the field.

```
╔══════════════════════════════════════════════════════╗
║                  Field Properties                      ║
╠══════════════════════════════════════════════════════╣
║  Name:      [ photo            ]      Type: [ Button ▼]║
║  User name: [|                 ]                       ║
║  ┌Appearance┐ Options  Actions                         ║
║  ┌─Border:──────────────────────────────────────────┐ ║
║  │  ☐ Border Color      ▓      Width: [ Thin     ▼]  │ ║
║  │  ☐ Background Color  ▓      Style: [ Solid    ▼]  │ ║
║  └───────────────────────────────────────────────────┘║
║  ┌─Text:────────────────────────────────────────────┐ ║
║  │                                    ▓              │ ║
║  │  Font: [ Helvetica Bold     ▼]                    │ ║
║  │                              Size: [ 12 ] [▼]     │ ║
║  └───────────────────────────────────────────────────┘║
║                                                        ║
║  ☐ Read Only   ☐ Hidden   ☐ Required   ☐ Don't Print  ║
║                                                        ║
║                            [ Cancel ]  (( OK ))        ║
╚══════════════════════════════════════════════════════╝
```

Step 9: Field Properties Dialog-Appearance Tab

Activate the Appearance tab. We don't need to select a Border or Background Color due to our form's design. The button's text color isn't important because we aren't displaying the button title. We aren't going to require the photo for a submission, so make sure Required isn't checked.

```
╔══════════════════════════════════════════════════════╗
║                  Field Properties                      ║
╠══════════════════════════════════════════════════════╣
║  Name:      [ photo            ]      Type: [ Button ▼]║
║  User name: [                  ]                       ║
║  Appearance ┌Options┐ Actions                          ║
║  Highlight: [ None   ▼]   Layout: [ Icon only      ▼] ║
║                                                        ║
║  ┌─Button Face When:─┐   ┌─Button Face Attributes:──┐ ║
║  │ Up                │   │                 ┌───────┐ │ ║
║  │                   │   │                 │       │ │ ║
║  │                   │   │  [ Select Icon...]      │ │ ║
║  │                   │   │  [   Clear     ] │       │ │ ║
║  └───────────────────┘   │                 └───────┘ │ ║
║  [ Advanced Layout... ]  └──────────────────────────┘ ║
║                            [ Cancel ]  (( OK ))        ║
╚══════════════════════════════════════════════════════╝
```

Step 9: Field Properties Dialog-Options Tab

The Options tab allows you to select how the button appears when it's clicked and the general layout of the button. Is this instance, we set the

Highlight option to None. We don't want any user interaction when the image is clicked. The Layout option is set to Icon only. Then click the Advanced Layout button.

Step 9: Advanced Layout Dialog

The Advanced Layout dialog lets us scale an image we'll import into this button. Scaling can be done if the image is larger or smaller than the button's size. Scaling can also be set to be proportional, or it can vary horizontally and vertically. Here we choose to Always scale an image to fit the button and to scale it Proportionally.

Step 9: Select Appearance Dialog

After determining the scaling options, we need to select the button's icon. We do this back in the Field Properties dialog. Click the Select Icon button and you're asked to choose a PDF file to browse through. Here we've selected page one of the photos.pdf file. If the selected PDF contains multiple pages, a scroll bar appears allowing you to scroll through each page until you find the one you want. Click the OK button to confirm the selection.

Step 10

Image Number Field—Read Only

Now we'll add the image number field. This is a read-only field where we display the image number. A number is associated with each image we have to display. This number is how we know what image to send back to the user when they request the next image. In this example the images are numbered sequentially, meaning if a user is viewing image number 123451 and requests the next image, we'll package up and send data associated with image number 123452.

With the Acrobat Exchange's forms tool, create the field where the image number will be placed. The Field Properties dialog box appears asking for specifics about the new image number field.

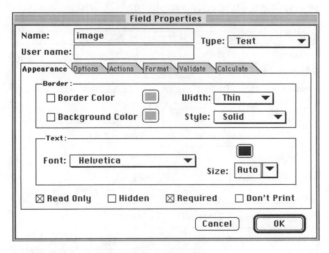

Step 10: Field Properties Dialog-Appearance Tab

Enter "image" as the field name and select Text as the field type. Leave the User Name field blank.

Activate the Appearance tab. We don't need to select a Border or Background Color due to our form's design. Make sure the text color is black. If it isn't, change it to black by clicking the Text Color chip. Select Helvetica as the Font and Auto as the Size. Finally select the Read Only checkbox. This text box will hold and display text, but it won't allow a user to enter any information.

Now activate the Format tab. The Format tab allows us to regulate the formatting of information entered into the field. Choose Number from the Category list and Decimal places to "0" from the Number Options list.

Now click the Field Properties dialog's OK button. The dialog closes, adding the field to the document.

Step 11

Description Field—Read Only

Next we'll create another read-only field to hold the description text. To create the field, choose the forms tool button on the Acrobat Exchange toolbar. Click the mouse button and drag out a rectangle defining the area where you want the text field. The Field Properties dialog box appears asking for specifics about the text field we're creating.

Step 11: Field Properties Dialog-Appearance Tab

Enter "description" as the field name and select Text as the field type. Leave the User Name field blank. It's only used to export a different field name with this field's value when the form is submitted.

Activate the Appearance tab. Here we're presented with options that affect the field's appearance. Our designer decided to create the field as a graphic so we don't have a Border or Background Color selected. If the designer didn't add a field graphic, the Acrobat forms plug-in provides options to create a field with an outline or a background color. Select a color the text will display by clicking the Text Color chip. Select Helvetica as the Font and Auto as the Size. The text is sized to fit the box we've just drawn.

Step 11: Field Properties Dialog-Options Tab

Now activate the Options tab. Here we'll enter the default text displayed in the field. Here we've entered "Baby rests". This is the description for our first entry.

Once you've completed your choices, click the OK button. The dialog closes, adding the field to the document.

Step 12

Cost Field

Now we'll move on to the cost field. This is a read-only field where we display the price to download an image. With Acrobat Exchange's forms tool selected, drag out a rectangle defining the area where you want to display the cost. The Field Properties dialog box appears asking for specifics about the field we're creating.

Step 12: Field Properties Dialog-Appearance Tab

Enter "cost" as the field name and select Text as the field type. Again we leave the User Name field blank. It's only used if we want to have a different field name exported with this field's value when the form is submitted.

Activate the Appearance tab. We don't need to select a Border or Background Color due to our form's design. Make sure the text color is black. If it isn't, change it by clicking the Text Color chip. Select Helvetica as the Font and Auto as the Size. Finally check the Read Only checkbox. This text box will hold and display text but it won't allow a user to enter any information.

Now activate the Format tab. The Format tab allows us to regulate the formatting of information entered into the field. Choose Number from the Category list. Set the number of decimal places we'll display to two. Choose Dollar as the Currency symbol we want to use. Pick a separator style and choose how negative numbers are to be displayed.

```
╔══════════════════════════════════════════════════════╗
║                    Field Properties                    ║
╠══════════════════════════════════════════════════════╣
║  Name:     cost                      Type: │ Text   ▼│ ║
║  User name:│                        │                  ║
║ ┌Appearance┐┌Options┐┌Actions┐┌Format┐┌Validate┐┌Calculate┐║
║                                                        ║
║  Category :           ┌─Category Options:───────────┐  ║
║   None        ⇧       │ Currency symbol: │ Dollar  ▼│ │║
║   Custom              │                              │ ║
║   Number              │ Decimal and 1000s style: │1,234.56 ▼││
║   Percentage          │                              │ ║
║   Date                │ Negative number style:       │ ║
║   Time                │ ● -$1,234.01                 │ ║
║   Special             │                    Decimal   │ ║
║                       │ ○ $1,234.01        places :  │ ║
║                   ⇩   │ ○ ($1,234.01)      │ 2   ▼│  │ ║
║                       │ ○ ($1,234.01)                │ ║
║  The number format is used for the display of numbers, including║
║  currency.                                             ║
║                           ┌────────┐  ┌──────────┐     ║
║                           │ Cancel │  │    OK    │     ║
║                           └────────┘  └──────────┘     ║
╚══════════════════════════════════════════════════════╝
```

Step 12: Field Properties Dialog-Format Tab

Now click the Field Properties dialog's OK button. The dialog closes, adding the field to the document.

Step 13

Previous and Next Buttons

The two buttons that allow us to request the next and previous images in a list are both similar to a submit button. The following instructions walk through creating the previous button. Follow the same process to create the next button.

To start, with Acrobat Exchange's forms tool selected, drag out a rectangle over the previous arrow on the PDF document. The Field Properties dialog appears, asking for specifics about the field we just created. Choose Button from the Type popup menu and enter "prev" as the button name.

Step 13: Field Properties Dialog-Appearance Tab

Activate the Appearance tab. Make sure the Border and Background checkboxes are not checked. The button doesn't display any text, so the text color selection isn't important.

Step 13: Field Properties Dialog-Options Tab

Activate the Options tab. Choose Invert from the Highlight popup menu, and Text only from the Layout popup menu. This creates a button that inverts the underlying area of the PDF file.

Step 13: Field Properties Dialog-Actions Tab

From the Actions tab, the button can be assigned an action. Select the Mouse Up option from the When this happens list. Next, click the Add button and choose Submit Form from the list of available action types.

Step 13: Add an Action Dialog

At this point we need to select an URL to process the form submission. Click the Select URL button and enter an URL. Choose to submit the fields in HTML Form and be sure all fields are selected to export.

URL and Field Selection

Enter a Universal Resource Locator [URL] for this link:

/scripts/i_library.pl

Export Format
- ○ Forms Data Format (FDF)
- ⦿ HTML Form (URL encoded)

Field Selection
- ☐ Include empty fields
- ⦿ All fields
- ○ All, except...   Select fields...
- ○ Only these...

Cancel   OK

Step 13: URL and Field Selection Dialog

To commit the settings, click the OK buttons in the URL and Field
Selection, Add an Action and Field Properties dialogs.

Step 14

Submit and Reset Buttons

Our two remaining fields correspond to the submit and reset buttons.
First we'll create the submit button. With Acrobat Exchange's forms tool
selected, drag out a rectangle defining the area where the submit button
is located. The Field Properties dialog box appears asking for specifics
about the field we're creating.

Field Properties

Name: submit   Type: Button ▼
User name:

Appearance Options Actions

Border:
- ☐ Border Color   ▢   Width: Thin ▼
- ☐ Background Color   ▢   Style: Solid ▼

Text:
Font: Helvetica Bold ▼   ▢
                              Size: 12 ▼

☐ Read Only   ☐ Hidden   ☐ Required   ☐ Don't Print

Cancel   OK

Step 14: Field Properties Dialog-Appearance Tab

Activate the Appearance tab. Again we don't need to select a Border or
Background Color due to our form's design. The button's text color isn't
important because we aren't displaying the button's title.

Step 14: Field Properties Dialog-Options Tab

The Options tab is where you select any special appearance options for
the button. In this instance we set the Highlight option to Invert. The
Layout option is set to Text only. Because we don't want any text to show
over our buttons, the Text entry for the Button face attributes is left
blank. The Button Face When option determines when the appearance
we set up is invoked. Here we want it to Invert on a mouse up event.

Step 14: Field Properties Dialog-Actions Tab

The Actions tab is where you select any action this field will invoke. Here we choose the Mouse Up event. Click the Add button and choose Submit Form from the list of available action types.

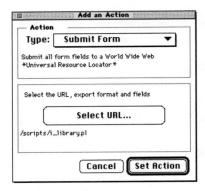

Step 14: Add an Action Dialog

Now we need to identify the URL that will process the form submission. Click the Select URL button and enter the URL we'll use to process this form.

Step 14: URL and Field Selection Dialog

Here we also choose to submit the data to the server in HTML format. We could submit in the FDF format but the Perl script we'll use to process the submission is set up to receive the data in HTML format. We also want to send All fields even though we have the option to just send a subset of the fields from the form. Once the proper selections are made, click the OK buttons in the URL and Field Selection, Add an Action, and Field Properties dialogs.

Step 15

Reset Button

Our final field is the reset button. With Acrobat Exchange's forms tool selected, drag out a rectangle defining the area where the reset button is located. The Field Properties dialog box appears asking for specifics about the field we're creating.

Step 15: Field Properties Dialog-Appearance Tab

Activate the Appearance tab. Again we don't need to select a Border or Background Color due to our form's design. The button's text color isn't important because we aren't displaying the button's title.

Step 15: Field Properties Dialog-Options Tab

The Options tab is where you select any special appearance options for the button. Is this instance we set the Highlight option to Invert. The Layout option is set to Text only. Because we don't want any text to show over our buttons, the Text entry for the Button face attributes is left blank. The Button Face When option determines when the appearance we set up is invoked. Here we want it to Invert on a mouse up event.

Step 15: Field Properties Dialog-Actions Tab

Now select the Actions tab. When a user clicks this button, we want the form to reset all its fields to their default values. To do this, select the Mouse Up item from the When this happens list. Click the Add button and the Add an Action dialog appears.

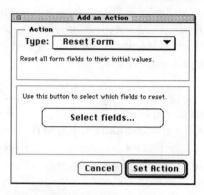

Step 15: Add an Action Dialog

From this dialog choose Reset Form from the list of available action types. Now we can also select the fields we want to reset. All fields is the default. Leave All fields selected for now.

Once the proper selections are made, click the OK button in the Add an Action and Field Properties dialogs.

We're ready to discuss setting up the back end of the process to receive information from this form.

Creating the PDF Images File

This example also uses one PDF file to store the collection of images. This file was created in QuarkXPress. Each image was placed on a separate page and a nine page PDF file was created. The Perl script we'll use sets the button appearance of the photo button to the contents of one of our pages from this file. Our example file is named "photo.pdf" and is stored in the same "C:\pdfs\" directory located on our server machine.

Creating the Perl Scripts

This example uses one Perl script on the server side of the transaction. The script processes the submission identifying a possible purchase or request for another image. A request for another image identifies which image is being viewed and forwards the next image and its accompanying information back to the client.

The script is "i_library.pl". It works with the form to process the submission. The form gathers name, address, city, state, zip, telephone, payment, account, and image number and sends it to the server for processing by a CGI script. The Perl script decodes the submission and returns a confirming HTML file or the next image to the client.

The following pages discuss creating the "i_library.pl" Perl script used for processing the form's submission on the server side of this transaction. The complete script is shown below. For this example to work, the script must exist as a file named "i_library.pl". This file is placed in the "scripts" directory in the IIS 4.0's root directory. Of course the IIS root directory and scripts directory were created automatically when we installed the Web server on our Windows NT machine.

Code Example: i_library.pl

```
1.    #!/usr/local/bin/perl
2.
3.    use CGI;
4.    use Acrobat::FDF;
5.
6.    my $q = new CGI;
7.    my $theFdf = Acrobat::FDF::new( );
8.    my $filename = "c:\\temp\\a" . (int( rand( 1000000
      ) ) + 1) . ".fdf";
9.    my $imageNum = $q->param('image');
10.   my $subType;
11.   my $normalApp = 0;
12.
13.   $subType = "prev" if( $q->param('prev') );
14.   $subType = "next" if( $q->param('next') );
15.   $subType = "submit" if( $q->param('submit') );
```

```perl
16.
17.  if( $subType eq "next" || $subType eq "prev" )
18.  {
19.    if( $subType eq "next" ){
20.      if( $imageNum eq "123459"){ $imageNum =
           "123451" }
21.      else{
22.        $imageNum = $imageNum + 1;
23.      }
24.    }
25.    elsif( $subType eq "prev" ){
26.      if( $imageNum eq "123451"){ $imageNum =
           "123459" }
27.      else{
28.        $imageNum = $imageNum - 1;
29.      }
30.    }
31.    else{
32.      &returnError( $q, 500, "Submission Method
         Error", "Unsupported submission type
         encountered." );
33.    }
34.    &create_fdf( $theFdf, $filename , $imageNum );
35.
36.    print $q->header('application/vnd.fdf');
37.
38.    open( IN, $filename ) || die "cannot open
         $filename for reading";
39.    binmode IN;
40.    binmode STDOUT;
41.    while( <IN> ){
42.      print $_;
43.    }
44.    close( IN );
45.    unlink( $filename );
46.  }
47.  else{
48.    if( $subType eq "submit" ){
49.      &send_thank_you( $q );
50.    }
```

```
51.      else{
52.         &returnError( $q, 500, "Submission Method
            Error", "Unsupported submission type
            encountered.");
53.      }
54.   }
55.   exit(0);
56.
57.   sub create_fdf
58.   {
59.      my $theFdf = shift;
60.      my $filename = shift;
61.      my $imageNum = shift;
62.
63.      if( $imageNum eq "123451" )
64.      {
65.         $theFdf->SetValue( "image", "123451", False );
66.         $theFdf->SetValue( "description", "Baby
            resting", False );
67.         $theFdf->SetValue( "cost", "\$12.00", False );
68.         $theFdf->SetAP( "photo", $normalApp, "",
            "c:\\pdfs\\photo.pdf", 1 );
69.      }
70.      elsif( $imageNum eq "123452" )
71.      {
72.         $theFdf->SetValue( "image", "123452", False );
73.         $theFdf->SetValue( "description", "Woman
            Laughing", False );
74.         $theFdf->SetValue( "cost", "\$18.00", False );
75.         $theFdf->SetAP( "photo", $normalApp, "",
            "c:\\pdfs\\photo.pdf", 2 );
76.      }
77.      elsif( $imageNum eq "123453" )
78.      {
79.         $theFdf->SetValue( "image", "123453", False );
80.         $theFdf->SetValue( "description", "Man
            Laughs", False );
81.         $theFdf->SetValue( "cost", "\$10.00", False );
82.         $theFdf->SetAP( "photo", $normalApp, "",
            "c:\\pdfs\\photo.pdf", 3 );
```

```
83.     }
84.     elsif( $imageNum eq "123454" )
85.     {
86.       $theFdf->SetValue( "image", "123454", False );
87.       $theFdf->SetValue( "description", "Machu
          Picchu", False );
88.       $theFdf->SetValue( "cost", "\$12.00", False );
89.       $theFdf->SetAP( "photo", $normalApp, "",
          "c:\\pdfs\\photo.pdf", 4 );
90.     }
91.     elsif( $imageNum eq "123455" )
92.     {
93.       $theFdf->SetValue( "image", "123455", False );
94.       $theFdf->SetValue( "description", "Pyramids",
          False );
95.       $theFdf->SetValue( "cost", "\$14.50", False );
96.       $theFdf->SetAP( "photo", $normalApp, "",
          "c:\\pdfs\\photo.pdf", 5 );
97.     }
98.     elsif( $imageNum eq "123456" )
99.     {
100.      $theFdf->SetValue( "image", "123456", False );
101.      $theFdf->SetValue( "description", "Sphinx",
          False );
102.      $theFdf->SetValue( "cost", "\$19.00", False );
103.      $theFdf->SetAP( "photo", $normalApp, "",
          "c:\\pdfs\\photo.pdf", 6 );
104.    }
105.    elsif( $imageNum eq "123457" )
106.    {
107.      $theFdf->SetValue( "image", "123457", False );
108.      $theFdf->SetValue( "description", "Diskette",
          False );
109.      $theFdf->SetValue( "cost", "\$12.00", False );
110.      $theFdf->SetAP( "photo", $normalApp, "",
          "c:\\pdfs\\photo.pdf", 7 );
111.    }
112.    elsif( $imageNum eq "123458" )
113.    {
114.      $theFdf->SetValue( "image", "123458", False );
```

```
115.        $theFdf->SetValue( "description", "Electric
            Socket", False );
116.        $theFdf->SetValue( "cost", "\$18.00", False );
117.        $theFdf->SetAP( "photo", $normalApp, "",
            "c:\\pdfs\\photo.pdf", 8 );
118.    }
119.    elsif( $imageNum eq "123459" )
120.    {
121.        $theFdf->SetValue( "image", "123459", False );
122.        $theFdf->SetValue( "description", "Medicine",
            False );
123.        $theFdf->SetValue( "cost", "\$11.00", False );
124.        $theFdf->SetAP( "photo", $normalApp, "",
            "c:\\pdfs\\photo.pdf", 9 );
125.    }
126.    else
127.    {
128.        $theFdf->SetValue( "image", "123451", False );
129.        $theFdf->SetValue( "description", "Baby
            rests", False );
130.        $theFdf->SetValue( "cost", "\$12.00", False );
131.        $theFdf->SetValue( "photo", "Get Being Used",
            False );
132.        $theFdf->SetAP( "photo", $normalApp, "",
            "c:\\pdfs\\photo.pdf", 1 );
133.    }
134.    $theFdf->SetFile( "/samples/photo/main.pdf" );
135.    $theFdf->Save( $filename );
136. }
137.
138. sub send_thank_you
139. {
140.    my $q = shift;
141.
142.    print $q->header;
143.    print $q->start_html('Thanks for your order', 0,
        0, 'BGCOLOR="#FFFFFF"');
144.    print $q->h1("Thanks for placing your order");
145.    print "We will process your order (not really)
        and contact you if there is a problem.\n\n";
```

```perl
146.    print "The information received was:   ";
147.    print "<PRE>\n";
148.    print "<BR>Your name is:        ", $q-
        >param('name'), "\n";
149.    print "<BR>Your company is:     ", $q-
        >param('company'), "\n";
150.    print "<BR>Your address is:     ", $q-
        >param('address'), "\n";
151.    print "<BR>Your city is:        ", $q-
        >param('city'), "\n";
152.    print "<BR>Your state is:       ", $q-
        >param('state'), "\n";
153.    print "<BR>Your ZIP code is:    ", $q-
        >param('zip'), "\n";
154.    print "<BR>Credit card type:    ", $q-
        >param('payment'), "\n<BR>\n";
155.    print "<BR>Image number ordered: ", $q-
        >param('image'), "\n";
156.    print "<BR>Image description:    ", $q-
        >param('description'), "\n";
157.    print "<BR>Cost:      ", $q->param('cost'), "\n";
158.    print "</PRE>";
159.    print $q->end_html();
160. }
161.
162. sub return_error
163. {
164.   my $q = shift;
165.   local ($status, $errtype, $message) = @_;
166.
167.   print $q->header( -status=>$status . ' ' .
       $errtype);
168.   print $q->start_html('CGI Program Error', 0, 0,
       'BGCOLOR="#FFFFFF"');
169.   print $q->h1( "This CGI program encountered an
       error: ", $errtype );
170.   print $message;
171.   print $q->hr;
172.   print $q->end_html();
173.   exit(1);
174. }
```

The Example Script

Let's take a detailed look at our example script. Line one of our script is used to declare the location of the Perl interpreter to use when running this script. In a UNIX environment this line would look something like this: #!/usr/local/bin/perl. Windows NT keeps track of which programs run which type of files, so we don't need to point out the path of the Perl interpreter to use.

Line three sets the variable we'll use to direct our e-mail. Here we'll send it to info@mix-media.com. Notice the '@' and the "." Have a '\' before them. These two characters actually have meaning to a computer. They can cause programs to execute certain functions. To prevent this from happening we put a "\" character in front of them announcing the next character is in fact a character and not a command we want executed. This is called escaping characters in a string.

```
1.   #!/usr/local/bin/perl
2.
3.   use CGI;
4.   use Acrobat::FDF;
5.
```

http://www.perl.org/CPAN/

Lines three and four tell Perl to use a module of pre-defined routines. These routines are kept in a Perl module file. The file is stored in the Libs directory of the Perl interpreter. On line three we use the CGI module. This module was written and is maintained by Lincoln Stien at MIT. Most modules are free and a comprehensive archive is available for FTP downloading. This CGI module contains a library of routines that decode form submissions and output HTML among other things. Line four tells Perl to use the FDF module located in the Acrobat sub-directory of the Libs directory. This module is available only from Adobe. It can construct an FDF response that a PDF form can use to flow data into its existing fields. To use this script, both modules must be downloaded and installed according to their instructions.

```
6.   my $q = new CGI;
7.   my $theFdf = Acrobat::FDF::new( );
8.   my $filename = "c:\\temp\\a" . (int( rand( 1000000
     ) ) + 1) . ".fdf";
```

```
9.    my $imageNum = $q->param('image');
10.   my $subType;
11.   my $normalApp = 0;
12.
```

On line six three things happen. First, we use the new operator to create a new instance of the CGI module. Second, we assign that reference to the variable $q. We use the my scoping declaration to insure this is a private variable. By default, anytime you create a variable, it is global. This causes problems if in other routines the same variable is referenced. By using the my scoping declaration, we insure the variable's private nature until the end of this code block.

On line seven we do the same for an instance of the Acrobat::FDF module. We create a new instance and assign it to the $theFdf variable. Again, this variable is scoped using the my declaration so that we don't collide with any similarly named variables.

On line eight we construct a string we'll use as a path to save the FDF file we create. The file is stored on our "C:\" drive in the temp directory. The file name is constructed by generating a random number. The rand() function takes a value and returns a semi-random number. The seed value we use is the one million. One is added to the value and it is converted to an integer. This number is concatenated to our path. Finally, the ".fdf" suffix is added to the string. Once this is completed, the string stored in the $filename variable will look something like this:

```
C:\temp\a854515.fdf
```

On line nine we access the param member function of our $q variable. . Remember, the $q is a reference to the CGI module. Inside the CGI module, the param() function is defined. It retrieves a value from a form submission. Here we retrieve the value stored in the image field. The value is then stored in our $imageNum variable.

The final two variables we declare are $subType and $normalApp. A zero is stored in $normalApp, and $subType is left for initialization on the next three lines of our script.

```
13.    $subType = "prev" if( $q->param('prev') );
14.    $subType = "next" if( $q->param('next') );
15.    $subType = "submit" if( $q->param('submit') );
16.
```

Lines 13, 14 and 15 all perform the same task. Since Acrobat submits the name of the button clicked with no value, we need to check to see which button was used to make this submission. We do this by checking for a field's inclusion in the submitted data. Line 13 states that "prev" is assigned to $subType if a field named "prev" is found in the submission. To accomplish this we again access the param() member function of the $q variable. If the "prev" field isn't found, nothing is assigned to the $subType variable. On lines 14 and 15 this is repeated, checking for the next and submit fields.

```
17.    if( $subType eq "next" || $subType eq "prev" )
18.    {
19.      if( $subType eq "next" ){
20.        if( $imageNum eq "123459"){ $imageNum =
           "123451" }
21.        else{
22.          $imageNum = $imageNum + 1;
23.        }
24.      }
```

On line 17 it becomes clear why we need to know which button was clicked to send the submission. Here, we check if $subType is now equal to "next" or "prev". If it is, we branch into a code block that will return the next or previous image information as FDF data.

On line 19 we check if $subType is set to "next". If it is, we need to adjust the image number to return the appropriate image. First we check if we're viewing the last image available. This example only has nine images, and the ninth image is numbered "123459". If this is the image number the user is viewing , we set the return image number to the first available image. This is image "123451". If we're not viewing our last image we just need to add one to the image number. This occurs on line 22.

```
25.      elsif( $subType eq "prev" ){
26.        if( $imageNum eq "123451"){ $imageNum =
```

```
          "123459" }
27.       else{
28.          $imageNum = $imageNum - 1;
29.       }
30.    }
```

If $subType wasn't set to "next", we check to see if it's set to "prev". If it is, on line 26, we check to see if we're viewing the first image in our list and if we are, set the return image number to "123459". This is the last or ninth image in the example. This gives sort of a loop to the list of images. If we aren't in this special case of being at the first image, we need to simply subtract one from our image number to identify the previous image to return.

```
31.    else{
32.       &return_error( $q, 500, "Submission Method
          Error", "Unsupported submission type
          encountered.");
33.    }
```

Lines 31-33 are a safety net in case we've somehow reached this point and don't have either a "prev" or "next" field. If this is the case, we return an HTML error page by calling the return_error() sub routine.

```
34.    &create_fdf( $theFdf, $filename , $imageNum );
35.
36.    print $q->header('application/vnd.fdf');
37.
38.    open( IN, $filename ) || die "cannot open
       $filename for reading";
39.    binmode IN;
40.    binmode STDOUT;
41.    while( <IN> ){
42.       print $_;
43.    }
44.    close( IN );
45.    unlink( $filename );
46. }
```

Line 34 calls our create_fdf() sub routine. This is the routing we use to generate the FDF data for the response. We pass the routine a reference to our FDF module object, the path we constructed, and the image number we've adjusted. We'll discuss this routine in detail shortly.

Once we've successfully constructed the FDF response, we need to begin returning the information to the user. On line 36 we access the header() member function of the $q variable. Here we indicate the mime type of the response is "application/vnd.fdf". Accessing the member functions of the CGI module is a great way to avoid errors common in print statements.

On line 38 we open the file indicated by our $filename variable and associate it with our input buffer. If this fails, the script dies and prints a message the server places in its log file. If we're successful, we change the mode the file is to read to binary. PDF and FDF files contain binary data, so we must change to binary mode for reading and writing. On lines 39 and 40 we set the mode to binary for our input file handle and our STDOUT file handle.

Lines 41-43 are a while loop we use to output the contents of the file we constructed. It reads as, while there is data left to read in the file, print it to STDOUT.

On line 44 we close the file handle we opened on line 38 and on line 45 we use the Perl unlink() function to delete the file we created on our server's hard drive to hold the FDF data.

```
48.   else{
49.     if( $subType eq "submit" ){
50.       &send_thank_you( $q );
51.     }
52.     else{
        &return_error( $q, 500, "Submission Method
        Error", "Unsupported submission type
53.       encountered.");
54.     }
55.   }
56.   exit(0);
```

If the $subType isn't "prev" or "next", we fall into the else branch that begins on line 47. Here we check for a $subType value of "submit". If found, we call our sub routine send_thank_you(). If $subType doesn't equal submit, we have an unsupported submission type. In that case, we call our return_error() sub routine on line 52.

If everything goes well, our script reaches line 55 and returns with an exit code of zero.

The create_fdf() Sub Routine

Next let's look at the create_fdf() sub routine. The routing begins on line 57. Lines 59-61 store references to the three parameters passed into the routine. We use the Perl shift function to shift the parameters into the locally scoped variable references. Line 59 shifts the first parameter into the variable $theFdf. The same names as the parameters were used to clarify what comes in and where it goes. Lines 60 and 61 receive the field name and adjusted image number.

```
57.  sub create_fdf
58.  {
59.    my $theFdf = shift;
60.    my $filename = shift;
61.    my $imageNum = shift;
```

On line 63 we check to see if the image number being requested is equal to "123451". If it is, we access the SetValue() member function of the FDF module, passing it three values. The first is a string containing the name of the field whose value we wish to set. Here we are setting image field to "123451". The second parameter is the value the field will be set to. The final parameter indicates if the FDF module should convert the value to a PDF name. Items in a PDF file can be named and later referenced to by name. This doesn't apply here, so we pass the value "False".

```
63.      if( $imageNum eq "123451" )
64.      {
65.        $theFdf->SetValue( "image", "123451", False );
66.        $theFdf->SetValue( "description", "Baby
           rests", False );
67.        $theFdf->SetValue( "cost", "\$12.00", False );
```

```
68.        $theFdf->SetAP( "photo", $normalApp, "",
           "c:\\pdfs\\photo.pdf", 1 );
69.      }
```

Lines 66 and 67 accomplish the same task for the description and cost fields. The values here are the actual text that will flow into the PDF file. Line 68 accesses the SetAP() or set appearance member function of the FDF module. The parameters we pass it tell the module we want to set the "photo" field. The second parameter is the value we stored in the $normalApp variable. Zero represents normal appearance. The third parameter is used to indicate if the field contains any sub appearances. Pass the empty string here since our photo field doesn't. The fourth parameter is the path on our server machine of the PDF file where the appearance can be found. The final parameter is the page number to use as the field's appearance.

Lines 70 through 125 repeat this process for each image the library makes available. The only difference is that the appropriate parameters are inserted for each individual image number.

```
70.      elsif( $imageNum eq "123452" )
71.      {
72.        $theFdf->SetValue( "image", "123452", False );
73.        $theFdf->SetValue( "description", "Woman
           Laughing", False );
74.        $theFdf->SetValue( "cost", "\$18.00", False );
75.        $theFdf->SetAP( "photo", $normalApp, "",
           "c:\\pdfs\\photo.pdf", 2 );
76.      }
77.      elsif( $imageNum eq "123453" )
78.      {
79.        $theFdf->SetValue( "image", "123453", False );
80.        $theFdf->SetValue( "description", "Man
           Laughs", False );
81.        $theFdf->SetValue( "cost", "\$10.00", False );
82.        $theFdf->SetAP( "photo", $normalApp, "",
           "c:\\pdfs\\photo.pdf", 3 );
83.      }
84.      elsif( $imageNum eq "123454" )
85.      {
```

```
86.          $theFdf->SetValue( "image", "123454", False );
87.          $theFdf->SetValue( "description", "Machu
             Picchu", False );
88.          $theFdf->SetValue( "cost", "\$12.00", False );
89.          $theFdf->SetAP( "photo", $normalApp, "",
             "c:\\pdfs\\photo.pdf", 4 );
90.      }
91.      elsif( $imageNum eq "123455" )
92.      {
93.          $theFdf->SetValue( "image", "123455", False );
94.          $theFdf->SetValue( "description", "Pyramids",
             False );
95.          $theFdf->SetValue( "cost", "\$14.50", False );
96.          $theFdf->SetAP( "photo", $normalApp, "",
             "c:\\pdfs\\photo.pdf", 5 );
97.      }
98.      elsif( $imageNum eq "123456" )
99.      {
100.         $theFdf->SetValue( "image", "123456", False );
101.         $theFdf->SetValue( "description", "Sphinx",
             False );
102.         $theFdf->SetValue( "cost", "\$19.00", False );
103.         $theFdf->SetAP( "photo", $normalApp, "",
             "c:\\pdfs\\photo.pdf", 6 );
104.     }
105.     elsif( $imageNum eq "123457" )
106.     {
107.         $theFdf->SetValue( "image", "123457", False );
108.         $theFdf->SetValue( "description", "Diskette",
             False );
109.         $theFdf->SetValue( "cost", "\$12.00", False );
110.         $theFdf->SetAP( "photo", $normalApp, "",
             "c:\\pdfs\\photo.pdf", 7 );
111.     }
112.     elsif( $imageNum eq "123458" )
113.     {
114.         $theFdf->SetValue( "image", "123458", False );
115.         $theFdf->SetValue( "description", "Electric
             Socket", False );
116.         $theFdf->SetValue( "cost", "\$18.00", False );
```

```
117.        $theFdf->SetAP( "photo", $normalApp, "",
            "c:\\pdfs\\photo.pdf", 8 );
118.    }
119.    elsif( $imageNum eq "123459" )
120.    {
121.        $theFdf->SetValue( "image", "123459", False );
122.        $theFdf->SetValue( "description", "Medicine",
            False );
123.        $theFdf->SetValue( "cost", "\$11.00", False );
124.        $theFdf->SetAP( "photo", $normalApp, "",
            "c:\\pdfs\\photo.pdf", 9 );
125.    }
```

Line 126 is our catch all handler. If an unrecognized image number is encountered, the information and photo of our first image is returned.

```
126.    else
127.    {
128.        $theFdf->SetValue( "image", "123451", False );
129.        $theFdf->SetValue( "description", "Baby
            rests", False );
130.        $theFdf->SetValue( "cost", "\$12.00", False );
131.        $theFdf->SetValue( "photo", "Get Being Used",
            False );
132.        $theFdf->SetAP( "photo", $normalApp, "",
            "c:\\pdfs\\photo.pdf", 1 );
133.    }
```

The final three lines of the sub routine set the file reference for the FDF file. This tells the PDF viewing application which PDF document is the owner of the FDF data.

Line 135 saves the FDF data file to the path name we constructed and stored in the $filename variable. On line 136 the sub routine finishes, returning control to its calling routine.

```
134.    $theFdf->SetFile( "/samples/photo/main.pdf" );
135.    $theFdf->Save( $filename );
136. }
137.
```

The send_thank_you() Sub Routine

The send_thank_you( ) sub routine returns a simple HTML page that confirms a client's order. The routine is comprised of the code block from line 138 to 160. One parameter is passed into the routine. This is a reference to our CGI module. Line 140 of the script uses the Perl shift function to assign the parameter to a local variable $q. The name was kept the same to help identify the $q parameter that is passed in and assigned to the local variable also named $q.

```perl
138.  sub send_thank_you
139.  {
140.    my $q = shift;
141.
142.    print $q->header;
143.    print $q->start_html('Thanks for your order', 0,
        0, 'BGCOLOR="#FFFFFF"');
144.    print $q->h1("Thanks for placing your order");
145.    print "We will process your order (not really)
        and contact you if there is a problem.\n\n";
146.    print "The information received was:  ";
```

On lines 142 through 144 we use the member functions of the CGI module to output HTML. Line 142 outputs the required header. Line 143 adds the open HTML tag, a title and a body tag with background color information. Line 144 adds a level one heading. It's much simpler to add HTML using the CGI module methods. On lines 145 and 146 we output plain text using the print Perl function.

```perl
147.    print "<PRE>\n";
148.    print "<BR>Your name is:      ",
        $q->param('name'), "\n";
149.    print "<BR>Your company is:      ",
        $q->param('company'), "\n";
150.    print "<BR>Your address is:      ",
        $q->param('address'), "\n";
151.    print "<BR>Your city is:       ",
        $q->param('city'), "\n";
152.    print "<BR>Your state is:      ",
        $q->param('state'), "\n";
```

```
153.    print "<BR>Your ZIP code is:      ",
        $q->param('zip'), "\n";
154.    print "<BR>Credit card type:      ",
        $q->param('payment'), "\n<BR>\n";
155.    print "<BR>Image number ordered: ",
        $q->param('image'), "\n";
156.    print "<BR>Image description:     ",
        $q->param('description'), "\n";
157.    print "<BR>Cost:      ", $q->param('cost'), "\n";
158.    print "</PRE>";
159.    print $q->end_html();
160.  }
```

From line 147 to line 158 we print the contents of the form fields. Again we use the param routine of the CGI module to access each field by name. Finally, on line 159 we output the required closing HTML tags and exit the sub routine.

The return_error() Sub Routine

The return_error() sub routine is another simple solution that sends an HTML response to the client if an error occurs.

On line 165 we call the Perl local operator to create local references to the four parameters passed to this routine.

```
162.  sub return_error
163.  {
164.    my $q = shift;
165.    local ($status, $errtype, $message) = @_;
166.
167.    print $q->header( -status=>$status . ' ' .
        $errtype);
168.    print $q->start_html('CGI Program Error', 0, 0,
        'BGCOLOR="#FFFFFF"');
169.    print $q->h1( "This CGI program encountered an
        error: ", $errtype );
170.    print $message;
171.    print $q->hr;
172.    print $q->end_html();
173.    exit(1);
174.  }
```

Line 167 prints the result of the CGI module's header member function. To this function we pass a status parameter containing the error code status followed by a space and the description of the error that occurred. Line 168 adds the document's title and body tags.

On line 169 we add a level one header informing the user an error occurred. The type of error is concatenated to the string to further identify the problem. Line 170 adds the message passed to the sub routine. This should be text that will help the user track down the source of their problem. Line 171 outputs a horizontal rule HTML tag and line 172 completes the file by outputting the required close body and HTML tags.

On line 173 we call the Perl exit() function, passing it a value of one to inform the interpreter an error has occurred. Finally, on line 174 the sub routine ends.

Run the Example

http://www.activestate.com/

To run the example, place the "i_library.pl" Perl script in your IIS "scripts" directory. Perl must be configured to run with IIS. ActiveWare provides a compatible version of Perl and instructions for integration with IIS.

Also, place the "photo.pdf" in your server's "C:\pdfs\" directory. The remaining PDF file and the three HTML files should be placed in the same directory on your server so that you can access them through your browser. Place them in a "photo" directory so they can be accessed as "http://your server/photo/.

In order to generate FDF, a shared library on Unix or an ActiveX server component on Windows must be installed on the server machine.

http://www.adobe.com/ada/ acrosdk/fdf.html

In this case the FdfAcX.dl and the FdfTk.dll are copied into our \winnt\system32\ directory. Any directory with execute permissions will do. If you're using an NTFS formatted hard drive, be sure the DLLs also have execute permission.

Once the files are copied, the FdfAcX.dll needs to be registered with the system. To do this, from the command line, cd into the directory containing the FdfAcX.dll. Then enter regsvr32 FdfAcX.dll. Be sure that FDF.pm is copied into the proper location in your Perl directory structure. With Perl 5.004 or newer, this is in the \lib\site\Acrobat directory.

The Unix FDF toolkit comes with a Perl script that walks you through its suggested installation.

Now enter the form's URL in your browser window. Enter some information into the form fields and click the submit button.

Résumé Submission

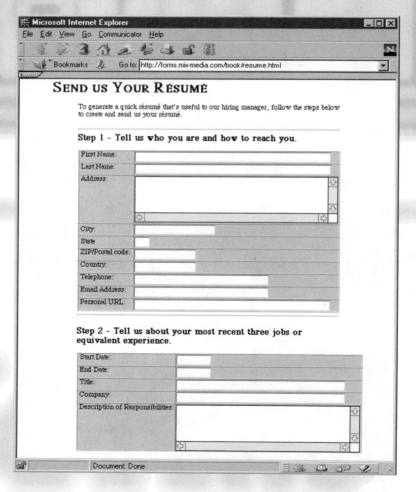

Overview

This example demonstrates how to construct a résumé form that gathers employment information from hopeful candidates, and emails a formatted version to a predefined recipient such as the director of recruiting. The example allows the user to enter their information into an HTML form document.

Physical Requirements

The following list is a description of the setup used to create this example. The actual components are:

UNIX server running the LINUX operation system
Apache Web Server 1.2
Perl 5.004 for Unix
Sendmail Unix mail utility
Netscape Navigator 3.x or Netscape Communicator 4.04 or newer with Acrobat
Plug-in or Microsoft Internet Explorer 4.0 or newer with Acrobat Plug-in

Physical Setup the Example Uses

The example runs on an Apache Web Server 1.2. The operating system the server runs on is LINUX. Perl 5.0 is installed on the server machine in the "usr/local/bin" directory. After the installation, the Perl script used to send the resume is placed in the server's cgi-bin directory.

In this example checking for valid submission data takes place through JavaScript in the browser window. However, we still use a Perl script to package and send the resume submission through e-mail. The Apache server requires that the "resume.pl" script we use to process the form's submission reside in the "cgi-bin" directory in the root folder for our Web server. The script's been granted execute permission.

We have installed Netscape Communicator 4.04 and Microsoft Internet Explorer 4.0 on our client machine.

Creating the Necessary Files

To get this example to work, we need to put two files on the server. The first is an HTML file that is the form the client interacts with and the second is the Perl script we'll use to process the form submission.

Although we check the form fields with a JavaScript routine on the client we still use a Perl script to mail the submission to the proper recipient.

Creating the HTML File

This example uses an HTML file as its client-side interface. This HTML form allows users to enter information relevant to submitting their resume information. The form takes a first name, last name, address, city, state, ZIP code, telephone number, email address, and a personal URL. It accepts information for each of the applicant's two most recent jobs. This includes start and end dates, title of their position, company, and a description of their responsibilities. The form also accepts information about the applicant's academic history. Information for two degrees includes the type of degree, year completed, field of study and the school or institution. Finally, the form allows for personal information such as interests or hobbies.

This form contains JavaScript, which validates the submission. A dialog box describing the problem is displayed if any information is missing or incomplete. Once the submission passes this checkpoint, the data is sent to a Perl script on the server, where it is packaged up and mailed to the hiring manager.

The designer constructed the HTML form file visually using Claris HomePage. The JavaScript was added using a text editor. The next steps discuss creating the client side form of this transaction.

The Form Field Names

This HTML document contains the following form fields:

fname
lname
address
city
state
zip

telephone
email
personalurl
start1
end1
title1
company1
desc1
start2
end2
title2
company2
desc2
degree1
grad1
field1
school1
degree2
grad2
field2
school2
other
submit

Examining the HTML code

You can use any visual HTML tool to create the page or you can type the
HTML using a text editor. The following is the complete HTML example. We'll discuss the parts of the file over the next few steps.

```
1.    <HTML>
2.    <HEAD>
3.      <META HTTP-EQUIV="Content-Type"
CONTENT="text/html; charset=iso-8859-1">
4.      <TITLE>Create Your Resume</TITLE>
5.    <SCRIPT>
6.    <!-- Hide from old browsers
7.    function verify()
8.    {
9.      checktext();
10.     flag=0;
11.     i=1;
```

```
12.      while ( ( i<=18 ) && ( flag==0 ) )
13.      {
14.        alert( "Verifying " + fieldnames[i] );
15.        if
      (document.forms[0].elements[fieldnames[i]].value=
      ="")
16.          flag=1;
17.        if (flag)
18.        {
19.          document.forms[0].action="
           javascript:error(i)";
20.          break;
21.        }
22.        else
23.            i++;
24.      }
25.    }
26.
27.    function error(n)
28.    {
29.      switch( fieldnames[n] )
30.      {
31.        case "fname":
32.          s1 = "The First Name";
33.        break;
34.        case "lname":
35.          s1 = "The Last Name";
36.        break;
37.        case "address":
38.          s1 = "The Address";
39.        break;
40.        case "city":
41.          s1 = "The City";
42.        break;
43.        case "state":
44.          s1 = "The State";
45.        break;
46.        case "zipcode":
47.          s1 = "The ZIP code";
48.        break;
```

```
49.        case "country":
50.          s1 = "The Country";
51.        break;
52.        case "telephone":
53.          s1 = "The Telephone";
54.        break;
55.        case "email":
56.          s1 = "The E-Mail";
57.        break;
58.        case "start1":
59.          s1 = "The First Start Date";
60.        break;
61.        case "end1":
62.          s1 = "The First End Date";
63.        break;
64.        case "title1":
65.          s1 = "The First Job Title";
66.        break;
67.        case "company1":
68.          s1 = "The First Company Name";
69.        break;
70.        case "desc1":
71.          s1 = "The First Job Description";
72.        break;
73.        case "grad1":
74.          s1 = "The First Degree Type";
75.        break;
76.        case "field1":
77.          s1 = "The First Field or Major";
78.        break;
79.        case "school1":
80.          s1 = "The First School Name";
81.        break;
82.        case "other":
83.          s1 = "The Other Information";
84.        break;
85.        default:
86.          s1 = "A";
87.        break;
88.      }
```

```
89.       alert( s1 + " field is required and is
             empty!\r\rPlease complete it and try
             again.");
90.     document.forms[0].action="/cgi-bin/resume.cgi";
91.   }
92.
93.   function checktext()
94.   {
95.     s1=document.forms[0].address.value;
96.     if ( (s1.length>750) )
97.       alert("The string is too long in the Address
98.             field.");
99.     s1=document.forms[0].desc1.value;
100.    if ( (s1.length>750) )
101.      alert("The string is too long in the Job
                Description #1 field.");
102.
103.    s1=document.forms[0].desc2.value;
104.    if ( (s1.length>750) )
105.      alert("The string is too long in the Job
                Description #2 field.");
106.
107.    s1=document.forms[0].other.value;
108.    if ( (s1.length>750) )
109.      alert("The string is too long in the other
                information field.");
110.  }
111.
112.  function makeArray(n)
113.  {
114.    this.length=n;
115.    for( i=1; i<=n; i++ )
116.    this[i]=0;
117.    return this;
118.  }
119.
120.  fieldnames=new makeArray(18);
121.  fieldnames[1]="fname";
122.  fieldnames[2]="lname";
123.  fieldnames[3]="address";
```

```
124.  fieldnames[4]="city";
125.  fieldnames[5]="state";
126.  fieldnames[6]="zipcode";
127.  fieldnames[7]="country";
128.  fieldnames[8]="telephone";
129.  fieldnames[9]="email";
130.  fieldnames[10]="start1";
131.  fieldnames[11]="end1";
132.  fieldnames[12]="title1";
133.  fieldnames[13]="company1";
134.  fieldnames[14]="desc1";
135.  fieldnames[15]="grad1";
136.  fieldnames[16]="field1";
137.  fieldnames[17]="school1";
138.  fieldnames[18]="other";
139.
140.  <!--  -->
141.  </SCRIPT>
142.
143.  </HEAD>
144.  <BODY BGCOLOR="#FFFFFF">
145.  <FORM ACTION="http://forms.mix-media.com/cgi-
      bin/resume.pl" ENCTYPE="x-www-form-encoded"
      METHOD="POST" onSubmit="verify()">
146.  <H2>
147.  <FONT SIZE=+3>S</FONT>END US <FONT
      SIZE=+3>Y</FONT>OUR <FONT
      SIZE=+3>R</FONT>&Eacute;SUM&Eacute;</H2>
148.  <BLOCKQUOTE>To generate a quick r&eacute;sum&ea-
      cute; that's useful to our hiring manager, follow
      the steps below to create and send us your r&ea-
      cute;sum&eacute;.
149.  <H3>
150.  <HR>Step 1 - Tell us who you are and how to reach
      you.</H3>
151.  <TABLE BORDER CELLSPACING=0 CELLPADDING=0 BG-
      COLOR="#CCCCCC">
152.  <TR ALIGN=LEFT>
153.  <TD ALIGN=LEFT VALIGN=TOP
      BGCOLOR="#CCCCCC"> First Name: </TD>
```

```
154.  <TD ALIGN=LEFT VALIGN=TOP><INPUT NAME="fname"
      TYPE="text" MAXLENGTH=64 SIZE="50"
      MAXLENGTH=40></TD>
155.  </TR>
156.  <TR>
157.  <TD ALIGN=LEFT VALIGN=TOP
      BGCOLOR="#CCCCCC"> Last Name: </TD>
158.  <TD ALIGN=LEFT VALIGN=TOP><INPUT NAME="lname"
      TYPE="text" MAXLENGTH=40 SIZE="50"></TD>
159.  </TR>
160.  <TR>
161.  <TD ALIGN=LEFT VALIGN=TOP
      BGCOLOR="#CCCCCC"> Address: </TD>
162.  <TD ALIGN=LEFT VALIGN=TOP><TEXTAREA NAME="ad-
      dress" TYPE="text" WRAP=PHYSICAL ROWS="4"
      COLS="48" MAXLENGTH=128></TEXTAREA></TD>
163.  </TR>
164.  <TR>
165.  <TD ALIGN=LEFT
      BGCOLOR="#CCCCCC"> City: </TD>
166.  <TD VALIGN=LEFT><INPUT NAME="city" TYPE="text"
      MAXLENGTH=20 SIZE="20"></TD>
167.  <TR>
168.  <TD ALIGN=LEFT
      BGCOLOR="#CCCCCC"> State </TD>
169.  <TD VALIGN=LEFT><INPUT NAME="state" TYPE="text"
      MAXLENGTH=3 SIZE="3"></TD>
170.  </TR>
171.  <TR>
172.  <TD ALIGN=LEFT VALIGN=TOP
      BGCOLOR="#CCCCCC"> ZIP/Postal
      code: </TD>
173.  <TD VALIGN=LEFT><INPUT NAME="postal" TYPE="text"
      MAXLENGTH=15 SIZE="15"></TD>
174.  </TR>
175.  <TR>
176.  <TD ALIGN=LEFT VALIGN=TOP
      BGCOLOR="#CCCCCC"> Country: </TD>
177.  <TD VALIGN=LEFT><INPUT NAME="country" TYPE="text"
      MAXLENGTH=40 SIZE="15"></TD>
```

```
178.  </TR>
179.  <TR>
180.  <TD ALIGN=LEFT VALIGN=TOP
      BGCOLOR="#CCCCCC"> Telephone: </TD>
181.  <TD ALIGN=LEFT VALIGN=TOP><INPUT NAME="tel"
      TYPE="text" MAXLENGTH=34 SIZE="34"></TD>
182.  </TR>
183.  <TR>
184.  <TD ALIGN=LEFT VALIGN=TOP
      BGCOLOR="#CCCCCC"> Email Address: </TD>
185.  <TD ALIGN=LEFT VALIGN=TOP><INPUT NAME="email"
      TYPE="text" MAXLENGTH=80 SIZE="34"></TD>
186.  </TR>
187.  <TR>
188.  <TD ALIGN=LEFT VALIGN=TOP
      BGCOLOR="#CCCCCC"> Personal URL: </TD>
189.  <TD ALIGN=LEFT VALIGN=TOP><INPUT NAME="url"
      TYPE="text" MAXLENGTH=80 SIZE="50"></TD>
190.  </TR>
191.  </TABLE>
192.  <HR>
193.  <DL>
194.  <H3>Step 2 - Tell us about your most recent three
      jobs or equivalent experience.</H3>
195.  <TABLE BORDER CELLSPACING=0 CELLPADDING=0
      BGCOLOR="#CCCCCC">
196.  <TR>
197.    <TD ALIGN=LEFT VALIGN=TOP> Start
      Date: </TD>
198.    <TD VALIGN=TOP><INPUT NAME="start1" TYPE="text"
      MAXLENGTH=8 SIZE="8"></TD>
199.  </TR>
200.  <TR>
201.    <TD VALIGN=TOP> End Date: </TD>
202.    <TD VALIGN=TOP><INPUT NAME="end1" TYPE="text"
      MAXLENGTH=8 SIZE="8"  ></TD>
203.  </TR>
204.  <TR>
205.    <TD ALIGN=LEFT
      VALIGN=TOP> Title: </TD>
```

```
206.     <TD ALIGN=LEFT VALIGN=TOP><INPUT NAME="title1"
         TYPE="text" MAXLENGTH=43 SIZE="43"></TD>
207.   </TR>
208.   <TR>
209.     <TD ALIGN=LEFT
         VALIGN=TOP> Company: </TD>
210.     <TD ALIGN=LEFT VALIGN=TOP><INPUT NAME="com-
         pany1" TYPE="text" MAXLENGTH=43 SIZE="43"></TD>
211.   </TR>
212.   <TR>
213.     <TD ALIGN=LEFT VALIGN=TOP> Description of
         Responsibilities:</TD>
214.     <TD ALIGN=LEFT VALIGN=TOP><TEXTAREA
         NAME="desc1" TYPE="text" WRAP=PHYSICAL ROWS="7"
         COLS="43" MAXLENGTH=750></TEXTAREA></TD>
215.   </TR>
216.   </TABLE>
217.    
218.   <TABLE BORDER CELLSPACING=0 CELLPADDING=0
         BGCOLOR="#CCCCCC">
219.   <TR>
220.     <TD ALIGN=LEFT VALIGN=TOP> Start
         Date: </TD>
221.     <TD VALIGN=TOP><INPUT NAME="start2" TYPE="text"
         MAXLENGTH=8 SIZE="8"></TD>
222.   </TR>
223.   <TR>
224.     <TD VALIGN=TOP> End Date: </TD>
225.     <TD VALIGN=TOP><INPUT NAME="end2" TYPE="text"
         MAXLENGTH=8 SIZE="8"  ></TD>
226.   </TR>
227.   <TR>
228.     <TD ALIGN=LEFT
         VALIGN=TOP> Title: </TD>
229.     <TD ALIGN=LEFT VALIGN=TOP><INPUT NAME="title2"
         TYPE="text" MAXLENGTH=43 SIZE="43"></TD>
230.   </TR>
231.   <TR>
232.     <TD ALIGN=LEFT
         VALIGN=TOP> Company: </TD>
```

```
233.    <TD ALIGN=LEFT VALIGN=TOP><INPUT NAME="com-
        pany2" TYPE="text" MAXLENGTH=43 SIZE="43"></TD>
234.    </TR>
235.    <TR>
236.      <TD ALIGN=LEFT VALIGN=TOP> Description of
        Responsibilities:</TD>
237.      <TD ALIGN=LEFT VALIGN=TOP><TEXTAREA
        NAME="desc2" TYPE="text" WRAP=PHYSICAL ROWS="7"
238.    COLS="43" MAXLENGTH=750></TEXTAREA></TD>
239.    </TR>
240.    </TABLE>
241.    <HR>
242.    <H3>Step 4 - Tell us about your education and/or
        equivalent experience.</H3>
243.    <TABLE BORDER CELLSPACING=0 CELLPADDING=0
        BGCOLOR="#CCCCCC">
244.    <TR>
245.      <TD ALIGN=RIGHT VALIGN=BOTTOM>Degree
        #1: </TD>
246.      <TD ALIGN=LEFT VALIGN=BOTTOM><SELECT NAME="de-
        gree1" SIZE="1">
247.    <OPTION SELECTED>None
248.    <OPTION>High School
249.    <OPTION>Associate of Arts
250.    <OPTION>Associate of Sciences
251.    <OPTION>Bachelor of Arts
252.    <OPTION>Bachelor of Sciences
253.    <OPTION>Master of Arts
254.    <OPTION>Master of Sciences
255.    <OPTION>Ph.D or other advanced degree
256.    </SELECT></TD>
257.    </TR>
258.    <TR>
259.      <TD ALIGN=RIGHT VALIGN=BOTTOM> Year
        Completed: </TD>
260.      <TD ALIGN=LEFT VALIGN=BOTTOM><INPUT
        NAME="grad1" TYPE="text" MAXLENGTH=4
        SIZE="5"></TD>
261.    </TR>
262.    <TR>
```

```
263.    <TD ALIGN=RIGHT VALIGN=BOTTOM> Field or
        Major: </TD>
264.    <TD ALIGN=LEFT VALIGN=BOTTOM><INPUT
        NAME="field1" TYPE="text" MAXLENGTH=43
        SIZE="45"></TD>
265.    </TR>
266.    <TR>
267.    <TD ALIGN=RIGHT VALIGN=BOTTOM> School or
        Institution: </TD>
268.    <TD ALIGN=LEFT VALIGN=BOTTOM><INPUT
        NAME="school1" TYPE="text" MAXLENGTH=80
        SIZE="45"></TD>
269.    </TR>
270.    </TABLE>
271.     
272.    <TABLE BORDER CELLSPACING=0 CELLPADDING=0 BG-
        COLOR="#CCCCCC">
273.    <TR>
274.    <TD ALIGN=RIGHT VALIGN=BOTTOM>Degree
        #2: </TD>
275.    <TD ALIGN=LEFT VALIGN=BOTTOM><SELECT NAME="de-
        gree1" SIZE="1">
276.    <OPTION SELECTED>None
277.    <OPTION>High School
278.    <OPTION>Associate of Arts
279.    <OPTION>Associate of Sciences
280.    <OPTION>Bachelor of Arts
281.    <OPTION>Bachelor of Sciences
282.    <OPTION>Master of Arts
283.    <OPTION>Master of Sciences
284.    <OPTION>Ph.D or other advanced
        degree</SELECT></TD>
285.    </TR>
286.    <TR>
287.    <TD ALIGN=RIGHT VALIGN=BOTTOM> Year
        Completed: </TD>
288.    <TD ALIGN=LEFT VALIGN=BOTTOM><INPUT
        NAME="grad1" TYPE="text" MAXLENGTH=4
        SIZE="5"></TD>
289.    </TR>
```

```
290.    <TR>
291.      <TD ALIGN=RIGHT VALIGN=BOTTOM> Field or
        Major: </TD>
292.      <TD ALIGN=LEFT VALIGN=BOTTOM><INPUT
        NAME="field1" TYPE="text" MAXLENGTH=43
        SIZE="45"></TD>
293.    </TR>
294.    <TR>
295.      <TD ALIGN=RIGHT VALIGN=BOTTOM> School or
        Institution: </TD>
296.      <TD ALIGN=LEFT VALIGN=BOTTOM><INPUT
        NAME="school1" TYPE="text" MAXLENGTH=80
        SIZE="45"></TD>
297.    </TR>
298.    </TABLE>
299.    <P>
300.    <HR>
301.    <H3>Step 5 - Tell us more about yourself.</H3>
        We want to know what makes you, well, <I>you</I>.
        List hobbies, activities you enjoy, sports you
        play, and anything else you think we might like to
        know about you:
302.    <P>
303.    <TEXTAREA NAME="other" ROWS="7" COLS="43"
        MAXLENGTH=750 WRAP=PHYSICAL></TEXTAREA>
304.    <P>
305.    <HR>
306.    <H3>Step 6 - Submit your
        r&eacute;sum&eacute;.</H3>Once you've reviewed
        your information, click the Submit button below.
        Your r&eacute;sum&eacute; will be formatted and
        emailed to the department you indicated in section
        2.
307.    <P>We'll be in touch to let you know we received
        it.
308.    <BR>
309.    <BR>
310.    <INPUT NAME="name" TYPE="submit" VALUE="Submit">
311.    <BR> </DL>
312.    </BLOCKQUOTE>
```

```
313    </FORM>
314.   </BODY>
315.   </HTML>
```

Examining the HTML Code

This example's opening lines of HTML provide a standard opening for any HTML file. Line one is the tag declaring that what will follow is an HTML file. Line two begins the head of the file. Here we add a title for display in the browser window while the file is being viewed. Line three was added by our visual editing tool. It defines the MIME type, the content type and the character set used by this file. This information isn't necessary but is becoming widespread with more and more visual editors.

On line five this file becomes more complicated. Here we add the script tag. This informs the browser that the following information is a script or a series of scripts defining routines we intend to use during display of this HTML file. Everything inside the <SCRIPT> tag until the </SCRIPT> tag defines an executable statement. Some browsers don't support this functionality so on line six we take the precaution of commenting out all the information that might confuse them. If we move to line 140 we can see the end comment tag informing old browsers that they can begin paying attention to the HTML file again. As far as the JavaScript is concerned line seven is where things begin happening.

```
1.     <HTML>
2.     <HEAD>
3.       <META HTTP-EQUIV="Content-Type"
       CONTENT="text/html; charset=iso-8859-1">
4.       <TITLE>Create Your Resume</TITLE>
5.     <SCRIPT>
6.     <!-- Hide from old browsers
7.     function verify()
8.     {
9.       checktext();
10.      flag=0;
11.      i=1;
12.      while ( ( i<=18 ) && ( flag==0 ) )
13.      {
14.        alert( "Verifying " + fieldnames[i] );
```

```
15.        if
   (document.forms[0].elements[fieldnames[i]].value=
   ="")
16.          flag=1;
17.      if (flag)
18.      {
19.         document.forms[0].action="
            javascript:error(i)";
20.         break;
21.      }
22.      else
23.          i++;
24.    }
25.  }
```

The JavaScript

On line seven we define a function named verify( ). Verify is called to check the data for omissions before the form sends the data to the server. If an error is detected, a dialog is displayed informing the user which field they've omitted. Let's walk through the verify function. On line nine the function calls another routine, checktext(). We'll look at this function next but for now it's enough to know the checktext() function makes sure too many characters haven't been entered in any of the fields. On line 11 we initialize the variable "i" to one. This is our loop variable.

After checking each field for too many characters, we want to check for empty fields. We do this by looping through the list of fields the document maintains. Line 12 is where our loop begins. We check each field's value to see if it's equal to, "", the empty string. If it is, we set the form's action to the error() function. The error function is then called instead of the action that sends the form to the server for processing. If the value of the field is not the empty string, " ", then we increment our loop variable and try the next field.

```
27.  function error(n)
28.  {
29.    switch( fieldnames[n] )
30.    {
31.      case "fname":
32.        s1 = "The First Name";
```

```
33.        break;
34.        case "lname":
35.          s1 = "The Last Name";
36.        break;
37.        case "address":
38.          s1 = "The Address";
39.        break;
40.        case "city":
41.          s1 = "The City";
42.        break;
43.        case "state":
44.          s1 = "The State";
45.        break;
46.        case "zipcode":
47.          s1 = "The ZIP code";
48.        break;
49.        case "country":
50.          s1 = "The Country";
51.        break;
52.        case "telephone":
53.          s1 = "The Telephone";
54.        break;
55.        case "email":
56.          s1 = "The E-Mail";
57.        break;
58.        case "start1":
59.          s1 = "The First Start Date";
60.        break;
61.        case "end1":
62.          s1 = "The First End Date";
63.        break;
64.        case "title1":
65.          s1 = "The First Job Title";
66.        break;
67.        case "company1":
68.          s1 = "The First Company Name";
69.        break;
70.        case "desc1":
71.          s1 = "The First Job Description";
72.        break;
```

```
73.        case "grad1":
74.          s1 = "The First Degree Type";
75.        break;
76.        case "field1":
77.          s1 = "The First Field or Major";
78.        break;
79.        case "school1":
80.          s1 = "The First School Name";
81.        break;
82.        case "other":
83.          s1 = "The Other Information";
84.        break;
85.        default:
86.          s1 = "A";
87.        break;
88.      }
89.    alert( s1 + " field is required and is
                empty!\r\rPlease complete it and try
                again.");
90.    document.forms[0].action="/cgi-bin/resume.cgi";
91.  }
```

Define the error function

Lines 27 to 91 define the error function. This function is called from the verify() routine if a field is left blank. The function receives the field number and then performs three tasks. First it enters a switch state-ment. The switch statement takes the value stored in the array "fieldnames" at "fieldnames[n]" and offers several options or cases that can be executed if that case is met. On line 31, the first of 18 cases is presented. Here we check to see if the field name is equal to "fname" and if it is, we copy the string, "The first name", into the s1 variable. If the fieldnames[n] does not equal "fname", the next case is evaluated until a match is found. If no match is found, line 85 contains a default case that handles all other instances. Switch statements are only available in browsers that support JavaScript 1.2 or newer.

The final two actions the error function performs are to put up a dialog box informing the user as to which field is empty and then to set the form's action back to the CGI script we want to handle the submission. This putting up the alert dialog is accomplished on line 89. The JavaScript alert() routine is responsible for displaying the dialog box.

We call alert( ) and pass it a string to display in the dialog box. The string we pass it is the combination of the s1 variable with the "field is required and is empty! Please complete it and try again." added or concatenated to it. Line 90 is where the form's action is set back to "/cgi-bin/resume.pl" Remember that when we detected an error, we set the form's action to the error( ) function. Now we set it back so that any corrected submission will be directed to the proper URL.

```
93.    function checktext()
94.    {
95.      s1=document.forms[0].address.value;
96.      if ( (s1.length>750) )
97.        alert("The string is too long in the Address
98.               field.");
99.      s1=document.forms[0].desc1.value;
100.     if ( (s1.length>750) )
101.       alert("The string is too long in the Job
                  Description #1 field.");
102.
103.     s1=document.forms[0].desc2.value;
104.     if ( (s1.length>750) )
105.       alert("The string is too long in the Job
                  Description #2 field.");
106.
107.     s1=document.forms[0].other.value;
108.     if ( (s1.length>750) )
109.       alert("The string is too long in the other
                  information field.");
110.   }
```

Checktext() function

The checktext( ) function performs a simple length check on four fields. Most browsers enforce length limits on text fields, but just in case we'll access these field's content and check their length with JavaScript.

On line 95 we copy the contents of "document.forms[0].address.value" into the s1 variable. This looks complicated but actually it's very straight-forward. JavaScript organizes documents into objects. The JavaScript object we use to access the field's contents is the document object.

```
document
```

Each JavaScript document object contains an array of forms objects. An HTML document can have more than one form, but this document contains only a single form. On line 99 we access the document object's first form object.

```
document.forms[0]
```

Remember JavaScript arrays are zero based. This means the first object in the array is actually object number zero. Our next step is to access the field of the form we want to examine. This is done by accessing the forms[0] object's address field. Each form object contains a list of the fields it contains. They are stored and referenced by their name.

```
document.forms[0].address
```

At this point we have a reference to the field we're interested in examining. The property of the address field we want to look at is its value. The value property is the string the text field contains.

```
document.forms[0].address.value
```

This value is what we store in the s1 variable. The s1 variable is a JavaScript object as well and it has properties also. On line 100 we access the s1 object's length property. If it's greater than 750 characters in length we put up an alert dialog warning the user there has been an error.

The rest of the routine checks both description fields and the other field for length violations.

```
112.    function makeArray(n)
113.    {
114.       this.length=n;
115.       for( i=1; i<=n; i++ )
116.         this[i]=0;
117.       return this;
118.    }
```

The makeArray() function

The next function we'll discuss is makeArray(). This is a simple routine we use to allocate space for an array of a number of elements. On line 114 we set the length of the object to the number of items passed into the function. On line 115 we start a loop. The loop initializes each item of our array object to zero. Finally on line 117 we return a reference to this object so it can be referenced later.

```
120.  fieldnames=new makeArray(18);
121.  fieldnames[1]="fname";
122.  fieldnames[2]="lname";
123.  fieldnames[3]="address";
124.  fieldnames[4]="city";
125.  fieldnames[5]="state";
126.  fieldnames[6]="zipcode";
127.  fieldnames[7]="country";
128.  fieldnames[8]="telephone";
129.  fieldnames[9]="email";
130.  fieldnames[10]="start1";
131.  fieldnames[11]="end1";
132.  fieldnames[12]="title1";
133.  fieldnames[13]="company1";
134.  fieldnames[14]="desc1";
135.  fieldnames[15]="grad1";
136.  fieldnames[16]="field1";
137.  fieldnames[17]="school1";
138.  fieldnames[18]="other";
139.
140.  <!-- -->
141.  </SCRIPT>
142.
143.  </HEAD>
```

Executing new makeArray()

Line 120 of the file makes use of our makeArray() function. As the file is read by the browser, it registers each function definition and on line 120 it encounters the makeArray(18) function. The browser realizes it isn't a definition and executes the function. The browser allocates space for an array of 18 objects and returns a reference to it in the fieldnames array variable. Lines 121 to 138 see us setting each member of the array to a string value. Here we set each spot in the array to a corresponding field name in the HTML document.

Line 143 is the close comment tag that instructs non-JavaScript aware browsers to start paying attention again. Line 141 closes the </SCRIPT> tag and line 142 closes the </HEAD> of the HTML document.

```
144.  <BODY BGCOLOR="#FFFFFF">
145.  <FORM ACTION="http://forms.mix-media.com/cgi-
      bin/resume.pl" ENCTYPE="x-www-form-encoded"
      METHOD="POST" onSubmit="verify()">
146.  <H2>
147.  <FONT SIZE=+3>S</FONT>END US <FONT
      SIZE=+3>Y</FONT>OUR <FONT
      SIZE=+3>R</FONT>&Eacute;SUM&Eacute;</H2>
148.  <BLOCKQUOTE>To generate a quick r&eacute;sum&ea-
      cute; that's useful to our hiring manager, follow
      the steps below to create and send us your r&ea-
      cute;sum&eacute;.
149.  <H3>
150.  <HR>Step 1 - Tell us who you are and how to reach
      you.</H3>
```

Body of the HTML document

The body of the HTML document begins on line 144. Here we set the background color to, "#FFFFFF", white. Line 145 opens a form tag and sets the action to invoke our CGI script. We tell the browser to encode the submission information and indicate the POST method is used to send information to the server. The final item defined in the <FORM> tag is the onSubmit tag. We set its value to our verify() function. This informs JavaScript aware browsers to invoke the verify() function when the form is told to submit its data.

Lines 147 to 150 add HTML to the file that is responsible for drawing the page heading, and provide a brief explanation of the page's purpose, a horizontal rule, and a subhead that identifies the first table of text data entry fields.

HTML Tables

This file contains five tables that are used to gather our résumé information. The first table displays the text all the fields used to gather personal information such as name, address, etc.

```
151.   <TABLE BORDER CELLSPACING=0 CELLPADDING=0 BG-
       COLOR="#CCCCCC">
152.   <TR ALIGN=LEFT>
153.   <TD ALIGN=LEFT VALIGN=TOP
       BGCOLOR="#CCCCCC"> First Name: </TD>
154.   <TD ALIGN=LEFT VALIGN=TOP><INPUT NAME="fname"
       TYPE="text" MAXLENGTH=64 SIZE="50"
       MAXLENGTH=40></TD>
155.   </TR>
```

Line 151 uses the HTML TABLE tag to start a table. Here we set the border around the table to 0 pixels in width. Cell spacing and padding is set to 0. The table's background color is set to, "#CCCCCC", light gray.

Once the table is set up we begin adding rows and cells to the table. On line 152 we use the table row tag, <TR>, to open a table row. Inside the tag we set the text alignment to left. Once we open a table row, we can add as many cells as we want with the table detail tag, <TD>.

On line 153 we add the row's first cell. We set the alignment to left and the vertical alignment to top. We also set the cell's background color to "#CCCCCC", light gray. Now we add the text. This cell contains a non-breaking space, then the text, "First Name:" followed by another non-breaking space. This is all the cell contains, so we close the cell.

This row contains two cells and the second holds the text input field. The field's type is "text", its name is "fname", its initial value is the null string "", it's long enough to show 50 characters, and it accepts 40 characters. This field will hold the applicant's first name. Now we're ready to close the cell using the </TD> tag.

```
156.   <TR>
157.   <TD ALIGN=LEFT VALIGN=TOP
       BGCOLOR="#CCCCCC"> Last Name: </TD>
158.   <TD ALIGN=LEFT VALIGN=TOP><INPUT NAME="lname"
       TYPE="text" MAXLENGTH=40 SIZE="50"></TD>
159.   </TR>
```

```
160.  <TR>
161.  <TD ALIGN=LEFT VALIGN=TOP
      BGCOLOR="#CCCCCC"> Address: </TD>
162.  <TD ALIGN=LEFT VALIGN=TOP><TEXTAREA NAME="ad-
      dress" TYPE="text" WRAP=PHYSICAL ROWS="4"
      COLS="48" MAXLENGTH=128></TEXTAREA></TD>
163.  </TR>
164.  <TR>
165.  <TD ALIGN=LEFT
      BGCOLOR="#CCCCCC"> City: </TD>
166.  <TD VALIGN=LEFT><INPUT NAME="city" TYPE="text"
      MAXLENGTH=20 SIZE="20"></TD>
167.  <TR>
168.  <TD ALIGN=LEFT
      BGCOLOR="#CCCCCC"> State </TD>
169.  <TD VALIGN=LEFT><INPUT NAME="state" TYPE="text"
      MAXLENGTH=3 SIZE="3"></TD>
170.  </TR>
171.  <TR>
172.  <TD ALIGN=LEFT VALIGN=TOP
      BGCOLOR="#CCCCCC"> ZIP/Postal
      code: </TD>
173.  <TD VALIGN=LEFT><INPUT NAME="postal" TYPE="text"
      MAXLENGTH=15 SIZE="15"></TD>
174.  </TR>
175.  <TR>
176.  <TD ALIGN=LEFT VALIGN=TOP
      BGCOLOR="#CCCCCC"> Country: </TD>
177.  <TD VALIGN=LEFT><INPUT NAME="country" TYPE="text"
      MAXLENGTH=40 SIZE="15"></TD>
178.  </TR>
179.  <TR>
180.  <TD ALIGN=LEFT VALIGN=TOP
      BGCOLOR="#CCCCCC"> Telephone: </TD>
181.  <TD ALIGN=LEFT VALIGN=TOP><INPUT NAME="tel"
      TYPE="text" MAXLENGTH=34 SIZE="34"></TD>
182.  </TR>
183.  <TR>
184.  <TD ALIGN=LEFT VALIGN=TOP
      BGCOLOR="#CCCCCC"> Email Address: </TD>
```

```
185.   <TD ALIGN=LEFT VALIGN=TOP><INPUT NAME="email"
       TYPE="text" MAXLENGTH=80 SIZE="34"></TD>
186.     </TR>
187.   <TR>
188.   <TD ALIGN=LEFT VALIGN=TOP
       BGCOLOR="#CCCCCC"> Personal URL: </TD>
189.   <TD ALIGN=LEFT VALIGN=TOP><INPUT NAME="url"
       TYPE="text" MAXLENGTH=80 SIZE="50"></TD>
190.   </TR>
191.   </TABLE>
```

The same procedure is followed for eight more rows of this table.

Another HTML Table

Our next table displays five fields used to gather employment history information. This HTML document uses two tables to gather employment information. We'll discuss the structure of the first of these tables below.

```
195.   <TABLE BORDER CELLSPACING=0 CELLPADDING=0 BG-
       COLOR="#CCCCCC">
196.   <TR>
197.     <TD ALIGN=LEFT VALIGN=TOP> Start
       Date: </TD>
198.     <TD VALIGN=TOP><INPUT NAME="start1" TYPE="text"
       MAXLENGTH=8 SIZE="8"  ></TD>
199.   </TR>
```

Line 195 uses the HTML TABLE tag to start a table. Here we set the border around the table to 0 pixels in width. Cell spacing and padding is set to 0. The table's background color is set to "#CCCCCC", light gray.

On line 196 we use the table row tag, <TR>, to open a table row. On line 197 we begin the row's first cell. We set the alignment to left and the vertical alignment to top. We also set the cell's background color to "#CCCCCC", light gray. Now we add the text. This cell contains a non-breaking space, then the text "Start Date:" followed by another non-breaking space.

This row contains two cells and the second holds the text input field. The field's type is "text", its name is "start1", its initial value is the null string "", it's long enough to show 8 characters, and it accepts 8 characters.

```
200.    <TR>
201.      <TD VALIGN=TOP> End Date: </TD>
202.      <TD VALIGN=TOP><INPUT NAME="end1" TYPE="text"
        MAXLENGTH=8 SIZE="8"  ></TD>
203.    </TR>
204.    <TR>
205.      <TD ALIGN=LEFT
        VALIGN=TOP> Title: </TD>
206.      <TD ALIGN=LEFT VALIGN=TOP><INPUT NAME="title1"
        TYPE="text" MAXLENGTH=43 SIZE="43"></TD>
207.    </TR>
208.    <TR>
209.      <TD ALIGN=LEFT
        VALIGN=TOP> Company: </TD>
210.      <TD ALIGN=LEFT VALIGN=TOP><INPUT NAME="com-
        pany1" TYPE="text" MAXLENGTH=43 SIZE="43"></TD>
211.    </TR>
212.    <TR>
213.      <TD ALIGN=LEFT VALIGN=TOP> Description of
        Responsibilities:</TD>
214.      <TD ALIGN=LEFT VALIGN=TOP><TEXTAREA
        NAME="desc1" TYPE="text" WRAP=PHYSICAL ROWS="7"
        COLS="43" MAXLENGTH=750></TEXTAREA></TD>
215.    </TR>
216.    </TABLE>
```

The same procedure, as shown in lines 200 to 203, is followed for four more rows of this table.

Last HTML table

Our document's last table displays four fields used to gather educational information. This HTML document uses two tables to gather this information. Just as with the work history tables, here we'll discuss the structure of the first of these identical tables. The only difference is that the field names must be different. This insures the data can be differentiated by the CGI script on the server.

```
242.    <H3>Step 4 - Tell us about your education and/or
        equivalent experience.</H3>
243.    <TABLE BORDER=0 CELLSPACING=0 CELLPADDING=0 BG-
        COLOR="#CCCCCC">
244.    <TR>
245.      <TD ALIGN=RIGHT VALIGN=BOTTOM>Degree
        #1: </TD>
246.      <TD ALIGN=LEFT VALIGN=BOTTOM><SELECT NAME="de-
        gree1" SIZE="1">
247.      <OPTION SELECTED>None
248.      <OPTION>High School
249.      <OPTION>Associate of Arts
250.      <OPTION>Associate of Sciences
251.      <OPTION>Bachelor of Arts
252.      <OPTION>Bachelor of Sciences
253.      <OPTION>Master of Arts
254.      <OPTION>Master of Sciences
255.    <OPTION>Ph.D or other advanced degree
256.    </SELECT></TD>
257.    </TR>
```

Line 242 adds HTML to the file that is responsible for drawing the text explaining step 4's purpose. Line 243 uses the HTML TABLE tag to start the education table. Here we set the border around the table to 0 pixels in width. Cell spacing and padding is also set to 0. The table's background color is set to "#CCCCCC", light gray.

On line 244 we use the table row tag, <TR>, to open a table row. On line 245 we begin the row's first cell. We set the alignment to right and the vertical alignment to bottom. Next we add the text. This cell contains the text "Degree #1:" followed by a non-breaking space.

The second cell in this row contains a <SELECT> menu listing types of qualifying degrees. The field's name is "degree1" and its size is 1. Lines 247 to 255 add options to our select menu. The first option is the one displayed by default and it displays as "None".

```
258.    <TR>
259.      <TD ALIGN=RIGHT VALIGN=BOTTOM> Year
        Completed: </TD>
```

```
260.    <TD ALIGN=LEFT VALIGN=BOTTOM><INPUT
        NAME="grad1" TYPE="text" MAXLENGTH=4
        SIZE="5"></TD>
261.    </TR>
262.    <TR>
263.    <TD ALIGN=RIGHT VALIGN=BOTTOM> Field or
        Major: </TD>
264.    <TD ALIGN=LEFT VALIGN=BOTTOM><INPUT
        NAME="field1" TYPE="text" MAXLENGTH=43
        SIZE="45"></TD>
265.    </TR>
266.    <TR>
267.    <TD ALIGN=RIGHT VALIGN=BOTTOM> School or
        Institution: </TD>
268.    <TD ALIGN=LEFT VALIGN=BOTTOM><INPUT
        NAME="school1" TYPE="text" MAXLENGTH=80
        SIZE="45"></TD>
269.    </TR>
270.    </TABLE>
```

The remaining three rows of this table are structurally identical. Each row contains two cells. The first cell of a row displays some text and the second cell presents a text field used to capture user input. The first cell of the second row is defined on line 263. We set the text alignment to right and the vertical alignment to bottom. This cell contains a non-breaking space, and the text, "Field or Major:", followed by a non-breaking space.

The second cell of each row holds a text-input field. On line 268 the field's type is "text" and its name is "school1". It's long enough to show 45 characters and it accepts 80 characters.

The </TABLE> is closed on line 270. In the actual HTML file, there is another identical table that follows this one. The input field names are different but the structure of the table is identical. If you're using a text editor, once the first table is completed, copy and paste it after the first table. Then simply change the input field names.

```
299.    <P>
300.    <HR>
301.    <H3>Step 5 - Tell us more about yourself.</H3>
```

```
        We want to know what makes you, well, <I>you</I>.
        List hobbies, activities you enjoy, sports you
        play, and anything else you think we might like to
        know about you:
302.    <P>
303.    <TEXTAREA NAME="other" ROWS="7" COLS="43"
        MAXLENGTH=750 WRAP=PHYSICAL></TEXTAREA>
304.    <P>
305.    <HR>
306.    <H3> Step 6 - Submit your
        r&eacute;sum&eacute;.</H3>
        Once you've reviewed your information, click the
        Submit button below. Your r&eacute;sum&eacute;
        will be formatted and emailed to the department
        you indicated in section 2.
307.    <P>We'll be in touch to let you know we received
        it.
308.    <BR>
309.    <BR>
310.    <INPUT NAME="submit" TYPE="submit"
        VALUE="submit">
311.    <BR> </DL>
312.    </BLOCKQUOTE>
313     </FORM>
314.    </BODY>
315.    </HTML>
```

The remaining HTML in this file displays some textual instructions and provides a text area to enter other information pertinent to the applicant. Line 303 adds a text area. The field's type is <TEXT AREA>,and its name is "other". It's 43 columns wide and seven rows high. It accepts up to 750 characters.

On line 310 we add a submit button. We use the browser's default appearance so no background image is indicated. Its name, type, and value are all set to equal submit. This HTML creates the button the user clicks on to submit their resume information to the server for processing.

Lines 313-315 close the form, body, and the HTML document itself.

Creating the Perl Script

This example uses an HTML file as its interface to the user. The form gathers fname, lname, address, city, state, zip, country, telephone, email, and personal URL and sends it to the server for processing by a CGI script. This example uses a Perl script to process the submitted information. The Perl script decodes the submission, formats the information and electronically mails it to the human resources department.

The following pages discuss creating the Perl script used for processing the form's submission on the server side of this transaction. The complete script is shown below. For this example to work the script must exist as a file named "resume.pl". This file is placed in the "cgi-bin" directory in the Apache Server's root directory. The script must have execute privileges or an error will be returned.

Code Example: resume.pl

```
1.    #!/usr/local/bin/perl
2.
3.    $sendto     = "info\@mix-media.com";
4.    $xmailer    = "CGI Resume Mail Gateway [v1.0]";
5.    $sendmail   = "/usr/lib/sendmail -t -n";
6.
7.    &parse_form_data(*FORM_DATA);
8.    &send_mail();
9.    &send_thank_you();
10.   exit(0);
11.
12.   sub parse_form_data
13.   {
14.       local (*FORM_DATA) = @_;
15.
16.       local ( $request_method, $query_string,
          @key_value_pairs, $key_value, $key, $value);
17.
18.       $request_method = $ENV{'REQUEST_METHOD'};
19.
20.       if($request_method eq "GET")
21.       {
```

```
22.              $query_string = $ENV{'QUERY_STRING'};
23.          }
24.      elsif($request_method eq "POST")
25.          {
26.              read(STDIN, $query_string,
                 $ENV{'CONTENT_LENGTH'});
27.          }
28.      else
29.          {
30.              &return_error (500, "Server Error",
                 "Server uses unsupported method");
31.          }
32.
33.      @key_value_pairs = split(/&/,
         $query_string);
34.
35.      foreach $key_value (@key_value_pairs)
36.          {
37.              ($key, $value) = split (/=/,
                  $key_value);
38.              $value =~ tr/+/ /;
39.              $value =~ s/%([\dA-Fa-f][\dA-Fa-f])/pack
                 ("C", hex ($1))/eg;
40.
41.              if (defined($FORM_DATA{$key}))
42.          {
43.                  $FORM_DATA{$key} = join ("\0",
                     $FORM_DATA{$key}, $value);
44.          }
45.          else
46.          {
47.                  $FORM_DATA{$key} = $value;
48.          }
49.          }
50.  }
51.
52.  sub send_mail
53.  {
54.     local (*FORM_DATA) = @_;
55.
```

```
56.     open (SENDMAIL, "| $sendmail");
57.

58.     print SENDMAIL "From: ", $FORM_DATA{'email'},
        "\n";
59.     print SENDMAIL "To: ", $sendto, "\n";
60.

61.     print SENDMAIL "Reply-To: ",
        $FORM_DATA{'email'}, "\n";
62.     print SENDMAIL "Subject: Resume Submission\n";
63.     print SENDMAIL "X-Mailer: ", $xmailer, "\n";
64.     print SENDMAIL "X-Remote-Host: ",
        $ENV{'REMOTE_ADDR'}, "\n";
65.     print SENDMAIL "Cc: \n";
66.

67.     print SENDMAIL "\n\nName/Address/Etc\.";
68.     print SENDMAIL "\n", $FORM_DATA{'first'};
69.     print SENDMAIL " ", $FORM_DATA{'last'};
70.     print SENDMAIL "\n", $FORM_DATA{'address'};
71.     print SENDMAIL "\n", $FORM_DATA{'city'};
72.     print SENDMAIL ", ", $FORM_DATA{'state'};
73.     print SENDMAIL " ", $FORM_DATA{'postal'};
74.     print SENDMAIL "\n",
        $FORM_DATA{'country'},"\n";
75.     print SENDMAIL "\n\n", "Telephone: ",
        $FORM_DATA{'tel'};
76.     print SENDMAIL "\n", "E-mail Address: ",
        $FORM_DATA{'email'};
77.     print SENDMAIL "\n", "Personal URL:   ",
        $FORM_DATA{'url'};
78.

79.     print SENDMAIL "\n\n", "Employment History";
80.  ##   First Company Entry
81.     if($FORM_DATA{'start1'})
82.     {
83.       if($FORM_DATA{'end1'})
84.       {
85.         print SENDMAIL "\n\n",
        $FORM_DATA{'start1'};
86.         print SENDMAIL "\-", $FORM_DATA{'end1'};
87.       }
```

```
88.        else
89.        {
90.          print SENDMAIL "\n\n",
             $FORM_DATA{'start1'};
91.          print SENDMAIL "\-";
92.        }
93.     }
94.     if($FORM_DATA{'title1'})
95.     {
96.       print SENDMAIL "\n", $FORM_DATA{'title1'};
97.     }
98.     if($FORM_DATA{'company1'})
99.     {
100.       print SENDMAIL "\n", $FORM_DATA{'company1'};
101.     }
102.     if($FORM_DATA{'desc1'})
103.     {
104.       print SENDMAIL "\n", $FORM_DATA{'desc1'};
105.     }
106.
107. ##   Second Company Entry
108.     if($FORM_DATA{'start2'})
109.     {
110.       if($FORM_DATA{'end2'})
111.       {
112.         print SENDMAIL "\n\n",
             $FORM_DATA{'start2'};
113.         print SENDMAIL "\-", $FORM_DATA{'end2'};
114.       }
115.       else
116.       {
117.         print SENDMAIL "\n\n",
             $FORM_DATA{'start2'};
118.         print SENDMAIL "\-";
119.       }
120.     }
121.     if($FORM_DATA{'title2'})
122.     {
123.       print SENDMAIL "\n", $FORM_DATA{'title2'};
124.     }
```

```perl
125.    if($FORM_DATA{'company2'})
126.    {
127.      print SENDMAIL "\n", $FORM_DATA{'company2'};
128.    }
129.    if($FORM_DATA{'desc2'})
130.    {
131.      print SENDMAIL "\n", $FORM_DATA{'desc2'};
132.    }
133.
134.    print SENDMAIL "\n\n", "Education";
135.    if(!($FORM_DATA{'degree1'} eq "None"))
136.    {
137.      print SENDMAIL "\n", $FORM_DATA{'degree1'};
138.      print SENDMAIL "\n", $FORM_DATA{'grad1'};
139.      print SENDMAIL "\n", $FORM_DATA{'field1'};
140.      print SENDMAIL "\n", $FORM_DATA{'school1'};
141.    }
142.    if(!($FORM_DATA{'degree2'} eq "None"))
143.    {
144.      print SENDMAIL "\n\n",
145.      $FORM_DATA{'degree2'};
         print SENDMAIL "\n", $FORM_DATA{'grad2'};
146.      print SENDMAIL "\n", $FORM_DATA{'field2'};
147.      print SENDMAIL "\n", $FORM_DATA{'school2'};
148.    }
149.    print SENDMAIL "\n\n", "Other Information";
150.    print SENDMAIL "\n", $FORM_DATA{'other'},
        "\n";
151.
152.    close (SENDMAIL);
153. }
154.
155. sub send_thank_you
156. {
157.    local (*FORM_DATA) = @_;
158.
159.    print "Content-type: text/html\n\n";
160.
161.    print "<HTML>\n";
162.    print "<HEAD>\n";
```

```
163.     print "<TITLE>CGI Resume
         Submission</TITLE>\n";
164.     print "</HEAD>\n";
165.     print "<BODY><BR>\n";
166.     print "<H1>Thanks for Your
         Application</H1>\n";
167.     print "We will review your qualifications and
         contact you shortly." "\n";
168.     print "Thanks again:", $FORM_DATA{'fname'}," ",
         $FORM_DATA{'lname'},".",<BR><BR>\n";
169.     print "<HR>\n";
170.     print "<BR>\n";
171.     print "</BODY></HTML>\n";
172. }
173. sub return_error
174. {
175.     local ($status, $errtype, $message) = @_;
176.
177.     print "Content-type: text/html\n";
178.     print "Status: ", $status, " ", $errtype,
         "\n\n";
179.     print "<HTML>\n";
180.     print "<HEAD>\n";
181.     print "<TITLE>CGI Program Error</TITLE>\n";
182.     print "</HEAD>\n";
183.     print "<BODY><BR>\n";
184.     print "<H1>This CGI program encountered a ",
         $errtype, "</H1>\n";
185.     print $message;
186.     print "<HR>\n";
187.     print "<BR>\n";
188.     print "</BODY></HTML>\n";
189.     exit(1);
190. }
```

The Resume Script

Let's take a detailed look at our resume script. Line one of our script is used to declare the location of the Perl interpreter to use when running this script.

Line three sets the variable we'll use to direct our e-mail. Here we'll send it to info@mix-media.com. Notice the '@' and the "." Have a '\' before them. These two characters actually have meaning to a computer. They can cause programs to execute certain functions. To prevent this from happening we put a "\" character in front of them, announcing the next character is in fact a character and not a command we want executed. This is called escaping characters in a string.

```
1.   #!/usr/local/bin/perl
2.
3.   $sendto      = "info\@mix-media.com";
4.   $xmailer     = "CGI Resume Mail Gateway [v1.0]";
5.   $sendmail    = "/usr/lib/sendmail -t -n";
6.
7.   &parse_form_data(*FORM_DATA);
8.   &send_mail();
9.   &send_thank_you();
10.  exit(0);
```

Lines seven and eight are the core of our script. They are the sub routines we call to do the work for us. The first, parse_form_data (), gathers and decodes the information sent to us by the client. It then sends that information via e-mail to info@mix-media.com. When this is completed, the sub routine return_thanks () returns an HTML thank you page to the client that submitted the information. Finally, the Perl script exits, returning a result code of zero. This signals that everything went without a problem.

The parse_form_data() Sub Routine

Now let's take a detailed look at our parse_form_data() sub routine. Line 12 of our script is used to declare the following instructions are part of our parse_form_data sub routine. Every instruction between the open curly bracket on line 13 and the close curly bracket on line 50 is included in this routine. On line 14 we call the Perl local routine to create a reference to the argument passed to the routine. Perl passes arguments to its routines through the @_ associative array. If this is unfamiliar, we've simply created a reference to the submitted form data that this sub routine and the main routine can share. On line 16 we create some more local space to store information we'll copy out of the submission.

```
12.    sub parse_form_data
13.    {
14.        local (*FORM_DATA) = @_;
15.
16.        local ( $request_method, $query_string,
               @key_value_pairs, $key_value, $key, $value);
```

The two most popular methods for submitting information to an HTTP server are POST and GET. Information sent to a server via the GET method is stored in the QUERY_STRING environment variable. If it's sent via a POST to the server the data is placed in the STDIN buffer and its length is placed in the CONTENT_LENGTH environment variable. This architecture requires that we check for the method of submission in order to locate the form data. On line 14 we determine just how the information was sent to this script by calling the $ENV{} function and passing 'REQUEST_METHOD' as the parameter. This returns the submission method and stores it in the $request_method local variable. On line 15 we compare what's stored in $request_method with the string "GET". If they're equal we again call $ENV{} but this time with 'QUERY_STRING' as the parameter. This stores the submission information in the local variable $query_string.

```
18.        $request_method = $ENV{'REQUEST_METHOD'};
19.
20.        if($request_method eq "GET")
21.        {
22.            $query_string = $ENV{'QUERY_STRING'};
23.        }
```

If what's stored in $request_method isn't equal to "GET", on line 19 we check to see if it's equal to "POST". If it is, we need to read the form data from the standard input buffer. To do this, we call the read() command. However, the read command requires three parameters. First it needs to know from where it is to read the information. Second is where it is to put the information it reads, and third, it needs to know how much information it's supposed to read. By invoking the read() command and passing it STDIN (the standard input buffer) as to where we want it to read from, calling $query_string as to where we want to store the information we read, and retrieving the length of the data we're suppose to read by calling $ENV{'CONTENT_LENGTH'}, we accomplish this task.

```
24.      elsif($request_method eq "POST")
25.      {
26.          read(STDIN, $query_string,
             $ENV{'CONTENT_LENGTH'});
27.      }
```

In case the $request_method isn't either GET or POST we provide a catch all that calls our return_error sub routine. This returns an HTML page informing the user we didn't know what to do with their request. It then exits the script without processing the submission.

```
28.      else
29.      {
30.          &return_error (500, "Server Error",
             "Server uses unsupported method");
31.      }
```

After we receive the information and properly store it in the $query_string local variable our next task is to format and decode it. We know the HTTP protocol requires the client to separate each key/value pair with the ampersand character. Using this information, we can use the Perl split() command to store each key/value pair in an array. Line 33 accomplishes this by splitting the query string at each ampersand and storing it in the key_value_pairs array.

```
33.      @key_value_pairs = split(/&/,
         $query_string);
```

Once we have the key/value information in an array, we need to break it into its key and value components. The HTTP protocol requires each field and its value be separated by the equals character. As we loop through each entry, line 37 splits the field name and its value and stores the two in the $key and $value local variables. Line 38 uses the Perl translate command to replace any "+" characters with a space. This is necessary because the client has done the reverse and replaced any space with "+" characters before transmitting the data to the server. Line 39 is another type of translation. Here we use the substitute command to revert all characters that have been converted to their hexadecimal equivalent back to their original ASCII values. The substitute command contains a regular expression that looks for a "%" followed by two characters. These two characters are stored in a variable $1. The expression then is evaluated by the e option converting the value stored in $1 into its ASCII equivalent. Finally the "g" option searches the initial string and replaces all occurrences on the hexadecimal value with its ASCII equivalent. Needless to say a lot happens in this little line.

We finally have our data in a state that we're ready to store. Line 41 checks for an existing entry for this field. If there is already an entry we call the join command to append this value to the existing values in our array on line 43. If the field doesn't yet exist we add it and its value to the $FORM_DATA associative array on line 47.

```
35.        foreach $key_value (@key_value_pairs)
36.        {
37.          ($key, $value) = split (/=/,
             $key_value);
38.          $value =~ tr/+/ /;
39.          $value =~ s/%([\dA-Fa-f][\dA-Fa-f])/pack
             ("C", hex ($1))/eg;

41.          if (defined($FORM_DATA{$key}))
42.        {
43.              $FORM_DATA{$key} = join ("\0",
                 $FORM_DATA{$key}, $value);
44.          }
45.        else
46.        {
47.              $FORM_DATA{$key} = $value;
48.          }
49.        }
50.    }
```

The entire purpose of the parse_form_data() sub routine is to format and decode the form submission data. At this point that task is accomplished. Now let's examine our send_mail() subroutine.

```
52.    sub send_mail
53.    {
54.      local (*FORM_DATA) = @_;
55.
```

```
56.     open (SENDMAIL, "| $sendmail");
57.
58.     print SENDMAIL "From: ", $FORM_DATA{'email'},
        "\n";
59.     print SENDMAIL "To: ", $sendto, "\n";
60.
61.     print SENDMAIL "Reply-To: ",
        $FORM_DATA{'email'}, "\n";
62.     print SENDMAIL "Subject: Resume Submission\n";
63.     print SENDMAIL "X-Mailer: ", $xmailer, "\n";
64.     print SENDMAIL "X-Remote-Host: ",
        $ENV{'REMOTE_ADDR'}, "\n";
65.     print SENDMAIL "Cc: \n";
66.
67.     print SENDMAIL "\n\nName/Address/Etc\.";
68.     print SENDMAIL "\n", $FORM_DATA{'first'};
69.     print SENDMAIL " ", $FORM_DATA{'last'};
70.     print SENDMAIL "\n", $FORM_DATA{'address'};
71.     print SENDMAIL "\n", $FORM_DATA{'city'};
72.     print SENDMAIL ", ", $FORM_DATA{'state'};
73.     print SENDMAIL "  ", $FORM_DATA{'postal'};
74.     print SENDMAIL "\n",
        $FORM_DATA{'country'},"\n";
75.     print SENDMAIL "\n\n", "Telephone: ",
        $FORM_DATA{'tel'};
76.     print SENDMAIL "\n", "E-mail Address: ",
        $FORM_DATA{'email'};
77.     print SENDMAIL "\n", "Personal URL:   ",
        $FORM_DATA{'url'};
78.
79.     print SENDMAIL "\n\n", "Employment History";
```

Now we're ready to start sending the e-mail. On line 56 we open a file handle to the sendmail application. Our $sendmail variable contains a pipe "|" character. Instead of opening a file, this character indicates we want to open a command so we can write to it. Putting the pipe at the beginning indicates we want to write to the process. If we put the pipe at the end of the path, we could read the output from the command. In either case, we receive a file handle to the command from open. We store this file handle in the SENDMAIL variable. Once we have this file handle, we can print our response to it. From line 58 to 65 we print e-mail addressing information to the sendmail command. Sendmail uses this information to properly forward the e-mail. Once our message is addressed, we start outputting our message. Lines 67 to 77 print HTML through our SENDMAIL file handle.

```
80.     ##   First Company Entry
81.     if($FORM_DATA{'start1'})
82.     {
83.       if($FORM_DATA{'end1'})
84.       {
85.         print SENDMAIL "\n\n",
       $FORM_DATA{'start1'};
86.         print SENDMAIL "\-", $FORM_DATA{'end1'};
87.       }
88.       else
89.       {
90.         print SENDMAIL "\n\n",
          $FORM_DATA{'start1'};
91.         print SENDMAIL "\-";
92.       }
93.     }
94.     if($FORM_DATA{'title1'})
95.     {
96.       print SENDMAIL "\n", $FORM_DATA{'title1'};
97.     }
98.     if($FORM_DATA{'company1'})
99.     {
100.      print SENDMAIL "\n", $FORM_DATA{'company1'};
101.    }
102.    if($FORM_DATA{'desc1'})
103.    {
104.      print SENDMAIL "\n", $FORM_DATA{'desc1'};
105.    }
```

From lines 80 to 105 we gather our employment history information from $FORM_DATA and print it to the SENDMAIL file handle. From lines 134 we process educational history. On line 135, if degree1 is not equal to "None", we retrieve the specific degree information and print it to SENDMAIL. If it is equal to "None" we print the string "No first degree." to SENDMAIL.

```
134.    print SENDMAIL "\n\n", "Education";
135.    if(!($FORM_DATA{'degree1'} eq "None"))
136.    {
137.      print SENDMAIL "\n", $FORM_DATA{'degree1'};
138.      print SENDMAIL "\n", $FORM_DATA{'grad1'};
139.      print SENDMAIL "\n", $FORM_DATA{'field1'};
140.      print SENDMAIL "\n", $FORM_DATA{'school1'};
141.    }
142.    if(!($FORM_DATA{'degree2'} eq "None"))
143.    {
144.      print SENDMAIL "\n\n",
          $FORM_DATA{'degree2'};
145.      print SENDMAIL "\n", $FORM_DATA{'grad2'};
146.      print SENDMAIL "\n", $FORM_DATA{'field2'};
147.      print SENDMAIL "\n", $FORM_DATA{'school2'};
148.    }
```

From lines 149 to 150 we print the remaining applicant information, and on line 153 we close the SENDMAIL file handle. Once SENDMAIL is closed, the mail is sent to its recipient.

```
149.    print SENDMAIL "\n\n", "Other Information";
150.    print SENDMAIL "\n", $FORM_DATA{'other'},
151.    "\n";
152.
153.    close (SENDMAIL);
154.  }
```

The send_thank_you() Sub Routine

Line 45 of our script is used to declare the following instructions are part of our send_thank_you() sub routine. On line eleven we call the Perl local command to create a reference to the associate array passed to this script's main routine. Again we create a reference to the submitted form data that this sub routine and the main routine can share. By the time we call this routine, we've formatted and decoded the information in the parse_form_data() routine.

On line 157 we use the print command to output a minimum HTTP response header. The line informs the client the file they're about to receive is of the "text/html" MIME type. The print command sends data to the standard output buffer (STDOUT). This is where the server looks for a response to send back to the client.

```
155.   sub send_thank_you
156.   {
157.      local (*FORM_DATA) = @_;
158.
159.      print "Content-type: text/html\n\n";
160.
161.      print "<HTML>\n";
162.      print "<HEAD>\n";
163.      print "<TITLE>CGI Resume
          Submission</TITLE>\n";
164.      print "</HEAD>\n";
165.      print "<BODY><BR>\n";
166.      print "<H1>Thanks for Your
          Application</H1>\n";
```

From line 161 we begin printing HTML to STDOUT as our reply. On line 168 we continue printing HTML combined with our $FORM_DATA to STDOUT as our reply. On line 171 we print the required closing HTML and on line 172 the routine ends.

```
167.      print "We will review your qualifications and
          contact you shortly." "\n";
168.      print "Thanks again", $FORM_DATA{'fname'}," ",
          $FORM_DATA{'lname'},".",<BR><BR>\n";
169.      print "<HR>\n";
170.      print "<BR>\n";
171.      print "</BODY></HTML>\n";
172.   }
```

The return_error() Sub Routine

Our return_error() sub routine is a very simple solution that sends an HTML response to the client advising them that an error occurred. Line 173 of our script is used to declare the instructions that follow are part of our return_error() sub routine. On line 175 we call the Perl local command to create a local reference to the three parameters passed to this routine.

On line 177 we use the print command to output the content-type member of the HTTP response header. On line 178 we add the status to the header and append two newline characters signifying the response header's end. Line 179 outputs the opening HTML needed to construct the reply. On lines 184 and 185 we combine the $errtype and $message into our response and then print the HTML required to complete the response file. In conclusion we call the Perl exit() command passing it "1" so the script will exit knowing an error has been encountered.

```
173.  sub return_error
174.  {
175.     local ($status, $errtype, $message) = @_;
176.
177.     print "Content-type: text/html\n";
178.     print "Status: ", $status, " ", $errtype,
         "\n\n";
179.     print "<HTML>\n";
180.     print "<HEAD>\n";
181.     print "<TITLE>CGI Program Error</TITLE>\n";
182.     print "</HEAD>\n";
183.     print "<BODY><BR>\n";
184.     print "<H1>This CGI program encountered a ",
         $errtype, "</H1>\n";
185.     print $message;
186.     print "<HR>\n";
187.     print "<BR>\n";
188.     print "</BODY></HTML>\n";
189.     exit(1);
190.  }
```

Run the Example

To run the example, place the "resume.pl" Perl script in your Apache Server's "cgi-bin" directory. Place the "resume.html" file on your server in a directory that you can access through your browser. Make sure the user account the server uses has permission to execute the script. Now enter the form's URL in your browser window. Enter some information into the form fields and click the submit button.

University Course Enrollment

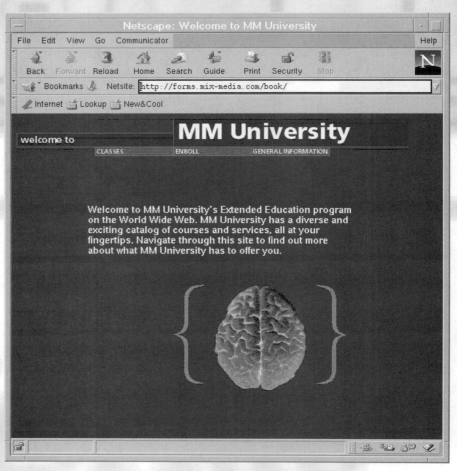

Overview

This example demonstrates how to construct a multi-page form application that allows a user to review a fictional university's course offerings.

General information available includes course descriptions, class listings, general information about the university, and an enrollment form.

Physical Requirements

The following list is a description of the setup used to create this example. The actual components are:

Windows NT Server version 4.0
Microsoft Internet Information Server 4.0
Microsoft Access98
Netscape Navigator 3.x or Netscape Communicator 4.04 or newer with Acrobat Plug-in or Microsoft Internet Explorer 4.0 or newer with Acrobat Plug-in
Adobe Acrobat Exchange 3.1 or newer with Adobe Forms Plug-in 3.5 or newer.

Physical Setup the Example Uses

The example runs on a Microsoft Internet Information Server 4.0 (IIS) running on a Windows NT 4.0 Server.

We've added a "courses" table to our Access database and configured it to accept connections from user "Adobe", password "book". The table has ten fields that correspond to the fields of our enrollment form. They are:

fname
mname
lname
address
city
state
zip

ssnumber
homephone
email

For security reasons, the university database is the only one this user and password can access.

For this example we're using the active server pages to manage the connection to the database. We use SQL to generate the responses to the database queries. Active server pages use VBScript to access the database through ODBC. With VBScript we can access information stored in the database, perform calculations, and return HTML documents constructed from the information requested. This example uses SQL commands to generate and retrieve a student's course information.

To query the database and gather information about the connected employee we'll use ASP scripts. These scripts return information to our HTML forms and forward valid submissions back to the Access database.

We have installed Microsoft Internet Explorer 4.0 and Acrobat Reader 3.01 on our client machine. Additionally, Internet Explorer has the Acrobat plug-in located in its plug_in directory. This allows PDF files to be viewed directly in the Internet Explorer window.

Creating the Necessary Files
To get this complete example to work, we need to put nine document files on the server. The files are:

1 HTML file for the welcome screen
1 HTML file for current course offerings
1 PDF file for general information and a map of how to reach the school
1 HTML form file for course enrollment

Current Course files
3 HTML files, one for each Class description
1 ASP file that returns current class enrollment status

Form Processing file

1 ASP file that returns enrollment confirmation or denial

In this example, the course enrollment status files will be generated dynamically. When they're accessed, the Access database is queried and the current class list is displayed.

Creating the Welcome HTML file

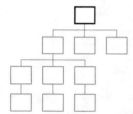

This example uses an HTML file as its initial contact screen. This welcome screen is contained in one HTML file and is named "index.html". It's a simple file that provides confirmation to the user that they're in the right place. From the welcome screen you can access the list of classes offered, some general information about the school, and how to enroll for classes.

This form application demonstrates general principles that can be applied to any event registration application. You can use any visual HTML tool to create the page or you can type in the HTML using a text editor. The following is the complete HTML example. We'll discuss the parts of the file over the next few steps.

```
1.    <HTML>
2.    <HEAD>
3.       <TITLE>Welcome to MM University</TITLE>
4.    </HEAD>
5.    <BODY BGCOLOR="#FFFFFF" LINK="#D70000"
      ALINK="#F4FC58" VLINK="#D70000"
      BACKGROUND="/images/background.gif">
6.    <P> </P>
7.    <P><A HREF="/images/title.map"><MAP NAME="title">
8.    <AREA SHAPE=RECT COORDS="119,46,238,60"
      HREF="courses.html">
9.    <AREA SHAPE=RECT COORDS="240,46,358,60"
      HREF="enrollment.html">
10.   <AREA SHAPE=RECT COORDS="360,46,478,60"
      HREF="general_info.pdf">
```

```
11.   </MAP><IMG ISMAP USEMAP="#title"
      SRC="/images/welcome_title.gif"
      ALT="Welcome" WIDTH=600 HEIGHT=60 BORDER=0
      ALIGN=BOTTOM></A><BR></P>
12.   <BR>
13.   <BR>
14.   <BR>
15.   <TABLE BORDER=0 CELLSPACING=6 WIDTH=640>
16.     <TR>
17.       <TD VALIGN=top ALIGN=LEFT WIDTH="20%">
18.         <P>  </TD>
19.         <TD VALIGN=TOP COLSPAN=3>
20.         <P><B><FONT SIZE="+1" FACE="Helvetica"
21.         COLOR="#FFFFFF">
22.         Welcome to MM University's Extended
            Education program on the World Wide Web.
            MM University has a diverse and exciting
            catalog of courses and services, all at
            your fingertips. Navigate through this
            site to find out more about what MM
            University has to offer you.</FONT></B></P>
23.         <P>
24.       </TD>
25.     </TR>
26.     <TR>
27.       <TD WIDTH="20%">
28.         <P>
29.       </TD><TD VALIGN=TOP WIDTH="20%">
30.         <P>
31.       </TD><TD VALIGN=TOP COLSPAN=2>
32.         <P><IMG SRC="/images/home_brain.jpeg"
            WIDTH=286 HEIGHT=198
33.         BORDER=0 ALIGN=BOTTOM>
34.       </TD>
35.     </TR>
36.   </TABLE>
37.   </BODY>
38.   </HTML>
```

Examining the HTML Code

This example's opening lines of HTML provide a standard opening for any HTML file. Line one is the tag declaring that what will follow is an HTML file. Line two begins the head of the file. Inside the HEAD tags we add a title that will display in the browser window while the file is being viewed.

On line five we define the color for text, the background, the links, the visited links, the a links, and an image to use as the background for the file. Here we set the background to use the image to "background.gif". We provide a path to the image stored on our server in the images directory, "/images/background.gif".

After we've established these basic settings, we begin adding items to the file that will display in the window. Next we add our title graphic.

The title image is part of an image map. The block of HTML code from lines 7-11 identifies a server- and client-side image map. To insure compatability with older browsers that don't handle image maps, we set an anchor tag as an HREF to the map file on the server. The map file describes a set of rectangles and the URL they each link to when clicked. Instead of submitting a request to the server, recent browsers have the ability to decipher image map information themselves. The <MAP></MAP> defined on lines 7-11 provides information to the client for this purpose. It defines three rectangles and the URLs they reference.

Lines 12-14 add a break tag to increase the space between the title graphic and the table we use to display our initial greeting.

```
1.   <HTML>
2.   <HEAD>
3.     <TITLE>Welcome to MM University</TITLE>
4.   </HEAD>
5.   <BODY BGCOLOR="#FFFFFF" LINK="#D70000"
     ALINK="#F4FC58" VLINK="#D70000"
     BACKGROUND="/images/background.gif">
6.   <P> </P>
7.   <P><A HREF="/images/title.map"><MAP NAME="title">
8.   <AREA SHAPE=RECT COORDS="119,46,238,60"
     HREF="courses.html">
```

```
9.     <AREA SHAPE=RECT COORDS="240,46,358,60"
       HREF="enrollment.html">
10.    <AREA SHAPE=RECT COORDS="360,46,478,60"
       HREF="general_info.pdf">
11.    </MAP><IMG ISMAP USEMAP="#title"
       SRC="/images/welcome_title.gif"
       ALT="Welcome" WIDTH=600 HEIGHT=60 BORDER=0
       ALIGN=BOTTOM></A><BR></P>
12.    <BR>
13.    <BR>
14.    <BR>
```

Adding the table

Lines 15 to 39 add the table we use to display our greeting and brain
graphic. Line 15 uses the HTML <TABLE> tag to start a table. We set the
border around the table to 0 pixels in width, the spacing between each
cell in the table to six pixels, and the width of the table to exactly 640 pixels. On line 16 we use the table row tag, <TR>, to open a table row. Once
we open a table row we can add as many cells as we want with the table
detail tag, <TD>.

```
15.    <TABLE BORDER=0 CELLSPACING=6 WIDTH=640>
16.      <TR>
17.        <TD VALIGN=TOP ALIGN=LEFT WIDTH="20%">
18.          <P>  </TD>
```

On line 17 we add our row's first cell. We set the text alignment to Left
and the vertical text alignment to Top. This forces text in the cell to be left
aligned from the top of the cell. Next we define a relative width of 20%.
This instructs the browser to draw the cell to 20% of the table's width. If
we defined the table as a percentage of the window, all these width values
would be recalculated when the browser window is resized. Since our
table is exactly 640 pixels, this cell will always be 20% of the table width
or 128 pixels wide. We want this cell to be blank so we don't add any text.
Instead we add an HTML non-breaking space character, . Finally
we close the cell with the </TD> tag.

```
19.          <TD VALIGN=TOP COLSPAN=3>
20.          <P><B><FONT SIZE="+1" FACE="Helvetica"
21.          COLOR="#FFFFFF">
```

```
22.              Welcome to MM University's Extended
                 Education program on the World Wide Web.
                 MM University has a diverse and exciting
                 catalog of courses and services, all at
                 your fingertips. Navigate through this
                 site to find out more about what MM
                 University has to offer you.</FONT></B></P>
23.         </TD>
24.     </TR>
```

On line 19 we add another cell to our currently open row. We set the vertical text alignment to Top and we set the number of columns this cell will span to three. This allows text in this cell to extend the width of three columns. We use the Bold tag and set the font color to #FFFFFF, white, and increase the point size by one point. This gives us a larger, bold font for the text we're about to display. Line 22 is the text we'll draw in the cell and the closing tags for </FONT>and </B>. The cell is closed,</TD>, on line 23. On line 24 the first row is closed using the </TR> tag.

Our table only has two rows. On line 26 we open the second and begin adding cells. Line 27 and 29 define cells we use for spacing purposes. Notice that both rows have three cells. This is a valuable organizational tool to help keep tables consistent. On line 33 a cell is added that contains an image. We provide the image information so that it is consistent with the <IMG> tag. On line 34 we close the row and on line 36 we close the table.

```
26.     <TR>
27.        <TD WIDTH="20%">
28.          <P>
29.        </TD><TD VALIGN=TOP WIDTH="20%">
30.          <P>
31.        </TD><TD VALIGN=TOP COLSPAN=2>
32.          <P><IMG SRC="/images/home_brain.jpeg"
             WIDTH=286 HEIGHT=198
33.          BORDER=0 ALIGN=BOTTOM>
34.        </TD>
35.     </TR>
36.     </TABLE>
37.     </BODY>
38.     </HTML>
```

By the end of line 37, we've completed all the definitions needed to create the welcome page. All that remains to do is close the HTML file's </BODY> tag and then close the </HTML> file itself.

Creating the Courses HTML File

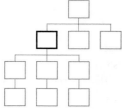

This page is also contained in one HTML file and is named "courses.html". It's a simple file that lists all Humanities courses offered in the Fall MM University's curriculum. A student can click on any of the course listings to view a detailed description of the course. Information regarding the course instructor is also provided in the description of the course.

```
1.    <HTML>
2.    <HEAD>
3.       <TITLE>Humanities Class Listings</TITLE>
4.    </HEAD>
5.    <BODY BGCOLOR="#FFFFFF" LINK="#D70000"
      ALINK="#F4FC58" VLINK="#D70000"
      BACKGROUND="/images/background.gif">
6.    <P><A HREF="/images/title.map"><MAP NAME="title">
7.       <AREA SHAPE=RECT COORDS="119,46,238,60"
         HREF="courses.html">
8.       <AREA SHAPE=RECT COORDS="240,46,358,60"
         HREF="employee_info.pdf">
9.       <AREA SHAPE=RECT COORDS="360,46,478,60"
         HREF="general_info.pdf">
10.   </MAP><IMG ISMAP USEMAP="#title"
      SRC="/images/humanities_title.gif"
      ALT="Courses" WIDTH=600 HEIGHT=60 BORDER=0
      ALIGN=BOTTOM></A><BR>
11.   <BR>
12.   <BR>
13.   <BR>
14.   <TABLE BORDER=0 CELLSPACING=6 WIDTH=600>
15.      <TR>
16.         <TD ALIGN=LEFT WIDTH="25%">
17.            <P>
```

```
18.        </TD><TD VALIGN=TOP COLSPAN=3 ALIGN=LEFT
           WIDTH="75%">
19.          <P><B><FONT SIZE="+1" FACE="Helvetica"
      COLOR="#FFFFFF">For listings in other
      Departments, go to the Table of Contents or look
      them up through the Index.</FONT></B> <BR>
20.           
21.        </TD></TR>
22.     <TR>
23.       <TD WIDTH="25%">  </TD>
24.         <TD WIDTH="25%">
25.         <P>
26.       </TD><TD WIDTH="25%">
27.         <P>
28.       </TD><TD WIDTH="25%">
29.         <P>
30.       </TD></TR>
31.     <TR>
32.       <TD WIDTH="25%">
33.         <P>
34.       </TD><TD WIDTH="25%">
35.         <P>
36.       </TD><TD WIDTH="25%">
37.         <P>
38.       </TD><TD WIDTH="25%">
39.         <P>
40.       </TD></TR>
41.     <TR>
42.       <TD VALIGN=TOP WIDTH="25%">
43.         <P>
44.       </TD><TD VALIGN=TOP ALIGN=LEFT
           BGCOLOR="#000000" WIDTH="25%">
45.        <P><B><FONT SIZE="+1" FACE="Helvetica"
           COLOR="#FFFFFF">Anthropology</FONT> </B>
46.         </TD><TD VALIGN=TOP BGCOLOR="#000000"
           WIDTH="25%">
47.         <P><B><FONT SIZE="+1" FACE="Helvetica"
           COLOR="#FFFFFF">Philosophy</FONT> </B>
48.         </TD><TD VALIGN=TOP BGCOLOR="#000000"
           WIDTH="25%">
```

```
49.        <P><B><FONT SIZE="+1" FACE="Helvetica"
           COLOR="#FFFFFF">Art History</FONT> </B>
50.        </TD></TR>
51.      <TR>
52.        <TD VALIGN=TOP WIDTH="25%">
53.          <P>
54.        </TD><TD VALIGN=TOP WIDTH="25%">
55.    <P><FONT SIZE="+1" FACE="Helvetica"
       COLOR="#FFFFFF"><A HREF="urban_anth.html">Urban
       Anthropology</A></FONT>
56.        </TD><TD VALIGN=TOP WIDTH="25%">
57.        <P><FONT SIZE="+1" FACE="Helvetica"
           COLOR="#FFFFFF">
           <A HREF="philosophy.html">Philosophy
           101</A></FONT> 
58.        </TD><TD VALIGN=TOP WIDTH="25%">
59.          <P><FONT SIZE="+1" FACE="Helvetica"
             COLOR="#FFFFFF">
             <A HREF="art_history.html">Renaissance Art
             in Rome, 1400-1600</FONT> </A>
60.        </TD></TR>
61.    </TABLE>
62.    </BODY>
63.    </HTML>
```

Examining the HTML Code

This example's opening lines of HTML provide the same standard opening for each HTML file in this application. Line one through five defines the basic settings used to set up the HTML file. Line six adds our title graphic.

The title image for this page is also an image map. Lines six through ten create an anchor to a server-side image map and a complete server-side image map. The server-side map is the file located at "/images/title.map". It's a file that defines three rectangles and the URLs each rectangle references. The client-side <MAP></MAP> also defines three rectangles and the URLs they reference. This <MAP> can be interpreted by the browser so it doesn't need to query the server. It can process the mouse click in the image itself.

Lines 11-13 add break tags to increase the space between the title graphic and the table we use to display page information.

```
1.    <HTML>
2.    <HEAD>
3.       <TITLE>Humanities Class Listings</TITLE>
4.    </HEAD>
5.    <BODY BGCOLOR="#FFFFFF" LINK="#D70000"
      ALINK="#F4FC58" VLINK="#D70000"
      BACKGROUND="/images/background.gif">
6.    <P><A HREF="/images/title.map"><MAP NAME="title">
7.       <AREA SHAPE=RECT COORDS="119,46,238,60"
         HREF="courses.html">
8.       <AREA SHAPE=RECT COORDS="240,46,358,60"
         HREF="employee_info.pdf">
9.       <AREA SHAPE=RECT COORDS="360,46,478,60"
         HREF="general_info.pdf">
10.   </MAP><IMG ISMAP USEMAP="#title"
      SRC="/images/humanities_title.gif"
      ALT="Courses" WIDTH=600 HEIGHT=60 BORDER=0
      ALIGN=BOTTOM></A><BR>
11.   <BR>
12.   <BR>
13.   <BR>
```

Adding a table

Lines 14 to 61 add the table we use to display our list of courses offered at MM University. Line 14 uses the HTML <TABLE> tag to start a table. Here we set the border around the table to 0 pixels in width. We set the spacing between each cell in the table to six pixels and the padding from the edge of the cell to the point where text is drawn to 0 pixels. The table's size is set to exactly 600 pixels in width.

On line 15 we use the table row tag, <TR>, to open a table row. Once we open a table row, we can add as many cells as we want with the table detail tag, <TD>.

```
14.   <TABLE BORDER=0 CELLSPACING=6 WIDTH=600>
15.      <TR>
16.         <TD ALIGN=LEFT WIDTH="25%">
```

```
17.              <P>
18.          </TD><TD VALIGN=TOP COLSPAN=3 ALIGN=LEFT
             WIDTH="75%">
19.              <P><B><FONT SIZE="+1" FACE="Helvetica"
         COLOR="#FFFFFF">For listings in other
         Departments, go to the Table of Contents or look
         them up through the Index.</FONT></B> <BR>
20.               
21.          </TD></TR>
```

On line 16 we add our row's first cell. We set the relative width of the cell to 25%. This instructs the browser to draw the cell to 25% of the table's width. If we defined the table as a percentage of the window, all these width values would be recalculated when the browser window is resized. Since our table is exactly 600 pixels, this cell will always be 25% of the table width or 150 pixels wide. Again, we want this cell to be blank so we don't add any text. Instead we add an HTML non-breaking space character, " " to insure the cell will be drawn by all browsers. Finally we close the cell with the </TD> tag. On line 18-20 we add another cell with bold, white text four points larger than our normal text and then on line 21 we close the cell and row.

```
22.      <TR>
23.        <TD WIDTH="25%">  </TD>
24.          <TD WIDTH="25%">
25.          <P>
26.        </TD><TD WIDTH="25%">
27.          <P>
28.        </TD><TD WIDTH="25%">
29.          <P>
30.        </TD></TR>
```

This table has five rows. Lines 22-30 add the second set of cells that are empty, to control placement of text on the page. Lines 31-40 add the third. Notice that each row has four cells. This consistency helps keep cell alignment manageable. On line 60 we close the final row and on line 61 we close the table.

```
51.      <TR>
52.        <TD VALIGN=TOP WIDTH="25%">
```

```
53.              <P>
54.          </TD><TD VALIGN=TOP WIDTH="25%">
55.      <P><FONT SIZE="+1" FACE="Helvetica"
         COLOR="#FFFFFF"><A HREF="urban_anth.html">Urban
         Anthropology</A></FONT>
56.          </TD><TD VALIGN=TOP WIDTH="25%">
57.          <P><FONT SIZE="+1" FACE="Helvetica"
             COLOR="#FFFFFF">
             <A HREF="philosophy.html">Philosophy
             101</A></FONT> 
58.          </TD><TD VALIGN=TOP WIDTH="25%">
59.             <P><FONT SIZE="+1" FACE="Helvetica"
                COLOR="#FFFFFF">
              <A HREF="art_history.html">Renaissance Art
                in Rome, 1400-1600</FONT> </A>
60.          </TD></TR>
61.  </TABLE>  </P>
62.  </BODY>
63.  </HTML>
```

All that remains to do is close the HTML file's </BODY> tag and then close the </HTML> file itself.

Creating the Individual Course HTML Files

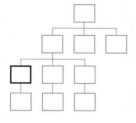

The individual pages detailing each course are also static HTML files. Below we'll discuss the creation of the Philosophy page that offers the Philosophy 101 course. The implementation for the other two courses is identical but won't be duplicated here. Again, this is a simple file that lists course specifics such as dates and times, cost, location, and a description. This file offers links to the three top-level pages in this application and a button that takes you to the registration form.

```
1.  <HTML>
2.  <HEAD>
3.     <TITLE>Philosophy of Plato:The Republic</TITLE>
4.  </HEAD>
5.  <BODY BGCOLOR="#FFFFFF" ALINK="#0000FF"
    VLINK="#551A8B"
    BACKGROUND="/images/background.gif">
```

```
6.    <P><A HREF="/images/title.map"><MAP NAME="title">
7.      <AREA SHAPE=RECT COORDS="119,46,238,60"
        HREF="courses.html">
8.      <AREA SHAPE=RECT COORDS="240,46,358,60"
        HREF="enrollment.html">
9.      <AREA SHAPE=RECT COORDS="360,46,478,60"
        HREF="general_info.pdf">
10.   </MAP><IMG ISMAP USEMAP="#title"
      SRC="/images/philosophy_title.gif"ALT="Philosophy
      " WIDTH=600 HEIGHT=60 BORDER=0
11.   ALIGN=BOTTOM></A><BR>
12.   <TABLE BORDER=0 CELLSPACING=6 WIDTH=600>
13.     <TR>
14.       <TD VALIGN=BASELINE ALIGN=LEFT WIDTH="33%">
15.         <P>
16.       </TD><TD VALIGN=TOP ALIGN=LEFT WIDTH=400>
17.         <P><B><FONT SIZE="+1" FACE="Helvetica"
            COLOR="#FFFFFF">Philosophy of Plato:The
            Republic</FONT></B><FONT SIZE="+1"
            FACE="Helvetica" COLOR="#FFFFFF">Section:
18.         122.1</FONT> <BR>
19.          
20.       </TD></TR>
21.     <TR>
22.       <TD VALIGN=TOP WIDTH="33%">
          <P><FONT SIZE="+1" FACE="Helvetica"
23.       COLOR="#FFFFFF">June 24- August 12, 1997<BR>
24.       Monday, Wednesday, Friday</FONT><BR>
25.       11am -12:00pm<BR>
26.   <BR>
27.         Downtown</P>
28.         3 semester Units</P>
29.         $250.00</FONT> <BR>
30.          
31.       </TD><TD VALIGN=TOP ALIGN=LEFT WIDTH=400>
            <P><FONT SIZE="+1" FACE="Helvetica"
            COLOR="#FFFFFF">This course attempts to
            develop the basic skills of constructing
            arguments for positions in which one
            believes, of meeting objections with
            reason, and of analyzing arguments and
            criticizing them effectively. Offered
```

```
32.                    every other Fall semester.</P>
                       <P>Instructor: Stephen Decker, Ph. D.,
                       received his degree in philoshopy from
                       Boston University. He spent ten years
                       living as a monk, studying the effects of
                       complete silence on the soul. His work has
                       been published in numerous scholarly
                       journals and the professor is currently at
                       work on a biography of Mahatma Ghandi. </FONT>
33.        </TD></TR>
34.      <TR>
35.        <TD WIDTH="33%">
36.          <P>
37.        </TD><TD WIDTH=400>
38.          <P>
39.        </TD></TR>
40.      <TR>
41.        <TD WIDTH="33%">
42.          <P>
43.        </TD><TD WIDTH=400>
44.          <P>
45.        </TD></TR>
46.      <TR>
47.        <TD WIDTH="33%">
48.          <P>
49.        </TD><TD WIDTH=400>
50.  <P><A HREF="/scripts/register.asp?course=2055">
     <IMG SRC="/images/register.gif" WIDTH=121
     HEIGHT=15 BORDER=0 ALIGN=TOP></A>
51.  <A HREF="courses.html">
     <IMG SRC="/images/return_index.gif" WIDTH=121
     HEIGHT=15 BORDER=0 ALIGN=TOP></A>
52.        </TD></TR>
53.  </TABLE>
54.  </BODY>
55.  </HTML>
```

Examining the HTML Code

Lines one through five define the basic settings used to set up the HTML file. Lines 6-10 construct our title as an image map.

```
1.   <HTML>
2.   <HEAD>
3.     <TITLE>Philosophy of Plato:The Republic</TITLE>
4.   </HEAD>
5.   <BODY BGCOLOR="#FFFFFF" ALINK="#0000FF"
     VLINK="#551A8B"
     BACKGROUND="/images/background.gif">
```

On line six we open an <A></A> tag. We provide an HREF to a file on our server, "/images/title.map" as the target. To this we add a <MAP></MAP> tag. This is our client-side image map information. This MAP named "title" consists of three rectangles. If the mouse is clicked in any of these areas, the browser requests the HREF associated with the area. This information can be processed by the browser, saving time and a submission to the server. For older browsers, mouse down in this area will send a request to the server where the correct URL to return will be determined. By including both server-and client-side image mapping, we cover all bases and incorporate a great feature on our page.

```
6.   <P><A HREF="/images/title.map"><MAP NAME="title">
7.     <AREA SHAPE=RECT COORDS="119,46,238,60"
       HREF="courses.html">
8.     <AREA SHAPE=RECT COORDS="240,46,358,60"
       HREF="enrollment.html">
9.     <AREA SHAPE=RECT COORDS="360,46,478,60"
       HREF="general_info.pdf">
10.  </MAP><IMG ISMAP USEMAP="#title"
     SRC="/images/philosophy_title.gif"ALT="Philosophy"
     WIDTH=600 HEIGHT=60 BORDER=0 ALIGN=BOTTOM></A><BR>
```

Adding a table

Lines 11 to 53 add the table we use to display our courses descriptions. Line 11 uses the HTML TABLE tag to start a table. Here we set the border around the table to 0 pixels in width. We set the spacing between each cell in the table to six pixels and the padding from the edge of the cell to the point where text is drawn to 0 pixels. The table's size is set to exactly 600 pixels in width.

On line 12 we use the table row tag, <TR>, to open a table row. Once we open a table row, we can add as many cells as we want with the table detail tag, <TD>.

```
11.   <TABLE BORDER=0 CELLSPACING=6 WIDTH=600>
12.     <TR>
13.       <TD VALIGN=BASELINE ALIGN=LEFT WIDTH="33%">
14.         <P>
15.       </TD><TD VALIGN=TOP ALIGN=LEFT WIDTH=400>
16.         <P><B><FONT SIZE="+1" FACE="Helvetica"
17.         COLOR="#FFFFFF">Philosophy of Plato:The
            Republic</FONT></B><FONT SIZE="+1"
            FACE="Helvetica" COLOR="#FFFFFF">Section:
            122.1</FONT> <BR>
18.          
19.       </TD></TR>
```

On line 13 we add the row's first cell. We set the relative width of the cell to 33%. This instructs the browser to draw the cell to 33% of the table's width. Since our table is exactly 600 pixels, this cell will always be 33% of the table width or 198 pixels wide. Again, we want this cell to be blank so we don't add any text. Instead we add an HTML non-breaking space character, " ", to insure the cell will be drawn by all browsers. Finally we close the cell with the </TD> tag. On line 15-19 we add another cell that spans 400 pixels. It displays text using bold, white text one size larger than our normal text. On line 19 we close the row.

```
20.     <TR>
21.       <TD VALIGN=TOP WIDTH="33%">
22.       <P><FONT SIZE="+1" FACE="Helvetica"
          COLOR="#FFFFFF">June 24- August 12, 1997<BR>
23.       Monday, Wednesday, Friday</FONT><BR>
24.       11am -12:00pm<BR>
25.   <BR>
26.         Downtown</P>
27.         3 semester Units</P>
28.         $250.00</FONT> <BR>
29.          
30.       </TD><TD VALIGN=TOP ALIGN=LEFT WIDTH=400>
31.         <P><FONT SIZE="+1" FACE="Helvetica"
            COLOR="#FFFFFF">This course attempts to
            develop the basic skills of constructing
            arguments for positions in which one
            believes, of meeting objections with
```

```
      reason, and of analyzing arguments and
      criticizing them effectively. Offered
      every other Fall semester.</P>
32.   <P>Instructor: Stephen Decker, Ph. D.,
      received his degree in philoshopy from
      Boston University. He spent ten years
      living as a monk, studying the effects of
      complete silence on the soul. His work has
      been published in numerous scholarly
      journals and the professor is currently at
      work on a biography of Mahatma Ghandi. </FONT>
33.   </TD></TR>
```

Starting on line 20, we add the second row of our table. This row has only one cell. It contains information pertinent to the date and time of the course. The font is requested to be Helvetica and the color is set to white. The size of the type is increased one unit.

The second cell or detail of this table row contains a brief description of the course. This is drawn using the same type specifications as the paragraph above. If a user doesn't have the requested font or they have a specific font chosen in their browser preferences, they won't see the font Helvetica. If they're cooperative, they will.

```
34.   <TR>
35.   <TD WIDTH="33%">
36.      <P>
37.   </TD><TD WIDTH=400>
38.      <P>
39.   </TD></TR>
40.   <TR>
41.   <TD WIDTH="33%">
42.      <P>
43.   </TD><TD WIDTH=400>
44.      <P>
45.   </TD></TR>
```

Starting on line 33, we add two more rows containing blank cells to increase the space between this and the final row of our table.

```
46.      <TR>
47.        <TD WIDTH="33%">
48.          <P>
49.        </TD><TD WIDTH=400>
50.    <P><A HREF="/scripts/register.asp?course=2055">
       <IMG SRC="/images/register.gif" WIDTH=121
       HEIGHT=15 BORDER=0 ALIGN=TOP></A>
51.    <A HREF="courses.html">
       <IMG SRC="/images/return_index.gif" WIDTH=121
       HEIGHT=15 BORDER=0 ALIGN=TOP></A>
52.        </TD></TR>
```

The final row of our table starts on line 45. Here we open the row and on the next line we add a cell that doesn't contain any information. On line 48 we add another cell that contains two images. These images, when clicked, take us to the registration page and the main courses page, respectively.

```
53.    </TABLE>
54.    <BODY>
55.    <HTML>
```

All that remains to do is close the table, the body, and the HTML file itself.

Creating the General Information PDF File

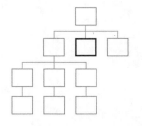

The PDF file that displays information on how to get to the college is a single page. The PDF file displays a map locating the college. This information is read only. However, since it's a PDF file, it looks great when it's printed, and it can be scaled up or down to fit a user's personal needs.

The designer used Adobe Illustrator to construct the original map and page. The file was then distilled into PDF format. The resulting PDF is placed on the server just like any HTML file. Users can download the file for future viewing or, if they have the Acrobat plug-in for their browser, they can view the file directly in their browser's window.

Creating the Course Enrollment HTML Form

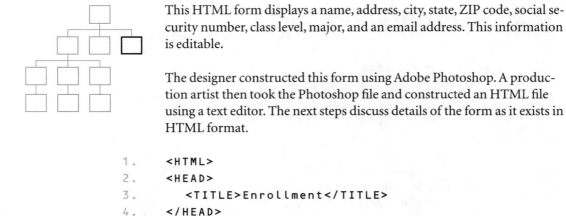

This HTML form displays a name, address, city, state, ZIP code, social security number, class level, major, and an email address. This information is editable.

The designer constructed this form using Adobe Photoshop. A production artist then took the Photoshop file and constructed an HTML file using a text editor. The next steps discuss details of the form as it exists in HTML format.

```
1.    <HTML>
2.    <HEAD>
3.       <TITLE>Enrollment</TITLE>
4.    </HEAD>
5.    <BODY BGCOLOR="#COCOCO" LINK="#D70000"
      ALINK="#F4FC58" VLINK="#D70000"
      BACKGROUND="/images/background.gif">
6.    <FORM ACTION="/scripts/u_register.asp"
      METHOD="POST">
7.    <P><A HREF="/images/title.map"><MAP NAME="title">
8.       <AREA SHAPE=RECT COORDS="119,46,238,60"
         HREF="courses.html">
9.       <AREA SHAPE=RECT COORDS="240,46,358,60"
         HREF="employee_info.pdf">
10.      <AREA SHAPE=RECT COORDS="360,46,478,60"
         HREF="general_info.pdf">
11.   </MAP><IMG ISMAP USEMAP="#title"
      SRC="/images/enroll_title.gif" ALT="Enrollment
      Form" WIDTH=600 HEIGHT=60 BORDER=0
      ALIGN=BOTTOM></A>
12.   <BR>
13.   <BR>
14.   <BR>
15.   <A NAME="top"></A>
16.   <TABLE BORDER=0 WIDTH=600>
17.      <TR>
18.         <TD WIDTH="25%"> </TD>
19.         <TD COLSPAN=3 WIDTH="75%">
```

```
20.              <B><FONT SIZE="+1" FACE="Helvetica"
                 COLOR="#FFFFFF">Please select one of the
                 following means of enrolling. For course
                 detail, refer to our </FONT>
21.              <FONT SIZE="+1" FACE="Helvetica"
                 COLOR="#AF0000">
                 <A HREF="courses.html">"course
                 description"</A></FONT>
22.              <FONT SIZE="+1" FACE="Helvetica"
                 COLOR="#FFFFFF">page.</FONT></B>
23.          </TD>
24.      </TR>
25.      <TR>
26.          <TD WIDTH="25%"> </TD>
27.          <TD COLSPAN=3 WIDTH="75%"> </TD>
28.      </TR>
29.    </TABLE>
30.    <TABLE BORDER=0 WIDTH=600>
31.      <TR>
32.          <TD WIDTH="25%"> </TD>
33.          <TD WIDTH="25%"> </TD>
34.          <TD WIDTH="50%"> </TD>
35.      </TR>
36.      <TR>
37.          <TD WIDTH="25%"> </TD>
38.          <TD VALIGN=TOP WIDTH="25%">
39.             <IMG SRC="/images/phone_arrow.gif"
                 WIDTH=150 HEIGHT=16 ALIGN=TOP> 
40.          </TD>
41.          <TD VALIGN=TOP COLSPAN=2 WIDTH="50%">
42.             <B><FONT SIZE="+1" FACE="Helvetica"
                 COLOR="#FFFFFF">(415) 430-1000 Please have
                 your Visa or MasterCard ready.</FONT></B>
43.             <BR>
44.          </TD>
45.      </TR>
46.      <TR>
47.          <TD WIDTH="25%"> </TD>
48.          <TD WIDTH="25%"> </TD>
49.          <TD WIDTH="50%"> </TD>
```

```
50.        </TR>
51.      <TR>
52.        <TD WIDTH="25%"> </TD>
53.        <TD VALIGN=TOP WIDTH="25%">
54.          <P><IMG SRC="/images/fax_arrow.gif"
             WIDTH=150 HEIGHT=16
55.          ALIGN=TOP> 
56.        </TD>
57.        <TD VALIGN=TOP COLSPAN=2 WIDTH="50%">
58.          <B><FONT SIZE="+1" FACE="Helvetica"
             COLOR="#FFFFFF">(415)430-1001 If using a
             credit card, fax this entire page. For
             purchase order enrollments fax: (415)
             430-1002.</FONT></B>
59.          <BR>
60.        </TD>
61.      </TR>
62.      <TR>
63.        <TD WIDTH="25%"> </TD>
64.        <TD WIDTH="25%"> </TD>
65.        <TD WIDTH="50%"> </TD>
66.       </TR>
67.      <TR>
68.        <TD WIDTH="25%"> </TD>
69.        <TD VALIGN=TOP WIDTH="25%">
70.          <IMG SRC="/images/mail_arrow.gif"
             WIDTH=150 HEIGHT=15
71.          ALIGN=TOP> 
72.        </TD>
73.        <TD VALIGN=TOP COLSPAN=2 WIDTH="50%">
74.          <B><FONT SIZE="+1" FACE="Helvetica"
             COLOR="#FFFFFF">Print and return this
             entire page. Mail to: Dept. M, MM
             University, 350 Pacific Ave., San
             Francisco, CA 94105</FONT></B>
75.  <BR>
76.        </TD>
77.      </TR>
78.      <TR>
79.        <TD WIDTH="25%"> </TD>
```

```
80.            <TD WIDTH="25%"> </TD>
81.            <TD WIDTH="50%"> </TD>
82.        </TR>
83.        <TR>
84.            <TD WIDTH="25%"> </TD>
85.            <TD VALIGN=TOP WIDTH="25%">
86.              <IMG SRC="/images/net_arrow.gif" WIDTH=150
                  HEIGHT=16 ALIGN=TOP> 
87.            </TD><TD VALIGN=TOP COLSPAN=2 WIDTH="50%">
88.              <B><FONT SIZE="+1" FACE="Helvetica"
                  COLOR="#FFFFFF">Complete this page and
                  submit. Be sure to enter your correct
                  return e-mail address.</FONT></B>
89.              <BR>
90.            </TD>
91.        </TR>
92.        <TR>
93.            <TD WIDTH="25%"> </TD>
94.            <TD WIDTH="25%"> </TD>
95.            <TD WIDTH="50%"> </TD>
96.        </TR>
97.        <TR>
98.            <TD WIDTH="25%"> </TD>
99.            <TD WIDTH="25%"> </TD>
100.           <TD WIDTH="50%"> </TD>
101.       </TR>
102.       <TR>
103.           <TD WIDTH="25%"> </TD>
104.           <TD WIDTH="25%"> </TD>
105.           <TD WIDTH="50%"> </TD>
106.       </TR>
107.   </TABLE>
108.   <TABLE BORDER=0 WIDTH=600>
109.       <TR>
110.           <TD WIDTH="20%"> </TD>
111.           <TD VALIGN=TOP COLSPAN=4 WIDTH="80%">
112.             <BR>
113.             <HR ALIGN=LEFT>
114.           <FONT SIZE="+2" FACE="Helvetica"
                COLOR="#FFFFFF">student information:</FONT>
```

```
115.          <BR>
116.         </TD>
117.       </TR>
118.       <TR>
119.         <TD WIDTH="20%"> </TD>
120.     <TD VALIGN=TOP COLSPAN=4 WIDTH="80%"> </TD>
121.       </TR>
122.       <TR>
123.         <TD VALIGN=TOP COLSPAN=2 WIDTH="40%">
124.           <B><FONT FACE="Helvetica"
              COLOR="#FFFFFF">first name</FONT></B><BR>
              <INPUT TYPE="text" NAME="fname" VALUE=""
              SIZE=40>
125.         </TD>
126.         <TD COLSPAN=2 WIDTH="40%">
127.           <B><FONT FACE="Helvetica"
              COLOR="#FFFFFF">last name</FONT></B><BR>
              <INPUT TYPE="text" NAME="lname" VALUE=""
              SIZE=40>
128.         </TD><TD WIDTH="20%">
129.           <B><FONT FACE="Helvetica"
              COLOR="#FFFFFF">mi</FONT></B><BR> <INPUT
              TYPE="text" NAME="mi" VALUE="" SIZE=20>
130.         </TD>
131.       </TR>
132.       <TR>
133.         <TD VALIGN=TOP COLSPAN=2 WIDTH="40%">
134.           <FONT FACE="Helvetica" COLOR="#FFFFFF">
              street address</FONT></B><BR> <INPUT
              TYPE="text" NAME="address" VALUE=""
              SIZE=40>
135.         </TD>
136.         <TD VALIGN=TOP WIDTH="20%">
137.           <B><FONT FACE="Helvetica" COLOR="#FFFFFF">
              apt #</FONT></B><BR> <INPUT TYPE="text"
              NAME="apt" VALUE="" SIZE=20>
138.         </TD>
139.         <TD WIDTH="20%"> </TD>
140.         <TD WIDTH="20%"> </TD>
141.       </TR>
```

```
142.     <TR>
143.       <TD COLSPAN=2 WIDTH="40%">
144.         <B><FONT FACE="Helvetica" COLOR="#FFFFFF">
             city</FONT></B><BR><INPUT TYPE="text"
             NAME="city" VALUE="" SIZE=40>
145.       </TD>
146.       <TD VALIGN=TOP WIDTH="20%">
147.         <B><FONT FACE="Helvetica" COLOR="#FFFFFF">
             state</FONT></B><BR><INPUT TYPE="text"
             NAME="state" VALUE="" SIZE=20>
148.       </TD>
149.       <TD VALIGN=TOP WIDTH="20%">
150.         <B><FONT FACE="Helvetica"COLOR="#FFFFFF">
             zip</FONT></B><BR><INPUT TYPE="text"
             NAME="zip" VALUE="" SIZE=20>
151.       </TD><TD WIDTH="20%"> </TD>
152.     </TR>
153.     <TR>
154.       <TD WIDTH="20%">
155.         <B><FONT FACE="Helvetica" COLOR="#FFFFFF">
             year in school</FONT></B><BR><INPUT
             TYPE="text" NAME="year" VALUE="" SIZE=20>
156.       </TD>
157.       <TD VALIGN=TOP WIDTH="20%">
158.         <B><FONT FACE="Helvetica" COLOR="#FFFFFF">
             major</FONT></B><BR><INPUT TYPE="text"
             NAME="major" VALUE="" SIZE=20>
159.       </TD>
160.       <TD VALIGN=TOP WIDTH="20%"> </TD>
161.       <TD VALIGN=TOP WIDTH="20%">
162.         <B><FONT FACE="Helvetica" COLOR="#FFFFFF">
             social security #<INPUT TYPE="text"
             NAME="ssnumber" VALUE=""
             SIZE=20></FONT></B>
163.       </TD><TD WIDTH="20%"> </TD>
164.     </TR>
165.     <TR>
166.       <TD COLSPAN=2 WIDTH="40%">
167.         <B><FONT FACE="Helvetica" COLOR="#FFFFFF">
             e-mail address</FONT></B><BR><INPUT
             TYPE="text" NAME="email" VALUE="" SIZE=40>
```

```
168.        </TD>
169.        <TD WIDTH="20%"> </TD>
170.        <TD VALIGN=TOP ROWSPAN=2 COLSPAN=2 WIDTH="40%">
171.          <FONT SIZE="+1" FACE="Helvetica"
              COLOR="#FFFFFF">Your social security number
              is used to identify and maintain your
              academic record. Providing your number is
              voluntary and is requested by the authority
              of Regents of MM University</FONT>
172.        </TD>
173.      </TR>
174.      <TR>
175.        <TD WIDTH="20%"> </TD>
176.        <TD WIDTH="75%"> </TD>
177.      </TR>
178.    </TABLE>
179.    <TABLE BORDER=0 WIDTH=600>
180.      <TR>
181.        <TD WIDTH="20%"> </TD>
182.        <TD VALIGN=TOP COLSPAN=4 WIDTH="80%">
183.          <BR>
184.          <HR ALIGN=LEFT>
185.          <FONT SIZE="+2" FACE="Helvetica"
              COLOR="#FFFFFF">courses:</FONT>
186.        <BR>
187.        </TD>
188.      </TR>
189.      <TR>
190.        <TD WIDTH="20%"> </TD>
191.        <TD COLSPAN=5>
192.          <FONT SIZE="+1" FACE="Helvetica"
              COLOR="#FFFFFF">The course section number
              is essential for processing your
              enrollment. You'll find it at the end of
              the course description following the fee.
              You may copy this form as needed. Students
              with special needs please call (555)
              555-1212.</FONT>
193.        </TD>
194.      </TR>
```

```
195.     <TR>
196.       <TD WIDTH="20%"> </TD>
197.       <TD COLSPAN=5> </TD>
198.     </TR>
199.     <TR>
200.       <TD VALIGN=TOP COLSPAN=2>
201.         <B><FONT FACE="Helvetica" COLOR="#FFFFFF">
             course title</FONT></B><BR><INPUT
             TYPE="text" NAME="course1" VALUE=""
             SIZE=40>
202.       </TD>
203.       <TD VALIGN=TOP>
204.         <B><FONT FACE="Helvetica" COLOR="#FFFFFF">
             section#<BR> <INPUT TYPE="text"
             NAME="section1" VALUE=""
             SIZE=20></FONT></B>
205.       </TD>
206.       <TD VALIGN=TOP>
             <B><FONT FACE="Helvetica" COLOR="#FFFFFF">
             fee($)</FONT></B><BR><INPUT TYPE="text"
             NAME="cost1" VALUE="" SIZE=10>
207.       </TD>
208.       <TD> </TD>
209.     </TR>
210.     <TR>
211.       <TD VALIGN=TOP COLSPAN=2>
212.         <B><FONT FACE="Helvetica" COLOR="#FFFFFF">
             course title</FONT></B><BR><INPUT
             TYPE="text" NAME="course2" VALUE=""
             SIZE=40>
213.       </TD>
214.       <TD VALIGN=TOP>
215.         <B><FONT FACE="Helvetica" COLOR="#FFFFFF">
             section#<BR><INPUT TYPE="text"
             NAME="section2" VALUE=""
             SIZE=20></FONT></B>
216.       </TD>
217.       <TD VALIGN=TOP>
218.         <B><FONT FACE="Helvetica" COLOR="#FFFFFF">
             fee($)</FONT></B><BR><INPUT TYPE="text"
             NAME="cost2" VALUE="" SIZE=10>
```

```
219.        </TD>
220.          <TD> </TD>
221.      </TR>
222.      <TR>
223.        <TD VALIGN=TOP COLSPAN=2>
224.          <B><FONT FACE="Helvetica" COLOR="#FFFFFF">
             course title</FONT></B><BR><INPUT
             TYPE="text" NAME="course3" VALUE="" SIZE=40>
225.        </TD>
226.        <TD VALIGN=TOP>
227.          <B><FONT FACE="Helvetica" COLOR="#FFFFFF">
             section#<BR><INPUT TYPE="text"
             NAME="section3" VALUE=""
             SIZE=20></FONT></B>
228.        </TD>
229.          <TD VALIGN=TOP>
230.          <B><FONT FACE="Helvetica" COLOR="#FFFFFF">
             fee($)</FONT></B><BR><INPUT TYPE="text"
             NAME="cost3" VALUE="" SIZE=10>
231.        </TD>
232.          <TD> </TD>
233.      </TR>
234.  </TABLE>
235.  <TABLE BORDER=0 WIDTH=600>
236.      <TR>
237.        <TD WIDTH="20%"> </TD>
238.        <TD VALIGN=TOP COLSPAN=4 WIDTH="80%">
239.          <BR>
240.          <HR ALIGN=LEFT>
241.          <FONT SIZE="+2" FACE="Helvetica"
             COLOR="#FFFFFF">payment:</FONT></P>
242.          <BR>
243.        </TD>
244.      </TR>
245.      <TR>
246.        <TD WIDTH="20%"> </TD>
247.        <TD COLSPAN=4 WIDTH="80%">
248.          <FONT SIZE="+1" FACE="Helvetica"
             COLOR="#FFFFFF">To pay by check, make
             check payable to MM University. To use
```

```
                   either Visa or MasterCard, check the
                   appropriate box and complete every
                   section.</FONT>
249.               <BR>
250.            </TD>
251.         </TR>
252.         <TR>
253.            <TD WIDTH="20%"> </TD>
254.            <TD VALIGN=TOP COLSPAN=4
                WIDTH="80%"> </TD>
255.         </TR>
256.         <TR>
257.            <TD VALIGN=TOP WIDTH="20%"> </TD>
258.            <TD VALIGN=TOP WIDTH="20%">
259.               <FONT SIZE="+1" FACE="Helvetica"
                   COLOR="#FFFFFF">Visa </FONT><BR>
                   <INPUT TYPE="radio" NAME="payment"
                   VALUE="visa">
260.            </TD>
261.            <TD VALIGN=TOP WIDTH="20%">
262.               <P><FONT SIZE="+1" FACE="Helvetica"
                    COLOR="#FFFFFF"> Mastercard </FONT>
                   <BR><INPUT TYPE="radio" NAME="payment"
                   VALUE="mastercard">
263.            </TD>
264.            <TD VALIGN=TOP WIDTH="20%">
265.               <P><FONT SIZE="+1" COLOR="#FFFFFF">
                   Expiration Date</FONT><BR><INPUT
                   TYPE="text" NAME="expdate" VALUE="" SIZE=20>
266.            </TD>
267.            <TD VALIGN=TOP WIDTH="20%">
268.               <FONT SIZE="+1" FACE="Helvetica"
                   COLOR="#FFFFFF">Account Number</FONT><BR>
                   <INPUT TYPE="text" NAME="accnt" VALUE=""
                   SIZE=20>
269.            </TD>
270.         </TR>
271.         <TR>
272.            <TD VALIGN=TOP COLSPAN=5
273. WIDTH="100%"><P><HR></TD>
274.         </TR>
```

```
275.  </TABLE>
276.  <TABLE BORDER=0 WIDTH=600>
277.    <TR>
278.      <TD WIDTH="20%"> </TD>
279.      <TD VALIGN=TOP>
280.        <INPUT TYPE="image"
             SRC="/images/register.gif" WIDTH=121
              HEIGHT=15 BORDER=0 ALIGN=TOP>
281.        <A HREF="#top"><IMG
             SRC="/images/backtotop.gif" WIDTH=121
             HEIGHT=15 BORDER=0 ALIGN=TOP></A>
282.      </TD>
283.      <TD WIDTH="20%"> </TD>
284.      <TD WIDTH="20%"> </TD>
285.    </TR>
286.  </TABLE>
287.  </FORM>
288.  </BODY>
289.  </HTML>
```

The Form Field Names

The fields we want to display on this HTML form are as follows:

fname	ssnumber
mi	email
lname	major
address	year
city	course
state	section
zip	cost

The form is a single HTML file that gathers the above field information and submits it to an Active Server Page that enters the information in an Access database on the host server machine. Lines one through five define the basic settings used to set up the HTML file. Line seven adds our title graphic. Line six is new. It declares this file is a form and indicates the action the browser should take when the submit button is clicked. Here the CGI application sends the submission to /scripts/u_register.asp.

The form wants the submission information encoded, and the method used to send the information to the server is the POST method.

```
1.    <HTML>
2.    <HEAD>
3.      <TITLE>Enrollment</TITLE>
4.    </HEAD>
5.    <BODY BGCOLOR="#C0C0C0" LINK="#D70000"
      ALINK="#F4FC58" VLINK="#D70000"
      BACKGROUND="/images/background.gif">
6.    <FORM action="/scripts/u_register.asp"
      method="POST">
```

On line seven we open an <A></A> tag. We provide an HREF to a file on our server, "/images/title.map" as the target. To this we add a <MAP></MAP> tag. This is our client-side image map information. This MAP named "title" consists of three rectangles. If the mouse is clicked in any of these areas, the browser requests the HREF associated with the area. This information can be processed by the browser, saving time and a submission to the server. For older browsers, mouse down in this area will send a request to the server where the correct URL to return will be determined. By including both server-and client-side image mapping, we cover all bases and incorporate a great feature on our page.

```
7.    <P><A HREF="/images/title.map"><MAP NAME="title">
8.      <AREA SHAPE=RECT COORDS="119,46,238,60"
        HREF="courses.html">
9.      <AREA SHAPE=RECT COORDS="240,46,358,60"
        HREF="employee_info.pdf">
10.     <AREA SHAPE=RECT COORDS="360,46,478,60"
        HREF="general_info.pdf">
11.   </MAP><IMG ISMAP USEMAP="#title"
      SRC="/images/enroll_title.gif" ALT="Enrollment
      Form" WIDTH=600 HEIGHT=60 BORDER=0
      ALIGN=BOTTOM></A>
```

Constructing a table

This file is constructed using five tables to display our information. The first table displays images and text describing how to enroll in a course at the University. The second table contains all the fields used to gather personal information: name, address, etc. The third table holds course enrollment choices for the submission. The fourth table contains payment information fields and the fifth table contains the submission buttons.

Table one is similar to the tables in the other pages in this example. We'll examine tables two and five.

Line 108 uses the HTML <TABLE> tag to start a table. Here we set the border around the table to 0 pixels in width. No cell spacing or padding is indicated. The table's size is set to exactly 600 pixels in width.

Once the table is set up we begin adding rows and cells to the table. On line 109 we use the table row tag, <TR>, to open a table row. Once we open a table row we can add as many cells as we want with the table detail tag, <TD>.

```
108.   <TABLE BORDER=0 WIDTH=600>
109.      <TR>
110.        <TD WIDTH="20%"> </TD>
111.        <TD VALIGN=TOP COLSPAN=4 WIDTH="80%">
112.          <BR>
113.          <HR ALIGN=LEFT>
114.        <FONT SIZE="+2" FACE="Helvetica"
           COLOR="#FFFFFF">student information:</FONT>
115.          <BR>
116.        </TD>
117.      </TR>
```

On line 110 we add the row's first cell. We set the relative width of the cell to 20%. This instructs the browser to draw the cell to 20% of the table's width. Since our table is exactly 600 pixels, this cell will always be 20% of the table width or 125 pixels wide. Again, we want this cell to be blank, so we don't add any text. Instead we add an HTML non-breaking space character, " ", to insure the cell will be drawn by all browsers. Finally we close the cell with the </TD> tag. On line 111 we add another cell that spans four columns. It displays a horizontal rule and white text that is 2 points larger than our normal text. The horizontal rule or <HR> is the rule displayed above the text. On line 117 we close the row.

```
118.      <TR>
119.        <TD WIDTH="20%"> </TD>
120.      <TD VALIGN=TOP COLSPAN=4 WIDTH="80%"> </TD>
121.      </TR>
122.      <TR>
```

```
123.        <TD VALIGN=TOP COLSPAN=2 WIDTH="40%">
124.           <B><FONT FACE="Helvetica"
               COLOR="#FFFFFF">first name</FONT></B><BR>
               <INPUT TYPE="text" NAME="fname" VALUE=""
               SIZE=40>
125.        </TD>
126.        <TD COLSPAN=2 WIDTH="40%">
127.           <B><FONT FACE="Helvetica"
               COLOR="#FFFFFF">last name</FONT></B><BR>
               <INPUT TYPE="text" NAME="lname" VALUE=""
               SIZE=40>
128.        </TD><TD WIDTH="20%">
129.           <B><FONT FACE="Helvetica"
               COLOR="#FFFFFF">mi</FONT></B><BR> <INPUT
               TYPE="text" NAME="mi" VALUE="" SIZE=20>
130.        </TD>
131.     </TR>
```

On line 122 we start the first row that contains information in the table. On line 123 we add the row's first cell. We set the relative width of the cell to 40% and set it to span two columns. This cell contains two more items. First we put a <BR> tag to return to the start of the next line. Next, on line 124, we add an input field. The field's type is "text", its name is "fname", its initial value is the null string " ", and it accepts 40 characters. This field will hold the applicant's first name. Now we're ready to close the cell using the </TD> tag.

We repeat this exact construction for the next two cells in this row. This allows us to capture the student's last name and middle initial.

```
132.     <TR>
133.        <TD VALIGN=TOP COLSPAN=2 WIDTH="40%">
134.           <FONT FACE="Helvetica" COLOR="#FFFFFF">
               street address</FONT></B><BR> <INPUT
               TYPE="text" NAME="address" VALUE=""
               SIZE=40>
135.        </TD>
136.        <TD VALIGN=TOP WIDTH="20%">
137.           <B><FONT FACE="Helvetica" COLOR="#FFFFFF">
               apt #</FONT></B><BR> <INPUT TYPE="text"
               NAME="apt" VALUE="" SIZE=20>
```

```
138.          </TD>
139.          <TD WIDTH="20%"> </TD>
140.          <TD WIDTH="20%"> </TD>
141.      </TR>
142.      <TR>
143.        <TD COLSPAN=2 WIDTH="40%">
144.          <B><FONT FACE="Helvetica" COLOR="#FFFFFF">
              city</FONT></B><BR><INPUT TYPE="text"
              NAME="city" VALUE="" SIZE=40>
145.        </TD>
146.        <TD VALIGN=TOP WIDTH="20%">
147.          <B><FONT FACE="Helvetica" COLOR="#FFFFFF">
              state</FONT></B><BR><INPUT TYPE="text"
              NAME="state" VALUE="" SIZE=20>
148.        </TD>
149.        <TD VALIGN=TOP WIDTH="20%">
150.          <B><FONT FACE="Helvetica"COLOR="#FFFFFF">
              zip</FONT></B><BR><INPUT TYPE="text"
              NAME="zip" VALUE="" SIZE=20>
151.        </TD><TD WIDTH="20%"> </TD>
152.      </TR>
```

The next two rows each add four cells of information to their row. On line 132 we start the second row in the table. Line 133 adds the row's first cell just like the first row's. We set the relative width of the cell to 40% and set it to span two columns. This cell contains three items. The first item is a <BR> tag to return to the start of the next line. The second is another input field. The field's type is "text", its name is "address", its initial value is the null string "", and it accepts 40 characters. Now we'll close the cell using the </TD> tag.

We repeat this exact construction for the next three cells in this row. This allows us to capture the student's apartment number. Notice that this row has one more cell than the first row. The final two cells in this row are blank. They're included to ease alignment of other cells on following rows.

```
153.      <TR>
154.        <TD WIDTH="20%">
```

```
155.        <B><FONT FACE="Helvetica" COLOR="#FFFFFF">
            year in school</FONT></B><BR><INPUT
            TYPE="text" NAME="year" VALUE="" SIZE=20>
156.    </TD>
157.    <TD VALIGN=TOP WIDTH="20%">
158.        <B><FONT FACE="Helvetica" COLOR="#FFFFFF">
            major</FONT></B><BR><INPUT TYPE="text"
            NAME="major" VALUE="" SIZE=20>
159.    </TD>
160.    <TD VALIGN=TOP WIDTH="20%"> </TD>
161.    <TD VALIGN=TOP WIDTH="20%">
162.        <B><FONT FACE="Helvetica" COLOR="#FFFFFF">
            social security #<INPUT TYPE="text"
            NAME="ssnumber" VALUE=""
            SIZE=20></FONT></B>
163.    </TD><TD WIDTH="20%"> </TD>
164.    </TR>
```

The row starting on line 153 has five cells of information. Line 154 adds a cell, setting its relative width to 20% of the table. This cell contains three items. The first item is a <BR> tag to return to the start of the next line. The second is another input field. The field's type is "text", its name is "year", its initial value is the null string "", and it accepts 20 characters.

We repeat this exact construction for the next four cells in this row. Here we capture the student's major and social security number. Notice that this row contains two blank cells. They're included for alignment purposes.

```
165.    <TR>
166.    <TD COLSPAN=2 WIDTH="40%">
167.        <B><FONT FACE="Helvetica" COLOR="#FFFFFF">
            e-mail address</FONT></B><BR><INPUT
            TYPE="text" NAME="email" VALUE="" SIZE=40>
168.    </TD>
169.    <TD WIDTH="20%"> </TD>
170.    <TD VALIGN=TOP ROWSPAN=2 COLSPAN=2 WIDTH="40%">
171.        <FONT SIZE="+1" FACE="Helvetica"
            COLOR="#FFFFFF">Your social security number
            is used to identify and maintain your
            academic record. Providing your number is
```

```
          voluntary and is requested by the authority
          of Regents of MM University</FONT>
172.      </TD>
173.    </TR>
174.    <TR>
175.      <TD WIDTH="20%"> </TD>
176.      <TD WIDTH="75%"> </TD>
177.    </TR>
178.  </TABLE>
```

The row starting on line 165 goes back to a three-cell layout. Line 166 adds a cell, setting its relative width to 40% of the table and spanning two columns. This cell contains three items. The first item is the "e-mail" text, the second is a <BR> tag to return to the start of the next line, and the third is an input field. The field's type is "text", its name is "email", its initial value is the null string "", and it accepts 40 characters.

This structure is repeated with this exact construction for the remaining two cells in this row. Here we add an explanation of why your social security number is requested.

The final row of this table consists of blank cells. They are included to maintain a pleasant space between this and the start of the third table.

```
276.  <TABLE BORDER=0 WIDTH=600>
277.    <TR>
278.      <TD WIDTH="20%"> </TD>
279.      <TD VALIGN=TOP>
280.        <INPUT TYPE="image"
            SRC="/images/register.gif" WIDTH=121
             HEIGHT=15 BORDER=0 ALIGN=TOP>
281.        <A HREF="#top"><IMG
            SRC="/images/backtotop.gif" WIDTH=121
             HEIGHT=15 BORDER=0 ALIGN=TOP></A>
282.      </TD>
283.      <TD WIDTH="20%"> </TD>
284.      <TD WIDTH="20%"> </TD>
285.    </TR>
286.  </TABLE>
```

```
287.   </FORM>
288.   </BODY>
289.   </HTML>
```

The final table contains the graphics and buttons used to submit the form. Line 276 uses the HTML <TABLE> tag to start a table. Here we set the border around the table to 0 pixels in width. No cell spacing or padding is indicated. The table's size is set to exactly 600 pixels in width.

Once the table is set up, we begin adding rows and cells to the table. On line 277 we use the table row tag, <TR>, to open a table row. Once we open a table row, we can add as many cells as we want with the table detail tag, <TD>.

The row starting on line 277 uses a five-cell layout. Line 278 adds a cell setting its relative width to 20% of the table. The first cell in this row is blank. The next two contain linked images, one being the submission button and the other a link back to the courses offered page.

Lines 286-289 close the table, form, body, and finally the HTML document itself.

Creating the Access Database

This example uses a Microsoft Access database to store information submitted by a client. Although Access is a popular database it isn't recommended as an industrial strength Web database. If your site demands thousands of transactions per day, another database designed to handle higher levels of transactions is a better choice. However, for our simple university enrollment form, its architecture is more than sufficient.

In this example we'll create a database using the Microsoft Access application and add two tables to it. This database will exist on our server and we'll connect to it using ODBC drivers.

Step 1

Create the database
Our first step is to create the database. Open Microsoft Access and choose new from the file menu. Create a blank database. Name it "university.mdb" and save it on the Web server machine.

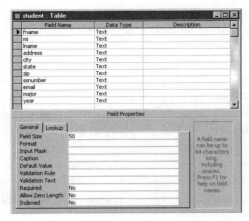

"student" table set-up

Add the "student" table

Now we need to add the "student" table where we'll store the student information that is submitted via our form. To do this we choose Table from the Insert menu. I like to add tables using the design view option but use whatever method you're most familiar with. Add the following fields to the table we just created:

Field Name	Data Type	Description
fname	Text	First name
mi	Text	Middle initial
lname	Text	Last name
address	Text	Address
city	Text	City
state	Text	State
zip	Text	ZIP Code
ssnumber	Text	Social Security Number
email	Text	E-mail address
major	Text	Major field of study
year	Text	Year in school

Add the "registered" table

The second table we'll use is the one that contains the information regarding students registered in a course. To do this, again choose Insert: Table from the Microsoft Access Menu. Choose the design view and add the following fields:

Field Name	Data Type	Description
section	Text	Section number of the course
lname	Text	Registered students last name
fname	Text	Registered students first name
year	Text	Year ranking in school
major	Text	Major field of study
paid	Text	Has the student paid or not

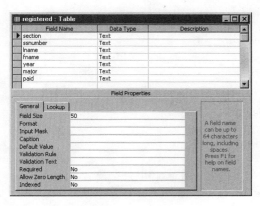

"registered" table set-up

Step 4

Create the ODBC data source

Once the database exists, we must create the ODBC data source. The first step in doing this is to verify the Microsoft Access ODBC driver is installed on the Windows NT Server. To check for this, open the ODBC Administrator in the server's control panel. The list of available drivers is displayed in the window. If you don't see Microsoft Access Driver "(*.mdb)" in the list, install it from the Microsoft Access setup program. When you run the setup program, choose the custom setup option and install the Data Access Object. This will install the Access ODBC drivers. After completion, check back in the ODBC Administrator control panel to verify the installation was a success.

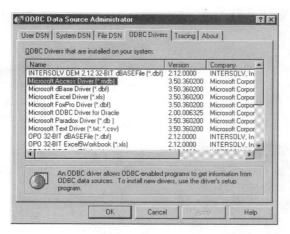

ODBC Data Source Administrator

Configure the Data Source

Once you've verified the correct drivers are installed, again open the ODBC Administrator. It lists all registered user data sources. User data sources are set up for individual users that log onto the system. This isn't what we want. We need a data source that's available to processes that run on the server. These type of data sources are called system data sources. To create a new system data source, click the "System DSN…" button. The System Data Sources dialog box appears listing all available system data sources.

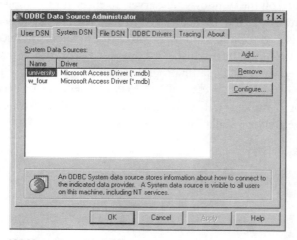

ODBC Data Source Administrator

Now click the "Add…" button. The Add Data Source dialog appears and asks you to select an ODBC driver. Select the Microsoft Access Driver and click the okay button.

ODBC Microsoft Access Setup dialog

Now we should be presented with the ODBC Microsoft Access Setup dialog. Here we need to accomplish three things. We need to name the data source, we need to supply a description of the data source, and we need to select the file for this data source. Enter "university" as the name and "Course Registration Information" as the description. Finally click the Select button and locate the database file we created in step 2. To enact the settings, click the OK button. The "university" data source should be viewable in the System Data Sources dialog. When the college data source is visible, close the dialog. It's now available through ODBC connectivity.

ODBC Microsoft Access Setup dialog

Creating the ASP Scripts

This example uses two Active Server Pages on the server side. The "u_classlist.asp" ASP processes the request for a current students enrolled list and returns an HTML file to a user's browser. The "u_register.asp" ASP inserts a student's registration in the database and returns an HTML file used to display up to the minute enrollment information.

For this example to work, the ASPs must exist as a file in the "scripts" directory in the IIS Server's root directory.

Code Example: u_classlist.asp

```
1.    <%
2.        Dim dbConn'// Database connection object
3.        Dim szSelect   '// SQL for database selection
4.        Dim szResponse   '// Query return
5.
6.        '// Set up connection and run query
7.        Set dbConn =
          Server.CreateObject("ADODB.Connection")
8.        dbConn.Open "dsn=university;uid=;pwd="
9.        szSelect = "SELECT * FROM registered WHERE
          section = '" & Request("class") & "'"
10.       Set szResponse = dbConn.Execute(szSelect)
11.   %>
12.   <HTML>
13.   <HEAD>
14.      <TITLE>Class Registration</TITLE>
15.   </HEAD>
16.   <BODY BGCOLOR="#FFFFFF" ALINK="#0000FF"
      VLINK="#551A8B"
      BACKGROUND="/images/background.gif">
17.   <BR>
18.   <BR>
19.   <P><A HREF="/images/title.map"><MAP NAME="title">
20.      <AREA SHAPE=RECT COORDS="119,46,238,60"
         HREF="courses.html">
21.      <AREA SHAPE=RECT COORDS="240,46,358,60"
         HREF="enrollment.html">
22.      <AREA SHAPE=RECT COORDS="360,46,478,60"
         HREF="general_info.pdf">
23.   </MAP><IMG ISMAP USEMAP="#title"
      SRC="/images/register_title.gif"
24.   ALT="Registration List" WIDTH=600 HEIGHT=60
      BORDER=0
25.   ALIGN=BOTTOM></A></P>
26.
```

```
27.    <BR>
28.    <BR>
29.    <BR>
30.    <BR>
31.
32.    <TABLE BORDER=0 CELLSPACING=6 WIDTH=600>
33.      <TR>
34.        <TD WIDTH="20%"> </TD>
35.        <TD VALIGN=TOP COLSPAN=3 ALIGN=LEFT
           WIDTH="60%">
36.          <P><B><FONT SIZE="+2" FACE="Helvetica"
37.          COLOR="#FFFFFF">registered
             students</FONT></B><BR>
38.        </TD>
39.        <TD WIDTH="20%"> </TD>
40.      </TR>
41.      <TR>
42.        <TD VALIGN=TOP WIDTH="20%"> </TD>
43.        <TD VALIGN=TOP ALIGN=LEFT BGCOLOR="#000000"
           WIDTH="20%">
44.          <P><FONT SIZE="+1" FACE="Helvetica"
             COLOR="#FFFFFF">last
45.  name</FONT>
46.        </TD>
           <TD VALIGN=TOP BGCOLOR="#000000"
47.        WIDTH="20%">
             <P><FONT SIZE="+1" FACE="Helvetica"
48.          COLOR="#FFFFFF">first
49.  name</FONT>
50.        </TD>
51.        <TD VALIGN=TOP BGCOLOR="#000000"
           WIDTH="20%">
52.          <P><FONT SIZE="+1" FACE="Helvetica"
53.          COLOR="#FFFFFF">year</FONT>
54.        </TD>
55.        <TD VALIGN=TOP BGCOLOR="#000000"
           WIDTH="20%">
56.          <P><FONT SIZE="+1" FACE="Helvetica"
57.          COLOR="#FFFFFF">major</FONT>
58.        </TD>
```

```
59.      </TR>
60.    <% While Not szResponse.EOF %>
61.      <TR>
62.        <TD VALIGN=TOP WIDTH="20%"> </TD>
63.        <TD VALIGN=TOP WIDTH="20%">
64.          <FONT SIZE="+1" FACE="Helvetica"
             COLOR="#FFFFFF">
65.           <% =szResponse("lname") %> </FONT>
66.        </TD>
67.        <TD VALIGN=TOP WIDTH="20%">
68.         <FONT SIZE="+1" FACE="Helvetica"
            COLOR="#FFFFFF">
69.           <% =szResponse("fname") %> </FONT>
70.        </TD>
71.        <TD VALIGN=TOP WIDTH="20%">
72.          <FONT SIZE="+1" FACE="Helvetica"
             COLOR="#FFFFFF">
73.           <% =szResponse("year") %> </FONT>
74.        </TD>
75.        <TD VALIGN=TOP WIDTH="20%">
76.          <FONT SIZE="+1" FACE="Helvetica"
             COLOR="#FFFFFF">
77.           <% =szResponse("major") %> </FONT>
78.        </TD>
79.      </TR>
80.    <%
81.    szResponse.MoveNext
82.    Wend
83.    %>
84.    <% dbConn.Close %>
85.    </TABLE>
86.    </BODY>
87.    </HTML>
```

The u_classlist.asp Active Server Page

Active server pages combine Visual Basic Scripting and HTML. The way
it works is anything between the <% and %> keys instructs the server to
run the information through an interpreter. This provides a procedural
methodology for HTML execution. Any characters outside the scope of
the <%...%> combination is designated HTML and returned to the
client as is.

```
1.    <%
2.    Dim dbConn'// Database connection object
3.    Dim szSelect  '// SQL for database selection
4.    Dim szResponse  '// Query return
5.
6.    '// Set up connection and run query
7.    Set dbConn =
      Server.CreateObject("ADODB.Connection")
8.    dbConn.Open "dsn=university;uid=;pwd="
9.    szSelect = "SELECT * FROM registered WHERE
      section = '" & Request("class") & "'"
10.   Set szResponse = dbConn.Execute(szSelect)
11.   %>
```

The code here is recognized by the server and executed. Line one opens the code block. Lines two through four declare in memory three objects. One stores a reference to our database connection, the second is where we store the SQL string we send to the database for execution, and the third is where we store the database's response.

Lines six to nine are all the code we need to connect to and query the database. On line seven we access the server object's CreateObject() method. We pass it the string "ADODB.Connection". This instantiates the DLL we use to access the ODBC datasource. On line eight we access the Open() method, passing it the DSN, UID, and PWD needed to connect to the datasource. The DSN we created was "university". We didn't set any security on the database, so we don't require a user name or password. On line nine we store the SQL string we'll pass to the database. Now we're ready to query the database. On line 10 we set the szResponse variable to the result of dbConn.Execute(). The execute method is what sends the SQL string we pieced together to the datasource. The response received back is the course listing we'll use to display to the user.

```
12.   <HTML>
13.   <HEAD>
14.     <TITLE>Class Registration</TITLE>
15.   </HEAD>
16.   <BODY BGCOLOR="#FFFFFF" ALINK="#0000FF"
      VLINK="#551A8B"
      BACKGROUND="/images/background.gif">
17.   <BR>
```

```
18.    <BR>
19.    <P><A HREF="/images/title.map"><MAP NAME="title">
20.      <AREA SHAPE=RECT COORDS="119,46,238,60"
         HREF="courses.html">
21.      <AREA SHAPE=RECT COORDS="240,46,358,60"
         HREF="enrollment.html">
22.      <AREA SHAPE=RECT COORDS="360,46,478,60"
         HREF="general_info.pdf">
23.    </MAP><IMG ISMAP USEMAP="#title"
       SRC="/images/register_title.gif"
24.    ALT="Registration List" WIDTH=600 HEIGHT=60
       BORDER=0
25.    ALIGN=BOTTOM></A></P>
26.
27.    <BR>
28.    <BR>
29.    <BR>
30.    <BR>
```

Lines 12 through 16 of our file output the standard HTML to the client. Since the code block closed on line 11, IIS stops processing the text as instructions and simply sends it back to the client.

On line 19 we construct another client- and server-side image map. In case an older browser that can't handle client-side image maps clicks the image, a request is made for the /images/title.map file. The mouse coordinates accompany the request. The server recognizes the "map" file type and uses the mouse coordinates to determine if the click occured in one of the map file's defined rectangles. If there's a match, the user is redirected to the corresponding URL. If a browser that can perform client lookups is used, this look up and redirection occurs on the client side without any further requests of the server.

```
32.    <TABLE BORDER=0 CELLSPACING=6 WIDTH=600>
33.      <TR>
34.        <TD WIDTH="20%"> </TD>
35.        <TD VALIGN=TOP COLSPAN=3 ALIGN=LEFT
           WIDTH="60%">
36.          <P><B><FONT SIZE="+2" FACE="Helvetica"
37.          COLOR="#FFFFFF">registered
```

```
                    students</FONT></B><BR>
38.          </TD>
39.          <TD WIDTH="20%"> </TD>
40.       </TR>
```

On line 32 we open a table and begin adding rows using the <TR></TR> tags. The page we begin outputting is the same as all the others in the example.

```
41.       <TR>
42.          <TD VALIGN=TOP WIDTH="20%"> </TD>
43.          <TD VALIGN=TOP ALIGN=LEFT BGCOLOR="#000000"
             WIDTH="20%">
44.             <P><FONT SIZE="+1" FACE="Helvetica"
                COLOR="#FFFFFF">last
45.  name</FONT>
46.          </TD>
             <TD VALIGN=TOP BGCOLOR="#000000"
47.          WIDTH="20%">
                <P><FONT SIZE="+1" FACE="Helvetica"
48.             COLOR="#FFFFFF">first
49.  name</FONT>
50.          </TD>
51.          <TD VALIGN=TOP BGCOLOR="#000000"
             WIDTH="20%">
52.             <P><FONT SIZE="+1" FACE="Helvetica"
53.             COLOR="#FFFFFF">year</FONT>
54.          </TD>
55.          <TD VALIGN=TOP BGCOLOR="#000000"
             WIDTH="20%">
56.             <P><FONT SIZE="+1" FACE="Helvetica"
57.             COLOR="#FFFFFF">major</FONT>
58.          </TD>
59.       </TR>
```

Lines 41-59 add one row of the table. This row contains the column heads for the information we'll return from the database. The columns reflect the registered student's last name, first name, their year in school and their major field of study. Notice that the background of the row is set to Black "#000000" on line 43.

```
60.     <% While Not szResponse.EOF %>
```

Line 60 is where the fun begins. Here we again use the <% %> tag to inform the server more code is to be executed. Line 60 starts a while loop. The loop continues while the variable szResponse has not reached its end of file marker, (EOF).

```
62.        <TD VALIGN=TOP WIDTH="20%"> </TD>
63.        <TD VALIGN=TOP WIDTH="20%">
64.          <FONT SIZE="+1" FACE="Helvetica"
             COLOR="#FFFFFF">
65.           <% =szResponse("lname") %> </FONT>
66.        </TD>
67.        <TD VALIGN=TOP WIDTH="20%">
68.          <FONT SIZE="+1" FACE="Helvetica"
             COLOR="#FFFFFF">
69.           <% =szResponse("fname") %> </FONT>
70.        </TD>
71.        <TD VALIGN=TOP WIDTH="20%">
72.          <FONT SIZE="+1" FACE="Helvetica"
             COLOR="#FFFFFF">
73.           <% =szResponse("year") %> </FONT>
74.        </TD>
75.        <TD VALIGN=TOP WIDTH="20%">
76.          <FONT SIZE="+1" FACE="Helvetica"
             COLOR="#FFFFFF">
77.           <% =szResponse("major") %> </FONT>
78.        </TD>
79.      </TR>
80.    <%
81.    szResponse.MoveNext
82.    Wend
83.    %>
```

Now that we've entered the while loop, we again switch back to outputting HTML. On line 62 we add an empty cell to the row and on line 63 we add another cell. This time the text inserted will be added dynamically. On line 65 we encounter another piece of code. This single instruction tells the server to output the "name" field's value of the szResponse variable. The "=" sign instructs the server to print the result in place to the file being returned. This outputting of fields from the szResponse variable occurs again on lines 69, 73, and 77. Remember , we're still in that while loop. On line 81 we access the MoveNext( ) method of the szResponse variable to get the next record returned from our earlier database query. This loop continues outputting each record as a row in our table until we reach the EOF marker of the szResponse variable. At this point we fall out of the while loop. The loop's end is identified by the Wend operator on line 82.

```
84.    <% dbConn.Close %>
85.    </TABLE>
86.    </BODY>
87.    </HTML>
```

On line 84 we execute the Close member function of the database connection object. The required closing </TABLE>, </BODY>, and </HTML> tags are added on lines 85-87 and the Active Server Page file ends.

The u_register.asp Active Server Page

This example's second Active Server Page receives a submission from the enrollment.html file, inserts pertinent information into the ODBC data source, and returns an HTML page showing the total number of courses in which the applicant has registered.

Code Example: u_register.asp

```
1.     <%
2.       '// Declare objects in memory
3.       Dim dbConn'// Database connection object
4.       Dim sqlInsert '// SQL for database selection
5.       Dim szSelect  '// SQL for database selection
6.       Dim szResponse  '// Query return
7.
8.       '// Set up connection and run query
9.       Set dbConn =
       Server.CreateObject("ADODB.Connection")
10.      dbConn.Open "dsn=university;uid=;pwd="
11.
```

```
12.    If Request("section1") <> "" Then
       insert_course(Request("section1"))
13.    If Request("section2") <> "" Then
       insert_course(Request("section2"))
14.    If Request("section3") <> "" Then
       insert_course(Request("section3"))
15.
16.    szSelect = "SELECT * FROM registered WHERE
       ssnumber = '" & Request("ssnumber") & "'"
17.    Set szResponse = dbConn.Execute(szSelect)
18.
19.    Sub insert_course(section)
20.      sqlInsert = "INSERT INTO REGISTERED (section,
         ssnumber, lname, fname, year, major, paid)"
21.      sqlInsert = sqlInsert & " VALUES ( "
22.      sqlInsert = sqlInsert & "'" & section & "', "
23.      sqlInsert = sqlInsert & "'" &
         Request("ssnumber") & "', "
24.      sqlInsert = sqlInsert & "'" & Request("fname")
         & "', "
25.      sqlInsert = sqlInsert & "'" & Request("lname")
         & "', "
26.      sqlInsert = sqlInsert & "'" & Request("year")
         & "', "
27.      sqlInsert = sqlInsert & "'" & Request("major")
         & "', "
28.      If Request("accnt") = "" Then
29.        sqlInsert = sqlInsert & "'no')"
30.      Else
31.        sqlInsert = sqlInsert & "'yes')"
32.      End if
33.      Set szResponse = dbConn.Execute(sqlInsert)
34.    End Sub
35.
36.  %>
37.  <HTML>
38.  <HEAD>
39.    <TITLE>Registration Confirmation</TITLE>
40.  </HEAD>
```

```
41.   <BODY BGCOLOR="#FFFFFF" ALINK="#0000FF"
      VLINK="#551A8B"
      BACKGROUND="/images/background.gif">
42.   <BR>
43.   <BR>
44.   <P><A HREF="/images/title.map"><MAP NAME="title">
45.      <AREA SHAPE=RECT COORDS="119,46,238,60"
         HREF="courses.html">
46.      <AREA SHAPE=RECT COORDS="240,46,358,60"
         HREF="enrollment.html">
47.      <AREA SHAPE=RECT COORDS="360,46,478,60"
         HREF="general_info.pdf">
48.   </MAP><IMG ISMAP USEMAP="#title"
      SRC="/images/register_title.gif"
49.   ALT="Registration List" WIDTH=600 HEIGHT=60
      BORDER=0
50.   ALIGN=BOTTOM></A></P>
51.
52.   <BR>
53.   <BR>
54.   <FONT SIZE="+2" FACE="Helvetica" COLOR="#FFFFFF">
55.   Thank you. You are currently registered in the
      courses listed below.</FONT>
56.   <BR>
57.   <BR>
58.
59.   <TABLE BORDER=0 CELLSPACING=6 WIDTH=600>
60.      <TR>
61.         <TD WIDTH="20%"> </TD>
62.         <TD VALIGN=TOP COLSPAN=3 ALIGN=LEFT
            WIDTH="60%">
63.            <P><B><FONT SIZE="+2" FACE="Helvetica"
64.            COLOR="#FFFFFF">course list</FONT></B><BR>
65.         </TD>
66.         <TD WIDTH="20%"> </TD>
67.      </TR>
68.      <TR>
69.         <TD VALIGN=TOP WIDTH="20%"> </TD>
70.         <TD VALIGN=TOP ALIGN=LEFT BGCOLOR="#000000"
            WIDTH="20%">
```

```
71.              <P><FONT SIZE="+1" FACE="Helvetica"
                 COLOR="#FFFFFF">last
72.              name</FONT>
73.          </TD>
74.          <TD VALIGN=TOP BGCOLOR="#000000"
             WIDTH="20%">
75.              <P><FONT SIZE="+1" FACE="Helvetica"
                 COLOR="#FFFFFF">first
76.              name</FONT>
77.          </TD>
78.          <TD VALIGN=TOP BGCOLOR="#000000"
             WIDTH="20%">
79.              <P><FONT SIZE="+1" FACE="Helvetica"
80.              COLOR="#FFFFFF">section</FONT>
81.          </TD>
82.          <TD VALIGN=TOP BGCOLOR="#000000"
             WIDTH="20%">
83.              <P><FONT SIZE="+1" FACE="Helvetica"
84.              COLOR="#FFFFFF">payment recieved</FONT>
85.          </TD>
86.      </TR>
87.
88.  <% While Not szResponse.EOF %>
89.     <TR>
90.        <TD VALIGN=TOP WIDTH="20%"> </TD>
91.        <TD VALIGN=TOP WIDTH="20%">
92.          <FONT SIZE="+1" FACE="Helvetica"
             COLOR="#FFFFFF">
93.          <% =szResponse("lname") %></FONT>
94.        </TD>
95.        <TD VALIGN=TOP WIDTH="20%">
96.          <FONT SIZE="+1" FACE="Helvetica"
             COLOR="#FFFFFF">
97.          <% =szResponse("fname") %></FONT>
98.        </TD>"
99.        <TD VALIGN=TOP WIDTH="20%">
100.          <FONT SIZE="+1" FACE="Helvetica"
              COLOR="#FFFFFF">
101.          <% =szResponse("section") %></FONT>
102.        </TD>"
```

```
103.          <TD VALIGN=TOP WIDTH="20%">
104.          <FONT SIZE="+1" FACE="Helvetica"
              COLOR="#FFFFFF">
105.          <% =szResponse("paid") %></FONT>
106.        </TD>
107.      </TR>
108.
109.  <%
110.  szResponse.MoveNext
111.  Wend
112.   %>
113.  <% dbConn.Close %>
114.
115.  </TABLE>
116.  </BODY>
117.  </HTML>
```

On examination, the first 36 lines of our file are instructions meant for execution. The default language for Active Server Pages is VB Script. All instructions in ASPs are placed inside <% %>.

```
3.      Dim dbConn'// Database connection object
4.      Dim sqlInsert '// SQL for database selection
5.      Dim szSelect  '// SQL for database selection
6.      Dim szResponse '// Query return
```

Lines three through six of our ASP declare in memory space for several variables we'll need. The first stores a reference to the database connection. The second stores the string that we use to hold the SQL needed to insert information into the database. The third holds the string used to select all classes which the user is registered. We declare the variable on line six a variable to hold the response from the database query.

```
9.      Set dbConn =
Server.CreateObject("ADODB.Connection")
10.     dbConn.Open "dsn=university;uid=;pwd="
```

On lines nine and ten we add a database connection object and open the connection. Line nine accesses the server object's CreateObject() method. The "ADODB.Connection" string identifies the server object we use. Line ten calls the Open() method of the connection object. The parameter passed is "dsn=university;uid=;pwd=;". This identifies the DSN, the UID and the PWD of the datasource we'll connect.

```
12.     If Request("section1") <> "" Then
        insert_course(Request("section1"))
13.     If Request("section2") <> "" Then
        insert_course(Request("section2"))
14.     If Request("section3") <> "" Then
        insert_course(Request("section3"))
```

Lines 12-14 check for a value in the Request object and if that value isn't the NULL string, call the insert_course() sub routine. The value we look for is the contents of the section field from our "enrollment.html" form. If a value is submitted, it's stored in the database by the insert_course() sub routine. In the real world an application would validate the section number before trying an insertion.

```
16.     szSelect = "SELECT * FROM registered WHERE
        ssnumber = '" & Request("ssnumber") & "'"
17.     Set szResponse = dbConn.Execute(szSelect)
```

After inserting the submission, we select all records for the user and store them in the szSelect variable. Line 16 stores the SQL string used. Here we want to select all matches from the registered table where the ssnumber field is equal to the ssnumber sent via the "enrollment.html" form. After the SQL statement is constructed, we send it to the database for execution. This is done on line 17 by calling the Execute() method of the database connection object. We store the result in the szResponse variable.

```
19.     Sub insert_course(section)
20.       sqlInsert = "INSERT INTO REGISTERED (section,
          ssnumber, lname, fname, year, major, paid)"
21.       sqlInsert = sqlInsert & " VALUES ( "
22.       sqlInsert = sqlInsert & "'" & section & "', "
23.       sqlInsert = sqlInsert & "'" &
          Request("ssnumber") & "', "
24.       sqlInsert = sqlInsert & "'" & Request("fname")
          & "', "
```

```
25.        sqlInsert = sqlInsert & "'" & Request("lname")
           & "', "
26.        sqlInsert = sqlInsert & "'" & Request("year")
           & "', "
27.        sqlInsert = sqlInsert & "'" & Request("major")
           & "', "
28.        If Request("accnt") = "" Then
29.          sqlInsert = sqlInsert & "'no')"
30.        Else
31.          sqlInsert = sqlInsert & "'yes')"
32.        End if
33.        Set szResponse = dbConn.Execute(sqlInsert)
34.      End Sub
35.
36.    %>
```

The remaining section of our initial code block defines the insert_course() sub routine. The purpose of this routine is to take a section and insert the submitted information into the registered students table of our database. Lines 20-32 assemble the SQL string we'll need. Each line appends a string value to the sqlInsert string. The values are retrieved from the request object. The values correspond to those submitted by the enrollment form. The only lines that differ are 28-32. Here we check for a value submitted in the accnt field. In a real world application we'd charge the credit card, but here we just check to see if any value was entered. If the user entered anything at all, we indicate they've paid. Otherwise, if the field was empty, we mark the paid field "no".

On line 33 we send the string we've constructed to the datasource for execution. The result is placed in the szResponse variable. On line 36 we have %>, signifying the close of the code block.

```
37.    <HTML>
38.    <HEAD>
39.      <TITLE>Registration Confirmation</TITLE>
40.    </HEAD>
41.    <BODY BGCOLOR="#FFFFFF" ALINK="#0000FF"
       VLINK="#551A8B"
       BACKGROUND="/images/background.gif">
```

Lines 37-41 output standard HTML opening the document, creating a minimal head and then opening the document's body. To the body tag we add attributes setting the background color and the color of the links on the page.

```
44.    <P><A HREF="/images/title.map"><MAP NAME="title">
45.       <AREA SHAPE=RECT COORDS="119,46,238,60"
          HREF="courses.html">
46.       <AREA SHAPE=RECT COORDS="240,46,358,60"
          HREF="enrollment.html">
47.       <AREA SHAPE=RECT COORDS="360,46,478,60"
          HREF="general_info.pdf">
48.    </MAP><IMG ISMAP USEMAP="#title"
       SRC="/images/register_title.gif"
49.    ALT="Registration List" WIDTH=600 HEIGHT=60
       BORDER=0
50.    ALIGN=BOTTOM></A></P>
```

Lines 44-50 construct the same client- and server-side image map found on each HTML file in this example. We double up here to accommodate users with older browsers. Newer browsers can process image map information themselves. Older browsers need the help of the server to process mouse clicks on images. For a more detailed description of the client- and server-side image maps, refer to the u_classlist.asp example.

```
52.    <BR>
53.    <BR>
54.    <FONT SIZE="+2" FACE="Helvetica" COLOR="#FFFFFF">
55.    Thank you. You are currently registered in the
       courses listed below.</FONT>
56.    <BR>
57.    <BR>
```

On lines 54 and 55 we add the heading informing the user what information will follow. The text size is increased two units, the text face requested is Helvetica, and the color is set to "#FFFFFF", or white.

```
59.    <TABLE BORDER=0 CELLSPACING=6 WIDTH=600>
60.       <TR>
61.          <TD WIDTH="20%"> </TD>
```

```
62.        <TD VALIGN=TOP COLSPAN=3 ALIGN=LEFT
           WIDTH="60%">
63.          <P><B><FONT SIZE="+2" FACE="Helvetica"
64.          COLOR="#FFFFFF">course list</FONT></B><BR>
65.        </TD>
66.        <TD WIDTH="20%"> </TD>
67.      </TR>
```

On line 59 we open a table and begin adding rows. The first row begins on line 60 and closes on line 67. It's used to form the course list heading.

```
68.      <TR>
69.        <TD VALIGN=TOP WIDTH="20%"> </TD>
70.        <TD VALIGN=TOP ALIGN=LEFT BGCOLOR="#000000"
           WIDTH="20%">
71.          <P><FONT SIZE="+1" FACE="Helvetica"
             COLOR="#FFFFFF">last
72.          name</FONT>
73.        </TD>
74.        <TD VALIGN=TOP BGCOLOR="#000000"
           WIDTH="20%">
75.          <P><FONT SIZE="+1" FACE="Helvetica"
             COLOR="#FFFFFF">first
76.          name</FONT>
77.        </TD>
78.        <TD VALIGN=TOP BGCOLOR="#000000"
           WIDTH="20%">
79.          <P><FONT SIZE="+1" FACE="Helvetica"
80.          COLOR="#FFFFFF">section</FONT>
81.        </TD>
82.        <TD VALIGN=TOP BGCOLOR="#000000"
           WIDTH="20%">
83.          <P><FONT SIZE="+1" FACE="Helvetica"
84.          COLOR="#FFFFFF">payment recieved</FONT>
85.        </TD>
86.      </TR>
```

Our next row has five cells. These cells are the columns we'll use to display course registration information. The first cell is empty, but the following four fields hold the last name, first name, section number of the course and whether or not the student has paid.

```
88.    <% While Not szResponse.EOF %>
89.      <TR>
90.        <TD VALIGN=TOP WIDTH="20%"> </TD>
91.        <TD VALIGN=TOP WIDTH="20%">
92.          <FONT SIZE="+1" FACE="Helvetica"
             COLOR="#FFFFFF">
93.          <% =szResponse("lname") %></FONT>
94.        </TD>
95.        <TD VALIGN=TOP WIDTH="20%">
96.          <FONT SIZE="+1" FACE="Helvetica"
             COLOR="#FFFFFF">
97.          <% =szResponse("fname") %></FONT>
98.         </TD>"
99.        <TD VALIGN=TOP WIDTH="20%">
100.         <FONT SIZE="+1" FACE="Helvetica"
             COLOR="#FFFFFF">
101.         <% =szResponse("section") %></FONT>
102.        </TD>"
103.         <TD VALIGN=TOP WIDTH="20%">
104.         <FONT SIZE="+1" FACE="Helvetica"
             COLOR="#FFFFFF">
105.         <% =szResponse("paid") %></FONT>
106.        </TD>
107.      </TR>
108.
109.  <%
110.  szResponse.MoveNext
111.  Wend
112.   %>
```

On line 88 we have another line of code. Here we start a while loop. The loop continues as long as the szResponse variable hasn't reached its end of file marker. On line 89 we again output HTML constructing another row of our table. Next we'll add five cells that contain data describing courses in which the student is registered.

The first cell of this row is again a blank placeholder. The second contains the student's last name. It's retrieved from the szResponse returned by the database query we made at the beginning of the script. To retrieve this value we enclose the function in the <% %> delimiters.